D1252891

HOW TO BECOME
A MUSICAL CRITIC

Da Capo Press Music Reprint Series

Music Editor
BEA FRIEDLAND
Ph.D., City University of New York

HOW TO BECOME
A MUSICAL CRITIC

BERNARD SHAW

EDITED WITH AN INTRODUCTION BY

DAN H. LAURENCE

DA CAPO PRESS · NEW YORK · 1978

Library of Congress Cataloging in Publication Data

Shaw, George Bernard, 1856-1950.
  How to become a musical critic.

  (Da Capo Press music reprint series)
  Reprint of the ed. published by Hill and
Wang, New York.
    1. Music—England—London. 2. Musical
criticism. 3. Music—Analysis, appreciation.
I. Title.
  [ML286.8.L5S36 1978] 780'.942   77-26653
  ISBN 0-306-77569-7

This Da Capo Press edition of *How to Become a Musical Critic*
is an unabridged republication of the edition published
in New York in 1961. It is reprinted by arrangement
with the Society of Authors.

Published by Da Capo Press, Inc.
A Subsidiary of Plenum Publishing Corporation
227 West 17th Street, New York, N.Y. 10011

HOW TO BECOME
A MUSICAL CRITIC

HOW TO BECOME
A MUSICAL CRITIC

BERNARD SHAW

EDITED WITH AN INTRODUCTION BY

DAN H. LAURENCE

HILL AND WANG
New York

To
GEORGINA CHAWORTH MUSTERS
—the "only one Judy"—
who knew and understands
GBS better than any of us

CONTENTS

HOW TO BECOME A MUSICAL CRITIC

CONTENTS

INTRODUCTION

"I could make deaf stockbrokers read my two pages on music," Shaw once wrote in reference to his criticism in *The World*, "the alleged joke being that I knew nothing about it. The real joke was that I knew all about it."

Shaw's extraordinary musical knowledge resulted from an exposure to music almost from infancy. The Shaws were naturally a musical family: "All the women could 'pick out tunes' on the piano," Shaw reminisced in the preface to *Immaturity*, "and support them with the chords of the tonic, subdominant, dominant, and tonic again. Even a Neapolitan sixth was not beyond them. My father played the trombone . . . My eldest uncle [William] . . . played the ophicleide, a giant keyed brass bugle, now superseded by the tuba . . . My Aunt Emily played the violoncello. Aunt Shah [Charlotte] . . . used the harp and tambourine." Shaw's mother had a mezzo-soprano voice "of remarkable purity of tone," which she developed under the mesmeric influence of a singing-teacher friend, George John Vandeleur Lee. Lee's "method" she eventually passed on to her son, who, as a boy, aspired to be an operatic baritone. It was Lee who first took young George to the opera, and it was his Amateur Musical Society concerts in Dublin's Antient Concert Rooms, in which Mrs Shaw was a frequent participant, which gave the boy much of his earliest knowledge of the Italian opera repertoire. At fifteen Shaw could "sing and whistle from end to end leading works by Handel, Haydn, Mozart, Beethoven, Rossini, Bellini, Donizetti and Verdi," and all this he owed, as he acknowledged in the preface to *London Music*, to "the meteoric impact of Lee, with his music, his method, his impetuous enterprise and his magnetism, upon the little Shaw household."

The extent to which this early—and profound—influence left its mark upon Shaw is reflected in the emphasis on music prevalent throughout his writing. Music is a dominant element in the five novels written between 1879 and 1884, and in the prefaces which subsequently were provided for them. *The Irrational Knot* opens with a satire on "Music for the People" workingmen's concerts sponsored by well-intentioned but benighted Christian Socialist parsons and social-conscious "society" folk (a subject Shaw was to expound upon with more seriousness in Francis Hueffer's *Musical Review* in 1883): "Tickets will be distributed to the families of working men by the Rev. George Lind . . . Symphony in F: Haydn. Arranged for four English concertinas by Julius Baker. Mr. Julius Baker; Master Julius Abt Baker; Miss Lisette Baker (aged 8); and Miss Totty Baker (aged 6½). . . . Song: Rose softly blooming: Spohr. Miss Marian Lind. . . . Nigger melody. Uncle Ned. Mr. Marmaduke Lind, accompanied by himself on the banjo."

In *Cashel Byron's Profession* the prizefighter hero of the novel translates into pugilistic terms his understanding of the battle between Wagner and his critics: "I made out from the gentleman's remarks that there is a man in the musical line named Wagner, who is what you might call a game sort of composer; and that the musical fancy, though they can't deny that his tunes are first-rate, and that, so to speak, he wins his fights, yet they try to make out that he wins them in an outlandish way, and that he has no real science."

But it is in *Love Among the Artists* that Shaw most fully reveals the extent of his knowledge of music and the powerful influence it has exerted upon him. His protagonist, Owen Jack, is a modern composer-genius of Beethovenesque intensity and ferocity, intractable and violent in his contempt for the second-rate, and demoniacally possessed as he composes:

Jack was alone, seated at the pianoforte, his brows knitted, his eyes glistening under them, his wrists bounding and re-bounding upon the keys, his rugged countenance transfigured by an expression of extreme energy and exaltation. He was playing from a manuscript score, and was making up for the absence of an orchestra by imitations of the instruments. He was grunting and buzzing the bassoon parts, humming when the violoncello had the melody, whistling for the flutes, singing hoarsely for the horns, barking for the trumpets, squealing

INTRODUCTION

for the oboes, making indescribable sounds in imitation of clarionets and drums, and marking each *sforzando* by a toss of his head and a gnash of his teeth. At last, abandoning this eccentric orchestration, he chanted with the full strength of his formidable voice until he came to the final chord, which he struck violently, and repeated in every possible inversion from one end of the keyboard to the other.

When Jack's Fantasia for pianoforte and orchestra is accepted for performance by Manlius, the conductor of the Antient Orpheus Orchestra, and the Polish lady pianist who is performing with the orchestra misjudges the speed of a movement under the direction of Manlius, Jack impetuously springs to the conductor's desk and, in an explosion of sound, conducts the rehearsal himself:

"Louder," roared Jack. "Louder. Less noise and more tone. Out with it like fifty million devils." And he led the movement at a merciless speed. . . . It was an insensate orgie of sound. Gay melodies, daintily given out by the pianoforte, or by the string instruments, were derisively brayed out immediately afterwards by cornets, harmonized in thirds with the most ingenious vulgarity. Cadenzas, agilely executed by the Polish lady, were uncouthly imitated by the double basses. Themes constructed like ballads with choruses were introduced instead of orthodox "subjects." . . . The Polish lady, incommoded by the capricious and often excessive speed required of her, held on gallantly, Jack all the time grinding his teeth, dancing, gesticulating, and by turns shshsh-shing at the orchestra or shouting to them for more tone and less noise.

Music is equally important as an element in Shaw's dramatic works. Mozart's *Don Giovanni*, which motivates the entire play, sets the mood and the scene specifically for the "Don Juan in Hell" sequence of *Man and Superman*, with the stage directions calling for "a ghostly violoncello palpitating on the same note endlessly" and "wailings from uncanny wind instruments." The Act III mystical rite in *The Tragedy of an Elderly Gentleman* (the fourth play in the *Back to Methuselah* cycle) opens with "Invisible trumpets utter[ing] three solemn blasts in the manner of

xiii

Die Zauberflöte," after which "organ music of the kind called sacred in the nineteenth century begins." In *Passion, Poison, and Petrifaction*, by way of contrast, a choir of invisible angels ends the burlesque with an unexpected rendition of "Won't You Come Home, Bill Bailey," and a pianoforte duet of a wedding march (*Lohengrin*, surely) climaxes the tomfoolery *The Music Cure*.

A considerable number of Shaw's dramatic characters are, to one degree or another, musicians. Clementina Buoyant is addicted to the saxophone, with which she charms alligators. Randall Utterword trills a flute solo of "Keep the Home Fires Burning" as the curtain descends on bomb-torn England at the end of *Heartbreak House* (the play itself is labelled a "fantasia"). Andrew Undershaft parades with Major Barbara's Salvation Army band, blaring away on a trombone. Charteris in *The Philanderer*, describing Julia's heartbreak, makes his point by sounding a discordant chord on Grace's piano, doing so, incidentally, by sitting on the bass end of the keyboard. Iddy Hammingtap in *The Simpleton* sermonizes on harp music. Count O'Dowda, Fanny's patrician parent, finds "Beethoven's music coarse and restless, and Wagner's senseless and detestable. I do not listen to them: I listen to Cimarosa, to Pergolesi, to Gluck and Mozart." Lady Corinthia Fanshawe, the "Richmond Park nightingale" of *Press Cuttings*, is "devoted to music and can reach F in alt with the greatest facility—Patti never got above E flat." Alastair Fitzfassenden, who marries the millionairess Epiphania, has "a startlingly loud singing voice of almost supernatural range"; he can "sing Caruso's head off," but "Nature unfortunately forgot to endow him with a musical ear."

The plays themselves, as Shaw revealed, were conceived on musical principles, being opera without music. His dialogues were frequently envisaged as duets, trios, and quartets. In the casting of the plays Shaw insisted on variety in pitch; Candida, for example, should be a contralto, Marchbanks a tenor, Morell a baritone, Prossy a soprano, and Burgess a bass. A conversation in which people all speak at the same speed and pitch, Shaw contended, is extremely disagreeable.

It might be propounded that, even had Shaw never written any formal musical criticism, we should still have been able to detect, from his plays and novels, that he was, as Eric Blom writes in the latest edition of Grove, "one of the most brilliant critics . . . of music, who have ever worked in London, or indeed anywhere." Fortunately conjecture is unnecessary, for the criticism does exist and, with the publication of the present volume, which complements the four volumes of *Star* and *World* criticism collected by Shaw in his Standard Edition as *London Music* and *Music in London*, the full range of Shaw's musical criticism may, for the first time, be examined in perspective.

Since music was the subject Shaw knew best, it is not surprising that his first journalistic experience should have been that of a musical critic. It is, however, unlikely that the editor of any London publication would knowingly have engaged the journalistic services of a stripling of twenty, fresh from provincial Dublin, for so specialised an assignment. The employment, as Shaw explained in the autobiographical essay which provides the title for this volume, came as the result of a deception played upon the non-related Captain Donald Shaw, editor of *The Hornet*, a satirical weekly. Vandeleur Lee, whose virtues apparently did not include moral scruple, palmed himself off on editor Shaw as a musical critic and privately arranged for his prodigy to pen the notices. It was a mutually advantageous arrangement, for both attended the concerts and operatic performances on complimentary tickets, and the Shaw household benefited from the additional income while Lee enjoyed the dubious distinction of being thought a journalist by his acquaintances and pupils. Donald Shaw eventually sensed he was being hoodwinked, but the editor and the ghost never met. The one major drawback, as Shaw subsequently noted, was that he had no opportunity to correct proofs of his material.

The deception was, however, sustained for nearly a year. Shaw's first contribution, a review of Frederic Cowen's opera *Pauline*, appeared in the issue of 29 November 1876, and his last, a satirical portrait of "A Typical 'Popular' Vocalist," in the issue of 26 September 1877. In later years Shaw was to claim that the paper expired shortly thereafter, due principally to the negative effect of his criticisms. This was a Shavian exaggeration, for in actuality *The Hornet* survived until February 1880.

Shaw also alleged that the editor "had mutilated and inter-polated my notices horribly," but he was often guilty of this type of hyperbole, the same extravagant charges of mutilation later being levelled, quite unjustifiably, against James Huneker, who collected Shaw's *Saturday Review* dramatic criticism into two volumes under the title *Dramatic Opinions and Essays.* Among all the *Hornet* contributions (preserved by Shaw in a large cutting-book), only one Wagner article—not included in the present volume—reveals any serious "anti-Wagnerism," and this is now known, from extant correspondence, to have been drafted by another hand, revised by "Lee" at the editor's request, and then re-revised by the editor. As for "puffs," which Shaw alleged the editor had frequently inserted, it is difficult to find in the entire body of the criticism more than a handful of real compliments, and this praise, when it appears, has the ring of sincerity; the artists thus extolled were to continue to receive Shaw's nod of approval in subsequent criticism and reminiscence. Only in the praise bestowed upon Sterndale Bennett's overture to *Parisina* (28 March 1877) does there appear to be ground for suspicion.

The criticism in *The Hornet* does reveal, however, that Shaw at twenty had already developed a remarkable capacity for detect-ing the weaknesses of musical performances. He expatiated on the importance of *ensemble* versus the "star system" in opera, on "scratch" performances, on inadequate rehearsal-time, on clumsy staging and ugly décor. He attacked (as he was later to do in Shakespearean productions) the vulgarisation and mutilation of classic works. He harped on the audience's bad manners and on the national insensibility to good music. He scored "the absurdity of being the only music-patronizing nation in the world which systematically tolerates opera delivered in a foreign tongue." And he single-handedly attacked the ballad-concert system fostered by music-publishers to promote their publications, at which lead-ing singers performed and thus advertised the wares of the pub-lisher, receiving in return a royalty on all copies sold (an interest-ing variation of a vice which was to become known in twentieth-century American musical circles as "payola").

In his early criticism Shaw was frequently ruthless, his crusading zeal leading him to an emulation of David's slaying of his tens of thousands. The legendary Tamberlik in his celebrated duet in Rossini's *Otello*, we were told, for the C sharp "substituted a strange description of shriek at about that pitch. The audience, ever appreciative of vocal curiosities, redemanded it." A Liszt composition was described as having "a brief *andante* of advanced commonplace." The sharpness of the flute-playing of Oluf Svendsen, it was suggested, constituted "an unhappy craving to be conspicuous at any cost." The ghost apprentice had not yet learned how to substitute the rapier for the bludgeon.

More than seven years elapsed before Shaw had an opportunity to return to musical criticism, but this long hiatus, during which Shaw had devoted himself largely to literary exercise (but also to the study of harmony, counterpoint, and temperament), resulted in a development of style and an improvement in articulation which are instantly apparent when one compares Shaw's criticism of the analytical programme of Liszt's *Mazeppa* in 1877 with that of the *Inferno* in 1885, or his contemporary description of Wagner's performance as a conductor in London with the retrospective portrait in "Herr Richter and His Blue Ribbon." The maturing critic focused his attention upon many of the same faults which had been targets of his earlier attack, but his approach had become more subtle, his assault more controlled, his brash self-assurance tempered by time and experience into a colourful and charming egotism. In the criticism of the mid-1880's the reader already has a presentiment of the imminence of that effervescent personality now known to us as Corno di Bassetto.

But it must not be supposed that Corno was conceived as spontaneously or with as much facility as Shaw and T. P. O'Connor led us to believe. It is true that Shaw joined the editorial staff of *The Star* at its inception in January 1888, under the editorship of O'Connor and his two brilliant young assistants, H. W. Massingham and Ernest Parke. And it is equally true that after a week or two of thwarted attempts, via *The Star*'s leaders, to turn the Liberal paper into a Socialist one, Shaw was obliged to withdraw from the staff. "Dear Chief," he wrote to O'Connor, "This is my resignation. I am not worth my salt to the Star; and you will be more at your ease without having constantly to suppress my articles.... So I must give myself the sack; though what

is to become of you and Massingham when you have no one to
guide you through the mists of sentimental Utopianism is more
than I can foresee. The special Providence that protects children
be your safeguard!"

The romantic tale woven by Shaw, and later embroidered by
O'Connor in his *Memoirs of an Old Parliamentarian*, is that
Massingham, being unwilling to lose his young Socialist friend,
reminded T. P. that the paper had no musical critic, and that
Shaw, having an extraordinary knowledge of music, would be the
ideal man for the position. To this O'Connor claimed he instantly
agreed, for he knew that Shaw "had just emerged from that
desolating interval in life in which employment either does not
exist or is sparse and fitful; and I had gone through so much
agony in the same interval of my life that I could not think of
putting a man back into the abyss from which he had only just
emerged."

Unfortunately, there isn't a grain of truth in the story. Shaw
resigned on 9 February 1888, noting in his diary on the 10th that
he went to the *Star* office in Stonecutter Street for the last time,
during which visit he wrote a sub-leader and arranged with
O'Connor to write occasional signed articles and to send notes.
For several months, as a free-lance journalist, he made odd contributions to *The Star*, but he was contributing with greater
frequency to the *Pall Mall Gazette* and, at the same time, providing art criticism for *The World*. There was no question of his
becoming musical critic of *The Star*; the position already was
filled. Anyone examining the pages of *The Star* for the bulk of
the year 1888 will find its musical criticism signed "Musigena," a
pseudonym which masked the identity of a fellow-Socialist,
E. Belfort Bax, the uncle of Arnold Bax. In June 1888 Shaw
gravitated towards the job that was eventually to be his by accepting Massingham's offer that he cover those occasional musical
events which conflicted with performances being reviewed by
Bax. In July, when Bax was preparing to leave for a holiday in
Zürich, he arranged with Shaw to serve as his substitute. Thereafter, until early in 1889, Shaw continued as second-string critic.
It was not until February 1889 that Shaw replaced Bax completely and, in need of a pseudonym, created his *alter ego*. Corno

di Bassetto, after months of anonymity, made his presence known to readers of *The Star* on February 15th.

London suddenly found itself being entertained by a weekly column of "Musical Mems" that was an olla-podrida of wit and wisdom on music, drama, socialism, bicycling, prizefighting, and anything else its author cared to throw in for good measure. Shaw had found his ideal *métier*, and at a cost to *The Star* of only three guineas a week. "There never was such musical criticism on land or flood," O'Connor later boasted, but when Shaw wrote to him in March 1890 to ask for an increase in salary, O'Connor demurred. *The Star*, he replied, could do very well without Shaw. A second letter of resignation followed immediately: "The giving up of the Musical Mems will be a gigantic—a Himalayan mistake. However, a wilful man must have his way." As O'Connor did not call his bluff, Shaw wrote *finis* to Corno di Bassetto in May 1890; a week later he contracted with Edmund Yates to do a column on music for *The World*, where for more than four years the initials "G.B.S." were to appear weekly. These articles represented his most mature musical journalism; they also constituted his valediction as a professional musical critic.

Any assessment of Shaw's nineteenth-century musical criticism must include several ineluctable facts. No critic of his time—no performer for that matter—possessed so thorough a knowledge and understanding as Shaw did of the Italian repertory which dominated the London musical scene. This, however, did not blind him to other musical values, as it seemed to do many of his colleagues. Few were so quick as Shaw in recognising the genius of Wagner; at virtually the same moment that Shaw was extolling Wagner's contribution, not only as a great musician, but as a profound thinker and moralist, Ruskin was proclaiming that "of all the affected, sapless, soulless, beginningless, endless, topless, bottomless, topsiturviest, scrannelpipiest, tongs and boniest doggrel of sounds I ever endured the deadliness of, that eternity of nothing [*Die Meistersinger*] was the deadliest." Shaw also perceived the profound significance of the music of Bach at a time when few in England were ready and able to appreciate it; he called it the music, not of the past, but of the future. And he championed the cause of Mozart, whose "German music with

Italian words" had not yet received the full recognition that Shaw insisted be accorded it. Mozart, to Shaw, was the greatest of all the musicians. "He taught me how to say profound things," Shaw once told Ferruccio Busoni, "and at the same time remain flippant and lively."

Perhaps most important of all, Shaw perceived clearly the ineptitude of British music as produced by the pedantic "university school" of composers, who dictated British musical taste. He scorned the works of men like Sterndale Bennett, Cowen, Macfarren, and Sullivan "the organist of Chester-square," academicians all. As Ernest Newman noted in his *Sunday Times* review of *Music in London* in 1932, "Shaw turned upon the spectacle of the English musical world of the day an eye unclouded by tradition, a judgment unaffected by social or official considerations. He declined to take people like the Parrys and the Stanfords and the rest of them seriously as composers, or the colleges as the providentially appointed trainees of the musical youth of the nation." To Shaw nineteenth-century British music was "a little Mozart and water."

When the non-academic Elgar appeared on the horizon at the turn of the century, Shaw was certain that British music had taken a decisive step forward. "I consider," he wrote to the editor of the *Morning Post* in 1911, "that the history of original music, broken off by the death of Purcell, begins again with Sir Edward Elgar." Elgar, he expostulated in an interview at Glastonbury in 1916, "is the first musician who, after a century of imitation of Handel, Mendelssohn and Spohr, began to write music like an Englishman." The older British composers were killed by the academic system, he insisted; the younger ones were *making* style and were full of experiments. "I hold the view," he concluded, "that after two hundred years during which our abler men would not touch music, we are now coming into our own again as a great musical nation." The emergence of Vaughan Williams, Walton, Britten, Bax, and Bliss as contributors to twentieth-century musical development more than fulfils the prophecy. But it is not unusual that Shaw should have been right in this instance; as Ernest Newman pointed out, "time has proved the rightness of nine contemporary estimates of his out of ten."

INTRODUCTION

That Shaw occasionally blundered in his evaluations cannot be questioned; he never claimed to be infallible, though he once exclaimed jocularly, in *The World*, that the first precept in a contemplated book, *Advice to Old Musicians*, would run, "Dont be in a hurry to contradict G.B.S., as he never commits himself on a musical subject until he knows at least six times as much about it as you do." He overestimated Gounod and undervalued Berlioz, though Newman suggested one reason for this might have been that the works of Berlioz were not too intelligently performed in London in the 1890's. More interestingly, he misjudged Brahms. In 1876 he cited the piano quartet in G minor as an " example of the genius of a master of whom we in this country know far too little," but subsequent evaluations were less complimentary and, certainly, less valid. To a friend he privately confided, in 1893, "Brahms is just like Tennyson, an extraordinary musician, with the brains of a third-rate village policeman." Later he was to apologise for failing to recognise and appreciate Brahms's unfamiliar idiom, and to attempt to excuse himself on the ground that even Beethoven had denounced Weber's Euryanthe overture as a string of diminished sevenths, but the fact remains that his devotion to Wagner apparently blinded him to the achievement of Brahms, much as Eduard Hanslick's infatuation with Brahms had led him to become one of Wagner's bitterest opponents (to Shaw's great disgust).

The errors of judgment were, however, comparatively few. For the most part, Shaw instinctively recognised the true artist and rejected the false one. And though he wrote less frequently of music in the twentieth century than he had in the nineteenth, his acumen was never blunted. He kept abreast of the times, at least as much as the B.B.C.'s programming would permit, and in the twentieth century he was as self-assured about Richard Strauss as he had been about Wagner in the nineteenth, as confirmed in his opinion of Beecham and Boult as he had been in that of Costa and Richter. In 1914 he commented, in a letter to Cedric Glover, "I always applaud Schönberg and Scriabin vigorously because they are enlarging our musical material so usefully ... I was quite proud of myself for guessing which was to be the final chord of the fifth Orchestral Piece, which was more than I had been able to do in the four previous ones." In his last years he kept a shelf of orchestral scores, uniformly bound in vegetarian vellum, beside his Bechstein, and even in his ninety-fourth year he continued to play and, quaveringly, to sing the scores of Mussorgsky's *Boris Godunov*, Verdi's *I Masnadieri*, Strauss's *Ariadne auf Naxos*, and Elgar's *Dream of Gerontius*. Iconoclastic to the end, he refused to indulge in the practice of old men by reminiscing nostalgically about the past to prove that things were better then. Almost with his dying breath he insisted that we sing better today than our grandparents did.

For three-quarters of a century Bernard Shaw appraised the British musical scene. He wrote with logic, wit, directness, conscience, courage, and a liveliness of intellect which was unique in his time and remains so in ours. The musical journalism he produced is as brilliant as any that literate man can ever hope to see. Leonard Bernstein, in his recently published *The Joy of Music*, contends that "the only way one can really say anything about music is to write music." It is obvious that Bernstein has not read Shaw.

DAN H. LAURENCE

LONDON, *August* 1960

EDITOR'S NOTE

The materials in this volume were published originally in a variety of styles, reflecting the idiosyncrasies of numerous editors and compositors. When Shaw reprinted some of his early writings in his Collected Edition (and, subsequently, in the reset Standard Edition), he gave them uniformity by revising the texts to conform with his own established style. This style, however, was in many respects more idiosyncratic than that of any of the predecessors whose typographical peculiarities he was rejecting. His reforms ranged inconsistently from the retention of archaic spellings (*shew* for *show*) to the introduction of strange new ones (*advertizing* and *wernt*), and he had stubborn convictions about the elimination of quotation marks, apostrophes, and italics.

Since the present edition is intended to complement the Standard Edition, the editor and publisher have, albeit reluctantly, undertaken to follow Shaw's dicta in all matters of spelling and punctuation within his texts, as well as in matters of general style and design. Except for a few corrections of obvious misprints, the texts are otherwise faithfully reproduced, with editorial emendations inserted in square brackets.

The unsigned writings included in the volume have been identified from examination of Shaw's unpublished diaries, notebooks, account books, correspondence, holograph manuscripts, and cuttings books, and from marked files of journals in which they were published.

The editor wishes to acknowledge gratefully the invaluable assistance of the following persons in the preparation of this book: Mr and Mrs T. Edward Hanley, Mr Stanley Pryor, librarian of *The Star* and *News Chronicle*, Mrs Woltraud Hatsfeld, Mr Andrew Block, Mr S. Geduld, Miss Monique Russ, Mr Eric Batson, Miss Barbara Smoker, and Mr Allen B. Veaner, Head, Photographic Department, Harvard College Library. He is indebted also to Mr John Wardrop for reading proof.

D. H. L.

PRELUDE

HOW TO BECOME A MUSICAL CRITIC

(*The Scottish Musical Monthly, December* 1894; reprinted
in *The New Music Review*, New York, *October* 1912)

My own plan was a simple one. I joined the staff of a new daily
paper as a leader writer. My exploits in this department spread
such terror and confusion that my proposal to turn my attention
to musical criticism was hailed with inexpressible relief, the subject being one in which lunacy is privileged. I was given a column
to myself precisely as I might have been given a padded room in
an asylum; and from that time up to the other day—a period of
nearly seven years—I wrote every week, in that paper or another,
an article under the general heading "Music," the first condition
of which was, as a matter of good journalism, that it should be as
attractive to the general reader, musician or non-musician, as any
other section of the paper in which it appeared. Most editors do
not believe that this can be done. But then most editors do not
know how to edit. The late Edmund Yates, who did, believed
in a good musical column as an important reinforcement to a
journal. He placed a whole page of The World at the disposal of
his musical critic. And the success of this page proved that in the
hands of a capable writer music is quite as good a subject from
the purely journalistic point of view as either painting or the
drama, whilst the interest taken in it is much more general than
in party politics, the stock exchange, or even the police intelligence. Let me add that Edmund Yates had no more special
interest in music than he had in chemistry; for young musical
critics should be warned that of all editors for their purposes, the
musical-amateur editor is the very worst. Only, let me in justice
add, too, that the critic who is a musical amateur and nothing
else is equally objectionable.

I

HOW TO BECOME A MUSICAL CRITIC

It is quite clear that if musical criticism is to win from all papers the space and consideration allowed it in The World, the critics must be persons of considerable accomplishment. There are three main qualifications for a musical critic, besides the general qualification of good sense and knowledge of the world. He must have a cultivated taste for music; he must be a skilled writer; and he must be a practiced critic. Any of these three may be found without the others; but the complete combination is indispensable to good work. Take up any of our musical papers —those which are taken in by the organist as The Lancet is taken in by the doctor—and you will find plenty of articles written by men of unquestionable competence and even eminence as musicians. These gentlemen may write without charm because they have not served their apprenticeship to literature; but they can at all events express themselves at their comparative leisure as well as most journalists do in their feverish haste; and they can depend on the interest which can be commanded by any intelligent man who has ordinary powers of expression, and who is dealing with a subject he understands. Why, then, are they so utterly impossible as musical critics? Because they cannot criticize. They set to work like schoolmasters to prove that this is "right" and that "wrong"; they refer disputed points to school authorities who have no more authority in the republic of art than the head master of Eton has in the House of Commons; they jealously defend their pet compositions and composers against rival claims like ladies at a musical at-home; they shew no sense of the difference between a professor teaching his class how to resolve the chord of the dominant seventh and a critic standing in the presence of the whole world and its art, and submitting his analysis of the work of an artist whose authority is at least equal to his own. A man may have counterpoint at his finger ends; but if, being no more than a second-rate music teacher, he petulantly treats composers of European reputation as intrusive and ignorant pretenders who ought to be suppressed—a very different thing from genuine criticism, however unfavorable, of their works—he obviously puts himself out of the question as a member of the staff of any general newspaper or magazine.

HOW TO BECOME A MUSICAL CRITIC

It is not so easy to cite instances of writers who fail because, being critics, they have neither literary skill nor musical culture. A man cannot become an expert in criticism without practicing on art of some kind; and if that art is not music, then he naturally confines himself to the art he is accustomed to handle, writing about it if he has the requisite literary faculty, and if not, teaching it. As to the literary artist who is neither musician nor critic, he has every inducement to devote himself to pure literature, like Mr Stevenson or Mr Rudyard Kipling, and no temptation whatever to eke out his income by sham musical criticism. But since, for the purposes of journalism, the literary qualification is the main one—since no editor who is supplied with entertaining "copy" ever asks whether it is criticism or gossip, or cares whether its technology is a bit sounder than the sham sailing directions given in Gulliver's ship, cases are not lacking of journalists taking the post of musical critic merely because it is the only opening that presents itself, and concealing their deficiencies by plenty of descriptive reporting and scraps of news about music and musicians. If such a critic has critical and musical faculty latent in him, he will learn his business after some years; but some writers of this sort have not the faculty, and never learn.

It is worth remarking here—at least I cannot resist mentioning it—that the experienced editor has usually found the mere musician critic so useless on a paper, and the mere journalist critic so sufficient for all purposes, that the critic whose articles are at all readable by people who only read to be amused is usually suspected by his fellow journalists of being a musical impostor, a suspicion which reaches absolute certainty in the mind of his editor. When my own articles on music first began to attract some attention, the cream of the joke was supposed by many persons to be the fact that I knew nothing whatever about music. Several times it happened to me to be introduced to admirers who, on discovering from my reply to the question, "What put it into your head to write about music?" that I did so because it happened to be the art I knew most about, have turned away cruelly disappointed and disillusioned by this prosaic explanation, which seemed to rob my exploits of all their merit.

3

Even when the hypothesis of my total ignorance became untenable, I still used occasionally to encounter people who appealed to me to candidly admit that my knowledge of music did not extend to its technicalities. They missed, I imagine, the Mesopotamianism of the sort of musical writing which parades silly little musical parsing exercises to impress the laity exactly as the performances of the learned pig impress the rustics at a fair.

A critic who does not know his business has two advantages. First, if he writes for a daily paper he can evade the point, and yet make himself useful and interesting, by collecting the latest news about forthcoming events, and the most amusing scandal about past ones. Second, his incompetence can be proved only by comparing his notice of a month ago with his notice of today, which nobody will take the trouble to do. Any man can write an imposing description of Madame Calvé, or of Slivinski, but if you turn back to his description of Miss Eames or of Sapellnikoff, you will find, if he is no critic, that the same description did duty for them also, just as it did duty, before he was born, for Catalani and Pasta, Cramer and Czerny. When he attempts to particularize the special qualities of the artists he criticizes, you will find him praising Sarasate and Paderewski for exactly those feats which their pupils, Miss Nettie Carpenter and Miss Szumowska, are able to copy to the life. Whether he is praising or blaming, he always dwells on some of the hundred points that all players and executants have in common, and misses the final ones that make all the difference between mediocrity and genius, and between one artist and another.

I know this by my own experience. Nearly twenty years ago a musician who wished to help me accepted a post as musical critic to a London paper. I wrote the criticisms; and he handed the emoluments over to me without deduction, contenting himself with the consciousness of doing generously by a young and forlorn literary adventurer, and with the honor and glory accruing from the reputed authorship of my articles. To them I owe all my knowledge of the characteristics of bad criticism. I cannot here convey an adequate impression of their demerits without overstepping the bounds of decorum. They made me miserable at the time; but I did not know even enough to understand that what was torturing me was the guilt and shame which attend ignorance and incompetence. The paper, with my assistance, died, and my sins are buried with it; but I still keep, in a safe hiding place, a set of the critical crimes I contributed to it, much as a murderer keeps the bloodstained knife under which his victim fell.[1] Whenever I feel that I am getting too conceited, or am conscious of crediting myself with a natural superiority to some younger brother of the craft, I take myself down by reading some of that old stuff—though indeed the bare thought of it is generally sufficient. And yet neither in literary ability nor musical knowledge was I unpardonably deficient at that time. I should have been a very decent critic for my age, if only I had known how to criticize. Not knowing that, however, my musical knowledge and power of literary expression made me much more noxious than if I had been a mere newsman in music and a phrasemonger in journalism. When I broke out again, about ten years later, I had graduated as a critic, as a writer, and as a citizen (a most important item) by constant work as an author, a critic of books, pictures, and politics, a public speaker, and a social reformer, including the function of the wirepuller and committee man, as well as of the theorist and Utopian. All this had nothing to do with music; yet, in my musical criticism, it made all the difference between an execrable amateur and a reasonably competent workman. I was enormously helped as a critic by my economical studies and my political practice, which gave me an invaluable comprehension of the commercial conditions to which art is subject. It is an important part of a critic's business to agitate for musical reforms; and unless he knows what the reforms will cost, and whether they are worth that cost, and who will have to pay the bill, and a dozen other cognate matters not usually included in treatises on harmony, he will not make any effective impression on the people with whom the initiative rests—indeed he will not know who they are. Even his artistic verdicts will often be aimed at the wrong person. A manager or an artist cannot be judged fairly by any critic who

---

[1] It is from this set of "critical crimes," carefully preserved by Shaw for three-quarters of a century, that *The Hornet* selections reprinted in the present volume are drawn.

does not understand the economic bearings of profits and salaries. It is one thing to set up an ideal of perfection and complain as long as it is not reached; but to blame individuals for not reaching it when it is economically unattainable, instead of blaming the conditions which make it unattainable; or to blame the wrong person—for instance, to blame the artist when the fault is the manager's, or the manager when the fault is the public's—is to destroy half your influence as a critic. All the counterpoint or literary brilliancy in the world will not save a critic from blunders of this kind, unless he understands the economics of art.

I need say no more as to the accomplishments of a musical critic, because I have already brought myself face to face with an economic difficulty in my own path. The emoluments of a musical critic are not large. Newspaper proprietors offer men from a pound a week to five pounds a week for musical criticism, the latter figure being very exceptional, and involving the delivery of a couple of thousand words of extra brilliant copy every week. And, except in the dead season, the critic must spend most of his afternoons and evenings, from three to midnight, in concert rooms or in the opera house. I need hardly say that it is about as feasible to obtain the services of a fully-qualified musical critic on these terms as it would be to obtain a pound of fresh strawberries every day from January to December for five shillings a week. Consequently, to all the qualifications I have already suggested, I must insist on this further one—an independent income, and sufficient belief in the value of musical criticism to sustain you in doing it for its own sake whilst its pecuniary profits are enjoyed by others. And since this condition is so improbable in any given case as to take my subject completely out of the range of the practicable, I may as well stop preaching, since my sermon ends, as all such sermons do, in a demonstration that our economic system fails miserably to provide the requisite incentive to the production of first-rate work.

I

MUSICAL BUZZINGS OF A
GHOST APPRENTICE

(*The Hornet*, 1876–77; unsigned)

The English opera season is at length over. For a time, at
least, theatre-going lovers of music must be content with the
brassy delights of pantomime and the affecting symphonies which
accompany the development of transformation scenes. Mr Carl
Rosa has started on a provincial tour, which will, we hope, prove
as successful as his London season has been. During that season
he has not hesitated to depart from managerial precedent so far
as to keep his promises, and he has fairly carried out his program
of discarding the star system and aiming at excellence of *ensemble*.
For this he deserves our gratitude, rather than the reproaches
with which he has been assailed for enlisting Mr Santley as "a
star," and for excluding Mozart's operas from his repertory.
Cavillers would do well to bear in mind that avoiding the star
system does not mean engaging none but second-rate artists.
When an *impresario* offers us an impoverished orchestra, incompetent subordinates, and defective *mise en scène* in order to meet
the sensational terms of popular *prime donne*: then we have just
cause for complaint. But Mr Carl Rosa has not done this. On the
contrary, his company is in all respects improved since the acces-
sion of Mr Santley.

As to the clamorers for Mozart, their importunity practically
amounts to asking for a display of weakness in the production of
works which demand all the highest qualifications which the
most gifted artists can bring to their work. We have had an
opera of Wagner's [The Flying Dutchman] very creditably produced; we have had Fidelio, which some—notably those who

speak of Mozart's works as trifles—declare the greatest of operas; we have had Pauline, specially written by one of our own composers; and if we are not satisfied, Mr Carl Rosa is not to blame in the matter.

The only special event of the closing week was a morning performance of Faust, for the benefit of the society for the relief of distressed Americans, the part of Marguerite being undertaken for this occasion by Madame Van Zandt, who, like the other artists, volunteered her services. Under these circumstances, a minute criticism of the lady's performance would be uncalled for. It will suffice to say that, with the exception of a trifling hitch in the church scene, she sang the music correctly, and achieved a floral success. We would suggest, however, that in future the persons who kindly undertake to throw bouquets should study the score beforehand, and offer their tributes at the proper opportunities. On Wednesday last, bouquets dropped promiscuously throughout the performance, and one, bearing a message of peace and charity, fell most inappropriately into the hands of Mephistopheles. The military band in the fourth act played strepitously—most offensively so, indeed. Mr Ludwig, who appeared as Valentine, effectually spoiled his song by delivering the words with a strong foreign inflection: an affectation which cannot be too strongly reprehended.[1] In other respects, the cast was the same as usual, Miss Yorke being conspicuous by her meritorious impersonation of Siebel.

On Tuesday, the 28th ult., Cagnoni's opera The Porter of Havre was performed before a rather limited audience. This pretty opera holds a position somewhat analogous to that of Marta. It is not great, but it is never disagreeable. It contains some beautiful numbers, the orchestration (in the style of Meyerbeer) is solid, and the plot, though absurdly constructed, is entertaining. Above all, in some of its scenes are familiar pictures of home life—impossible on the Italian stage—the power of presenting which is one of the most charming attractions afforded by English opera.

[1] Ludwig was the professional name adopted by Irish tenor William Ledwidge. Throughout Shaw's early critical years—until, in fact, the custom waned—he disparaged this practice by British musical artists of masking their national origin with foreign names and mannerisms.

The last two nights were devoted to Fidelio and The Water Carrier. The association of these is the more appropriate as it gives us an opportunity of tracing the extent to which Beethoven followed Cherubini—his acknowledged model—in the structure of his only opera. As performed by the Carl Rosa company, the dialogue is retained according to the intention of the composers, and we escape the recitative impertinences with which Balfe and others have vulgarized these works for representation on the Italian stage.

13 *December* 1876

The only novelty at the Saturday Popular Concert on the 2nd instant was a Sonata for pianoforte and violin by Rheinberger, introduced by Madame Norman Neruda and Mr Hallé. It was unfortunately placed at the end of the program, and neither the romantic beauty of the work, nor the ordinary politeness due to the artists, availed to secure it a hearing until the last overcoat in the hall was comfortably buttoned and everybody prepared to rush forth at the first notes of the *coda*. It is not calculated to advance our national reputation that these concerts should be so largely frequented by foreigners, who naturally conclude that our pursuit of music is mere fashionable affectation, and that we are incapable of behaving ourselves properly.

20 *December* 1876

Mazeppa, a symphonic poem for orchestra, by F. Liszt, was performed for the first time in England, at the Crystal Palace on the 9th inst. The program introduces the work as "a gigantic musical picture of the terrible three days' ride related in Victor Hugo's soul-stirring poem, and of the poet's allegorical representation of the unbridled flight of genius, and its final triumph through suffering and adversity." Then follows a brief dissertation on the comparative merits of Lord Byron and Victor Hugo as emotional poets; the usual thematic analysis of the music; and, finally, a reprint of the entire poem. It will be seen that no trouble was spared to enable the audience to realize the composer's intention, or to arouse their interest in his work.

The first portion is an *allegro agitato*, of which we are told: "This remarkable movement illustrates the three days' flight of the wild steed, and the almost indescribable anguish and despair of its human victim, as related in the first fourteen verses of the poem." It opens with a sudden clash of cymbals, at which the section of the audience which is not familiar with the eccentricities of higher development bursts out laughing. The sequel consists of rapid triplets, with a good deal of piccolo, drum, and cymbal, relieved by an effective melody for the brass: the whole producing an effect sufficiently entertaining, and at times very amusing, but not even remotely approaching the sublime. It may be revived at intervals with an alteration of program, as, for instance, "A Sudden Shower," "A Storm in a Teacup," or " Macbeth, The Witches' Cauldron," any of which it would illustrate more appropriately than the rushing of a wild horse, which is perhaps the only phenomenon of an exciting description that it does *not* suggest. After a brief *andante* of advanced commonplace, the "symphonic poem" concludes with an *allegro marziale*, in the constant modulations and stirring marches of which we see, not "glory and greatness achieved through suffering and adversity," but the favorite effects of the clever pianoforte transcriber achieved on a large scale through the resources of orchestra. Opinions respecting the work as a whole must depend altogether on the standard from which it is judged. If we consider it as a fantastic caprice designed to illustrate the more grotesque external incidents of the story, it deserves some admiration for its piquancy and skilful scoring. But if we apply the broad gauge, which the composer himself challenges, and look for a picture of complicated emotion, and a display of the powers of music much as we find in the symphonies of the great masters, we unhesitatingly condemn it as false art, due to the conception, not of a true musician, but of a charlatan.

Schubert's string quintet in C, Op. 163, beautiful though its themes are, is decidedly too long. The composer fell into the error—an habitual one with him—of developing the principal movements at a length quite disproportionate to his resources in variety of form, and hence the effect of the quintet as a whole is wearisome. Apart from this, the work is full of the melancholy tenderness characteristic of Schubert's style, and the compact central movements, with the quaint *scherzo* and funereal *trio*, are sources of unalloyed pleasure. It was moderately well played at the Monday Popular Concert on the 11th inst. by MM. Piatti, Ries, Zerbini, and Pezze, led by Herr Straus. Miss Anna Mehlig displayed her technical ability in a performance of Schumann's *Toccata* in C, Op. 7, and, being deservedly encored, played one of those mysterious *morceaux* which we are accustomed to hear on such occasions. She was also heard in Brahms's pianoforte quartet in G minor, and with Signor Piatti in a *polonaise* by Chopin. The arrangement of Brahms's quartet is unusual. It opens with the customary *allegro*, followed by an *intermezzo* with *trio*, the former melancholy in character, and played with muted violins. This is succeeded by an *andante*, which is perhaps the most important movement in the work. The *finale* is in the *rondo saltarello* form, so favored in modern instrumental music, and its performance elicited a burst of genuine applause. The entire work, though less striking than the quartet in C minor, recently introduced at the Popular Concerts, is a sufficient example of the genius of a master of whom we in this country know far too little.

3 January 1877

The past fortnight has been, musically speaking, nearly a blank. At Christmas the divine art is wont to retreat into private life! There are plenty of carols, but no concerts; and even the church bells, in hopelessly false intervals, ring out a special appeal to the public to be taken down from their cold eminence and consigned to the crucible. And as, in spite of our protests, they daily assert beyond dispute our national insensibility to music, it would be as well to comply with their demand and allow the hours to pass away undisturbed.

17 January 1877

In the present century of universal progress, no art, perhaps, has attained to such subtly-varied developments as that of advertizing. We used to hear that an outlay of some thousands in advertisements would ensure a return of cent. per cent. This, however, is now a vulgar and old-fashioned principle; and of late years the far more ingenious method of bringing one's wares into notoriety at the expense of the public has been brought nearly to perfection, especially by the music trade, abetted by the less independent singers of the day. Thus, a few of the leading firms have started musical journals in order to secure an impartial review for each work published by them, and a just exposure of the demerits of such trash as rival establishments may attempt to impose on the public. A more immediately remunerative plan is the institution of dreary entertainments known as "ballad concerts." It is well known that the best way to sell a song is to have it sung.

Consequently, when Messrs Blank and Co. announce a concert for which they have engaged the most eminent vocalists of the day, more is implied thereby than is evident to the unsophisticated concert-goer, who conceives the undertaking to be a legitimate speculation. He finds the concert stupid, but he does not attach any significance to the fact that all the uninteresting and worthless items which spin out the long program (excepting only those which constitute the attraction and are sung by artists who have achieved an independent position) are published by Messrs Blank and Co. Probably, if he did awaken to the true nature of the transaction, he would decline to contribute in future to the advertizing expenses of the enterprizing firm; and as such uninitiated frequenters of concert rooms are, as a rule, the only persons who pay for admission, the whole pernicious system of publishers' concerts would fall unsupported to the ground, bringing with it the concomitant nuisances of royalties and similar varieties of blackmail, alike degrading to art and oppressive to composers of real merit.

7 February 1877

On the 1st instant, at the Albert Hall, Mendelssohn's Lobgesang and Rossini's Stabat Mater were repeated. With the exception of Mr Sims Reeves, the cast was entirely different from that of last December. We are glad to note a decided improvement in the orchestra and chorus. The symphony preceding the vocal portions of the Hymn of Praise was very fairly played, especially the *allegretto*, in which the brass is little employed, and which is in itself perhaps the best part of the instrumental work. In following out the idea suggested by Beethoven's ninth symphony, the comparative weakness and paucity of invention displayed by Mendelssohn are emphasized by contrast; and whether from this reason or not, the symphonic prelude to the Lobgesang has always appeared to us an elaborate and lengthy working up of somewhat feeble materials. Mr Sims Reeves's delivery of the tenor music was full of devotional feeling, and the intensity of expression conveyed in the cry, Watchman, will the night soon pass? made a deep impression. Miss Anna Williams and Miss Braham sang out of tune, and the duet I waited for the Lord suffered for it.

In the Stabat Mater the principal parts were in the hands of Mesdames Lemmens-Sherrington and Antoinette Sterling, Messrs W. H. Cummings and R. Hilton. The last-named gentleman rendered the baritone music inartistically, and entirely failed to realize the sharp markings of the *Pro peccatis*. Miss Sterling was remarkable as usual for her earnest feeling and originality of style. If she would but deign to pay a little attention to phrasing and carefully avoid stooping to mannerism, she might take rank amongst the greatest of our oratorio singers. Madame Sherrington marred an otherwise satisfactory interpretation of the soprano music by the introduction of a shake very much out of keeping with the character of the Inflammatus.

In the duet *Quis est homo*, the trombones, which have become a nuisance to frequenters of the Albert Hall, exerted themselves with their usual offensiveness. It is true that Rossini marked the semiquaver emphasized by the trombones *fortissimo*, but the *maestro* had studied the instruments in the hands of artists, and not in the circus. The strangest thing is that Mr Barnby, who should know better, apparently approves of the hideous bark— there is really no other equivalent in the language—from which the audience visibly shrink. Excepting further a sharp drum, the orchestra was otherwise efficient.

HOW TO BECOME A MUSICAL CRITIC

28 *February* 1877

The second Crystal Palace concert of this year took place on Saturday afternoon, the 17th. The program included Cherubini's earnest and refined overture to Medea, Haydn's Oxford symphony, and an overture to Alfieri's tragedy of Saul, the latter being heard for the first—and possibly the last—time in England. It is a fair specimen of a modern concert overture, being provided with a program which instructs us as to the intention of the various passages. Thus, the trombone solos, which, we should mention, were played without any of the noisy vulgarity which our experience elsewhere has led us to associate with that instrument, are illustrative of the wrath of Saul; the harp indicates the soothing minstrelsy of David; and when a trumpet and side drum leave the orchestra and perform vigorously in the lobby, we know that the Philistines are approaching, and that the end of the overture is at hand. Excepting such brief suggestions as Beethoven prefixed to the movements of a very few of his works, or the fanciful titles which Schumann gave to his pianoforte pieces, detailed programs seem to be a complete mistake. They may impart a certain interest to a composition for those who are incapable of appreciating abstract music, but they do so at the expense of the dignity of an art whose true province is foreign to the illustration of commonplace and material detail. In the present case, however, the program is emotional rather than incidental, and Signor Bazzini's overture, if not strikingly original, is sufficiently entertaining to justify its introduction by Mr Manns.

Mlle Marie Krebs played Beethoven's fourth concerto in her characteristic style, crisply and steadily. Throughout the concert the orchestra acquitted themselves most satisfactorily. The performances to which we are accustomed in London seem to move in a narrow circle from weak incompetence or coarse violence to the perfection of lifeless finish, according to the incapacity, the misdirected energy, or the cold autocracy which distinguished the conductors. At Sydenham, thanks to Mr Manns, we can hear an orchestra capable of interpreting with refinement and expression the greatest instrumental compositions, more especially those of Beethoven. . . .

MUSICAL BUZZINGS OF A GHOST APPRENTICE

7 *March* 1877

The Quicksands of Honest Criticism

The Hornet regrets to have to inform its readers that it has been getting some grievous knocks lately, owing to its unreasonable tendency to be honest in the matter of musical criticism. Some weeks since it ventured to express itself strongly on the subject of advertizing songs, &c., at the expense of the public, by means of reviewing in journals conducted by publishing firms, royalties, ballad concerts, and similar disinterested undertakings of a culture-fostering description. The remarks were directed generally at a system which The Hornet believes detrimental to the advancement of music, because it reduces the concert room to the level of the market, and degrades the artist into what is vulgarly termed a "tout." No individuals were assailed and, sagacious and deeply versed in human nature as The Hornet is, it never occurred to it that anyone would claim the honor of being personally alluded to in the article. Closely though the cap might fit, it was not to be expected that many claimants for its honors would be forthcoming.

But The Hornet was deceived. Messrs Boosey and Co., the music publishers, of Regent-street, with unexpected candor, have confessed themselves hit by the random dart. They courteously add that the article was malicious and unfair, as to which The Hornet is perfectly content to allow the public to judge betwixt itself and Messrs Boosey. To complete the blow, they refuse to advertize any further in these columns—an announcement which has caused unspeakable dismay in the nest, and will, no doubt, speedily accomplish its financial ruin.

The Hornet publishes these facts because it is well that the public should be apprised of the difficulties which beset a critic who is resolved to do justice to himself and his duty to his readers. Not very long ago a certain colossal temple of art, erected to the memory of the late Prince Consort, goaded by the irreverent comments of a Hornet (who refused to accept a thousand performers as a substitute for a decent performance), endeavored to exclude the sensitive insect, evidently preferring to reserve their favors for more complaisant critics. The attempt meets with the success it deserves, and The Hornet will criticize such performances as impartially as ever.

Finally, as it is not fond of airing itself in its own columns, it will withdraw its injuries from the notice of its readers until again stimulated by some aspirant to the honors of counter concerts and stall-purchased criticism.

7 March 1877

Musical Reviews [Arthur Barraclough's *Observations on the Physical Education of the Vocal Organs*]

This is one of a large number of pamphlets which have been called forth by the success of certain works on the voice, which have recently come into general notice. Mr Barraclough, being, as we presume, a teacher of singing, has made some observations in the exercise of his profession which possess the merit of being quite incontrovertible, and strictly in accordance with the results of scientific research. Such, for instance, is the statement that voice production results from the action of muscles controlled by the will, that every period of activity must be followed by a period of repose, and that Nature's laws cannot be violated with impunity. If the public consider these facts sufficiently startling to call for an outlay of a shilling on a pamphlet embodying them, Mr Barraclough's book will probably have a large circulation. If, on the contrary, it should occur to them that the said facts are abundantly promulgated elsewhere, and are, indeed, the property of most intelligent schoolboys, they will lay down the Observations with a passing wonder why they should have been printed at all.

Mr Barraclough's special knowledge of voice production may be estimated by his references to singers as "vocal athletes," to "force of blast" as a condition of vocalization, and to physical exhaustion as a necessary consequence of singing which must be provided for, on the principle of training a prizefighter. He mentions that "the vocal ligaments are brought together," a fact which we would recommend him to test by the laryngoscope before issuing a second edition of his work. And to clergymen who suffer from loss of voice, he recommends daily practice at reading lessons, which would infallibly leave them without any voice at all, their affection not being [from] want of practice, as Mr Barraclough erroneously supposes, but an improper method of production, usually brought about by the endeavor to read with a sombre inflection not natural to them.

Matter of this kind, eked out to twentytwo pages by some commonplace remarks, and a misquotation of Shakespear, constitute the Observations on the Physical Education of the Vocal Organs, without throwing the smallest light, even suggestively, on one of the most important musical questions of the age, and, unfortunately, one of the most obscure.

21 *March* 1877

At the Albert Hall, on Thursday last, a portion of Bach's St Matthew Passion was performed by Mr Barnby's choir. We say a portion because the omissions were extensive, though, doubtless, justified by the necessity for accommodating a work of singular religious intensity to the tastes of an audience only half content to simulate an interest in what the majority·of them are incapable of appreciating. The full force of Bach's treatment of the scriptural narrative is of a kind which can be felt only by unsophisticated or highly cultivated communities. A modern metropolitan audience consists chiefly of persons who retain nothing of the simplicity which must have characterized a Leipzig congregation a hundred and fifty years ago, and who have not yet reached that stage of development at which the popularly dramatic element in music ceases to be indispensable; consequently, the works of the great cantor are listened to with cold respect, whilst enthusiasm is reserved for those compositions of a later date in which the passion is all on the surface, and in the rarest beauties of which is indicated a disquietude in sympathy with the unsettled march of modern ideas.

The accuracy with which the difficult choral parts were executed on Thursday evening testified to the care with which the work had been rehearsed. In the chorales, the effect of the voices, freed from the constraint of false temperament involved by accompaniment, was particularly agreeable. Unfortunately, Mr Barnby seems to lack that magnetic hold of the forces under his command which constitutes the gift of conducting, and a painful tendency to drag is always apparent in his choir. Mr Cummings undertook the arduous part of the Evangelist. He repeated the text as fast as possible, and with little regard to the dignity of the narrative. His attempts at expression were few and unfelicitous, and his intonation was occasionally defective. Mr Thurley Beale delivered the august words allotted to him mechanically. He made no effort in Twas in the cool of eventide, the only *aria* which he essayed. Miss Anna Williams sang the soprano music correctly, but without expression. In the *aria* For love of us, the tune was imperfect, and the reeds in the orchestra somewhat behind the flute *obligato*, which was played by Mr Svendsen. The result was rather startling than agreeable, and the audience were clearly somewhat bewildered.

Madame Antoinette Sterling alone displayed sufficient poetic power for the interpretation of the Passion music, her rendering of See the Savior's outstretched arm being especially excellent. She also sang Have mercy with great intensity, and her performance generally left nothing to be desired, except, perhaps, a little more purity of style. The violin *obligato* to the last-named song was very satisfactorily executed by Mr Pollitzer, and the orchestra throughout was fairly efficient, the score affording no opportunity for those strepitous displays which often distinguish performances under Mr Barnby's direction. Dr Stainer presided at the organ, and discharged his important functions with his usual ability.

28 *March* 1877

An extra Popular Concert was given on the afternoon of the 21st, for the performance of the first and fifth of Beethoven's posthumous quartets. The selection was an admirable one, for the two works in question illustrate some phases of feeling which belong peculiarly to the great master's individuality, and have been expressed in music by no other composer. The quartet in F major, Op. 135, contains one of those majestic slow movements which occur in Beethoven's earliest and latest works, and in which he has conveyed intense melancholy without any sacrifice of dignity or suggestion of morbid sentimentality. In the *scherzo* and *finale* of the E flat quartet is expressed the riotous humor which seems to have increased in recklessness with the years and troubles of the writer. In both works are to be found other beauties, of which it would be impossible to treat with the pen; but the characteristics above-mentioned contrast so strongly that they produce a striking effect when heard in succession, as was the case on Wednesday last. The executants were MM. Joachim, Ries, Straus, and Piatti. Herr Henschel was the vocalist, and was —thanks to his fine voice—received with marked favor. Madame Schumann played the Waldstein Sonata in a manner which would have sustained a comparison with the performance of any other artist save one—Madame Schumann herself. The sonata was certainly not rendered with her usual exquisite delicacy and feeling, a misfortune for which a very cold concert room and a very bad piano are probably responsible.

At the third concert of the Philharmonic Society, on the 22nd inst., Schumann's music to the last scenes of Goethe's Faust was performed for the first time in London. It probably astonished many hearers, in whose minds music to Faust was associated in idea with limelight and earthly passion. It may safely be asserted that there are fifty English readers familiar with the story of Gretchen for one who is acquainted with that strange flight into purely ideal regions, wherein the poet depicts the opening of the uneasy philosopher's immortal career. Speculations on the "eternal feminine" are more congenial to the German than to the English temperament. It is, consequently, improbable that many of the audience on Thursday last knew very clearly what they were to look for. When the object and scope of Schumann's music become more familiar to us, we will be better able to appreciate its thoroughness; for sustainedly earnest and beautiful as it undoubtedly is, it never once rises to a sublimity independent of the poem. Another novelty introduced at this concert was a scene from Tristan and Isolde, a music drama which, in order of development, is the latest of Wagner's works. It is not exactly a song in the ordinary acceptation of that term, for the sharpest amateur could never hope to whistle it. It is worked out with elaborate richness of orchestration, yet its brief lines have all the charm of simplicity. Despite its unfavorable place in the program, it was vehemently encored, and with this unreasonable demand Mrs Osgood complied, singing on both occasions with admirable taste and feeling.

Beethoven was represented by a terzetto in his Fidelio style and by the Choral Fantasia, the pianoforte part of which was excellently rendered by Miss Agnes Zimmermann. Indeed, we have never heard her play better—a fact which implies no trifling measure of merit. The orchestra, saving a few slight drawbacks, was satisfactory throughout the concert, and did justice to the late Sir Sterndale Bennett's Parisina, an overture which will compare without derogation with any of Mendelssohn's. They also distinguished themselves by the fire with which they executed the overture to Der Freischütz. A word of commendation is due to the unusual steadiness of the horns in the *adagio*.

11 *April* 1877

The forthcoming Wagner Festival at the Albert Hall, announced by Messrs Hodge and Essex, ought to prove the genuineness of our appreciation of the greatest of modern composers, by presenting to us his music divested of the attractions of the stage. Our Wagnerian education has, by the force of circumstances, hitherto been retrogressive. Lohengrin was the first work of the advanced school with which we became familiar; and this was not in itself inappropriate, for Lohengrin is the first opera in which Wagner is all himself. Its form is complete and symmetrical, and its construction exhibits no trace of the disturbing influence of the old style of Weber and Meyerbeer, which may be regarded as Wagner's starting point. This disturbing influence is so palpable in the incongruous mixture of old forms and new effects throughout the Tannhäuser that those who represented Wagner's music as inconsistent and chaotic were, for once, enabled to gratify their prejudice against the master with some degree of truth.

Yet this opera formed the next step in our experience of what has been absurdly called "the music of the future." It was inefficiently presented to us; and its vague outline, the natural product of the period of transition during which it was composed, was unsatisfactory to an audience whose hopes had been inspired by the perfect form of Lohengrin. But the retrograde from Lohengrin to Tannhäuser found a sort of homeopathic remedy in a further step back to Der Fliegende Holländer, in which the conflicting elements are as yet accommodated to oneanother, and which possesses what the other operas of Wagner grievously lack—human interest.

Such is the curious course which constitutes our preparation for the most advanced works of the composer who will shortly revisit us. How far it will be successful remains to be seen.

18 *April* 1877

On Wednesday, the 11th inst., the Bach choir—following their precedent of last year—gave a performance of the Mass in B minor, at the St James's Hall. In order that the Kyrie might be heard without interruption, the audience were invited to be seated at ten minutes before eight, an arrangement which the majority signified their appreciation of by arriving punctually at ten minutes past. The work was, however, listened to with attention; and the number who availed themselves of the pause before the Agnus Dei to leave the hall was, despite the great length of the Mass, unusually small. Considering the difficulties presented to an amateur chorus by the complicated polyphonic construction of Bach's music, the performance was a fairly satisfactory one. A few of the numbers dragged a little, and in all an extreme caution was evident, which interfered with that spontaneity which is essential to the full effect of massive choral works.

On the other hand, the choir displayed a praiseworthy accuracy and sense of the importance of their task. Many of the numbers of the Credo, which forms the grandest portion of the service, were followed by loud applause. Madame Lemmens-Sherrington and Madame Patey sang with their customary efficiency, the masterly duet *Detur unum Dominum, &c.* being rendered with particular success. Signor Foli was, as usual, in difficulties with his articulation, a peculiarity which the Latin language seems to render additionally prominent. Mr Cummings sang the tenor music as he sings always, which was, doubtless, gratifying to admirers of his voice and style.

HOW TO BECOME A MUSICAL CRITIC

The numerous *obligati* were well played as a rule, the difficult one to the Quoniam, for the horn, and that for the violin to the Benedictus, executed by MM. Wendtland and Straus, deserving particular notice. The exception was the flute-playing of Mr Svendsen, which was sharp throughout. As we have noticed the same want before with this artist, we are forced to conclude that it arises not from accidental circumstances, such as variation of temperature, but either from defective ear or an unhappy craving to be conspicuous at any cost. Herr Otto Goldschmidt conducted, and was warmly received by his choir.

25 April 1877

The announcement that the latest successor of Mario was to appear as Raoul, in Meyerbeer's Les Huguenots, attracted to Covent Garden Opera House a large audience desirous to judge of Signor Gayarré's powers from a part which affords every possible opportunity to an artist, both vocally and histrionically. Signor Mario's mantle has, by this time, been assumed by so many aspirants that it has become somewhat threadbare, and the public are slow to believe in its virtue. Some of the wearers have striking personal advantages, without either voices or dramatic ability. Some are singers who cannot act, others are actors who cannot sing. A great many can neither sing nor act nor look well —nor, in fact, offer any reasonable excuse for their appearance in opera at all, except that the public, not knowing any better, is content to endure them for a season.

Of this class Signor Gayarré is an illustrious example. We believe he once had a voice—and a robust voice, too—though not of remarkably fine quality, and to abuse its wreck without taste or artistic skill constitutes his present employment. His movements are awkward, and his few attitudes are suggestive of nothing but a self-complacency the grounds for which are wholly indiscernible. Why he should have been cast for a character such as Scribe's ingenuous and rash hero, when M. Capoul—who, though by no means immaculate, has, at any rate, some pretensions as an artist—was available, we are unable to guess. Signor Gayarré's Raoul was simply below criticism. After the most exciting situation in lyric drama—the duet in the fourth act of

Les Huguenots—he was honored with a single call. His C sharp in the duel septet evoked some applause. Except at these points, his performance seemed to produce no favorable impression. We hope it will be long before another such tenor appears, to be heralded with a flourish of puffery, and criticized with as much gravity as if he were really a singer.

2 *May* 1877

On Saturday, the 21st, the afternoon concert at the Crystal Palace was conducted by Herr Rubinstein, and the program consisted entirely of his works. For a reason which we will presently state, we shrink from the task of presenting a criticism of this remarkable performance. Greater pens than we can hope to wield have already told the world of the great pianist seizing his hearers by the ears with wings of golden fire. Highly popular essayists have circulated columns of exalted and original imagery, wherein we find Beethoven turning in his grave and gazing at the score of the Ocean symphony with admiring despair. Rubinstein is the Jupiter, the Cyclops, and the what other potent personality you will, of the pianoforte. One enthusiast, having apparently rushed straight from the exciting pages of Les Trois Mousquetaires into musical criticism, calls his idol "the d'Artagnan" of the instrument.

In short, after the approved fashion of modern Germany, our public prints have been pouring forth columns of such nauseous eulogy, not to say ignorant nonsense, on the works and performances of Herr Anton Rubinstein that, if Beethoven were not, fortunately for himself, beyond the reach of all journalism, whether penny daily or sixpenny weekly, it is not impossible that he would, indeed, turn in his grave with a characteristic grunt of disgust. For ourselves, we would out-Herod Herod in wild applause of the genius displayed by the great *virtuoso* at his concert, only—we wernt at it.

6 *June* 1877

The Wagner Festival

On the 29th of last month the last concert of the Wagner Festival took place at the Albert Hall. It is not, however, our intention to criticize any of the concerts in particular, but simply to make a few remarks about the festival generally. Herr Wagner, as a conductor, must be very unsatisfactory to an orchestra un-used to his peculiarities. He does not, as has been stated, lack vigor, but his beat is nervous and abrupt; the player's intuition is of no avail to warn him when it will come; and the *tempo* is capriciously hurried or retarded without any apparent reason. Herr Richter, whose assumption of the *bâton* was hailed by the band on each occasion with a relief rather unbecomingly ex-pressed, is an excellent conductor, his beat being most intelligible in its method, and withal sufficiently spirited. The orchestra acquitted themselves imperfectly as a rule, the inner parts dragging sometimes so much as to destroy the effect, more especially in such brisk contrapuntal movements as occur in Die Meistersinger.

The vocalists were of exceptional excellence. Frau Materna justified her great reputation, not only as to the brilliancy of her tone and her great powers of endurance, but in the equally im-portant matter of expressive delivery and distinct articulation. Frau von Sadler Grün's voice is of that rare quality which has some indefinable sympathy with melancholy. Her rendering ot Brangäne's ominous warning in the Tristan and Isolde conveyed the spirit of the verse to perfection, and her performance of Senta's music in Der Fliegende Holländer has fixed for us a high standard for future reference. No less remarkable was her singing as the woodbird in Siegfried. Owing to a severe cold, the mellow and powerful voice of Herr Unger was heard at a disadvantage. Herr Karl Hill made good his claim as a singer of the first rank by his expressive and refined singing of the parts of Vander-decken and King Mark.

At each concert Herr Wagner was received with tempestuous applause. On the 19th May he was presented with an address, and a laurel wreath was placed on his brow, which latter dis-tinction was probably more gratifying to his feelings than favorable to the dignity of his appearance. After the last concert he made a brief speech to the orchestra, expressing a satisfaction at their performance which we hope was sincere. Addresses were also presented to Herren Richter and Wilhelmj.

MUSICAL BUZZINGS OF A GHOST APPRENTICE

20 June 1877

The chief event of last week at Her Majesty's was the revival of Rossini's Otello, with Signor Tamberlik in the title *rôle*. Madame Nilsson's Desdemona was so fine a performance as to give intense interest to an occasion which would have been somewhat dull without it. In the last act especially, the effect on the audience was evidenced by the manner in which some untimely applause was suppressed. Equally moving was her acting in the *finale* of the second act. Henceforth her Desdemona may rank amongst the most remarkable of her impersonations.

In order to represent the operatic Othello respectably, a voice and some faculty for acting are indispensable. Signor Tamberlik possesses neither of these qualifications. He sings in a doubtful falsetto and his movements are unmeaning, and frequently absurd. For the C sharp in the celebrated duet *L' ira d' avverso fato*, he substituted a strange description of shriek at about that pitch. The audience, ever appreciative of vocal curiosities, eagerly redemanded it. Signor Carrion, as Roderigo, seemed laudably anxious to make as much of his part as possible, and succeeded—more, probably, to his own satisfaction than to that of the audience. He sang his music correctly, but the quality of his voice is not pleasant. M. Faure's Iago was generally understood to be a deeply-studied conception. Possibly it was, for there was no indication of it on the surface. His vocalization lacked the crispness necessary for Rossini's florid music, and his acting consisted merely of shaking hands warmly with his colleagues for no apparent reason. Signor Foli was an efficient Elmiro. His rendering of *Nel cor* was, however, rather slovenly. The orchestra was excellent; and Sir Michael Costa displayed unwonted animation. The various instrumental solos were [satis]factorily executed, particularly that for the horn, which precedes the second scene of the first act. The opera was well mounted, and the scenery appropriately handsome. Nevertheless, we doubt whether Othello's garden was happily placed in the bed of a river; and we are sure that the gondola of the Doge would glide all the more smoothly for a little lubrication.

HOW TO BECOME A MUSICAL CRITIC

27 June 1877

WAGNER AT COVENT GARDEN THEATRE

On the 16th inst. the popularity which Wagner's Flying Dutchman [earned] in the hands of Mr Carl Rosa last year was followed up by its production at Covent Garden, with Mlle Albani and M. Maurel in the principal parts. Some weeks ago we departed from the usual cautious reserve of critics as far as to predict a failure for the orchestral portion of the opera. Signor Vianesi's band has obligingly borne out our statement, but not without a faint effort to redeem its reputation. The strings and reeds were a little better than usual, whilst the brass exercised an unwonted self-denial in the matter of noise, and so added indecision and feebleness to their customary defects of coarse tone and absence of phrasing. The rendering of the picturesque and forcible overture was quite colorless; and throughout the opera the bold phrases which constantly recur were so meanly interpreted that those who had formed their expectations of the work from the spirited representation at the Lyceum must have been sadly disappointed by its new aspect under the *bâton* of Signor Vianesi. The scenic arrangements were elaborate, but not always appropriate. The phantom ship was represented by a substantial structure which moved with the deliberation of a canal barge, and in the last act came to pieces, or rather folded itself up with a gravity that tacitly rebuked all inclination to excitement. The violence of the waves sometimes lifted them entirely from their bed, and revealed strange submarine monsters disporting themselves in perpendicular jumps below. The billows in the opening storm were represented by an ingenious application of the principle of the corkscrew to a sheet of green canvas. The atmospheric effects were the most successful.

From Mlle Albani, as the acknowledged exponent of Wagner in this country, an interesting impersonation of Senta was expected. She was, as she always is, extremely conscientious, and the music displayed the clear beauty of her upper notes to great advantage. But Mlle Albani has not attained to that highest art which lies in the concealment of art, and consequently her acting lacked spontaneity, and had a melodramatic tinge wholly repugnant to the pure simplicity of the ideal Senta. Nevertheless, her performance may still claim a high degree of merit for its earnestness and the care with which it had evidently been studied. M. Maurel, as the Dutchman, looked very well, and sang very well. It is the more to be regretted that he should mistake fervid affectation for true acting, and so neutralize his great natural gifts. His demeanor suggested an inartistic self-consciousness, and in one or two situations he verged dangerously on the ridiculous. Signor Bagagiolo's fine voice carried him through the least intelligent impersonation of Daland we have ever witnessed. Signor Carpi was a tolerable Erik. Signor Rosario was an unsatisfactory pilot, and made nothing of the charming song in the first act. The small part of Mary was undertaken by Mlle Ghiotti. The choruses were executed without any regard to light and shade, and suffered accordingly, more especially the spinning song. The performance generally shews that Mr Gye has good material at his command if it could only be put to any good account. Its misuse is more to be deplored in the present case because it is not so much the reputation of Covent Garden which is at stake as the popularity already too long withheld from the works of Wagner.

27 June 1877

One of the most important musical events of the season took place at Her Majesty's Theatre on Saturday night, when Mlle Etelka Gerster, a lady who has already achieved a considerable reputation in Germany, made her *début* before an English audience, in the character of Amina in Bellini's La Sonnambula. Her success was a gratifying proof that our national habit of believing blindly (or, rather, deafly) in any worthless artistic material that *impresarios* think fit to impose on us, has not quite blunted our appreciation of genuine merit. Mlle Gerster is evidently a born musician. The quality of her voice, though not equally agreeable throughout its range, is generally clear and sympathetic. She sings up to F in *altissimo* with facility and fine tone. She phrases correctly, and her articulation is distinct, without being affected. She executes *roulade* with fluent rapidity, and does all her work with an intelligent certainty which only those

27

who possess the true musical temperament ever display. Her histrionic powers are so considerable as to ensure for her a celebrity in the future as an actress as well as a vocalist. When she acquires the perfect finish that comes from long experience, she will be qualified to take a place in the first rank of lyric artists. Her performance evoked the most enthusiastic recognition from the audience. We are so accustomed to the heartless applause of *claqueurs* at first appearances that it was quite a relief to hear the true ring of the outburst that followed the first few notes of the artist. *Ah non Credea* was rapturously encored; and Mlle Gerster received four calls at the conclusion of the opera, in addition to three between each act. She is to be congratulated on having made a remarkable and well-deserved success.

On Thursday last, Flotow's charming, but unpopular, Marta was produced before a limited audience. The difficulty of inducing the public to patronize this opera is the more curious as those who do venture on it invariably evince the greatest appreciation of its freshness and graceful flow of melody by constant *encores* and warm plaudits. However, there are reasons for its want of attraction. It is too long; it contains rather much of the Last Rose; it requires a faculty for light comedy, which is almost unknown on the lyric stage; and it is so comprehensible that the public are wont to consider it a waste of money to pay for it what would secure an opera by Beethoven, or some other master, equally intelligible to them.

If we may judge from the performance on Thursday, Marta is not a favorite with Sir Michael Costa. The overture was taken too rapidly at the *larghetto*, and too slowly at the *allegro*. The prelude to the second act was hurried, and the effect in both numbers was lost. We hear no such defects when Rossini is interpreted at the Haymarket. Of Mlle Chiomi's Marta there is nothing to be said, except that it was extremely unfinished, and that her intonation (from nervousness, possibly) was false throughout the first scene. Much more study will be necessary before Mlle Chiomi can be heard with pleasure in principal parts beside an artist so accomplished as Madame Trebelli, whose Nancy left nothing to be desired, either vocally or histrionically.

The part of Lionello is not suited to Signor Fancelli, but he acquitted himself very creditably under the circumstances. Signor del Puente was a moderately respectable Plunketto, and received for the *Chi mi Dirà* an *encore* which the conductor refused to recognize. Signor Zoboli was the Tristane. Some humor was displayed by the stage manager in the selection of costumes. Not content with the time-honored custom, which clothes the foster brothers in a garb such as no peasant ever wore at any period of the world's history, he introduced a company of soldiers in the attire of the Wars of the Roses. The attendants of Queen Anne were habited as Italians of the fifteenth century; and the monarch herself led the fashion, in a style obsolete about 150 years before her birth. These matters do not trouble the public much; but it is well to point them out occasionally, lest they should be carried too far.

27 June 1877

VOCALISTS OF THE SEASON. Signor Fancelli

Signor Fancelli is a fortunate man. He is a tenor with a voice. The time has been, and will be again, we hope, when no man could hold a leading position on the stage without varied artistic qualifications. At present a great deal of audacity, a little affectation, some judicious puffing, and sufficient lung power to make a noise at brief intervals for three hours or so complete the list of acquirements necessary for a *primo tenore*. If he be able to shout, he will do well to sing a bar or two occasionally in a light falsetto. The critics will fall into raptures over his exquisite management of the *mezza voce*, and the public will follow the critics. If he cannot do this, he has only to be careful not to lapse into inoffensiveness. Critics are only human, and they will attribute their anguish whilst listening to the tenor to anything sooner than to his defects. If they can see no excellences, they will invent some.

For instance, it is easy to say that a singer "phrases" well, because so few know what phrasing means. A certain tenor of this season, who is the very worst singer we ever heard, had this accomplishment specially manufactured for him by critics who felt it to be their duty to admire him, and who were at a loss to see what they should admire him for. Yet his case was by no means an exceptional one. For men who desire a reputation in art for which they have nothing to shew, Italian opera in England opens the only suitable field. In a state of affairs such as we have hinted at, it is obvious that (since the public always retain their natural predilection for what is good, beneath their affected raptures at what is merely imposture) an artist who has any real qualifications has a much fairer opportunity than if he were surrounded by really gifted rivals.

Such a qualification, and such an opportunity, Signor Fancelli possesses. He is not an actor, but what he does is done in earnest, and he sustains comparisons only with men who cannot act and who are not in earnest. There are exceptions, perhaps, but they are too few to affect him. He has a real voice, and a fine one, and in this respect he is about alone amongst our operatic tenors. Opera-goers hail him with delight as a relief from the hideous varieties of throaty vibration with which they have been sur-feited. His tasks this season have been arduous, and he has dis-charged them ably, as far as his gifts permitted him. That he is above the vanity which disdains a small contribution to the com-pleteness of a performance, he proved by undertaking the few bars in Otello sung by the gondolier passing without. The inevitable comparison with the two other tenors who figured in the cast proved immeasurably to his advantage. If Signor Fancelli's taste and histrionic power were only equal to his voice and sincerity of intention, we should have on our stage an accom-plished singer and actor. As it is, we have a most useful artist, and one that we always hear with pleasure.

4 *July* 1877

Vocalists of the Season. Mlle Albani

Mlle Albani has for some years past sustained the enterprise of Mr Gye in a range of those leading parts which stop short on the one hand of the florid brilliancy of Rosina and Caterina, and on the other of the weighty grandeur which we look for in Semira-mide and Lucrezia. Since her first appearance here she has steadily improved her position, and at present her hold of the musical public is assured. Mlle Albani's artistic abilities, though not of the rarest, are still of a very estimable order. She has to thank nature for a faculty for hard work, and a voice of the most beautifully clear quality in its highest register. Everything else she owes to her own unspared exertions. It is to be regretted that these exertions seem to be always directed to the attainment of new and often visionary excellences, and never to the remedying of defects which are painfully obvious, and which mar, more or less, her most admired performances. Her intonation is frequently false; and the fatal *tremolo* is already perceptible even in her clearest notes. No amount of talent could neutralize these two faults, which seem to gain ground every season.

Yet Mlle Albani is apparently unconscious of their existence, and wastes the attention that might correct them on evolving forced dramatic effects which only rob her achievements of the simplicity essential to really fine art. That the production of her voice is often forced, and always accompanied by ungraceful facial contortion, should, perhaps, be imputed to her illustrious master, Signor—or, as he delights to be styled, Commendatore—Lamperti. But it is none the less a serious drawback to the enjoyment of the spectator. She is said to be qualified by special training for the impersonation of Wagner's heroines, and consequently her Elsa, Elizabeth, and Senta have always been regarded with peculiar interest. There is no necessity for alluding in detail to her reading of the various parts in her extensive *repertoire*. All exhibit the same characteristics. Earnest study, anxious striving after effect, and the sensuous charm of her voice are to be set off against art which is not concealed, defective management of the breath, artificial gesture, and an absence of genius which can never be compensated [for] by talent, however sedulously cultivated. That she has no claims to [be] what is arbitrarily called a classical singer she proved by her indifferent performance at the Handel Festival last week. Nevertheless, it is but just to add that Mlle Albani's capabilities have proved sufficient to gain for her an enthusiastic following, and deservedly so; for conscientiousness, which we consider her greatest merit, can hardly be too highly esteemed. During her last visit to Paris her success, which we had not the pleasure of witnessing, was reported as extraordinary; and the appreciation evinced of her powers at her late appearance as Senta at Covent Garden was one of which any artist might justly be proud.

4 July 1877

THE HANDEL FESTIVAL

Another Handel Festival has passed away, bearing testimony in its progress to the undiminished popularity of our most imposing musical institution. The occasion, considering its magnitude, affords but little matter for comment. The stale wonderment which the great chorus never fails to elicit has already been exhausted; and Sir Michael Costa has probably enjoyed the triennial laugh in his sleeve over the journalistic exaggerations of the difficulties he has had to contend with. As a matter of fact, the time for regarding an *ensemble* of 4,000 performers as a prodigy has gone by; and the sooner we begin to consider the feasibility of adding another thousand or so to the number, and varying the *repertoire* a little, the longer our national interest in the Festival is likely to last. We do not mean to imply that the highest interests of music would be served by increasing a choir already so large as to entail conditions of performance incompatible with strict justice to the master. But a justification of such a course might be found in the increase of sensational attraction; for the aims of the Festival-givers necessarily are, firstly, commercial; secondly, phenomenal; and, lastly, artistic.

The performance of The Messiah on the first day was excellent in the choral numbers, and generally respectable in the *arias*. It would be invidious to select any particular chorus for mention. All were executed with perfect precision; and the text was enunciated with surprising distinctness. It is unfortunate that spirited renderings are considered incompatible with the safe conduct of large masses. However, all that could be done to relieve the somewhat mechanical rigidity of the great choruses by careful observance of *forte* and *piano* was done to the utmost, and the effect was, on the whole, stirring and impressive. The orchestra, though at times rather brassy, was satisfactory, the phrasing being conscientiously followed with the result of a fairly artistic reading. The solos were the weak points of the performance, except in a very few instances. Mlle Albani sang her first recitatives out of tune, and in the subsequent *arias* made no effect, Rejoice greatly being conspicuously weak. Madame Patey acquitted herself most meritoriously in the numbers allotted to her, which produced an impression due to her care and earnestness. Madame Edith Wynne, in I know that my Redeemer liveth, struck the first really sympathetic chord in her listeners, and suggested regrets that her share in the performance was not greater. Mr Cummings sang the tenor music in the first part feebly as [is] his wont, but with more finish than usual. Owing to the high pitch of the organ, Mr Sims Reeves was not available for the Passion music; but Mr Vernon Rigby reproduced his mannerisms with more success than usually falls to the lot of imitators. Mr Santley did not seem in as happy a mood as usual. Nevertheless, he sang Why do the nations and The trumpet shall sound as perfectly as could have been desired. Herr Henschel took the rest of the baritone music; and it is sufficient to say of him that his bad pronunciation was his misfortune, and his bad phrasing his fault.

The program for the second day was too varied to admit of detailed notice within our limits. In addition to the vocalists (Mlle Albani and Herr Henschel excepted) before mentioned, Mesdames Patti, Sherrington, and Suter, MM. Foli and Edward Lloyd sang—the last-named artist making a decided addition to his already high reputation. Mr Best played an organ concerto. The Israel in Egypt was given on the concluding day, according to custom. We cannot omit this opportunity of warning conductors against the common error of endeavoring to make all performances of The Messiah as like the Festival one as possible. The transept of the Crystal Palace is larger even than the Albert Hall; and the crashing brass and retarded rhythms which are appropriate enough to the vast Handel orchestra become misplaced and intolerably offensive in any smaller space.

1 *August* 1877

Few operas have suffered more from the pruning-knife of the stage manager than Meyerbeer's historical romance [Les

Huguenots]. The fifth act, performed as it usually is with the opening scene excised and the *finale* recklessly mutilated, rarely induces an audience to sit after midnight for its sake. This season it vanished entirely from the boards, its omission being justifiable on the principle that what cannot be done properly is best left undone. The remaining acts are so extensively and tastelessly curtailed that many critics, unacquainted with the score, have denounced the opera as a fragmentary arrangement of musical odds and ends. In its original form the work is undoubtedly too long for the most patient audience. But the method which has been adopted of extracting central portions from the concerted pieces, as in the *finale* to the second and third acts, is so barbarous that a reconstruction of the version for performance would be extremely desirable, until the public are prepared to devote two nights to one opera. The score contains nothing unworthy of a hearing. We are acquainted with no work of similar length which is more highly finished in all its parts; which contains such a profusion of original and varied melody without being eked out by conventional manufacture; which displays greater fertility in orchestral device; and which at the same time bears so exclusive a stamp of one individuality. The merits of Meyerbeer are now rarely disputed. The conservative critics, having glorified Mayer and Paisiello in order to disparage Rossini, at length praised Rossini at the expense of Meyerbeer; and now, nothing discouraged, invent rhapsodies about Meyerbeer for the purpose of depreciating Wagner.

1 *August* 1877

VOCALISTS OF THE SEASON. Sir Michael Costa

To those profane persons who have been moved to laughter by the appearance of the celebrated conductor amongst our "Vocalists," we address the assurance that no one has a more influential voice in regulating our operatic repasts than Sir Michael Costa. Nay, he is the most successful of our vocalists, for his voice never fails—and of whom else can as much be said?

The struggle for existence in modern London has been aptly described as a constant march against time. By dint of constantly beating time, Sir Michael has secured the foremost place in the very thin ranks of our conductors. His place is undisputed. With the exception of Mr August Manns, whose labors are confined to the nobler field of abstract music, he is the only chief under whose *bâton* orchestras display good training. The merits which he successfully cultivates are precision and refinement, and both go so far in music that their attainment alone would entitle him to his high position. Nevertheless, they are not everything. In rendering the heavily loaded scores of the composers of the new German school, and the well-filled compositions of Beethoven and even Meyerbeer, the music, if played correctly and steadily, will answer for itself. The combination of noise and commonplace which constitutes the usual accompaniment of an Italian opera requires little of artistic treatment, save the avoidance of coarseness. And in all such works the band swayed by Sir Michael Costa at Her Majesty's Theatre invariably gives complete satisfaction. It is only when they essay the light but exquisitely constructed scores of Mozart that we are compelled to admit that the rare delicacy and dash necessary to their effect is wholly wanting. The master who receives the fullest justice from Sir Michael is Rossini, to whose music he is wedded by taste and nationality. The works of the great Germans he attacks conscientiously, but without the keen relish which he exhibits when his own school is the subject of exposition. His ideas of speed are not uniformly satisfactory. Generally speaking, he errs on the side of slowness.

That highest faculty of a conductor, which consists in the establishment of a magnetic influence under which an orchestra becomes as amenable to the *bâton* as a pianoforte to the fingers, we do not give Sir Michael Costa credit for. Instead, he has the common power of making himself obeyed, and is rather the autocrat than the artist. To one who is only called on to direct competent players, this is amply sufficient. The performers are all able artists, who know that they will not be permitted to play carelessly, and this knowledge naturally ensures satisfactory results. When, as sometimes happens, an emergency arises and confusion reigns momentarily amongst his forces, Sir Michael quietly puts down his wand and allows the matter to remedy itself as best it can. He has acquired much fame from his conducting of the Handel Festival; but we have, on a former occasion, expressed our opinion that the difficulties of this achievement are fancifully exaggerated by the public. In conclusion, we are sorry to say that he has been guilty of some grave breaches of musical taste. It may be justifiable to rescore the oratorios of Handel, but no true musician can sympathize with Sir Michael Costa when he tampers with Beethoven, as he has done in more than one instance, by presumptuously reinforcing the brass parts with trombones.

8 *August* 1877

A not very brilliant season has been succeeded by a week of absolute stagnation, musically speaking. *Impresarios*, artists, and audiences have vanished from amongst us in quest of new singers, new triumphs, and such health as can be gained from the mountain winds of Switzerland, or the more economical atmosphere of the rearward apartments of apparently deserted premises. The critics are divided between operatic retrospects and the prospects of English opera during the autumn and winter with Mr Carl Rosa. We have so low an opinion of the merits of Italian opera in this country, and so steady a conviction that its downfall is only a question of time and musical culture, that we turn willingly to the rival enterprise which has relieved us from the absurdity of being the only music-patronizing nation in the world which systematically tolerates opera delivered in a foreign tongue. And, be it remembered, not in the language for which the music was written, but in a vile Italian substitute for the original French or German libretto.

Those persons who object to English versions on the score of their literary demerits are presumably unacquainted with the Italian language, or they would scarcely assert the superiority of the translations which we hear so maltreated by German, Spanish, Swedish, French, Irish, and American artists at our opera houses. The few Italian singers, mostly of minor importance, do even less justice to their native tongue than the foreigners, pronouncing their recitatives in a species of gabble which we can scarcely identify with the musical language which we have heard declaimed by Signor Salvini. In other countries the artists pay their audiences the compliment of mastering their speech, and presenting them with an intelligible and most enjoyable entertainment. The pre-eminence of Italian as the language of song has been urged to the serious detriment of opera in this country. English is the only tongue capable of enlisting the sympathy of the Englishman. It is far nearer to the German, in which the greatest operas have been written, than Italian; and it is also capable of greater variety of inflection and expression. It is more amenable to musical requirements than French. Once cultivated on the lyric stage, an example would be constantly before the public which might perhaps modify the corruption which the unfortunate vowel experiences in London. But these are secondary matters.

The great point is that English is our national tongue, and, therefore, the only one which should be tolerated in our national opera houses. When we are at last roused to draw comparisons between the dreary emptiness of the evening spent in Covent Garden or the Haymarket, listening to performances which are foreign in heart and form, and the familiar and sympathetically rendered versions which excite the enthusiasm of shilling galleries for even Wagner, it is certain that we should as soon think of going to hear Mr Irving in a German translation of Hamlet as to an Italian opera. After this hint of our views, we need scarcely add that Mr Carl Rosa has our warmest wishes for the success of the enterprise which he has inaugurated with so much energy.

22 August 1877

The Promenade Concerts at Covent Garden, which have become an institution during our unmusical autumns, are now in active operation. On last Wednesday, the first "classical" program of the season was performed, and its reception afforded another proof of the fallacy of the commonplace theory that the public dislike good music, which is so frequently advanced as an excuse for giving audiences the worst possible value for their money. The concert opened with the Anacreon overture, a work in which Cherubini, in addition to his constructive skill, displays a vivacity and fire which are not always to be found in his

37

polished and scholarly compositions. A movement from the beautiful fragment of a symphony in B minor by Schubert produced its usual effect, and the *scherzo* from Mendelssohn's Midsummer Night's Dream, although somewhat roughly performed, was encored.

The principal attraction, however, centred in the performance of the first of Mozart's three most popular symphonies, that in E flat. The manner in which it was executed by "the most eminent musicians of the day" suggested an unpleasant idea of the spirit in which they approached their work. Instead of an orchestra conscientiously endeavoring to do justice to a great work, the audience were entertained by the spectacle of a number of individuals bent on displaying the consummate ease with which they could rattle through so simple an affair as a score of Mozart's. There was much vigorous bowing, which was not necessary; there was no delicacy, which was the chief requisite; little attention was paid to the conductor, who is never in his element when dealing with high-class German music; and the result was, of course, the comparative failure of the symphony.

It was followed by a transcription for orchestra and military band of Handel's See the Conquering Hero comes, in which the delighted listeners had the pleasure of hearing the simultaneous explosions of six cornets, six horns, four euphoniums, one ophicleide, and seven trombones, in addition to the full orchestra of reeds and strings. The trumpets alone remained silent, probably in order to avoid undue noise. A selection from M. Gounod's new opera Cinq Mars revealed the unwelcome fact that the composer of Faust, in his last production, has fallen back on manufacture as a substitute for inspiration. As it comes from a first-rate establishment, it is manufacture of a good sort, but as music it is valueless. Signor Arditi's selection was satisfactorily performed, as his band contains many accomplished soloists, of whom we may particularize MM. Hughes and Lazarus as the best. Mr Howard Reynolds has a remarkable physical aptitude for the cornet, and plays with some taste; but his style is not at all legitimate. The remainder of the instrumental portion of the program was made up of popular dance music, one item being a polka by Signor Arditi, accompanied by the vigorous rataplans of a youthful contingent from the Coldstream Guards. . . .

The vocalists are not above the promenade concert average, and Mlle Dérivis, who displayed her weakness in *Batti, batti,* and the shadow song from Dinorah, is decidedly below it. Signor Gianini, the tenor, does his best. Signor Medica, the baritone, does his worst. It is impossible to witness the performance of this very young singer without a sensation compounded of mirth and pity. As he sings he repeatedly makes a stereotyped gesture with his disengaged hand, and glares about him with the eagle eye of affectation. He has no artistic style, but his voice is a noisy one, and he seems to delight in the sound of it. We expect modesty of demeanor even from singers who have just reason to be proud of their gifts, and Signor Medica, having neither the one nor the other, seems to have adopted the dignified principle that the best palliative of groundless arrogance is boundless absurdity.

22 *August* 1877

VOCALISTS OF THE SEASON. Mr Santley

Mr Santley is the best baritone singer with whom the London public is familiar. He has a voice; he knows how to produce it; he [has] acquired the art of managing his breath properly; and he conscientiously interprets the works which he sings without adding or subtracting a note. The taste of the present age has, it is true, voted all these accomplishments and gifts to be superfluous and old-fashioned. Your modern audience plausibly argues that it is no great feat for a man to sing if he has a voice, and clamors for the sensational performances of artists (foreigners preferred) who have mastered a few unpleasant tricks during the final shattering of the vocal organs, which usually precedes their appearance in public. It is the birthright of an Englishman to do as he likes; and if he chooses to pay through the nose for the privilege of hearing a French baritone sing through the nose, he can adduce in his defence the natural fitness of the transaction, and the fact that the national taste rarely gives itself the slightest trouble about artistic excellence.

There is always, however, a mass of persons in existence who possess more or less musical and, consequently, unfashionable taste; who profess to like what they know; and who have the far more valuable faculty of knowing what they like. They like Mr Santley because he is both a competent and an honest singer. He cannot boast of genius, and yet, at the present moment, he stands quite unrivaled in his position. At the opera houses his successors only disparage themselves by suggesting comparisons with him. In the concert room we have no choice between him and some estimable nonentity who merely fills a gap in the harmony. Since the lamented death, some years since, of Signor Agnesi, we have had no baritone of any serious pretensions established amongst us, and the result is that Charles Santley, who, though a very good singer, is neither a great nor a poetic artist, is, beyond dispute, the chief of his own department of the musical profession in England.

He has been much before the public in opera, and the introduction of Wagner's Flying Dutchman to London is probably due to his influence. If it be so, he rendered an important service to art progress at some expense to himself, for his exertions in the part of Vanderdecken were seriously, though, we hope, temporarily, detrimental to his voice, the music lying in great part much below his natural range. His greatest success was in the high and light *rôle* of Mikèli, in the Les Deux Journées of Cherubini. Although not unsuccessful in portraying simple pathos, acting is evidently no part of his vocation. His bearing on the stage is congenial and familiar, but quite unsuited for characters requiring dignity or refinement. His secession from the boards is, therefore, not to be regretted. He is seen to greater advantage on the concert platform and [with] the Handel orchestra, and he is removed from the temptation to cultivate an artificially weighty style which opera holds out.

We desire to emphasize our recognition of one of his merits as a man, if not a musician. It is that he is an Englishman who is not ashamed of his nationality. Despite the managerial pressure which must have borne on him at the outset of his career in favor of Sant, Santelli, Santalini, Saint Lis, and other seductive disguises, he had the courage to be "Mr Santley." We wish other native artists had the good sense to follow his example. Or if they must deceive themselves (they can scarcely imagine that they deceive the public) can they not do it with some show of plausibility? Why insult ordinary perception by putting an *o* after each syllable of a good Scotch name, as Burns often did with a line of poetry? Does not "Signor Talbo" sound, to say the least of it, a little disingenuous? If Mr Slater thinks his name more befitting a critic than a composer, can he not adopt the worthy name of Barry without misspelling it? There is no custom for which we have a more hearty contempt than that prevalent amongst our artists of adopting foreign names. It is a species of fraud on our national reputation as a musical people (such as it is), and is practiced only through affectation or a slavish regard for false conventionality.

5 September 1877

VOCALISTS OF THE SEASON. Mr Vernon Rigby

In the musical as in all callings, originality, or the power of creating an independent mode of exposition, is a gift possessed only by a few. Mr Vernon Rigby is not one of the few. Nor is he one of the musical mob—the vast army of singers who commence with an awkwardly-assumed style derived from their teachers and, in course of time, drift into respectable nothingness with no style at all. He has apparently recognized the fact that his own resources contain no germ of artistic individuality, and so has adopted at second-hand a pre-existing individuality which had done good service during many years of trial. Such a process has a delusive semblance of easiness about it. A public singer is successful. He makes his success in full view of everybody who chooses to study him. He is conspicuous on a platform. The lights are turned up. There is no deception. He who has eyes and ears can perceive how it is done.

After this manner, it appears to us, did Mr Vernon Rigby set to work to discover the potent spell of Mr Sims Reeves. He has succeeded in producing a counterfeit coin not altogether unacceptable to those who are unfamiliar with the original. The voice metal is genuine in both, though of a somewhat baser quality in the copy; but the distinctive stamp of the latter is an imitation, and, of course, an imitation correct only in trick and external flourish. Somehow the essence of the mysterious thing always escapes the imitator, who gains nothing for his pains but a set of sorry antics, and a rueful conviction that, after all, every true man's apparel does *not* fit your thief.

The apparel of Mr Sims Reeves, both artistic and material, is of more than usual eccentricity, and has so much of the grotesquely manneristic about it that it sits even on him oddly enough at times. But his is forgiven because it covers a spark of true feeling. When Mr Vernon Rigby puts it on, it covers nothing, but aspires to be attractive on its own account. That it fails needs not be said. But it does worse. It becomes irritating. The borrowed articles of the singer offend that sensitive appreciation of fitness in art which the really musical listener possesses, and, although we question very much whether there can be said to be a truth in impersonative art without a twisting of terms, still, for a singer to assume the mannerisms of a brother artist, instead of assuming an ideal character of his own conception, seems to us as false as anything may well be.

Yet Mr Vernon Rigby, though thus unwilling to rely on his own invention for a good style, is in other respects decidedly egotistical in his musical attitude. When he takes a leading part in an oratorio, which he frequently does, he gives his audience to understand that any interest in Handel or Haydn they may feel disposed to evince must be strictly subsidiary to their attention to the celebrated tenor who deigns to lend the lustre of his voice to the works of these composers. The critic who demurs to this, and who looks for breadth of style and regard to the due relation of the various parts to the entire composition, is likely to be considerably disappointed. Mr Rigby has a nice voice. We are sorry we cannot give him credit for his other accomplishments, seeing that they are not fairly his own, or exonerate him from artistic failings which, in our opinion, go far to nullify them.

26 September 1877

A TYPICAL "POPULAR" VOCALIST

Amongst artists, the struggle for existence resolves itself into a struggle for popularity. Popularity is attained by different persons in different ways. Twice or thrice in a century some gifted being appears, and, by an occult power, gains the idolatry of the public in a night or two, retaining it often for years after the last traces of the original fascination have succumbed to age, misuse, or the intoxication of success. Others enter the arena in humble guise, and toil laboriously in the pursuit of artistic excellence, their love of music sustaining them against the coldness of unscrupulous rivals who resent conscientiousness, and the indifference of the mob to exalted considerations of all kinds. They often have to wait, but, as a rule, the solid weight of genuine art material establishes itself at last, and that unassailably. Nevertheless, the process is a slow one for this age of quick returns and impatient aspirations; and a quicker method of succeeding is usually adopted.

The outward and visible signs of this royal road to popularity are of infinite variety, according to the ingenuity of the traveler. If a female vocalist (and such are the most brilliant professors of the science of claptrap) desire to shine in this way, she must bear in mind that her work begins from the moment her audience first catches sight of her. Let her then smile, and trip forth as captivatingly as possible. If she have to make her way through an orchestra, a little judicious embarrassment as she threads the row of fiddlers (who will tap their desks vigorously and so ensure a reception) will often lay the foundation of an enthusiastic *encore* before she utters a note. A prettily whispered conference with the conductor or accompanist will dispose of the suffrages of every youth present of average susceptibility. The fashion in which the sheet of music is held is of much importance, but no positive rule can be laid down respecting it. To dispense with the copy altogether is sometimes advisable as being impressive, but, perhaps, the most irresistible plan is to have a small card or scrap of paper on which the words are scribbled. A timely lapse of memory is useful when the singer has the gift of displaying confusion agreeably.

The purely musical portion of the task is of minor importance. If the song be English, the words must be pointedly delivered at the audience in a confidentially colloquial style. The pathetic parts should be drawled, and those notes made the most of which best display the power of the voice. In justice to all present, each line must be delivered to the right and left of the platform alternately, and the vocalist must bear in mind that it is impossible to smile too often. In Italian music, shakes must be introduced at every suitable or unsuitable opportunity. They must by no means be steadily delivered, as such a mode savors of old-fashioned classicalism, but shot forth in a series of jerks. During the process the pitch may be allowed to fall half a tone, but not more, as it might be difficult to regain the key with sufficient rapidity. Considerations of this kind are, however, immaterial, as very few persons will have the least idea as to whether the singer is in or out of tune. Applause should be promptly improved by reappearance and many obeisances. If an *encore* be doubtful, it should be accepted as a matter of generosity to the public.

From these few and unskilful hints may be gathered the manner in which popularity can be obtained without taste, culture, or voice. Those who adopt it are not necessarily devoid of these attributes, but they pervert rather than improve them. Of their school, more than one that we could name is a prominent professor of this theory; and in drawing attention to this *spurious imitation of real art*, we now remind them that, though speaking now in general terms, we may be led on some future occasion to particularize offenders.[1]

---

[1] Fortunately for the threatened "offenders," this was the last critical buzz of the ghost apprentice in *The Hornet*.

II

THE EMERGENCE OF
BASSETTO

(The 1880's)

MUSIC FOR THE PEOPLE

(*The Musical Review*, 10 and 17 *March* 1883; unsigned)

The employment of a generic term, such as "the people," to
denote one section of the community is not wholly defensible,
but the sanction of custom must be an excuse for its use in the
present instance; and, after all, it is a more complimentary expression than the "proletariat," or the "lower orders," and not
more open to question than the "working classes"—which last
is frequently adopted by toilers with the hand in a somewhat
invidious sense. By the people we mean the vast number of
struggling bread-winners whose life is passed outside the regions
of art, and beyond the reach of its ennobling influence. That the
art of music, with which we are especially concerned, has no
place, and can have no place, in the existence of an immense
majority of the population unless external action places it at
their command, will not be contended. The prices of admission
to concerts and opera in the metropolis are practically prohibitive except to persons in easy circumstances, and to a less
extent the same rule applies to the great provincial centres. On
the continent imperial and municipal authority assumes a more
parental aspect than with us, and the principle of subsidies is
universally recognized as the one means whereby the community
generally may be enabled to enjoy first-rate performances in the
theatre and the concert room. It would be idle to lament the
absence of such machinery at home. Great Britain is committed

45

to a policy of *laissez-faire* in art matters, or, more strictly speaking, in musical matters, and until a revolution occurs in our national method of treating the subject it is only to the philanthropic efforts of individuals that we can look, in the first instance, for an alteration of the musical famine under which so many suffer.

For a long period the matter was treated with profound indifference generally, but quite recently a feeling seems to have arisen in the minds of certain well-meaning persons that something might be done, and the result is the formation of two or three societies having for their direct and sole purpose the giving of cheap musical entertainments to those who can only afford a few pence for an evening's amusement. We say advisedly the result is the formation of these societies, for the practical outcome of the movement can scarcely be said to have commenced, owing either to the feebleness or misdirection of the efforts in the cause. The proceedings of an association styling itself the People's Concert Society have come under our observation once or twice, and it may be allowed that in this instance the executive seem to have some lucid idea of the nature of the work to be accomplished. A series of concerts was first tried about four years ago, at the hall of the Eleusis Club, a radical institution, in the King's-road, Chelsea, the programs of which consisted chiefly of instrumental chamber music, the movements of a trio or a sonata being frequently interspersed with vocal pieces. The latter were always of a superior class and were interpreted generally by efficient amateurs, the instrumental executants being professionals whose names are familiar in the musical world. The charges for admission were a penny and threepence. The society is still in existence, for we have heard of concerts being given of a similar nature at the East-end during the present season. Persons of Sabbatarian tendencies may be scandalized to hear that Sunday evening concerts have been tried at which a collection for expenses has taken the place of a charge for admission. Whether the society's operations have met with an encouraging amount of support we have no means of knowing, but it cannot be said that the measures taken to enforce the fact of its existence on the lethargic public mind have been as vigorous as could be wished. Perhaps a lack of capital has necessitated the adoption of a modest policy up to the present time.

In another instance, however, there has been an amount of trumpet-blowing worthy of the inauguration of a great work. If the promoters of the temperance music-hall movement are not triumphant in the task they have undertaken, it will certainly not be for want of sufficient advertizing. But it is questionable whether the attempt to work in two directions at once is not inimical to progress in either. Sobriety is a good thing and healthy amusement is another, but the working man's tastes will not be elevated by the association of music with total abstinence; for he will resent the attempt to dictate what he shall drink or avoid, and severely stay away from the coffee music-hall. Of course temperance people may come, but persons of moderate opinions, being denied the privileges which they can obtain in the theatres and ordinary music-halls, are not likely to avail themselves of entertainments so dearly purchased. Thus the Victoria Hall, which might be made a centre for the diffusion of art among the humbler ranks of society, only appeals to one section, and that a comparatively small one. The executive may reply that the spread of temperance principles is their primary object, music being merely employed as a helping influence in the cause. That may be, but it would be grossly unfair to gauge the tastes of the entire artisan class by the measure of success obtained in this instance. We have yet to learn what would be the result of an enterprise in which musical culture was made the first consideration, the liberty of the subject being fully maintained in matters of bodily refreshment.

A few remarks on the nature of the work actually carried on in the Victoria Hall may be desirable. The ballad concerts, given once or twice weekly, were at first sustained by professional aid, often given gratuitously—a system, it is needless to say, which could not be maintained for any length of time. Grave objections were made by ordinary concert-givers, but they were scarcely necessary, as the supply of competent performers was certain to fail after a while, and we believe the professionals are now receiving remuneration in the regular way. It would be unwise to judge hastily, but from the experience of two or three visits to the hall, we should imagine that the management underestimates, rather than overestimates, the critical capacity of its audiences. For example, at a so-called Scandinavian concert, given on the 13th ult., a number of weak songs, weakly interpreted, were received with polite indifference, *encores* being reserved for Beethoven's violin Romance in G, Op. 40, some Hungarian airs nicely rendered by Mlle Brousil, and a couple of Swedish melodies capitally sung by Mlle Enequist. A newly-formed choir gave a selection of part-songs very creditably, and these were also warmly received, while the dance-tunes, played by an indifferent band, went almost without a hand. At a rough guess, there may have been 1,500 people in the hall, and if the whole of them had been skilled musicians the verdict on each item could not have been more discriminating. The demeanor of all present was equally remarkable, perfect silence being preserved while the music was being performed; and the observer could not, therefore, fail to gain a favorable impression of the musical receptivity of the dwellers in and around the New Cut.

Perhaps the most successful and most generally satisfactory of all the associations in the metropolis whose operations come within the scope of the present inquiry is the Bow and Bromley Institute. Music is not the sole end and aim of this institution, but the art has a large place in its working, and its interests are furthered in a straightforward and practical manner. Here, every Saturday evening during the winter months, organ recitals are given, at which the most accomplished English and foreign performers appear, the charges for admission being sixpence and threepence. A means is hereby provided for enabling the humblest classes to become acquainted with at least one variety of the best music, performed in the best manner, at a nominal cost; and it is cheering to know that the movement has been attended by unequivocal success. Although the hall will accommodate 1,200 persons, the number of those who desire admission is generally in excess of these figures. Further, the programs are neither exclusively nor mainly composed of overtures and operatic selections; on the contrary, the works of Bach and Mendelssohn are largely drawn upon, and we have the best authority for saying that they are as highly appreciated as the lighter excerpts of the French school. The printed programs contain brief and pithy descriptions of the various pieces, enabling the audiences to follow the music with some intelligent interest. The Bow and Bromley Institute has also an excellent Choral Society, under the direction of Mr W. G. McNaught, and frequent performances are given of the most elaborate oratorios and cantatas. The work here, it should be noted, is carried out on strictly business-like principles, without any pretense at philanthropy or any intrusion of the goody-goody element. Herein, we believe, lies the secret of its success. There may be other institutions than those already named in which the diffusion of musical taste among the masses is made a feature, but, if so, their doings have not attained sufficient prominence to warrant attention in this place.

It has frequently been observed that true musical feeling is to be found in greater abundance in some of our large provincial centres than in the metropolis. This is unquestionably true in the sense that towns like Birmingham, Manchester, or Leeds are not of such unwieldy magnitude as to hinder general sympathy for and interest in any movement emanating from a central point in their corporate existence. We shall see later on how the vast size of London is directly inimical to the establishment of such an institution as the Birmingham Musical Association, on which some remarks may be fittingly offered in connection with our present subject. Three or four years ago it seems to have occurred to some influential residents in the hardware capital and its vicinity that the musical prestige which the town has long possessed might be extended by a more direct co-operation of the artisan class in the art and its cultivation. The result of this feeling was the formation of the above-named association, with Mr Jesse Collings, M.P., as its president. Birmingham possesses a magnificent Town-hall and various musical societies. The Mayor grants the use of the former, free of rent, and the assistance of the latter is secured for the concerts of the Association, which are given on Saturday evenings from October to April. The third annual report lies before us, and it is at once an interesting and [an] encouraging document. It appears that during the season 1881–82 twentyseven concerts were given, at which the average attendance was 2,629 persons. As the receipts average £45 : 11 : 7, it follows that the charge for admission equaled fourpence a head.

What kind of music was it, then, which drew these crowded assemblages of working people? The report furnishes an extremely satisfactory answer. Among the choral works which were performed in their entirety were Bennett's May Queen, Gounod's Gallia, Bridge's Boadicea, Gade's Crusaders, and Macfarren's May Day, together with selections from various oratorios and cantatas. Many of these were given with full orchestral accompaniment, and the following instrumental works were presented entire: Beethoven's Symphony in C, Mozart's Pianoforte Concerto No. 4, the Rosamunde ballet music, and a number of overtures. Upwards of 2,700 choralists and fifty instrumentalists took part in the concerts, the majority twice and many three times. As most of the societies to which these performers belong were remunerated by donations to their funds, it may fairly be said that the Birmingham Musical Association is a self-supporting concern, or, at any rate, no more dependent upon voluntary help than are the majority of our leading musical societies throughout the country. Thus firmly established, this enterprising body has of late busied itself with the formation of a special amateur band and chorus, to belong exclusively to the association. The invitations issued met with so warm a response that the limits of 250 originally assigned to the chorus and of seventy to the band were at once reached and even exceeded.

In face of such facts as these, it would be idle to deny the existence of an immense latent capacity for musical culture in the ranks of the people, and it only remains to inquire why the example of Birmingham is not generally followed, and especially in London. The primary difficulty in this overgrown Babylon is the absence of any central machinery which could be utilized for the purpose. Hammersmith and Stepney, Kentish Town and Rotherhithe lie practically as far away from one another as Liverpool and Manchester. It needs but little observation to prove that the outlying theatres and music-halls depend exclusively upon local audiences for patronage. High-class concerts given in any one of the four districts named would, therefore, have no concern for the dwellers in the other three. What we require is not one society, such as that of Birmingham, but a dozen; and unfortunately the resources of each district are not equal to the task of initiating any movement of the kind.

Help from without being practically out of the question, matters remain as they have always been, save for a few spasmodic attempts to cope with the difficulty. But another adverse influence is that anti-musical feeling which refuses to recognize the value of the art, save as a means to gain some other end. Our principal musical festivals have only been sustained by connecting them with philanthropic work, and in two directions at the present time in the metropolis music is relegated to the position of a handmaid in the cause of religion and sobriety. We have already seen how the promoters of the temperance movement utilize their opportunities at the Victoria Hall; but a far more lamentable misuse of means remains to be noticed. The purchase of Exeter Hall by the Young Men's Christian Association has afforded scope for the exercise of religious prejudices, which might, but for this circumstance, have been deemed incredible at the present day. Here is one of the finest halls in London, centrally situated, in possession of an excellent organ, and for well-nigh fifty years associated with musical celebrations on the grandest scale, doomed to re-echo nothing better than the celebrations of the Salvation Army. It would be as idle to attempt a serious argument with those who deem Handel, Bach, and Mendelssohn sinful as to enter upon a contest of logic with the inmates of Hanwell Asylum; but it is little less than exasperating to observe golden chances thrown away by those who are presumed to have a direct interest in the promotion of refining and civilizing influences among the masses. It is pleasant to note that in one or two instances—notably at Bristol and Leeds—a feeling is beginning to manifest itself in favor of the severance of the galling chains which have so long bound music and charity together, and it is therefore not too much to hope that some idea of the dignity and value of art will eventually find its way among those who undertake important schemes of a philanthropical nature in London. But at present the silver lining to the cloud is barely discernible.

HERR RICHTER AND HIS BLUE RIBBON

(The Dramatic Review, 8 February 1885*)*

Herr Richter's popularity as an orchestral conductor began, not in the auditorium, but in the orchestra. It dates from his first visit here in 1877 to conduct the Wagner festivals at the Albert Hall. At these concerts there was a large and somewhat clumsy band of about 170 players, not well accustomed to the music, and not at all accustomed to the composer, who had contracted to heighten the sensation by conducting a portion of each concert. It is not easy to make an English orchestra nervous, but Wagner's tense neuralgic glare at the players as they waited for the beat with their bows poised above the strings was hard upon the sympathetic men, whilst the intolerable length of the pause exasperated the tougher spirits. When all were effectually disconcerted, the composer's *bâton* was suddenly jerked upwards, as if by a sharp twinge of gout in his elbow; and, after a moment of confusion, a scrambling start was made. During the performance Wagner's glare never relaxed: he never looked pleased. When he wanted more emphasis he stamped; when the division into bars was merely conventional he disdained counting, and looked daggers—spoke them too, sometimes—at innocent instrumentalists who were enjoying the last few bars of their rest without any suspicion that the impatient composer had just discounted half a stave or so and was angrily waiting for them. When he laid down the *bâton* it was with the air of a man who hoped he might never be condemned to listen to such a performance again. Then Herr Richter stepped into the conductor's desk; and the orchestra, tapping their desks noisily with their bows, revenged themselves by an ebullition of delight and deep relief, which scandalized Wagner's personal admirers, but which set the fashion of applauding the new conductor, whose broad, calm style was doubly reassuring after that of Wagner. He, meanwhile, sat humbly among the harps until he could no longer bear to listen quietly to his own music, when he would rise, get into the way of the players, seek flight by no thoroughfares and return discomfited, to escape at last into the stalls and prowl from chair to chair like a man lost and friendless. As it is difficult to remain in the room with the greatest living composer without watching his movements, even at the risk of missing some of his music—which, after all, you will have other chances of hearing—you perhaps paid less attention to Herr Richter than he deserved.

After the Wagner festival nothing remarkable in the way of conducting occurred in London until the following year (1878), when, at a series of concerts given by Madame Viard-Louis, Mr Weist Hill achieved some extraordinary successes, which the London public would probably have recognized in the course of, say, ten years or so, had Madame Viard-Louis been able to prosecute her undertaking at a loss for so long. But this was impossible; and next year Herr Richter came again to conduct "Festival Concerts," so called because the managers knew that his reputation as conductor of the Bayreuth Festival was likely to attract the public far more than his artistic ability. In 1880, however, his position was secure; and since then we have had "Richter Concerts" annually. These concerts had many pleasant peculiarities, which their good example soon rendered less peculiar. The conductor seemed to be familiar with the music, and did not conduct at sight from a score from which he hardly ventured to raise his eyes lest he should lose his place. He did not pose and gesticulate like a savage at a war dance, nor did he, like an over-bred man of St James's, scorn to appear more impressionable than a regimental bandmaster. He seemed to think about his business rather than about himself, and, in rare snatches, when the band had fallen into perfect swing, about the music rather than about his business. In these ecstatic moments his extended arms would pulsate almost imperceptibly; and poetic admirers would compare him to a benignant bird balancing itself in a cloud of blond sunshine (the blond sunshine being diffused from his fair Saxon locks). A point missed would bring him quickly to earth, alert, yet still gracious; but a point overdone—nothing short of monumental stolidity could endure his eye then. For the rest, he could indicate the subdivisions of a bar when it was helpful to do so; and he declined to follow the fashion, set by acrobats of the pianoforte, of playing all *allegros* against time, on the principle that fastest is cleverest.

The public felt the gain in dignity, and respected Herr Richter for it, probably without knowing why. Then he let slip the secret that the scores of Wagner were not to be taken too literally. "How," exclaimed the average violinist in anger and despair, "is a man to be expected to play this reiterated motive, or this complicated figuration, in demisemiquavers at the rate of sixteen in a second? What can he do but go a-swishing up and down as best he can?" "What, indeed?" replied Herr Richter encouragingly. "That is precisely what is intended by the composer." So the relieved violinists went swishing up and down, and the public heard the hissing of Loki's fires in it and were delighted; whilst those who had scores and were able to read them said, "Oh! thats how it's done, is it?" and perhaps winked. And Herr Richter flourished, as he deserved; so that even when his band is positively bad, as it was once or twice at the German Opera last year, or weary and demoralized, as it cannot but become towards the end of a long concert in the stuffiness of St James's Hall, his credit shields them from the censure of the few who know, and from the suspicion of the many who dont. He has now been engaged to conduct the Birmingham Festival, and Sir Arthur Sullivan, who appreciates him better than the general public, whose admiration of a musical celebrity is always half superstitious, thinks that a post of such honor should have been given to a native conductor. He has suggested Mr Cowen, Mr Villiers Stanford, and Mr Barnby as competent substitutes. But Mr Villiers Stanford is an Irishman; Mr Cowen is a Jew; and Mr Barnby, though an industrious and enterprising musician, accustomed to deal with large choirs, has been more successful with new works like Verdi's requiem or Parsifal than with our stock oratorios, which somehow have a stale sound under his direction which Herr Richter has not yet succeeded in imparting to any performance entrusted to his care. Besides, Mr Barnby's reputation is local. If he were selected, dozens of other local celebrities, who doubtless consider themselves equally efficient, would raise the cry of favoritism, if not of downright jobbery. To select the only popular conductor who enjoys a European reputation was the least invidious course open to the Festival Committee; and it is difficult to imagine any alternative which would not have caused more general dissatisfaction both to the profession and to the public.

It is certainly true that Herr Richter, years before he had even chosen the profession in which he is so eminent, succumbed to those "temptations to belong to other nations" which the hero of Pinafore withstood. He is not an Englishman, and he does not even intend to become one: a course quite open to him, as Sir Arthur pointed out when reminded of the supremacy of the late Sir Michael Costa. Costa was an Englishman by domicile; and Sir Arthur himself, who was born a little westward of these shores, and who is of a darker and southerlier strain than the Saxon Richter, can claim no more. Since, however, we use a musical scale which is not specially English, but European and American also, we must go east of the Ural mountains or south of the Mediterranean to find a real "musical foreigner." Still, there is something in the remark of Sir Arthur Sullivan that "a German who cannot speak English appears oddly selected to conduct English choruses." It is less to the point that Herr Richter is not, as Costa was, conductor of the Sacred Harmonic Society and of the Italian opera, that being clearly so much the worse for the Italian opera, whilst the Sacred Harmonic, by appointing Mr Charles Hallé as successor to Costa, set the Birmingham committee the example of appointing a foreigner. And if the conductorship of a series of concerts of established reputation justified the position allowed to Costa, the Viennese conductor is qualified in that respect by the Richter concerts, which are not second in popularity or musical importance to any in London. Indeed, the increased alertness of our older institutions dates from the year in which Herr Richter gave them something tolerable to compete with. I have a particularly deadly-lively recollection of the seasons which immediately preceded his invasion; and I do not think he came a day too soon, nor have I ever met a musician who did. The objection that he is not a master of the English tongue, though invalid against a conductor of orchestral concerts or of German opera, deserves to be weighed when an English oratorio is to be performed. Orchestras only need to be sworn at; and a German is consequently at an advantage with them, as English profanity, except in America, has not

gone beyond a limited technology of perdition, extremely monotonous in the recurrent irritation set up by an unsatisfactory rehearsal. But choristers must have their pronunciation corrected
by somebody if we are ever to escape from that hearty British
"Thah wooaht Ee-li-jar," with which our choirs are accustomed
to denounce Mr Santley for troubling Israel's peace. Herr Richter
clearly cannot do this with authority. If anyone else will undertake to polish the elocution of the Birmingham choir in the course
of a few rehearsals, he has a fair claim—other things being equal
—as against the foreigner. Pending the production of his testi-
monials, we seem to bear with the foreigner very cheerfully.

THE INFERNO AT ST JAMES'S HALL

(The Dramatic Review, 15 February 1885)

Mr Walter Bache has now given us a dozen opportunities of
hearing the serious products of Franz Liszt. His twelfth orchestral
concert of the works of that eminent pianist, biographer, essayist,
patron of genius, Hungarian rhapsodist, and musical enthusiast
took place on the 3rd instant. The chief composition in the
program was "a symphony to Dante's Inferno, Purgatorio, and
Paradiso," particularly the Inferno. When, in order that allowance may be made for my personal bias, I declare at once that I
do not like this symphony, I consider that I am expressing myself
very moderately indeed; and were I to act strictly upon critical
precedents, I should proceed to prove to my own satisfaction
that the form of the symphony is wrong, the progressions forbidden, the decay of modern music largely attributable to its
influence, and the total result lamentably different to what might
have been expected had it occurred to Mozart to set the Divine
Comedy to music. But as all these remarks would be equally
appropriate to much modern music of which I am very fond, I
will forgo them, and content myself with thanking Mr Bache for
the opportunity of making up my mind that the Dante symphony, though doubtless a treat to the composer's disciples, is
not suited to my constitution. I shall justify as best I can my
opinion that the work is shallowly conceived and detestably

expressed; and the reader, if curious on the subject, can study the very different view advanced by Richard Pohl in his book about Franz Liszt, and judge between us. The shortest way would undoubtedly be to go and hear the symphony played; but this, with my experience of Mr Bache's concert fresh in my recollection, I distinctly decline to advise any sober person to attempt.

It is hard to say what the characteristics of Dante's Hell are. Turmoil, hurry, incessant movement, fire, roaring wind, and utter discomfort are there; but so they are also in a London house when the kitchen chimney is on fire. Convey these by music, and the music will be just as appropriate to the one situation as to the other. To convey nothing else is to miss the characteristic which differentiates the Inferno from any other noisy and unpleasant place; and this is what, as I think, Liszt has done: therefore I call his conception a shallow one. I am seriously of opinion that if the symphony were dubbed anew The Conflagration, and a careful analytical program compiled, assigning the various episodes of the *allegro* to The Alarm, The Fire Gaining Ground, Awakening of the Inmates and their Flight, Gathering of the Crowd, Arrival of the Engines, Exertions of Firemen and Struggle of Police with the Mob, with the Falling in of the Roof as a climax, not one of the audience would perceive the slightest incongruity between the music and the subject. The plan could be carried out to the end of the symphony. The Francesca episode might be labeled Complaint of the Lady of the House to Captain Shaw. To that gallant officer might be attributed the soothing recitative-like passage for the bass clarionet, at present supposed to represent the poet's sympathetic address to the unfortunate lovers. The *andante* would be appropriate to the mingled feelings of relief and regret following the extinction of the flames; the incidental fugue might portray the firemen searching the blackened ruins by lantern light; whilst the vocal conclusion would be in its place as the Thanksgiving of the Householder. The music is far more adequate to this program than to that of the composer, whose logic is like that of Shakespear's Welshman. "I warrant you shall find," says Fluellen, "in the comparisons between Macedon and Monmouth, that the situations, look you, is both alike. There is a river in Macedon; and there is also moreover a river in Monmouth; and there is salmons in both." There is haste, confusion, and discord in Dante's Hell; and there is haste, confusion, and discord in Liszt's symphony. So far, "the situations, look you, is both alike." But not a whit more alike than dozens of situations even more remote from the Divine Comedy than the one I have suggested. Dante's poem is unique because of those features of it that are not to be found elsewhere. Liszt's symphony is commonplace because disturbance and noise are commonplace. But to do justice to it on its own level, I admit that the degree of noise is not altogether commonplace. The symphony is exceptionally loud.

The proceedings begin at the gate of Hell with a phrase founded on that useful old favorite formerly known as the chord of the diminished seventh. This is delivered *fortissimo* by the three trombones and the tuba in unison, and repeated twice with modifications of increasing harshness. The effect is purely a question of the power of the trombones. Such as it is, it is just half what six trombones and two tubas would produce. As additional instruments could easily be procured from the band of the Grenadier Guards, who are accustomed to enhance similar effects at Promenade Concerts, Mr Bache, if he really likes this description of music, might find the reinforcement worth its cost. As it is, the result of the opening is to deafen and irritate the listener, and to leave him more than ever convinced that the art of using the trombone to express the terrors of the supernatural was born and died with Mozart, who would certainly have regarded a *fortissimo* passage for three trombones in unison in a serious work as an outrage on public decency. It is impossible, from lack of space, to follow the symphony point by point. The trombones go from bad to worse. Their parts, at first marked *ff*, soon appear with the three f's, in his enthusiasm for which Liszt outdoes the Farmers' Alliance. Volleys of strident barks from the brass alternate with shuddering triplets from the strings, and mingle with clarionets buzzing in their lowest register on the hackneyed Der Freischütz model; drum rolls that soon cease to convey anything to the worried ear except a monotonous thumping and stamping, like applause at a public meeting in a hotel breaking out on the floor above your bedroom in the middle of your first sleep; and all the howling and hurrying commonplaces of orchestral *diablerie* piled upon oneanother to exasperation point. When it was over on Friday evening, a majority of the audience, in spite of their disposition (which I shared) to make much of Mr Bache in return for his enterprise and devotion, shewed by their silence that the composer had gone too far in offering them this obscene instrumental orgy as a serious comment on a great poem.

The remainder of the work was so far Dantesque that it produced an impression which ordinary readers of the Divine Comedy often confess having experienced. They find the Purgatorio duller than the Inferno, and the Paradiso duller than either. For my own part I was in no humor to be consoled by elaborate prettinesses from harp and English horn, viola and flute, and so forth, for what I had just suffered. The choir of ladies, among whom were Mr Malcolm Lawson's votaresses of St Cecilia, furnished a pretty background to the orchestra; but they did not seem well accustomed to sing together; and the final Magnificat, monotonously exalting itself by modulations from one key to another a tone above, and accompanied by muted violins hissing like a badly-adjusted limelight, was not so soothing as it was intended to be. At last a senseless episode, like the duel in Don Giovanni gone mad, turned out to be the *coda*; and, with a final Hallelujah, the welcome end came.

Putting Dante and the pretensions of the composer to illustrate him out of the question, and regarding the work merely as an example of the resources of the orchestra, the symphony seems to me useless even from a student's point of view. Qualities of tone which have never been made effective except when used very sparingly are resorted to almost continuously. Combinations which have been used with delightful results elsewhere occur only to fall flat upon ears tortured beyond the desire of any orchestral combination except a few bars rest. Though in many places ethereal sweetness and smoothness have been so elaborately planned that a glance at the score raises pleasant expectations, the effect proves to be only a paper one; or perhaps the players are too far demoralized by the violence and strain of the context to do justice to the pretty platitudes which the composer has sought to worry, by mere stress of orchestration, into melody and beauty. If there be any of those charmingly piquant effects which decorate the Hungarian rhapsodies, they are so discounted as to be unnoticeable. Comparisons with Berlioz are suggested by the fact that his aims and method are imitated by Liszt, as they have been by Raff. But Liszt's range is very narrow as compared with that of Berlioz. He produces certain vigorous and strident effects which are acceptable until he gives you too much of them, which he invariably does: a notable example being his setting of the Rákóczy March, which was also in the program the other evening. But though he aims strenuously at Berlioz's formidable maximum of tone, he has not the secret of it, and degenerates into intolerable noise in the attempt to reach it. He never surprises you, as Berlioz does, by producing several different effects from combinations of the same instruments. He outdoes Berlioz in bidding for the diabolical by noise and fury; but he quite misses the strange nightmare sensation, the smell of brimstone, as Schumann called it, which characterized Berlioz's exploits in the infernal field. Pre-eminence in the infernal is, perhaps, hardly worth disputing; but one must compare Liszt with a composer against whom he is perceptibly measurable. To compare his works with those of Bach, Handel, and Mozart, or even with the occasional savage aberrations of Wagner and Beethoven, would dwarf him too absurdly.

A few other works were performed at the concert. There was the March of the Three Holy Kings, with its pretty *trio* in D flat, which I had sufficiently recovered from the Inferno to enjoy. A "dramatic scene" entitled Joan of Arc at the Stake, with happily very little stake and a great deal of Joan, was sung by Mademoiselle Alice Barbi, who will probably sing it, not with more pleasure to others, but with perhaps a little more comfort to herself, when she attains some additional skill in managing her breath. I offer the suggestion with due reserve, conscious that the lady is likely to know more of her art than I do. Mr Bache played the pianoforte concerto in E flat, and received a laurel crown of the dimensions of a life-buoy in

acknowledgment. I am sorry for the sake of my credit with him
that I came away unconverted.

THE BACH BI-CENTENARY

(The Dramatic Review, 28 March 1885)

The Bach choir is a body of ladies and gentlemen associated
under the direction of Mr Otto Goldschmidt "for the practice
and performance of choral works of excellence of various
schools." It made itself famous on the 26th April 1876, by
achieving the first complete performance in England of John
Sebastian Bach's setting of the High Mass in B minor. The work
disappointed some people, precisely as the Atlantic Ocean disappointed Mr Wilde. Others, fond of a good tune, missed in it
those compact little airs that can be learnt by ear and accompanied by tonic, sub-dominant, tonic, dominant, and tonic
harmonies in the order stated; or, pedantry apart, by the three
useful chords with which professors of the banjo teach their
pupils, in one lesson, to accompany songs (usually in the key of
G), without any previous knowledge of thoroughbass. As there
was nothing for those unfortunate persons who did not like the
Mass but to listen to it again and again until their state became
more gracious, the Bach choir repeated it in 1877, in 1879, and
again on Saturday last. As that day is supposed to be the 200th
anniversary of Bach's birthday, a special effort was made; the
performance was given in the Albert Hall; the society was reinforced by picked choristers from Henry Leslie's and other
noted choirs, to the total number of over five hundred singers;
and orchestral instruments that have fallen into disuse since
Bach's time were specially manufactured and studied by eminent
players for the occasion.

Those faults in the performance for which the conductor and
the choir can fairly be held responsible were not due to any want
of care or earnestness in preparation. One chorus, *Credo in
Unum Deum*, fell into confusion, the singers being apparently
bewildered by the burst of applause with which the audience had
just received the *Cum Sancto Spiritu*. This, however, was an

accident: the number was sung accurately at the last rehearsal; and had the conductor been in a position to stop and start afresh, or to repeat the chorus, the mistake would have been remedied. Here, for once, was an opportunity for the British public to set matters right by an *encore*. It is needless to add that the British public did not rise to the very simple occasion. Among the inevitable shortcomings may be classed the loss of effect in some of the brighter numbers—notably the *Pleni sunt cœli*—by the jog trot which seems to be Mr Goldschmidt's *prestissimo*. It is ungracious to complain of a conductor who has achieved a result so admirable and difficult as a good performance of the great Mass; and it is quite possible that Mr Goldschmidt may have experimentally determined that a single extra beat per second would endanger the precision upon which so much depends in Bach's polyphony; but there were moments on Saturday when the audience must have longed that Mr Goldschmidt would go ahead a little—when some may have profanely felt that one glass of champagne administered to the conductor would have made an acceptable difference in the effect. Mr Goldschmidt has, however, well earned his right to have his own opinion on the question; and he shewed when, in the *Gloria* and the *Cum Sancto Spiritu*, he got from B minor into D major, that he is capable, on occasion, of a flash of that spirit which earned for Bach himself the compliment that "in conducting he was very accurate; and in time, *which he generally took at a very lively pace*, he was always sure."

The renovation of the obsolete *oboe d' amore* (love-hautboy), and the execution of the trumpet parts upon the instrument for which they were written, instead of, as usual, upon the clarionet, proved very successful, and furnished a fresh illustration of the fact that our modern "orchestration" falls as far short of Bach's orchestral music as the medley of dance-tunes and stage thunder which constitutes a Parisian grand opera falls short of one of his cantatas. The *oboe d' amore* is pitched a third lower than the ordinary oboe. It fell into disuse in the last century. After some time its loss was felt; but unfortunately its place was then filled, in the scores of Rossini, Meyerbeer, and Wagner, by the English horn: an instrument which produces something of the plaintive

effect of the *oboe d' amore*, but the tone of which can be described
only as a mongrel compound of the snarling of a bad clarionet
and the whining of a bad oboe. The *oboe d' amore* has the true
oboe tone, and is far superior in dignity and sweetness to the
English horn. Whether it is equally manageable is best known to
Messrs Horton and Lebon, who have been at the pains to master
it; but if it be, I should not be sorry to see it finally banish the
English horn from the orchestra. A performance of the overtures
to William Tell and The Flying Dutchman with the English
horn parts taken by this new-old love-hautboy would furnish
an interesting test of the comparative merits of the instruments.
Perhaps the forthcoming South Kensington Exhibition [1] will be
so good as to arrange such a performance.

The rehabilitation of the old-fashioned trumpet was still more
interesting. Owing to the weakness of conductors, the indolence
or incompetence of players, and the ignorance of the public,
trumpet parts are habitually played upon the cornopean (I prefer
to give the thing its hideous English name): an instrument that,
accompanied by the harp, can, in skilful hands, draw tears from
a crowd at the door of a gin-palace by The Pilgrim of Love, or
Then youll remember me, but the substitution of which for the
trumpet in the concert room is an imposture and an outrage. It
is easier to play, however; and whenever trumpet players find a
conductor whom they dare trifle with, they play the cornopean.
On precisely the same ground, and with less injury to the general
effect, clarionetists might play their parts on the English concertina, which is far more like a clarionet in tone than a cornopean
is like a trumpet. The result of tolerating the easier instrument
has been that no composer now ventures to write for the easy
cornet passages that Handel never hesitated to write for the
difficult trumpet. Herr Julius Kosleck, of Berlin, shewed us on
Saturday that the old trumpet parts are as feasible as ever. He
brings out the high D with ease, executes shakes, rivals our finest

[1] The International Inventions Exhibition opened at South Kensington in May
1885. Division II, according to the official program, consisted "of Musical Instruments of a date not earlier than the commencement of the present century; and of
Historic Collections of Musical Instruments and Appliances . . ." Shaw purchased
a season ticket on 25th May and reviewed most of the variegated musical programs
at "the Inventions" from May to October in *The Dramatic Review*, *Our Corner*,
and *The Magazine of Music*.

flautists in the purity of the tone he produces in the upper register, and seems able to do, with his prodigiously long, straight instrument, all the feats that the first-cornet heroes of our military bands accomplish in their "*staccato* polkas," and the like double-tongueing atrocities. It is to be hoped that our native players will not suffer themselves to be beaten by the Berliner. The modesty which leads them to declare the trumpet too difficult for them has often been overcome by the simple argument of "No song, no supper," paraphrased for the occasion as "No trumpet, no engagement." Conductors can now reinforce their authority by threatening to send for Herr Kosleck.

The principal vocal parts were entrusted to Miss Anna Williams, Madame Patey, Mr Edward Lloyd, and Mr Kempton, who replaced Signor Foli, absent through illness. The audience, somewhat stunned by the stupendous choruses, hardly appreciated the delicacy and subdued fervor of the airs and duets, as to the execution of which it must suffice to say that the airs might have been worse, the duets might have been better, and both might have been more frequently rehearsed. This is a safe and widely-applicable critical formula, not disagreeably precise, and yet not inexpressive as critical formulæ go.

It is the custom of the Bach choir to give two concerts every year, concentrating themselves on the great composer at one, and avoiding him at the other. Thus the festival now in question was preceded by a concert at St James's Hall on the 19th of last month, when Mr C. H. H. Parry's setting of certain scenes from Shelley's Prometheus, composed for the Three Choirs Festival of 1880, was performed for the first time in London, as was also Friedrich Kiel's Star of Bethlehem. The latter work was quite new: Kiel, famous in Berlin as a learned teacher and contrapuntist, being little known in this country. The Star of Bethlehem is a short oratorio of excellent workmanship; and the composer, if his talent is not sufficiently many-sided to rank as genius, is yet so thoroughly qualified in other respects that our choral societies might well spend on his works some of the energy which they occasionally waste on composers that are not qualified at all. The English version has been adapted from the English Bible by Mr J. Maud Crament, himself a contrapuntist of some note, as an energetic helper of the Bach choir ought to be. It is, like his version of the Christus of the same composer, successful both from a musical and literary point of view.

One word on the economic side of these concerts. My program cost me more than it was worth, even as programs go. My seat also cost me more than it was worth, as seats at concerts go; but I was advised of that beforehand, and was at liberty to stay away if I did not like the price. But a program, once you are entrapped in St James's Hall, is an absolute necessity, because the last thing you can gather from an English vocalist is the lyric verse he is supposed to be singing; and you must, therefore, either refer to a book for the subject of the music, or trust to the singer's facial expression, which usually varies with the difficulty of the note rather than with the intensity of the dramatic situation. As the Bach choir is very rich, and allots the best seats privately to its members or their friends before the public are accommodated, it can surely afford to make its charges at least as low as those of heavily-handicapped individual concert-givers.

ENGLISH OPERA AT DRURY LANE

(*The Dramatic Review*, 11 *April* 1885; signed "Ignotus." Although this was the pseudonym of editor Edward Paget Palmer, Shaw identified himself as the author in his diary entry for 8 April 1885)

On Monday last, the Carl Rosa company opened their campaign at Drury Lane. They are as happy, healthy, and respectable as ever. They knock their voices about with their old confident robustness; their elocution fluctuates as of yore between artless colloquialism and toastmasterly magniloquence; and their acting is still the acting of Richardson's show. They are not yet tired of tacking tawdry strips of obsolete *cadenza* to the end of their songs, nor have they ceased to remind the judicious spectator, by their inveterate aping of the follies of the Italian lyric stage, of Artemus Ward's unlucky assumption of "an operatic voice" when serenading his sleeping wife. Nevertheless they are welcome. With a corrupt foreign school to lead them astray, no native school to reclaim them, and an ignorantly good-natured public to encourage them, they make the most of their opportunities, and treat their patrons far better on the whole than their Italian rivals treat theirs.

The opera performed on the opening night was Maritana. Poor Maritana! Its infinite blarney may keep its hotch-potch of bluster and sentiment alive longer than many more thoughtful works. There is not an original idea in it—not even an original turn given to a borrowed idea. The authorship of the inimitable Bunn is conspicuous in the singableness, the sentiment, and the outrageous absurdity of the lyrics. He never wrote words quite so pleasant to sing, so melting to hear, so irresistibly funny to read as those of When other lips and other hearts, but Let me like a soldier fall is by no means unworthy of him. A literary man who is not musical may always be detected by his inability to perceive the least merit in Bunn. Musicians know better, and envy Balfe and Wallace their librettist.

Don Cæsar de Bazan (variously called Sezzar and Scissor by the Carl Rosa artists) was impersonated by Mr Maas, who, not quite at ease with his breast "expanding to the ball," declined an enthusiastic *encore* for the song in which that heroic phenomenon is pre-figured, but repeated There is a flower that bloometh very willingly. Mr Maas's style is no longer heavily ecclesiastical, as it was some years ago, when he played Rienzi at Her Majesty's, and when Miss Georgina Burns made her first striking success in London as the Messenger of Peace. His voice is soft, rich, and unforced; and the delight of the public in it seems to be boundless. On the other hand, his gifts are not various. In passages where promptitude, force, and incisive declamation are required, Mr Maas is a trifle sleepy. Don Cæsar's warning to the captain of the guard, Know sir, who I am: Count of Garofa, &c. &c., is not very terrible as Mr Maas delivers it. In point of voice, the tenor was the best of the combatants; but there were traces of staleness and sluggishness about the fighting condition of the noble scamp that were all in favor of the captain of the guard.

Madame Georgina Burns as Maritana and Mr Ludwig as Don Jose obtained the usual *encores* for Scenes that are Brightest, and In Happy Moments. They were less successful in the duets of the first act, the soprano being hard and hurried, and the baritone hollow and toneless. In the concerted music they were far surpassed by Mr Maas and Miss Marian Burton, who listened to the voices with which they had to blend their own. Madame Georgina Burns and Mr Ludwig sang throughout as if they were stone-deaf to every part except those of Maritana and Don Jose.

Miss Marian Burton, though her voice is not yet quite solid, and although she appended a dreadful "ornament" to Hark, those Chimes, made a very favorable impression as Lazarillo by her appearance, her intelligent acting, and her sympathetic singing. Her phrasing is sometimes that of a not over-conscientious ballad singer, and, if not remedied, will prove a serious disqualification for parts of a higher order than Lazarillo; but Miss Marian Burton does not seem the sort of person to persist in bad habits when she is once made aware of them.

Lazarillo, by the bye, is an armorer's apprentice, a grimy, coaly, rusty person, with stains of the stithy on his shirt and skin, and with a scorched leathern apron on. Miss Marian Burton, however, turned out like the pastrycook in Genevieve de Brabant, in spotless lawn, impossibly dainty and clean. Now, as she has an opportunity of appearing in the last act at her very prettiest, in blue satin and lace, might she not sacrifice a little to realism by putting on the leathern apron and a touch or so of rust and soot during her apprenticeship to the brutal armorer? Surely the opera is unreal enough without such utterly incredible details as those of the costume and complexion she adopted on Monday night.

The chorus, regardless of the tanning sun of Spain, presented faces and arms of the whitest and pinkest, spoiling the scenery, and offending the eye. They also offended the ear. They are not, as many choruses are, voiceless; but the tone they produce—if tone it may be called—is coarse and unmusical at best, and execrable at worst. This is inexcusable, as any body of choristers can be made fairly efficient if trouble enough be taken with them. They make some attempt at acting too, as most choruses have done since the Meiningen company played Julius Cæsar here. Anyone desirous of a hearty laugh should hasten to witness the gesticulations of the Carl Rosa chorus as they listen to The Harp in the Air.

Maritana does not tax the ingenuity of the stage manager very heavily. Nevertheless, Mr Maas in the concerted piece, See the culprit, got into difficulties that could easily have been avoided. And the gymnastic feats of Miss Marian Burton with the muskets from which she has to withdraw the bullets should not be performed under the immediate supervision of the firing party.

Did Vincent Wallace regard the scene in which the Marquis and Marchioness appear as a harlequinade, with the clown and policeman omitted, and the pantaloon and the old woman retained? The effect is amusing, but not conducive to the dignity of English opera.

MANON

(The Dramatic Review, 16 *May* 1885)

In fitting the story of Manon Lescaut to the stage for M. Massenet, MM. Meilhac and Gille took for granted that their audience had read the novel upon which their libretto is founded. In France this assumption may have been justified, but the average Englishman is about as likely to have read the famous seventh volume of the Mémoires et aventures d'un homme de qualité produced by Prévost d'Exiles in 1731, as the average Frenchman is to have read Clarissa Harlowe. Those who find the libretto bewildering will do well to read the novel, which is prodigiously superior to the opera. The now scarce 1839 edition, with the vignettes of Tony Johannot, or the scarcer 1797 edition, exquisitely printed by Didot and illustrated by Lefevre, may be recommended to dainty readers. The much vaunted *édition de luxe* of 1875, with the preface by Alexandre Dumas *fils*, and the etchings by Leopold Flameng, will repay careful avoidance. Those who do not hold with M. Dumas that *"il n'y a de livres malsains que les livres mal faits"* had better read the novel before presenting a copy to the young lady of fifteen of whom much has been said of late in these pages.

When M. Jules Massenet descended on our shores for the first time in 1878 with an instrumental suite descriptive of scenes from

Macbeth, he established his reputation as one of the loudest of modern composers. Something of that *esprit de corps* which led a celebrated artillery regiment to sing with ungrammatical enthusiasm We are the boys that fears no noise seems to have determined him not to allow even a simple chord to a recitative to pass without a pluck at the strings and a slam on the drum capable of awakening the deaf. When the curtain descends on a thrilling "situation" he pours forth all his energy in a screeching, grinding, rasping *fortissimo* of extraordinary exuberance and vigor. He is perhaps better at a stage tumult than any living composer. Ever and anon there comes in Manon a number that stuns the hearer into drowsy good humor, and leaves him disposed to tolerate anything that gently tickles his exhausted ears and does not tax his attention too heavily. The quartet with chorus in the fourth act must be almost as audible on Waterloo Bridge as in the first row of stalls in Drury Lane Theatre.

About the music generally there is little to be said, but that little is in its favor. It is pretty, spirited, easy to follow, varied with considerable fancy and ingenuity, never dull, and only occasionally trivial or vulgar. As Manon is technically an *opéra comique*, the dialogue is spoken, and the speaking is accompanied by the old-fashioned *mélodrame*, or descriptive orchestral accompaniment, the effect of which is in every case happy. The instrumentation is so excessively strident at times that it would conceivably satiate even Liszt, whilst the immoderate fury to which the composer abandons himself at each climax of the drama, reminds one of the Verdi of Ernani and Il Trovatore; but on the whole the orchestral work has a distinct style, and is by no means a mere hotch-potch of borrowed effects. Of Wagnerism there is not the faintest suggestion. A phrase which occurs in the first love duet breaks out once or twice in subsequent amorous episodes, and has been seized on by a few unwary critics as a Wagnerian *leit motif.* But if Wagner had never existed, Manon would have been composed much as it stands now, whereas if Meyerbeer and Gounod had not made a path for M. Massenet, it is impossible to say whither he might have wandered, or how far he could have pushed his way.

The performance at Drury Lane on the 7th was favored by

the rare suitability of the parts to the artists who undertook them. "*J'ai l'humeur naturellement douce et tranquille*," said poor des Grieux to the Abbé Prévost; and Mr Maas, whatever his disposition may be, certainly has a voice and stage manner exceptionally *douce et tranquille*. He wins all the sympathy that readers of the novel feel, in spite of their moral sense, for the amiable hero whose honor rooted in dishonor stood, and whose faith unfaithful kept him falsely true. Manon, or Mannong, as they call her in their hearty English way at Drury Lane, was irresistible in the first two acts. Madame Marie Roze is not a first-rate singer, and time was when to have described her merely as a bad singer would have conveyed but a feeble impression of her shortcomings. When Tietjens's central place became vacant, Madame Marie Roze was put into it as a stopgap by a management at its wits' end to find a passable substitute. There is no room here to chronicle a tenth of the labors she undauntedly attacked in that extremity. When Lohengrin had to be played she took her voice in her hand (so to speak) and rushed through the part of Ortrud. When there was no Pamina left in England, she fell fearlessly on Mozart and was defeated with heavy loss to the hearers. The scars of that campaign are on her voice to this day. Yet through it all she disarmed the critics. Something pleaded for her in their manly breasts (it was certainly not any pre-eminent artistic excellence on her part), and she was allowed to clothe herself, unchallenged, with the prestige of *prima donna* at Her Majesty's Opera, London. It was supposed to be on the strength of this that America subsequently accepted her, and that she was hailed in the provinces as a great artist when she at last placed her services at the disposal of Mr Carl Rosa.

But it now appears to be delightfully and surprisingly true that there were better reasons for her success. She has returned to us with not only much more of her voice left than any reasonable person could have expected, but with new claims as an actress of remarkable ability. Her Carmen is as undeniably the best we have seen here as Madame Trebelli's is the best we have heard. She might be said to realize Mérimée's heroine down to her boots, were it not that the novelist expressly mentions Carmen's "white silk stockings with more than one hole in them," whereas on the stage Carmen's stockings appear intact. Manon is a fresh triumph for Madame Marie Roze. The intelligence and determination that have enabled her to achieve it are still masked by the infantine simplicity, the plaintive eyes, and the innocent beauty that used to blunt the critical pen and sweeten the critical ink. But the artlessness that was once only too genuine now conceals carefully premeditated acting, based on an exhaustive study of the original description of the character. Manon in the inn yard at Amiens, and in the little set of apartments in Paris, is more charming than any novelty the lyric stage has shewn us for some years past. No art can quite redeem the subsequent scenes from the repulsiveness of their moral infamy; but as the gilding is very thick, and the bustle incessant, the spectator finds it easier to laugh, to stare, and—if soft-hearted—to cry, than to think into the ethics of the case. As a singer Madame Marie Roze is far more judicious than she used to be. By giving up her old fashion of desperately assaulting vocal difficulties in the hope of vanquishing them by force or by good luck, she has saved her voice from serious deterioration; and it is now fairly clear and strong. In using it she makes the most of what she can do; and what she cannot do she gracefully dodges. She is to be congratulated on having made an extraordinary advance in her profession, and that, too, in a department of it which rarely receives a pretense of adequate attention.

Mr Ludwig, who plays the rascally soldier, Lescaut, once had some tone in his voice, and perhaps was capable of becoming an actor. But he has shaken all the tone away (most unfortunately managing to retain the voice), and, busy as he is posing, rolling the eye, and sawing the air, has no leisure even to think of acting. Yet his deportment as Lescaut is far more rational than that of Mr Burgon as des Grieux, senior, whose proceedings are so absolutely unaccountable as to exempt him from criticism. Yet the audience were pleased with Mr Burgon on the first night, and the strange signals he made with his hat, and his singing of Go wed some Maiden fair and tender must be recorded as popular successes. Mr Maas, by the bye, in altering I pray you, sir, do not mock me, into I pray *thee*, was disrespectful enough to *tutoyer* his father. Mr Lyall is as funny as usual in the part of

Guillot, introduced by the authors of the libretto to evade the disagreeably close relationship that exists in the story between the two lovers of Manon who procure her arrest. There are many pretty concerted pieces for the subordinate characters, and much lively choral work. In the riotous scene at the Amiens inn, where a crowd of passengers bawl and struggle for their luggage, the choristers for the most part adopt the tactics which have been allowed to pass in the riot scene in the Meistersinger, where the singers disregard their parts, shout whatever comes into their heads, and make as much noise as possible.

Mr Joseph Bennett has done his best to translate the French libretto into English that will fit the notes and yet comply with ordinary literary conditions. Nevertheless, quotations would be out of place here, as it is no part of the function of grave musical criticism to create uproarious mirth.

THE MARRIAGE OF FIGARO

(The Dramatic Review, 6 June 1885)

On this day last week Mr Carl Rosa concluded his triumphant season at Drury Lane by conducting a performance of Mozart's opera, Le Nozze di Figaro, now a hundred years old. A century after Shakespear's death it was the fashion for men, otherwise sane, to ridicule the pretensions of the author of Hamlet to intellectual seriousness, and to publish editions of his works prefaced by apologies for his childishness and barbarism, with entreaties to the reader to judge him indulgently as a man who "worked by a mere light of nature." At present, a century after Mozart's death, we have among us men, only partially idiotic, who hold similar language of the composer of Figaro, Don Giovanni, and Die Zauberflöte. Now the truth about Shakespear was never forgotten—never even questioned by the silent masses who read poetry, but skip notes, comments, and criticisms. And that the many heads of the mob are perfectly "level" on the subject of Mozart, is shewn by the fact that Figaro or The Don will still draw a house when nothing else will, though not a single perfectly satisfactory representation of either opera is on record. It

72

is true that the infallibility of the mob is as yet only a dogma of Mr Sydney Grundy's; but this matter does not rest on mob authority alone: Wagner, when not directly expressing his unmitigated contempt for his own disciples, delighted to taunt them by extoling Mozart; and Gounod, standing undazzled before Wagner and Beethoven, has confessed that before Mozart his ambition turns to despair. Berlioz formed his taste in ignorance of Handel and Mozart, much as a sculptor might form his taste in ignorance of Phidias and Praxiteles; and when he subsequently became acquainted with Mozart in his works, he could not quite forgive him for possessing all the great qualities of his idol Gluck, and many others of which Gluck was destitute, besides surpassing him in technical skill. Yet Berlioz admitted the greatness of Mozart; and if he did not fully appreciate him as the most subtle and profound of all musical dramatists, much less as his own superior in the handling of his favorite instrument, the orchestra, he never was guilty of the stupid fashion that has since sprung up of treating him as a sort of Papageno among composers.

This exordium is intended to help a few readers, who may have been perverted by the Papageno propagandists, to realize the magnitude of the task which Mr Carl Rosa successfully attempted last Saturday. For his own part, he came forward as a conductor to carry out his own reading of the work, and not as Mr Randegger does—and does very well—merely to keep the band together and accompany the singers. There is an old tradition that the Figaro overture should be played against time so as to finish within three and a half minutes. There are two hundred and ninetyfour bars in the overture; and there are only two hundred and ten seconds in three and a half minutes. Consequently seven bars have to be played every five seconds. This gives the most effective speed. But the conductor must keep it uniform throughout: he must not indulge in *rallentandos*. Unfortunately this is just what Mr Carl Rosa did. He lingered affectionately over the delightful little theme in A just before the repeat, and then spurted to make up for lost time. The orchestra responded gamely; and the final chord was passed well within the two hundred and tenth second; but the finish was a scramble, which was the greater pity as the *rallentando* which necessitated it was in bad taste. Mr Carl Rosa's conducting is marred by two bad habits of his: he hurries at every *crescendo*; and he prolongs his pet passages as much as possible. Physically, he gives himself much unnecessary trouble. Throughout the overture he actually made two down beats in each bar, as if the music were written in two-four instead of common time. In a less familiar work the effect might have been to confuse the players, and Mr Carl Rosa can hardly have steadied his own nerves by slashing the unoffending air nearly six hundred times in less than four minutes. However, if he did those things which he ought not to have done, he at least did not leave undone those things which he ought to have done. He conducted the performance instead of allowing the performance to conduct him; and the largest share of the effect produced would not have been produced had he not been there. His treatment of the *allegro maestoso* movement in the baritone *aria, Vedro, mentr' io sospiro*, revealed all its dignity, which must have surprised many Italian opera-goers present. In this case he reduced the speed to which we have become accustomed; and he did the same, but with questionable judiciousness, in the first section of the great *finale* to the second act, where the *allegro*, interrupted by the discovery of Susanna, is resumed in B flat at the words *Susanna, son morta*. On the other hand, he took Figaro's *aria, Aprite un po'*, at the beginning of the last act, at a rattling *allegro molto*, a quite unjustifiable proceeding, as it bothered Mr Barrington Foote and violated Mozart's direction *"moderato."* Later in the same act the movement marked *andante* in six-eight time, *Pace, pace, mio dolce tesoro*, was also taken far too quickly. There were three important omissions, besides those which have become customary. These were the duet *Via resti servita, madama brillante* for Susanna and Marcellina in the first act; the sestet *Riconosci in questo amplesso* in the third act, which was perceptibly weakened by the hiatus; and that extraordinary pæan of a base soul, *In quegl' anni*, for Don Basilio in the fourth act.

Before dealing more particularly with the singers, acknowledgment must be made of their general superiority in point of taste and conscientiousness to their Italian rivals as we last heard them at Covent Garden. They sang, with so few exceptions that they may all be stated here, faithfully what Mozart wrote. Madame Marie Roze, finding a few notes in *Deh vieni, non tardar* too low for her, sang them in the higher octave. Mr Barrington Foote in *Non più andrai* and Mr Burgon in *La Vendetta* embellished their parts by two very innocent (and easy) little scales, as merely human bassos always do and always will. Finally, in that song in which Mozart makes merry with the horns, Mr Barrington Foote altered the penultimate note with such disastrous effect that he will probably trust Mozart's judgment in future rather than his own. This was all. Lovers of music who have had, at Covent Garden, to submit to the vulgar liberties taken without public rebuke by Madame Pauline Lucca with such songs as *Voi che sapete*, or who have stared at the cool reliance upon popular ignorance with which Signor de Reszke used to omit the difficult passage of triplets and the F sharp in *Vedro, mentr' io sospiro*, against which Mr Ludwig so heroically bruises himself, will appreciate the fidelity of Mr Carl Rosa's artists, and will be glad to hear that they were applauded as heartily and encored as freely as if they had treated the audience to all the stale *fioriture* of their singing masters.

Madame Marie Roze was Susanna. She began very well, and remained so up to the middle of the second act, when her intonation became a little uncertain. Thenceforth she fell off vocally; and by the time the last act was reached she was singing much as the Marie Roze of ten years ago was wont to sing. Her acting was better, but she appeared too conscious of her own sprightliness, marred her dialogue by mirthless laughs, and was too tender-hearted to box Mr Barrington Foote's ears soundly in the garden scene. It would, perhaps, be inhuman to suggest that Mr Foote should try next time the effect of a vigorous pinch on the realism of Madame Marie Roze's acting. She would suffer; and probably he would too, subsequently; but the public would compensate both by the laughter and applause which make reputations behind the footlights. Miss Julia Gaylord, as Cherubino, delighted the audience by her vivacity, which indeed put her out of breath once or twice at critical moments. She made no attempt at the serious side—the Mozartian as distinct from the Beaumarchais side—of the page's calf-love for the countess, and was quite as impudent in her presence as elsewhere; but she did justice to as much as she could see of her part, sang *Voi che sapete* very prettily, and was encored heartily. Miss Georgina Burns played the countess. Her voice does not improve with use, but it is still brilliant. It may be said of nearly the whole cast that their voices are the worse for wear, instead of, as should be the case, the better. The exceptions are Mr Burgon, who did very well as Bartolo, and Mr Lyall, whose voice, if not very fresh or powerful, remains precisely as it was when the oldest inhabitant first heard it. As Basilio he had a grotesque hat and a red umbrella, and more Mr Lyall needs not to make him happy. Mr Barrington Foote's voice is not heavy enough for the music of Figaro, but his enunciation is very clear; and though he is not exactly a comedian, he is funny enough to pass for one on the lyric stage.

The orchestra, when playing the last section of the march in the third act, managed to get hideously out of tune, probably in consequence of the effect of the heat of the house on the wood wind instruments. With this exception they played admirably, as indeed any body of competent players could not help doing with such exquisite work in hand. The *fandango* was evidently designed by an artist capable of understanding the value of the opportunity offered by the only number in this wonderful opera that falls to the share of the dancer.

Though English performers in English opera are not quite so scarce as Italian performers in Italian opera, there was a mixture of nationalities at the Marriage of Figaro. The Countess was English and so was Figaro. The Count was Irish, Susanna French, Cherubino American, and the conductor German. The good humor of the audience was boundless. Besides the pre-arranged floral compliments to the *prime donne*, there was much cheering after the national anthem, and repeated calls for Mr Carl Rosa, who was at last led out by Mr Augustus Harris. As Mr Carl Rosa bowed himself off, a wreath was thrown, and Mr Augustus Harris snatched at it and made an unsuccessful attempt to lasso the retreating conductor with it. Failing, he disappeared in pursuit, and presently returned dragging Mr Carl Rosa forcibly with him, laurel crowned. Even after this Mr Carl Rosa had to come out again bowing. At the second bow he incautiously approached the footlights. Instantly there was a dead silence, broken only by a cry of "Speech! Speech!" Mr Carl Rosa blenched and precipitately dived behind the curtain; and the audience dispersed, highly pleased with him, with Mozart, and, for less obvious reasons, with themselves.

A SUBSTITUTE FOR STRAUSS

(The Dramatic Review, 27 June 1885)

When Herr Richter disbanded his orchestra on Monday last, London was left to face three months without concerts of high-class music. Only the well-to-do amateurs will be any the worse, for there is practically no regular provision made at any time throughout the year for the mass of people who like good orchestral music, but who cannot afford to spend more than a couple of shillings a week on gratifying their taste. Of weekly concerts of recognized excellence, we have two sets: the Saturday afternoons at the Crystal Palace in the winter and early spring, and the Richter concerts from spring to midsummer, with a few extra performances very late in the autumn or early winter. These concerts are not cheap enough for the people. A Crystal Palace Saturday Popular, taking place on a half-crown day, with an extra charge for admission to the concert room, a sixpenny program, and a railway journey, makes a larger hole in half-a-sovereign than many amateurs care to make in five shillings. The lowest charge for admission to a Richter concert is two-and-six-pence; and the analytic program, though fattened by six pages of advertisements, costs an additional shilling, for which it is perhaps the worst value in London. The consequent dependence of both series of concerts on the patronage of comparatively rich people is shewn by the fact that they cease when the moneyed classes leave London, and recommence when they return.

Yet music is never really out of season. Fashionable singers may go and come with the Mayfair birds of passage; but so do fashionable preachers: yet no one seriously proposes to close St Paul's or Westminster Abbey during the autumn. The moment our concerts reach the people, they will become independent of fashion and season; and until they are thus independent, it is useless to pretend that they are popular. One of the standard out-of-season entertainments is the promenade concert, decorated with huge blocks of ice that do not cool anyone, but only shew how independent music is of the weather. In spite of the fact that these concerts cater for two classes of people, each of which frightens the other away from them, they have proved beyond all question that classical music, a complete orchestra, and admission at one shilling, will attract a crowd in London. That is to say, one of our public needs is a weekly concert of good orchestral music for one shilling.

There is now such an opportunity of supplying this need as has never before arisen. The immense popularity of the yearly exhibitions at South Kensington is due, not to the interest of the people in fishery, in hygiene, or in inventions, but to their love of a crowd, a band, and "a gardens." The crowd satisfies the mere instinct of gregariousness; and the units of the crowd enjoy the garden much as the coster, as Mr Gilbert has quite accurately observed, "loves to lie a-basking in the sun." But the music ministers to an active taste. It turns the scale in favor of South Kensington against the parks, or the embankment, or any other accessible place where there is a crowd and some greenery. It attracts even those who dislike crowds and public gardens, just as the promenade concerts at Covent Garden Theatre attracted people who loathed every feature of a promenade concert except the orchestra. Hence a great deal of money has been and is daily being spent at the Kensington exhibitions on military bands.

But a military band is not an orchestra. The feats of the British bandsman with the clarionet are amazing: he achieves with ease fiddle passages which no student of the orthodox treatises on orchestration would dare to write for his instrument; yet he cannot be to the musician all that the violinist is. The most insinuating tenor saxhorn cannot make us forget the viola; nor can the contrabass helicon, as it wraps the stalwart soldier in its brazen coils, compel to its slow utterance the seismatic tremors of the double bass. Transcriptions of the overtures to William Tell and Masaniello, ballet music, selections from operas, Turkish patrols, and arrangements of The Lost Chord for cornet solo, afford small satisfaction to the masses who crave for symphonies, and are curious concerning the three manners of Beethoven.

Why, then, does not the Council of the Inventions Exhibition establish a first-rate orchestra at South Kensington? They cannot allege that it would cost too much: the mere imagination of the orchestra they might have had for the money which they have so ignorantly squandered on a small Austrian *quadrille* band, with an established reputation for being the very thing that we do not want here, makes the mouth of the musician in the London wilderness to water, and his teeth to gnash with disappointment. Here are a multitude of competent native or domiciled English players stranded at the closed doors of our opera houses and concert rooms, face to face with a music-loving multitude of Londoners thirsting for a good orchestra with a speciality for Beethoven's symphonies. Here, too, are the Inventions commissioners, with a unique market for bringing this supply and demand to equilibrium, and an opportunity of redeeming, by the same stroke, their exhibition from the reproach of being only a pretentious Cremorne or Rosherville. What, in this enviable position, have they done? They have engaged a foreign band, the speciality of which is not Beethoven's symphonies, but Strauss's sons' waltzes, which, even if people went to the Inventions to dance, would still be objectionable, not only because they are intolerably hackneyed, and have been so any time these fifteen years, in spite of the rest given to them by the popularity of Waldteufel and his slow waltz, but also because they remind us of the sheol of sensual vulgarity into which we suffered the French empire to lead us in the days when the beautiful Blue Danube first became rife among us.

The method of puffing this band adopted by the management was of a piece with the engagement. They advertized the sum they had agreed to pay Herr Eduard Strauss, and left the public to infer that the excellence of his band was in proportion to the largeness of the amount, which, it is as well to repeat, would have sufficed to engage an English orchestra equal to any in Europe. And they will probably justify their investment by pointing to the fact that audiences sufficient to overflow the Albert Hall crowd to see the dancing conductor, and to tap their feet

79

and wag their heads to the seductive swing of his numbers, accentuated by those neat flicks of the side drum and chirps from the piccolo in which much of the Strauss magic consists. But the duties of the Council are not fulfilled when a crowd is assembled. The promise of a mammoth Christy Minstrel show, a variety entertainment, or a prizefight, would mass the visitors to the Inventions in the Albert Hall at a stated hour: there would be a difference in the character and class of the audience, and possibly also in the subsequent history of England, but not in the number of heads. The Executive is practically availing itself of state aid to crush out private enterprises for the entertainment of the people. The theatres have suffered in all directions; and no fresh undertaking is likely to start handicapped by state competition. If under these circumstances the South Kensington authorities do not keep their exhibitions up to the highest practicable artistic standard, they will debase the moral and musical currency, and prevent private enterprise from restoring it. The safest, easiest, most profitable, and most creditable course open to them is to set at once about establishing a first-rate English orchestra on the foundations laid by Mr August Manns at the Crystal Palace, and by Mr Weist Hill at the Alexandra Palace. When the people have been educated by some years of popular concerts at which orchestral music of the highest class can be heard for a shilling, they will be better able to understand such entertainments as the "Historic Concerts," which will next month illustrate the steps by which Music progressed from the Missa brevis of Palestrina to the Wein, Weib, und Gesang waltzes which the Inventions Council offer us as the flower of modern European music.

A word of apology is due to Herr Eduard Strauss for grumbling so discourteously over his engagement. He has done all that he professed to do, and all that well-informed musicians expected. To quarrel with him because he has not astonished us as his father astonished our fathers nearly fifty years ago, or because he plays the sort of music that he is celebrated for playing, and was expressly engaged to play, would be unreasonable. The fault rests entirely with those Trustees of our metropolitan culture who blundered in art by neglecting a great opportunity of advancing music in England, and in economy by purchasing an inferior commodity abroad when a better was to be had for less money at home.

ART CORNER
(Extracts from a monthly series of notes on music, drama, and art, in *Our Corner*, 1885)

July 1885

We have had French opera at the Gaiety Theatre; but it has only served to shew the remarkable natural talent of Mlle Van Zandt, whose sole extraordinary qualification is an agile soprano voice with a range that includes E natural in *alt*. She is supported by a company of striking examples of the defects of the French school of singing, from which she is herself by no means free.

The Richter concerts, taking place on Monday evenings at St James's Hall, came to a close on June 22nd. Herr Richter's reception when he went to his desk at the first concert was so enthusiastic that he must feel assured that the musical amateurs of London have entire faith in him, and are ready to praise whatever he conducts without regard to the quality of the performance. Much of this faith is only fashionable superstition; but he won it honestly and takes no unfair advantage of it. The orchestra began the season admirably, and improved as it progressed, some of the performances being quite irreproachable, though there is a weak place or two in the wind band. The choir assisted in Beethoven's*Calm Sea and Prosperous Voyage, Brahms's Harz Mountains Rhapsody, and Berlioz's massive Symphonie Funèbre et Triomphale. The impression produced by these choral performances is that not one of the choristers individually possesses a voice, but that at this grave disadvantage they do wonders collectively. They certainly no longer spoil the concerts, as they did once or twice in former seasons. The performance of the Berlioz symphony was interesting, as it is in the list of works which the composer called "architectural" or "monumental," and in which he expressly sought to produce prodigious effects by the employment of prodigious resources. Thus the Symphonie Funèbre et Triomphale was planned for performance by a band

*As this new edition is reproduced photographically from the original edition, it perpetuates an uncharacteristic error by Shaw. The composer of "Calm Sea and Prosperous Voyage," it should be noted, was Mendelssohn, not Beethoven. D.H.L.

upwards of two hundred strong, including over one hundred and twenty wind instruments, drums, &c. Of course no such force was available at St James's Hall, and Berlioz would undoubtedly have repudiated such a paltry substitute as Herr Richter was able to offer. The effect was unsatisfactory; and the composer's reputation has been unfairly damaged by it: a result which those who were present at the production, on a similarly reduced scale, of the gigantic Te Deum at the Crystal Palace in April were quite prepared for. To play either of these works without at the very least doubling the ordinary numbers of a concert orchestra is as unjust to the composer as a performance of a Haydn quartet on the jew's harp would be.

Another novelty, at the same concert, was an overture by M. Eugen d'Albert, a young musician of whom great hopes were entertained during his connection with the South Kensington School of Music, now the Royal College. To musicians familiar with the later works of Wagner there is nothing novel or interesting in the overture, Mr d'Albert having sacrificed his individuality, doubtless with sincere devotion, at the Bayreuth shrine. His work was admirably played, but the significant coldness of the audience at the end was all the more conclusive. An orchestral piece from Liszt's Christus, representing the song of the Bethlehem shepherds, would have pleased better but for its tedious length, and the absolutely unreasonable character of much of the matter that spins it out. The first hundred bars contain some passages which shew that pastoral effects of instrumentation, hackneyed as they are, are not yet exhausted. If Liszt had spared us the inevitable sample of his would-be passionate and sublime manner which disturbs the movement later on, the shepherds' song might become popular. Most of the programs have included a Beethoven symphony, but perhaps the highest proof of Richter's ability as a conductor was his success with Mozart's symphony in E flat. Many of our conductors, who gain considerable credit by their achievements in our grandiose and sensational nineteenth-century music, are so completely beaten by Mozart that their performances have undermined the composer's immense reputation instead of confirming it. Herr Richter, however, held his own masterfully; and the only reputations damaged were those of the composers whose works were close enough to the E flat symphony in the program to suffer from the inevitable comparison. It was curious to observe in the two last movements of this work that the power of music to produce hysterical excitement when used—or abused—solely as a nerve stimulant, which is the only power that the nineteenth century seems to value it for, is used by Mozart with exquisite taste and irresistible good humor to relieve the audience from the earnest attention compelled by the more serious part of his work. Could he have foreseen that this half jocular side of his art would be that most seriously elaborated by his successors, and that his great compositions would appear as tame to some musicians of a later generation as a recitation from Shakespear presumably is to a howling dervish, his too early death might not have lacked consolation.

The Philharmonic concerts, which were not so well attended as they deserved, were conducted this year by Sir Arthur Sullivan, whose care and refinement have greatly improved the performances of the Philharmonic orchestra, but who certainly kills the music he conducts when vigor and impetuosity of treatment are required. The most important new works produced were a "symphonic poem" entitled Joan of Arc, by Moszkowski, the composer of the well-known Spanish dances for piano and four hands, and a symphony by Dvořák. Joan of Arc, a long and elaborate piece of program music, contains nothing very fresh, and a good deal that is decidedly stale. Herr Antonín Dvořák's symphony, which was conducted by the composer in person (as was Joan of Arc also), is in the key of D minor, and is numbered Opus 70. It suggests that a suite of gipsy songs and dance-tunes must have evolved, like an organism, into the higher form of a symphony. The quick transitions from liveliness to mourning, the variety of rhythm and figure, the spirited movement, the occasional abrupt and melancholy pauses, and the characteristic harmonic progressions of Bohemian music, are all co-ordinated in the sonata form by Herr Dvořák with rare success. To English ears his music seems to be particularly grateful, for Dvořák has become so popular that he has dedicated an early work of his to the English nation "with feelings of deep gratitude." It is so long since the English nation produced any particularly English music (having since Purcell's death compassed nothing but secondhand Handel, secondhand Mendelssohn, and lately a little secondhand Wagner of the Meistersinger sort) that they ought to appreciate this compliment from a composer so intensely national in his work as Dvořák. The subject of the dedication is a patriotic hymn entitled The Heirs of the White Mountain, by Vitězslav Hálek, translated by Dr Troutbeck. It was performed at St James's Hall, on the 13th May, by Mr Geaussent's choir. On the same occasion Mr A. C. Mackenzie's Jason was produced. The choir, though not very numerous, sang very well indeed, and the solo parts were undertaken by Madame Albani and Messrs Lloyd and Santley. Had the title of the work been Love in a Village, the adequacy and charm of the music would not have been questioned. Jason and Medea, unfortunately for Mr Mackenzie, have graver associations.

September 1885

New works of art do not come to light in London during the month of August. Picture shows are closed, and Music condescends to promenade concerts at which the orchestra serves as a blind to a drinking bar, the patrons of which pay most of the expenses, and hear least of the music. Thus Music exploits Vice; and Vice is probably none the worse for making the acquaintance of Music, though Music is undeniably a little the worse occasionally for her contact with Vice. But a large body of Londoners who, to our great disgrace, have no other opportunity than the promenade concerts of hearing an orchestra for a shilling, and who can afford no more, are enabled to hear an overture or two when they please, and occasionally a symphony or concerto. The Inventions Exhibition could and should have given these people what they want long ago; but the only orchestral concerts at South Kensington have been those of Herr Eduard Strauss, whose handful of players proved themselves a capital *quadrille* band, but did nothing to satisfy lovers of serious music, and were certainly not worth the large sum expended upon them by the Council of the Exhibition. They played dance music with a somewhat forced gaiety and dash, and ventured on a few good overtures, of which the conductor made but poor work. The rest of their programs contained arrangements of pretty drawing-room pieces, which were agreeable enough to those who knew of nothing better. Eduard Strauss is the youngest of three sons of Johann Strauss, who, with his celebrated band, made a sensation in London in the year of the Queen's coronation. That band, like its creator and conductor, now belongs to musical history only, though many persons undoubtedly believed last season that the Strauss at the Inventions was the celebrated Strauss, just as reasonably as the French peasants who voted for the imperatorship of Louis Napoleon believed that they were giving their suffrages to the hero of Austerlitz.

Johann Strauss had three sons, Johann, Josef, and Eduard; and he was determined that none of them should be musicians. But they all three baffled him. The waltzes of Johann the younger, the composer of the Blue Danube, caused his father's dance music to be almost forgotten. He had a Strauss orchestra; but he eventually devoted himself more and more to his present occupation of composing for the theatre. Die Fledermaus and other comic operas of his have been performed in London, at the Alhambra. Josef Strauss died some years ago after a visit to Russia. He too formed a Strauss orchestra, as did our recent visitor Eduard, who is said to have been trained, according to his father's wish, as an architect. He has the musical temperament of his family, but a musically endowed man may be either a Richter or a Christy Minstrel, according to his extra-musical qualifications. Eduard Strauss holds an intermediate position between the two extremes.

His only rivals at the Inventions Exhibition were military bands, notably those of the Grenadier and Coldstream Guards. The Grenadier band is popularly supposed to be the better of the two; and it is in fact by far the larger and more completely equipped. The compass of its intensity of sound is immense, the gradation from pp to ff (now frequently displayed at full length in claptrap marches of the Turkish Patrol pattern) lasting an extraordinarily long time. The conductor, Mr Dan Godfrey, is a popular hero on Saturday nights: the belief of the audience in him is boundless. But the Coldstream band, mechanically inferior as it is, is artistically the better of the two, Mr Thomas having the advantage of Mr Godfrey in point of refinement, although, like most English bandmasters, he is shy of doing more with his band than he is likely to be generally and vociferously thanked for. The position of a capable military bandmaster is not an easy one. He is largely dependent on the officers of the regiment, many of whom are pretty sure to consider coarse playing and trivial music the best value for their subscriptions. He has to insist ceaselessly on a delicacy in the playing of wind instruments which his men do not appreciate, until he has come victorious out of a long struggle with them. His power to enforce thorough practice and rehearsal, though despotic in comparison with that enjoyed by ordinary conductors, is discounted by the compulsion he himself is under to accept and train such players as chance sends him, instead of to select and engage the best talent in the town. And, worst of all, he is expected to be ready at a moment's notice with a string of trumpery marches and dances which deprave his own taste and those of his men; whilst anything more serious than the overture to William Tell brings him little, if any, immediate encouragement or credit. But in the long run good music would certainly repay him for the labor of getting it up. If Mr Thomas has the courage and perseverance to include an overture by Mozart or Beethoven, and at least one movement from a Beethoven symphony, in each of his Inventions programs; to stick to that policy; to induce the Council to advertize it; and to make it known as a speciality of his band, Mr Godfrey will soon be relegated to the second place in popular esteem, and the Coldstream Guards will have admittedly the first band in the service. The trouble of obtaining or making the necessary rearrangements of the orchestral scores ought not, at this time of day, to be considerable.

The Court band of the King of Siam, which plays certain compositions that have been handed down by aural tradition and have never, it is said, been committed to writing, plays occasionally at the Albert Hall. Their performance, though most of the visitors evidently find it merely outlandish, is not wholly beyond the range of Western sympathy. Some of the airs and instrumental effects are not unpleasant. The Siamese scale contains no leading note, and the attempts of the band to play God Save the Queen and other European airs are rather trying in consequence; but they succeed better with Scotch airs such as Auld Lang Syne, which is very like their own Pegu Affliction. But a little of the Siamese music goes, it must be confessed, a very long way.

November 1885

Another attempt to establish a standard musical pitch has been made and abandoned in despair. The King of the Belgians attacked the problem royally by decreeing that all military bands, musical schools, theatres, and other institutions subsidized by the Government throughout Belgium should tune to French pitch. Our minister at Brussels wrote to the Foreign Office quoting the decree. The Foreign Office, at a loss how to dispose of this communication, sent it on to the Royal Academy of Music as being presumably something in the line of that institution. The directors of the Academy thereupon convened a public meeting, which took place at St James's Hall on the 20th June last; and a very lively meeting it was. The upshot was the appointment of a committee to carry out certain resolutions which had been passed. This committee began by trying to get the pitch of our military bands authoritatively fixed by the War Office. But the Commander-in-Chief pleaded "financial and other difficulties too great to be overcome" and declined to trouble himself in the matter. The Committee, feeling that it would be presumptuous to persist in the face of difficulties which had daunted so brave and able a tactician as the Duke of Cambridge, abruptly dissolved itself, declaring that "the impossibility of controling the musical arrangements of her Majesty's forces renders such an establishment" (of a uniform pitch in accordance with that which prevails in Europe) "totally impracticable." And so the matter drops for the present.

The difficulty is, as usual, an economic one. For example, a flute such as is used by a professional player in a concert orchestra costs about thirty guineas. If the pitch for which that flute was constructed be altered so much that a new instrument will have to be substituted, then every professional flute player in the country will have to disburse thirty guineas for a new flute, and wait for a chance of partly recouping himself by selling the old one to some amateur who does not play in concert with other performers. The same heavy tax would, under the same conditions, fall on oboe, clarionet, and bassoon players. The outcry which a proposal to alter the pitch provokes from the orchestra may be imagined. But against it must be placed the outcry of the singers against the strain put upon their voices by the excessively high English pitch, and the protests of musicians against the performance of the music of Mozart and Handel in what are practically higher keys than those in which it was intended to be heard.

Our pitch is rather more than a semitone sharp to Handel's tuning fork, so that his compositions in the key of D are heard nowadays in what he would have called the key of E flat. The change is a disadvantage to tenor and soprano singers as far as their highest notes are concerned, though to contraltos and basses, whose lowest notes are of course facilitated by the rise in pitch, it is an advantage. Hence soprano and tenor singers protest against the high pitch, whilst contraltos advocate it. Mr Sims Reeves has sacrificed engagement after engagement at musical festivals sooner than sing to the high pitch set by the organs at such performances. Madame Nilsson and Madame Patti have insisted on French pitch at the opera. But Madame Patey declares that the high pitch is an improvement. She is a contralto. And so the battle rages between the vocalists and the instrumentalists, whilst the instrument makers take one side or the other according to their pecuniary interest or the difficulties created by the exigencies of construction. But a combination among our conductors, if they could be induced to agree as to the most desirable pitch, and to be inexorable in making the attainment of that pitch a condition of a player's engagement, would soon settle the question.

Expert players of wind instruments can modify the pitch of the notes they produce very considerably by their blowing, by turning the embouchure, drawing out mouthpieces, crooks, and tuning-slides, inserting washers, and other devices. They have to do this constantly even when playing at the pitch for which their instruments were designed, because mechanically perfect instruments are physical impossibilities. The upper octave of the flute, as far as it depends on the holes and keys of the instrument, is so sharp that it would be useless if the player could not flatten the notes by his method of blowing. Some players have such power of correcting mechanical defects by their embouchure that for the sake of certain advantages in power of tone they cause their flutes to be constructed in such a way that no ordinary player can use them. Players on reed instruments have less latitude of this kind; but except in the case of the clarionet they can by the aid of mechanical alterations vary the pitch within half a tone, which is quite sufficient for the purpose in question. The clarionet alone is said to be intractable, but as every clarionet player is expected to possess at least three instruments, in A, in B flat, and in C respectively, something can be done to meet the difficulty—if it really exists—by considering the A clarionet as a clarionet in B flat, which instrument many players improperly use almost exclusively. Brass instruments have resources in shanks and tuning-slides for flattening, and string instruments present no difficulty. Old Italian violins would be much improved by a return to thicker strings and removal of the fortifications which have been added in modern times to protect them against the strain of the high pitch. Nearly all the admitted difficulties can be got over without new instruments. Those that are supposed to be most formidable have been known to disappear with such alacrity before a determined conductor two minutes after they had been declared utterly insuperable by the player, that it may be doubted whether they are anything more than conservative excuses.

Perhaps the greatest obstacle to a reform is the expense of re-tuning great organs such as those in the Albert Hall and the Handel orchestra at the Crystal Palace, an operation which would cost a large sum per instrument, particularly if the alteration were not exactly a semitone, and so should necessitate the modification of every separate pipe and reed. If the proprietors of the organs could be induced to suffer this outlay, and if the War Office and the officers of the various regiments could be persuaded to make a tremendous investment in new clarionets, there would still have to be faced a certain amount of grumbling from the public and artistic agony on the part of conductors at the temporary falling off in the effect of orchestral performances which would inevitably follow a change of pitch. This would disappear when the players became accustomed to the new pitch; but in the meantime there would be much murmuring, and much crowing from the advocates of the high pitch. It will be seen that the matter is by no means a simple one, and that alteration involves unforeseen trouble in many quarters. The avoidance of such trouble in future is, however, one of the most tempting results of the establishment of a uniform pitch, not only throughout England, but throughout Europe.

December 1885

Mors et Vita, the sacred trilogy composed by M. Gounod for the last Birmingham Festival, and received there with something short of enthusiasm, was performed for the first time in London at the Albert Hall by Mr Barnby's choir on the 4th of November. M. Gounod is no Voltairean: he is the romantically pious Frenchman whose adoration of the Virgin Mother is chivalrous, whose obedience to the Pope is filial, and whose homage to his God is that of a devoted royalist to his king. It follows that he is not a deep thinker. But his exquisite taste, his fastidious workmanship, and an earnestness that never fails him even in his most childish enterprises, make him the most enchanting of modern musicians within the limits of his domain of emotion and picturesque superstition. Religious music is not now the serious work it used to be. One hundred and fifty years ago it was still possible for a first-rate intellect to believe that in writing for the Church its highest powers were enjoying their worthiest use. A Mass and a series of religious Cantatas embody the greatest achievements of John Sebastian Bach, the greatest composer of his age (which implies much more than that he was merely the greatest musician). Mozart, the immediate inheritor of Bach's supremacy, was so orthodox a man in his nonage that he exulted when, as he phrased it, Voltaire "died like a dog." Yet religion got no grip of his mature power. His reputation as a moralist and philosopher rests, not on his Masses, but on his two great operas, and on his allegorical music-play Die Zauberflöte, which might have been composed by a modern Positivist or Agnostic Socialist.

Beethoven's masterpiece, the Choral symphony, culminates in a setting of Schiller's Ode to Joy, a poem that might almost have been written by Shelley. After Beethoven, composers who, like Schumann, were thinkers as well as musicians, unconsciously dropped the Bible and the liturgy, and devoted themselves to secular poetry and to such works as the second part of Goethe's Faust. Berlioz was no exception: the Requiem Mass was to him only a peg to hang his tremendous music on; to a genuinely religious man the introduction of elaborate sensational instrumental effects into acts of worship would have seemed blasphemous. Mendelssohn was, like M. Gounod, no very profound thinker. The decay of what is called orthodoxy appeared quite as strikingly in its failure to call into action the highest faculties of philosophic composers who were not consciously heterodox, as in its overt repudiation by many commonplace persons at and about the revolutionary epoch. And so nowadays religious music means either a legend from scripture, melodramatically treated exactly as a legend from Hoffman or an opera libretto would be, or else a Mass in which the sensuous ecstasies of devotion and adoration, the hypnotic trances and triumphs which make religion a luxury, are excited in a refined fashion by all the resources of the accomplished musician, just as they are in a cruder way by the tambourines and cornets of the Salvation Army. Mors et Vita, like Rossini's Stabat Mater and Verdi's Requiem, belongs to this class; but in it there is also some of the descriptive melodrama of the modern oratorio.

Just as the introduction to the last act of M. Gounod's Roméo et Juliette is descriptive of the sleep of Juliet, so the introduction to the second part of his new sacred trilogy is entitled Somnus Mortuorum. The resurrection at the sound of the trumpets is then musically set precisely as if it were a scene in a ballet. A curious effect is produced by sharpening the fifth of the chord figured by the fanfares of the trumpets, which thus play the intervals of the augmented triad as if it were a common chord. As may be supposed, the resolution of the discord is somewhat urgently demanded by normal ears long before the dead are fairly awake. This central episode in the work is preceded by a requiem, and followed by scenes descriptive of the judgment and the new Jerusalem. Long before it is all over—it lasts three hours—one feels that a more vigorous composer would have made shorter work of it. At bottom, M. Gounod's piety is inane, and so, at bottom, his music is tedious. The charms of beauty and natural refinement without brains may be undeniable; but they pall. M. Gounod's religious music is beautiful; it is refined; it is negatively virtuous in the highest degree yet attained; the instrumentation is continuously delightful; the whole would realize a poetic child's conception of the music of angels. But men grapple with the problems of life and death in the nineteenth century in another fashion. Feeling that the consummate musician is a puerile thinker, we are compelled to deny that he is a great composer whilst admitting the loveliness of his music.

Of the performance it need only be said that Madame Albani, Miss Hilda Wilson, Mr Lloyd, and Mr Santley were fully efficient in the solo parts. The orchestra was admirable. The huge chorus sang accurately, and proved that they had been diligently drilled. The Albert Hall Choral Society is progressing, though there is still room for a considerable improvement both in tone and intelligent delivery. They might do better, considering their numbers and opportunities; but it can no longer be said of them as aforetime that they could not possibly do worse.

MUSICAL INSTRUMENTS AT THE INVENTIONS EXHIBITION

(Magazine of Music, August 1885)

No less satisfactory exhibition can be conceived than a collection of musical instruments surmounted by notices that visitors are requested not to touch. Even a Stradivarius violin is not pleasant to look at when it is standing on end in a glass case. You may not hold it to the light to make the lucid depths of the varnish visible; you must not foreshorten its curves by placing it in the position in which it should be played—the only position in which a fiddle does not remind you of a plucked fowl hanging by the neck in a poulterer's shop; you cannot hear the sound, apart from which it is the most senseless object extant; and your personal independence is irritated by the feeling that what prevents you from satisfying your curiosity by force of arms is not your conscience, but the proximity of a suspicious policeman, who is so tired of seeing apparently sane men wasting their time over secondhand fiddles and pianofortes, that he would probably rather arrest you than not, if only you would give him a pretext for the capture. A harpsichord with a glass lid on the keyboard is disappointing; but a clavichord similarly secured is downrightly exasperating; for if there is one instrument that every musician would like to try, it is the *wohltemperirte clavier* of Sebastian Bach.

To relieve such feelings, which must afflict all visitors to the gallery of the Albert Hall more or less, the Council of the Inventions Exhibition has arranged a series of historic concerts, at some of which a few of these instruments have already been heard. The six-stringed *viola di gamba* has actually raised the question whether it is not at least equal to the violoncello, instead of being the "nasal and ungrateful" instrument we have been taught to imagine it. But the few pieces played upon it by M. Jacobs were chosen to shew it to the greatest advantage, and certainly did not furnish an exhaustive test of its capacity. The old Italian violins were not played, as they are supposed to be already familiar to us. This, however, is a mistake. The Strads now in use by certain great violinists have all been tampered with to enable them to bear the tension of modern concert pitch. Take a Stradivarius or Amati fiddle, exactly as it left the maker's hand; fit it with the thick strings used in the seventeenth century; and an attempt to tune it at the pitch of the Albert Hall organ will probably spoil it or smash it. At the old pitch of Handel's tuning fork, which is a little flat to French pitch, the instrument would give us the true Stradivarius tone, which is just as strange to us as that of the *viola di gamba*. The excellence of the modernized Strad, with its added fortifications and its threadlike strings, is only obvious to the large class of amateurs whose imaginations, when prompted by an analytic program, discern divine harmonies in any plausible noise made in their presence. The

Council at South Kensington could not devise a more practically important experiment than a performance, at the old pitch, by some competent artist upon an authentic and untampered-with violin by Amati, Stradivarius, or Guarnerius, followed by a repetition of the piece at concert pitch on a modernized instrument by the same maker.

An old regal, a chamber organ, with flue pipes and one reed stop, was used at the historic concerts. It was a whole tone flat to the other instruments; but the discrepancy was easily overcome by transposition. The effect of Luther's Eine feste Burg, accompanied by the regal, was as fine as it would have been detestable had a modern harmonium been used. Small old-fashioned organs, in mean-tone temperament, are still to be found in some country churches; and the sweetness of their tone, and the smoothness of the chords and progressions played in the practicable keys upon them, will make many a church-goer grieve when they are replaced by modern equally-tempered instruments, with all the jangling abominations that represent power, and all the theatrical prettinesses that represent pathos to the nineteenth-century organ builder. The merits and limits of these old organs are those of the regal also.

The simple cross flute, with its six holes and one key, though still played by Christy Minstrels, itinerant musicians, and innumerable amateurs, is now known in the orchestra chiefly by traditions of the dislike which its imperfections provoked in Mozart and other great masters of instrumentation. Except in the quality of one or two of its upper notes, it proved greatly inferior to the modern Boehm instrument when directly contrasted with it at the historic concerts. There are a few pure and silvery notes at the top of its compass, and an occasional abjectly plaintive, but distinctly audible one, sprinkled here and there lower down. But the rest of its sounds are so weak that, at a little distance, they were lost in the tinkling of the harpsichord. Mozart's practice of doubling the flute part by a bassoon in the octave below, was probably suggested more by the necessity of reinforcing the weak places in the flute's compass than by any fancy for the effect of the two timbres in combination. The still older *flute-à-bec*, *flauto dolce*, or lansquenet flute, of which four sorts, treble, alto, tenor, and bass, were played in the simplest diatonic harmony, with a flaccid side drum of the kind used by showmen marking time, is a wooden flageolet, the most agreeable tones of which may be compared to the cooing of an old and very melancholy piping crow. The specimens used at the historic concerts were only approximately identical in pitch; and the piercing was of the roughest ante-Boehm order. The effect of the *flauti dolci* music was, on the whole, quaintly execrable.

So many abuses have come in with the modern pianoforte that its superiority to the harpsichord is not a subject for unmixed rejoicing. But its superiority is none the less undeniably vast. All that can now be said for the harpsichord is that it checkmated slovenly and violent playing; that it forced composers to cultivate clearness of construction and intelligent part writing; and that it preserves for us the intended effect of certain ornate passages, favored by Handel and Bach, which seem merely *rococo* when played on a pianoforte.

So far, these concerts of instrumental music, though excellently carried out, have been planned as exhibitions of old-fashioned chamber music only. It is greatly to be desired that some orchestral concerts be attempted with a view to reproducing the effects heard by Bach, Handel, Haydn, and Mozart, during what may be called the pre-clarionet period of orchestration. The Haydn orchestra might be revived by altering the ordinary proportions of string to wind players, multiplying the bassoons, and, of course, lowering the pitch, which should be done by thickening the strings used. The effect of this on the tone from the basses would be remarkable. There are various methods by which the pitch of wind instruments can be lowered, when the players are disposed to lower it, which they seldom are. The clarionet is an exception; but music in which the clarionet is used is practically modern music, and need not be included in the programs. The Bach orchestra, with its three trumpets, the first of them playing florid passages up to the high D, and its two *oboi d' amore*, was reproduced with splendid success at the Bach bi-centenary performance of the Mass in B minor last spring. The *oboe d' amore* has been resuscitated by the Mahillons at Brussels; and it amply justifies Bach's preference for it. In quality of tone it is purer, sweeter, and more dignified than the English horn; and it is certainly not less powerful. As to the trumpet, no instrument needs rehabilitation more urgently. In the show cases of modern instruments at the exhibition, dozens of cornets, many of them elaborately decorated and even bejeweled, are conspicuous; but only in one or two instances is a solitary trumpet, labeled "slide trumpet, for classical music," to be seen in a modest corner. These slide trumpets are not the instruments Bach wrote for. They are hard to play, and their tone is so vile that Herr Richter and other first-rate conductors connive at the substitution of the more manageable cornet. Though this is a musical fraud, and a deplorable one, it is certainly better to have a good cornet well played than a bad trumpet ill played. It has been repeatedly said that Bach's trumpet parts are impracticable; and they are commonly executed nowadays by the clarionet; but Julius Kosleck of Berlin has exploded that superstition by playing the first trumpet part of the great Mass at the highest English concert pitch on an old-fashioned straight trumpet, without missing a note. It is said that Mr Morrow, the well-known English trumpet player, has ordered a similar instrument. If this be true, there is some hope that what was once called "the heroick art" of playing the trumpet may be revived among us. We have had quite enough of the attempts of cornet players to produce genuine trumpet effects.

Besides the music of the past, the music of the future might have a place in the Inventions scheme. There are important classes of new instruments which are kept out of use because musicians have no opportunity of hearing them. Many of the pretended musical novelties in the Exhibition are, it is true, quite sufficiently illustrated by portraits of some distinguished person wiling away the tedium of high life by performing upon them. But on the other hand there are whole families of genuine additions to the resources of the orchestra that have not yet got further than a place in a few of our military bands. Probably not one student in the Royal Academy or Royal College of Music could "spot" a saxophone blindfold; and it is doubtful whether the name of the sarrusophone would convey any meaning to them. Yet a knowledge of the effect of applying the single and double

reed to metal instruments should surely form part of the education of the rising generation of composers. As yet the "recitals"
on new instruments have been of the nature of advertisements
rather than of experiments. In an exhibition of inventions, all the
practical publicity should not be appropriated to relics of the
past. Practical publicity for a musical instrument implies, not that
the public can see it, but that they can hear it.

SINGING, PAST AND PRESENT

(The Dramatic Review, 1 August 1885)

The most famous singing-master that ever lived was Porpora,
who was in his prime in the first half of the eighteenth century.
George Sand's novel Consuelo has made him known to the
general reader. That his pupils were extraordinary singers is not
a figment of the novelist's imagination. Specimens of the outrageous vocal feats which they habitually executed, and which
they compelled composers to devise for them, may be seen in
the works of Hasse, Porpora himself, Handel, and Mozart. The
only artists we have who can compare with these singers are our
circus acrobats, who make their living by performing athletic
impossibilities with grace, ease, and perfect tranquillity. These
acrobats are not exceptional men any more than soldiers and
sailors are exceptional men. Any boy of the proper age, and free
from deformity or marked physical disability, will do as well as
another for the purposes of the acrobat trainer in want of an
apprentice. Ordinary gentlemen who cannot rub the backs of
their heads against their heels without breaking their backs, or
sit down on the floor in the posture of a T square without split-
ting themselves, may rest assured that had they devoted themselves to the study of gymnastics at a sufficiently early age under
competent direction, they should by this time have been able to
converse with their friends in far more complicated attitudes
without inconvenience. And there is no doubt that our apparently
degenerate nineteenth-century singers, whom the contents of a
dozen ammoniaphones could not bring safely through the songs
written by Mozart in his boyhood for de Amicis and Rauzzini,

could, in the hands of Porpora, have done everything that Porpora's average pupils did. Exceptionally gifted people existed in Porpora's time, and exist now.

An artist's powers are partly native, partly acquired. Some people can do easily at the first challenge what costs others long training and teaching. But it is probable that, though the degree of skill that men and women are born with varies a good deal, the utmost additional skill that they can acquire by study is a constant quantity. For instance, if Porpora taught all he knew to each pupil, and we represent that quantity of imparted skill by the number 5, then a finished pupil of Porpora's would possess his or her natural gifts as a singer plus 5. Let us assume that nature does as much for the singer as art, and rate an average pupil's inherited capacity as 5 also. His total skill when trained by Porpora would then be represented by 10, consisting of natural skill 5, plus taught feats and trained skill 5. An exceptionally gifted person, a Caffarelli or Farinelli, would have natural skill equal to more than 5. Let us say, for Caffarelli, 7. Porpora added his 5 to the 7, leaving Caffarelli pre-eminent with a total of 12 as against the 10 of the average pupil of his master.

But let us now suppose that Caffarelli, instead of practically being given or sold when a child as an apprentice to Porpora, and sacrificing himself so completely to his profession as to have his soprano voice preserved artificially at the cost of his virility, had lived in our day; been educated in an ordinary English school; and had his attention turned to music by being assured, after attempting to sing Hybrias the Cretan, or Goodbye, to his sister's accompaniment, that he ought to study for the profession, because Lloyd and Santley get sums of guineas (variously stated at from five to a hundred and fifty by his friends) in one night for singing these very songs no better—to the friends' taste— than he. Caffarelli, if he cannot afford the terms of a private professor, accordingly takes his 7 of natural skill either to a conservatory, or academy, or college, or institute. At some of these, so far from adding to his 7, he may chance to have it reduced to 0 by the extinction of his voice. At any of them he is likely to gain 2 in elocution, style, &c., and to lose 3 in freshness of tone and soundness of voice. $7 + 2 - 3 = 6$. He comes out of his conservatory or academy with a loss of 1. All his average competitors have still, as in the eighteenth century, natural ability equal to 5; but they too lose 1 by their academic training; and so the average for trained singers is 4 as against 10 under Porpora's method and system. Thus the modern Caffarelli, scoring 6 to his competitors' 4, is still two above the average, and is therefore just as preeminent as the old Caffarelli, who scored 12 to his competitors' 10. Hence we have great singers now as our great-great-grandfathers had, although the acrobatic operas of Handel and the juvenile Mozart are inexecutable.

Of the results of private teaching it is better to say nothing. Every private teacher with whom I am or have ever been acquainted, has rediscovered Porpora's method, can explain it at considerable length, teaches exclusively on it, and is the only person in the world who can do so, all others being notorious quacks and voice destroyers. There are a great many unique persons in London, and most of them are teachers of singing. But even they will admit and lament that they cannot score Porpora's 5, because their pupils begin at too late an age, and obstinately refuse to spend six years over one page of exercises in the hope of being subsequently told, "Go forth, young man: you are now the greatest singer in the world." The difficulty, in fact, is not to implant that conviction in an ordinary English tenor, but to eradicate it. He feels it, without being told, in less than six months. So, even granting that our rediscoverers of Porpora's method really do add 3 out of his 5, and only miss the other 2 because no apprenticeship takes place, we are still left with an average of 8 (5 natural + 3 imparted) against Porpora's average of 10 (5 natural + 5 imparted).

Before we drop too many tears over this decadence of the art of singing, it is as well to consider whether all that we have lost is worth regretting. The old vocal acrobats were, like other acrobats, more anxious to dazzle the public and to make money as fast as possible than to make the highest use of their exceptional skill; and they used all the power that skill gave them to thwart composers who tried to save the opera house from sinking into a mere arena for the feats of vain singers. When Mozart was a boy, he dared not have written such easy music as Don Giovanni

99

for the stage. Nowadays, a composer hardly dare write anything so difficult as some of it has become. Mozart's lifelong fight was against supermusical virtuosity in singing; and when he became famous enough to have his own way, he wrote no more of his old Italian florid passages with skips of nearly two octaves between almost impossible intervals. The constantly cited music of the Queen of Night in the Zauberflöte, and the much more extravagant passages in Die Entführung aus dem Serail, are comparatively plain sailing: they require exceptional compass, but nothing comparable to acrobatic powers. Handel, who, when Cuzzoni refused to sing *Falsa imagine*, at once set about throwing her out of the window, bullied his singers into a wholesome fear of him; but he finally made up his mind that music could get on better without them; and, indeed, any reader of The Dramatic Review who will take the trouble to make himself acquainted with such of the music written for Porpora's pupils as can no longer be sung effectively by our best singers, will find that its impracticability is a distinct gain.

The history of stage speaking is much the same as that of stage singing. English actors were as famous throughout Europe in the sixteenth century as Italian singers were in the eighteenth. The plays of the pre-Shakespear period prove that the old dramatists, or rather stage poets, depended on their actors for effects of elocution which no modern actor can produce, or would dream of trying to produce. Chapman and Marlowe, with their passion for the grandiose, seem to have tempted these elocutionists to ruin their art by bombast and violence, exactly as Rossini and Verdi, in our century, have brought Italian opera singing to a condition in which the operatic tenor hardly takes precedence in popular estimation of the organ grinder and the penny ice man. The actors who abused their schooling and took to shouting found fate waiting for them in the plays of Shakespear. An actor who should habitually attempt to shout his way through Othello, Macbeth, or Lear would, by the ruin of his voice and the wreck of his moral and physical health, remove himself expeditiously from the stage. That the decadence of the old school, through the very excellence of which elocution had become the end and drama the means, was accelerated in this way, must appear very probable to anyone who has noted the quick work that Wagner's music makes with the shouting tenors and screaming sopranos who render Verdi so terrible to us. You cannot play Shakespear and live, unless you know how to speak rationally; and you cannot sing Wagner on the "tension of cords and force of blast" principle, with any prospect of lagging superfluous on the stage after a few years' work. All ambitious actors play Shakespear, and so, in self-preservation, must acquire a non-destructive method. Singers of Bayreuth music-dramas must do likewise. In this way Wagner's music is at present bringing about a busy revival of the art of singing, and is discrediting and destroying many ignorant and demoralized pretenders who have long infested the lyric stage, and who very naturally declare that Wagner's music means ruin to what they take to be the human voice. The same process is constantly in action. The Elizabethan and Victorian ages are striking examples of it; but the struggle between the poet and the player, the composer and the singer, both manifestations of the inward struggle in each man between the aspiring human side of him and the vain and greedy monkey side, are as busy in the centuries when art is happy and has no history as when it is disturbed by the advent of a Shakespear or a Mozart.

ENCORES

(Unsigned note in *The Dramatic Review*, 24 *October* 1885)

A hearty *encore* is not in its nature an appropriate subject for economic scrutiny, but not one in ten of such *encores* as have become habitual at Covent Garden is an expression of musical enthusiasm or gratitude to the artist who receives the pretended compliment. In every average audience there is a certain proportion of persons who make a point of getting as much as possible for their money—who will *encore*, if possible, until they have had a ballad for every penny in their shilling, with the orchestral music thrown in as a makeweight. There is also a proportion—a large one—of silly and unaccustomed persons who, excited by the novelty of being at a concert, and dazzled by the glitter and glory of the Bow-street temple of Art, madly applaud whenever anyone sets the example. Then there are good-natured people who lend a hand to encourage the singer. The honest and sensible members of the audience, even when they are a majority, are powerless against this combination of thoughtless good-nature, folly, and greed. And so the system becomes rooted, and can only be neutralized in an unsatisfactory way by favorite artists declining to be set down in the program for more than half the songs they intend to sing.

There are doubtless many concert-goers who *encore* from a genuine desire to hear over again a performance which has just given them great pleasure. One cannot help wondering whether their consciences ever ask them why they permit themselves to do at a concert what they would be ashamed to attempt elsewhere. Imagine the sincere encorist consuming a bath bun and asking the confectioner to give him another for nothing because the first was so nice. Yet that would be no more unreasonable than is the common practice of acknowledging the charm of Mr Sims Reeves's singing of Tom Bowling by a demand (without additional payment) for Come into the garden, Maud.

It is, however, of little help to dwell on an abuse without suggesting a remedy. The simplest one would be to send round the hat, with an announcement that as soon as the singer's terms for one song had been collected, the *encore* would be complied with. It would be amusing to witness the effect of such a measure on the enthusiastic crowd who surge about the orchestra at Covent Garden cheering Mr Lloyd and Mr Santley, and who next day recount the number of ballads they enjoyed over and above what they paid for. It might do much to convince them at last that *encores* are not nitrogenous food—singers cannot live on them. Also that beggars in broadcloth inside a theatre are not a whit more respectable morally than the beggars in rags outside.

FUGUE OUT OF FASHION

(*Magazine of Music, November* 1885)

To the average Briton the fugue is still an acute phase of a disease of dulness which occasionally breaks out in drawing rooms, and is known there as classical music. It has no pleasant tune in four strains to add to such stores of memory as Grandfather's Clock and Wait till the clouds roll by. Its style vaguely suggests organ music or church music. Its polyphonous development defies the amateur who picks up things by ear: not that Dutchman himself, who astonished the Philharmonic Society by playing chords on the flute when Sterndale Bennett was conductor, could have whistled a fugue. Those who are, comparatively speaking, connoisseurs, guess the piece to be "something by Handel." Outsiders, who have often wondered what a fugue may be, cease talking and listen curiously, generally with growing disappointment culminating in a relapse into whispered conversation. This is a relief to the player, who, conscious of having taken a desperate step in venturing on a fugue in a drawing room, becomes more and more diffident as the hush indicates that the company have adopted the unusual course of listening to the pianoforte. Many a player, under stress of too much attention, has lost heart; paused on the first dominant seventh that presented itself; and glided off into a waltz, which never fails to set all tongues going again except perhaps those of a few sentimental young people who have overpowering recollections of the last partner with whom they danced that very waltz. The classicists who rail at dance music should never forget the cluster of associations, rich with the bloom of youth and the taste of love, which the lounger, without the slightest previous knowledge of music, can gather from a waltz by Waldteufel.

Professional pianists, and those hardy amateurs who are not to be put out by any concentration or diffusion of the attention of their audience, usually confine themselves to their own compositions in the drawing room. They do not play fugues because they cannot write them. The standard precept runs:—"Learn thoroughly how to compose a fugue, and then *dont*"; and on the second clause of this they act perforce, since they have neglected the first for lack of the economic pressure which is needed to make the average man take serious pains with any subject. It does not pay an ordinary professor of music to learn double counterpoint any more than it pays a journalist to write Latin verses. Fugues are unsaleable: of the considerable number written every year by students, candidates for degrees, and organists, hardly one comes into the market, and for that one there is seldom a purchaser. As to the value of the practice in double counterpoint gained by fugal composition, all that can be said from a commercial point of view is that a musician can make as much money without it as with it. And even from an artistic point of view there are some plausible nothings to be said against the weary climb up Fux's Gradus ad Parnassum. If Beethoven had not worried himself as he did over counterpoint, we might have been spared such aberrations of his genius as the Mass in D. Cherubini's music might have been more interesting if he had not been stopped short by satisfaction with the scientific smoothness and finish which his technical resources enabled him to attain. Besides, one can pick up the art of fugue at any time if occasion should arise. Spohr never wrote a fugue until he had to furnish an oratorio with an overture. Then he procured a copy of Marpurg, looked at the rules, and wrote a respectable fugue without further preparation. Mozart tried his hand successfully at all sorts of contrapuntal curiosities the moment he came across examples of them. It may be true that the best contrapuntists were also the most skilful composers; but their good counterpoint was the result of their skill, and not their skill the result of their counterpoint. To study fugue, not for immediate use in composition, but for its own sake, eventually leads to writing it for its own sake, which means writing dry and detestable music. Such are the excuses at hand for the student who has privately made up his mind that life is not long enough for a thorough course of counterpoint.

Since even the most urgent advocates of such a course falter when the question is no longer one of learning how to write fugues, but of actually writing and publishing them, even the student whose aims are purely artistic finds himself at last debating whether fugue is not obsolete. Many have answered the question in the affirmative. The old-fashioned deliberate form no longer seems to express anything that modern composers are moved to utter. It is not the power to write fugues that is lost, it is the will. The St Paul proves that Mendelssohn could write elaborate fugues and embroider them with florid orchestral accompaniments; but the Elijah suggests that in his mature judgment these features of his earlier oratorio were but scholarly vanities. Meyerbeer and Donizetti were academic adepts; and Meyerbeer at least was never lazy, perfunctory, or hurried; yet neither of them made any considerable direct use of their knowledge: many comparatively unschooled composers, who only got up Marpurg as Spohr did, to write an Amen chorus or an oratorio prelude (just as a barrister gets up a scientific point when it happens to be the pivot of a case in which he holds a brief), have left more fugal counterpoint on record than either of them. Wagner wove musical tissues of extraordinary complication; but the device of imitation had no place in his method. The history of fugue as employed by the great composers during the last hundred and thirtyfive years, is one of corruption, decline, and extinction. Sebastian Bach could express in fugue or canon all the emotions that have ever been worthily expressed in music. Some of his fugues will be prized for their tenderness and pathos when many a melting sonata and poignant symphonic poem will be shelved for ever. Lamentation, jubilee, coquetry, pomposity, mirth, hope, fear, suspense, satisfaction, devotion, adoration— fugue came amiss to none of these in his hands. The old vocal counterpoint reached its zenith then, as the five-act tragedy in blank verse did in the hands of Shakespear. The decadence was equally rapid in both instances. Within half a century after Bach's death, Mozart was not only expressing emotions by means of music, but expressing them in the manner of a first-rate dramatist, as they are modified by the characters of the individuals affected by them. Like Bach, he was not merely an extraordinary man—Offenbach, strictly speaking, was that—but an extraordinary genius. And yet he made no use in his greatest work of the form which was as natural to Bach as the German language. The customary omission of the brisk little *fugato* at the end of Don Giovanni does not obscure the superlative excellence of that opera. In the Figaro there is not even a *fugato*. In the Zauberflöte the chorale sung by the two armed men is accompanied by some fugal writing of impressive beauty, which, with the Recordare of the Requiem, shews what Mozart could have done with the imitative forms had he preferred them. But this only gives significance to the fact that he did without them. In the last movement of the Jupiter symphony, and in the Zauber-flöte overture, the fugue and sonata forms are combined. But the overture is distinctly a *tour de force*, a voluntary reversion to an old form, undertaken by Mozart partly from his rare sympathy with what was noble and beautiful in the old school; partly because, in the overture to Don Giovanni, he had already produced a model for the modern opera overture which he could not himself surpass, and which remains unique to this day. The Jupiter *finale* is historically more important. It is the first notable instance of the nineteenth-century tendency to regard fugue, not as a vehicle of expression, but as a direct expression in itself of energy, excitement, and bustle. This view seized Beethoven, who took a great deal of trouble to acquire skill in double counterpoint and canon, in order to use it for certain *tours de force* which were much less successful than Mozart's. But in his natural characteristic works he used it only to produce a sort of spurious fugue or *fugato*, consisting of a vigorous subject treated with a fast and furious *stretto*, and then thrown aside. He had no command of the form: on the contrary, it commanded him. A particular effect to which it lent itself had caught his fancy, that was all. His *fugato* was invariably an ebullition of animal spirits. In it the parts had no vocal fitness: the accents of human emotion which occur in every bar of Bach's subjects and countersubjects are absent in Beethoven's fugal compositions. He brutalized the fugue as completely as he humanized the sonata. After his spurious fugue came Meyerbeer's spurious *fugato*, in which the subject, instead of being continued as countersubject to the answer, drops its individuality by merging in the harmony. In the prelude to Les Huguenots all the fugal effects which Meyerbeer cared for were produced in a striking way without the trouble of writing a bar of double counterpoint. Handel's fugal setting of the words He trusted in God that He would deliver Him. Let Him deliver Him, if He delight in Him! is a masterly expression of the hatred, mockery, and turbulence of an angry and fanatic mob. Meyerbeer, in the third act of his famous opera, obtained an effect of the same kind, sufficient for his purpose, by means of a sham fugue. This was his deliberate choice: he was perfectly competent to write a genuine fugue, and would un-doubtedly have done so had not the counterfeit suited the con-ditions of his work better.

Little mock fugal explosions are not uncommon now in opera. There is a ludicrous example in the overture to Vincent Wallace's Maritana. Verdi has occasionally threatened the theatre-goer with a display of fugal science, but the pretense has never been carried very far. Similar symptoms, also speedily suppressed, appear in the third act of Boïto's Mefistofele. Gounod often gives us a few pretty bars in canon, or a theme, with a bold skip or two at the beginning, introduced and answered in the rococo "dux and comes" style. There is a charming *fughetta* in the first act of Bizet's Carmen. But all these examples are either whims, pursued for a few measures and then abandoned, or exciting pantomime music to what is called by stage managers and prizefighters a rally. Wagner and Goetz, the only men of our time who have been, like Handel and Bach, great both as harmonists or chord writers and as contrapuntists or part writers, have not dealt in fugue. They have associated themes with definite ideas, and practiced all the combinations which their logic led them to in consequence. It has not led them to the device of imitation, which has been therefore left to men who, like the late Frederic Kiel of Berlin, have possessed great talent and industry without originality or genius. Imitation is often very pretty, and it always, by giving the part writing a definite and obvious aim, produces an air of intelligibility in the composition which is very welcome to the many people who are apt to get befogged when they endeavor to follow music of any complexity. But nowadays the life has gone out of it: we practice it principally for its own sake now and then, but never for the purpose of expressing subjective ideas.

PROGRAMS

(Magazine of Music, December 1885*)*

When the unsophisticated visitor from the country to the metropolis goes to a Richter concert, not because he knows or cares enough about music to make the faintest class distinction between the overture to La Gazza Ladra and the prelude to Tristan und Isolde, but because a Richter concert is one of the sounds of London, and therefore not to be missed by the complete tourist, his first experience is the payment of half-a-crown for admission. (Here let millionaire readers, who habitually pay half-guineas for stalls, forbear and read no more. The economic considerations which dictate this article have no weight with such.) His next is an encounter with a gentleman who carries a bundle of white pamphlets, and cries incessantly "Book of the words! Program! Book of the words!" A book will evidently not only be a guide through the unknown ways of a Richter concert, as to the nature of which the tourist's notions are of the vaguest, but will serve as a memento of the occasion in after years in the quiet country home. "One shilling, please," says the vendor. That is forty per cent. on the price already paid for admission. The visitor is staggered; but he is too much of a sportsman to grudge a shilling during a holiday trip, and he pays with assumed cheerfulness, privately adding the incident to his stock of instances of London roguery. Whilst waiting for the concert to begin, he opens his purchase and reads. It contains some historical information which is not of the slightest interest to him, and much technical detail which he does not understand. He can just gather that it becomes him to prepare with awe for the treat in store for him. Having always believed that the musicians in a band played by ear the tune agreed upon, whilst the basses improvised the harmony as they went along, he can make nothing of the references to the score. Vague notions of plan, pre-arrangement, and rehearsal oppress him with a sense of his own ignorance. He looks furtively at his neighbors; but they do not seem puzzled. They may, it is true, be only pretending to understand their "book of the words"; but no sign of imposture is perceptible. What can he do but imitate their serenity as best he can? When the band begins at last, he cannot make head or tail of the noise they are making. Occasionally they break into something like a tune, and then he smiles and beats time with his foot; but his neighbors frown and "shsh" angrily at him, and the tune is presently "developed" as the book calls it; that is, it becomes no tune at all. At the end of the concert he plucks up a little, and goes off to supper, after which he feels that now that it is all over he is glad he went. If asked subsequently whether he liked it, he will not reply directly, but will observe seriously that it was very fine—very fine indeed. But he has one solid grievance, if he chooses to ventilate it. He has been compelled to pay a shilling for a book of which only one page—the bare list of pieces, worth some fraction of a farthing—was of any use to him.

Take another case at the opposite extreme of musical culture. An experienced concert-goer and accomplished musician goes also to the Richter concert. He also requires only a list of the compositions to be performed. He has read over and over again, at the Crystal Palace and elsewhere, what Sir George Grove and Mr C. A. Barry have to say about the No. 3 Leonora overture. When "the movement comes to an impressive close on the tonic of the original key," he knows it without referring to a printed statement. He has read what Schumann said about Brahms and about everybody else, and he does not believe the little anecdotes as to what Beethoven said of "the young Franz Schubert." He objects to have his attention called to "remarkable modulations" that are only remarkable on paper. The old works he knows; and he would fain follow the new ones without being pestered and prejudiced at every step by somebody else's opinion, particularly when that opinion is only a forced remark made because the writer, being paid to say something, did not consider it honest to be silent even when he had nothing to say. Yet all this can the amateur not avoid unless, as many prudent matrons do, he cuts the advertisement from the newspaper and keeps it in his pocket for reference. Even then there may not be light enough to read small print by in a half-crown seat beneath the gallery. The chances are that he has to succumb to "One shilling, please," and to swallow the impertinences of the analyst with as few wry faces as possible. Occasionally, when the work is quite new, he derives an ill-natured satisfaction from the false estimates into which the analyst has been led by the necessity of judging the score by eye instead of by ear. For, though it is by no means safe to infer the intention of the composer from the achievement of any particular orchestra, still rasher is it to infer his achievement from his intention as expressed on paper. This, however, is neither here nor there; for the pleasure of finding out that an analyst is fallible is decidedly not worth a shilling. And when the work analyzed is a familiar one, as nine-tenths of the words performed at classical concerts are, not only is this gloomy triumph denied to the musician, but the analysis, instead of being a brand new essay on the work, is a stereotyped reprint that has done duty many times before, and will as many times again. It is quite maddening to calculate how this reduces the cost to the concert-giver, whilst the concert-goer cannot escape "One shilling, please."

And here we come to the interests of the general musical public, who approve of analytic programs as on the whole helpful and interesting. Professional concert-goers may both find and make useful memoranda in them, and they are particularly convenient when the critic goes to sleep during the performance of a new work, as, when the next thunderclap from the drum wakes him, he can, by referring to the analysis, guess how much he has lost during slumber. But were programs fifty times as convenient, a shilling is a shilling, and in this instance a shilling is too much. It is a monopoly price, and represents, not the cost of production of the book, but the utmost sum that a sufficient number of persons will reluctantly yield sooner than go without. Now this most pestilential principle assures the least happiness of the smallest number. Suppose the audience to consist of a thousand persons. Suppose that each of them will pay sixpence for a program, but that only five hundred will pay a shilling. A thousand programs will be printed in any case, the first time the experiment is tried. A return of £25 will, let us further suppose, satisfy the greed of the management. ("Greed" may not be polite, but, as has been already said, a shilling is a shilling.)

Now, in the interest of the greatest number, this return should be secured by the sale of the thousand programs at sixpence. But in the interest of the concert-giver, five hundred will be sold at a shilling, and only five hundred provided at the next concert. Five hundred of the audience will thus go programless, and the rest will suffer the exasperation of having had to submit to double extortion. And in the future the price will go up and the supply diminish, until a point is reached at which the profits decline instead of increase. For instance, it would not pay to raise the price to ten shillings, as nobody would buy at that price, and the expenditure for printing programs, which are valueless except as waste paper after a concert, would be a dead loss. The public, in short, will be "exploited" until it strikes. At present the demand for a shilling causes a partial strike; but there are sufficient "knobsticks"—*i.e.* compliers with the demand—to cover the loss occasioned by the strikers.

But a strike of purchasers on a rising market is foredoomed to failure. The only remedy lies in competition. Inside the concert room there can be no competition: the concert-givers have a monopoly there. But the monopoly ceases at the street door. If any private speculator, upon ascertaining the program of a concert from the advertisement in the daily papers, chooses to compile an analytic program, print it, sell it at the doors for ninepence, and gain for it a reputation for trustworthiness, the public will buy outside at ninepence instead of inside at a shilling. The concert-giver, after a few vain placards to the effect that authorized programs are to be had within only, will have to reduce his price to sixpence, only to be again underbid by the man outside. If the latter have the requisite qualities and capital, he will finally compel all concert-givers to contract with him for the supply of analytic programs, and he will conduct that branch of music publishing as a separate industry. The fear of competition from rival speculators would thenceforth prevent him from taking advantage of the transferred monopoly to re-establish the old extortionate prices. Nay, it is quite possible that by developing the practice of inserting advertisements in the programs, he might eventually find it to his interest to give them away gratuitously, embellished with handsome portraits of celebrated singers who have been soaped, or ammoniaphoned, or miraculously cured of a cough.

If no speculator is hardy enough to adopt this suggestion, the abuse will continue, and be aggravated as time goes on. One-and-sixpenny programs will soon appear, and we may yet pay half-a-crown for a pamphlet of stereotyped matter costing less than a penny to produce. Let the reader who has just paid a shilling for his program at one of the three recent Richter concerts, take that expensive volume and compare it with this Magazine (the circulation of which, by the bye, is not compulsory, as that of a concert program practically is), and consider whether something cheaper ought not to be forthcoming in this age of competitive license. Tender-hearted people who very properly mistrust modern cheapness, may note that a reduction in the price of programs would trench on profits and not on wages. Even profits would probably be increased in the long run by a concession to the impecuniosity of the art-loving middle classes; but it would be a waste of time to work this probability out in the hope of influencing such very bird-in-the-hand politicians as the monopolists who charge a shilling for an analytic program.

PALMY DAYS AT THE OPERA

(*Magazine of Music, January* 1886; unsigned)

When old-fashioned people deplore the decadence of the modern theatre, and regret the palmy days of the drama, superstitious ones are apt to take the desirability of palminess for granted, without troubling themselves to ascertain the exact conditions which constituted it. On inquiry, we are led to infer that long runs, elaborate scenery and dresses, efficient performance of minor parts, and prose dialogue, are degenerate; but that prompters, changes of program every night, poster playbills printed in blue color that adheres to everything except the flimsy paper, and "historical" costumes—*i.e.* costumes belonging to no known historic epoch—are palmy. Between the merits of these things, the young London play-goer can hardly judge; for he has no experience of palminess. There are many persons of culture still under thirty who are familiar with the palmy flat, vanishing from the scene with the scene-shifters' heels twinkling at its tail; who have touched the orchestra palisade from the front row of a palmily stall-less pit; who have seen the creations of Shakespear enter and quit the scene to the strains of Handel; and whose fingers have been a sorry sight after smudging the playbill for three hours. But these experienced critics are from the country, and began their playgoing careers whilst palminess and stock companies still lingered there, as they do, perhaps, to this day. But the West Londoner, who only visits first-class theatres, has only one way of studying palminess. He must go to the opera, where he will soon get quite enough of it to convince him that the theatre in John Kemble's time, when it was carried on much as Italian opera is now, had quite enough drawbacks to reconcile a reasonable man to the changes which have since taken place.

There are no long runs at the opera. Faust is played one night, and Lucia the next; Lohengrin follows, and so on. Here is a splendidly palmy training for the singers. No stagnation in one play for three hundred nights, until the characteristics of his part fasten themselves upon the actor as mannerisms, never afterwards to be got rid of. No rusting of one's powers of study by disuse, nor dawdling in drawing rooms when one should be busy with the divine art at rehearsal. No season passing away without a single performance of one of Mozart's operas, as seasons so often pass without a representation of Shakespear's plays. Development of powers in their fullest variety, by constant alternation of tragedy and comedy, classicism and romanticism, Italianism and Germanism; leading, of course, to enormous superiority of the lyric to the ordinary actor.

At this point it becomes somewhat obvious that the palmy theory lacks experimental verification. On the ordinary stage, crippled as it is supposed to be by long runs, everyone is expected to act; and the more important characters are expected to act very well. At the opera, the tenor is not expected to act at all; and the baritone, though admittedly an eminently dramatic figure, would not, if he condescended to spoken dialogue, stand the smallest chance of being allowed to play Rosencrantz at a revival of Hamlet at the Lyceum or Princess. And if, by bringing strong private influence to bear, he succeeded in getting cast for Bernardo, and attempted, at rehearsal, to apply to that part the treatment which gained general admiration for his Conte di Luna, he would undoubtedly be at once conveyed, under restraint, from the stage to bedlam. Fancy a Don Felix or a Benedick at any West-end theatre exhibiting the manners of an average Don

Juan or Count Almaviva! Conceive any respectable dramatic company daring to act that great and neglected work of Molière's, Le Festin de Pierre, as our opera singers usually act the masterpiece which Mozart founded on it. Yet musical critics frequently speak of the dramatic power and tragic intensity of the latest and absurdest Lucia or Traviata in terms which no sober critic of the kindred profession ever applies to the most skilful achievements of Mrs Kendal.

But, then, the variety of resource, the freedom from mannerism—from Middlewickism! Unhappily that has not come off yet. Operatic actors, so far from being free from mannerisms, wholly substitute mannerisms of the feeblest sort for acting; and as for variety of resource, there is not a penny to choose between an average *prima donna*'s treatment of any two of her parts, however dissimilar in conception. Her Lady Henrietta is exactly the same as her Marguerite; her Marguerite is not distinguishable by a deaf man from her Juliet, except by her dress and wig; and her Semiramis is only a swaggering Juliet. Even the few singers, male or female, who are specially celebrated for their acting, would be celebrated for their deficiency if they were placed in an equally prominent position in drama, and judged by the standard set by Ristori and Salvini.

As to the development of "study," or the power of learning new parts by constant change of program, it is to be noted that whereas the power of prompting and of taking a prompt during actual performance is becoming a lost art at our theatres, opera singers never venture before an audience without a prompter in the middle of the stage to pilot them through their business. As there is no possibility of sufficient rehearsal, it is part of their qualification, as it still is of the actor in the remote places where the palmy system is still rampant, to get through a part in which they are not even letter-perfect, much less note and letter-perfect. Who has ever heard an opera go absolutely without a hitch, except it was a very new opera which had been recently the subject of special effort in preparation, or a very old one played by a company of veterans? How many singers, when they have once picked up enough of their part to get through it without disgrace by dint of watching the prompter, ever give any further study to its details? At the ordinary theatres a hitch is as exceptional an occurrence as the forgetting of the Lord's Prayer, or the benediction by a Dean. Our actors gain both study and practice from long runs. It is true that they are condemned too often to play for months shallow and characterless parts which they get to the bottom of in a week; but that is the fault of the abject condition of the drama in England, and not of the system of long runs, which gives artists time to get thoroughly inside their parts, and frees them during considerable periods from daily rehearsals, to dawdle in the drawing room if they like, but also to study in the library, the picture gallery, the museum, the gymnasium, or the concert room, as their bodily or mental wants may suggest. The old system of a changed program every night and a hurried rehearsal every day meant insufficient time to prepare one's part, and no time at all to prepare oneself for playing it. To the actor as to other men, leisure means light. He may not always make a good use of his leisure; but in that case he will eventually succumb to competition of the men who do.

As to the advantage of having performances of the greatest operas each season, it may be admitted that a few great works are included in the narrow and hackneyed repertory of our opera houses; but it must at the same time be asked whether such performance as they get is in any sense worthy of them. Don Giovanni is certainly kept before the public; but in what plight? With fine movements omitted in the second act; with the recitatives gabbled through in a manner which could not be adequately described without the employment of abusive epithets; and with most of the parts played so as to inspire a faint wonder as to whether ten or twenty more earnest rehearsals, followed by a run of a hundred nights, would suffice to reveal them to the players. When this is all we can do for Don Giovanni we had better keep it on the shelf, as we now keep Shakespear when we have not time to take due trouble with him. The actor who knows one part, and consequently one play thoroughly, is superior to the actor who can scramble with assistance through a dozen. The one gets into the skin of one character: the other only puts on the clothes of twelve. One impersonation is worth more than many impostures. Long runs mean impersonations: palminess means imposture. Let us rejoice over the departure of the palmy days of the theatre.

LISZT

I

(The Dramatic Review, 10 April 1886)

"The favorite of Fortune" has revisited us at last, and is installed as the Grand Old Man of music. Many persons of literary and artistic tastes are now reading with genuine enthusiasm the newspaper chronicles of his pilgrimage—in all human probability his last pilgrimage—to the land of Purcell. Sonnets will spring—are springing daily, perhaps—from irrepressible impulses to worship the white-haired hero; the contemporary of Schumann, Berlioz, Chopin, Mendelssohn, and Goetz; who was sped on his career by Beethoven; who was the cherished friend of Wagner; who has all his life conversed with the immortals, and been envied by most of them for his pianoforte playing and his pluck before the public. You cannot read about such a man without emotion. If music be to you only a glorious dream, an unknown language transcending all articulate poesy, a rapture of angelic song, a storm-cloud of sublimity discharging itself into your inmost soul with thrilling harmonious thunder; then for you especially the voice of man's innate godhead will speak in whatever Liszt plays, whether he extemporizes variations on Pop goes the Weasel or faithfully re-utters for you the chromatic *fantasia* of Bach. The great player is to you no mere pianist: he is a host of associations—George Sand, Lamartine, Victor Hugo, Paris in the days of the Romantic movement, and what not and who not? Happy hero-worshiper! No generous infidel will grudge you your ecstasy, or untimely urge that it is intense in inverse ratio to your knowledge of music. Indeed, if one felt disposed to throw cold water on such genial transports, it would be difficult to find any just now to throw: Liszt having the gift that was laid as a curse upon the Scotch laird who made icy water bubble and boil by touching it.

Yet Liszt's associations do not by themselves entitle him to take precedence of many worthy citizens whose very names are unknown to history. The servant who opened Balzac's door to his visitors, and who must have been no mean connoisseur in creditors, was perhaps more interesting from this point of view than Liszt. As to the gentlemen who turn over the leaves for the pianists at St James's Hall, is there a great *virtuoso* with whom they are not familiar? What exciting tales they could tell of their breathless efforts to follow incredibly swift *prestos*; and what pleasant reminiscences they must enjoy of delicious naps stolen in the midst of dreamy *adagios* with a nice long repeat included within one open folio. For they sleep, these men: I have seen one of them do it at the elbow of a great artist, and have forgotten the music in contemplating the unfathomable satiety of the slumberer, and in speculating on the chances of his waking up in time for the *volte subito*. The eyes did not fail to open punctually; and their expression, unmistakeably that of the sleeper awakened, relieved me of the last doubt as to whether he had not been ecstatically drinking in the music with his eyes shut. What are Liszt's experiences compared to those of a man so prodigiously *blasé* that not Madame Schumann herself can fix his attention for the brief space of two pages? Clearly it is by his merit as a player or composer that Liszt's reputation must stand or fade.

There are not many people of anything like a reasonable age in England who have heard Liszt play. This statement may become false by the time it is printed—I hope it will; but at present it is true. That he was once a great player, one who far more than any interpreter of his time could play a sonata as the composer thought it, reading into every quaver the intention with which it was written there, is proved to us, as firmly as any such thing can be proved, by the crowning testimony of Wagner. Having the gift of governing men too, he was a great conductor as well as a great pianist. Whether he is as great as he was is just what we are all at present very curious to ascertain. We cannot expect him to formally undertake a public performance of Beethoven's Opus 106, his playing of which was ranked by Wagner as a creative effort; but there is abundant hope that he may be tempted to touch the keyboard at some concert at which only his presence can be promised. Already he has yielded to the desire of the Academy students; and the public wishes itself, for the nonce, a corps of Academy students and not a mob of mere ticket purchasers, whose applause and lionizing an artist is bound to mistrust if not to despise. Perhaps, under the circumstances, the best policy would be one of exasperation. Treat the master to a few examples of average British pianism; and a desperate longing to take the sound of it out of his ears, tempered by a paternal willingness to shew us what real playing is, may urge him to fulfil our hearts' desire.

Of Liszt's merits as a composer, those who heard his St Elizabeth at St James's Hall last Tuesday have, no doubt, their own opinion. To some of us his devotion to serious composition seems as hopeless a struggle against natural incapacity as was Benjamin Haydon's determination to be a great painter. To others the Dante symphony and the symphonic poems are masterpieces slowly but surely making their way to full recognition. Mr Bache has pressed the latter opinion hard upon us, and has backed it heavily. The present is not the time to insist with any grace on the former view. Fortunately, much of Liszt's music is admired on all hands. Sceptics who think it no more than brilliant, inspiriting, amusing, applaud as loudly as believers who revere it as significant, profound, and destined to endure with the works of Bach and Mozart. So, since we all enjoy it from one point of view or the other, we can very well unite in making as pleasant as possible the sojourn among us of an artist who has come clean-handed out of the press of three generations of frenzied nineteenth-century scramblers for pelf, and of whom even hostile critics say no worse than that he has failed only by aiming too high.

II

(*Pall Mall Gazette*, 2 *August* 1886; unsigned)

The foreboding that many of us must have felt last spring when Liszt left England with a promise to return has been verified by the news of his death at Bayreuth. Such news always comes too soon; but in this case Time has exacted less than his traditional due: three score and fifteen years were allowed to Liszt to work out what was in him. He had twice as long to utter himself as had Mendelssohn, who was only two and a half years his senior; or Mozart, who might have done things quite unimaginable in their effect on modern music if he had been allowed another thirty years of life. Of Liszt, we at least know that he said his say fully, such as it was. He was a Hungarian, born at Raiding in 1811, with the pianoforte at his fingers' ends. His career as a public player began when he was nine years old; and his success led him to Vienna and then to Paris, where he was excluded by his nationality from the Conservatoire and Cherubini's instruction. Of his plunge into the Romantic movement; his Saint-Simonianism; his Roman Catholicism; his connection with the Countess d'Agoult (Daniel Stern); his career in his middle age at Weimar, where he did for the opera what Goethe had done before for the theatre; his championship of Wagner, who became his son-in-law, and whose widow is his sole surviving child; his unique position as the idol of all the pianoforte students in the world—of all these we have been lately put in mind by the great overhauling of his history, which took place when he revisited us this year after nearly half a century's absence. He first played here at the Philharmonic Concerts in 1827. Fifteen years later he gave us another trial out of which we did not come with perfect credit. That was, perhaps, why he stayed away fortyfour years before he came again, and as an old man, half priest, half musician, stirred up all the hero-worship in our little world of music and all the lionizing in our big world of fashion. That little world will grieve awhile to learn that his third absence must be the longest of all. The big world will probably feel none the worse for having had something to talk about at breakfast this morning. Between it and the dead artist there was little genuine love lost. He cared so little for even dazzling it that he adopted the profession of pianist with repugnance, and abandoned it for that of conductor and composer as soon as he could afford to.

It was as a composer that Liszt wished to stand high in the esteem of his contemporaries, or—failing their appreciation—of posterity. Many musicians of good credit think that he judged himself rightly. Mr Bache, for instance, has given us concert after concert of his favorite master's works with a devotion that has extorted applause from audiences for the most part quite convinced that Liszt and Mr Bache were mistaken. Wagner, who spoke very highly of Liszt as a conductor, declared that his playing of Beethoven's greater sonatas was essentially an act of composition as well as of interpretation; he did not, however, commit himself on the subject of the Dante symphony or Mazeppa. There is a consensus of opinion in favor of Liszt as a player. His songs, too, have affected many musicians deeply; and though they are not generally familiar, their merit has not been at all emphatically questioned. His studies and transcriptions, if not wholly irreproachable in point of taste, shew an exhaustive knowledge of the pianoforte; and, unplayable as they are to people who attack a pianoforte with stiff wrists and clenched teeth, they are not dreaded by good pianists. The brilliancy and impetuous fantasy of his Hungarian Rhapsodies are irresistible, as Herr Richter has proved again and again at St James's Hall. But his oratorios and symphonic poems—especially the latter— have not yet won the place which he claimed for them. A man can hardly be so impressionable as Liszt was and yet be sturdy enough to be original. He could conduct Lohengrin like Wagner's other self, and could play Beethoven as if the sonatas were of his own moulding; but as an original composer he was like a child, delighting in noise, speed, and stirring modulation, and indulging in such irritating excesses and repetitions of them, that decorous concert-goers find his Infernos, his battles, and his Mazeppa rides first amusing, then rather scandalous, and finally quite unbearable. A pleasanter idea of the man can be derived from the many eulogies, some of them mere schoolgirl raptures, others balanced verdicts of great composers and critics, which, whether the symphonic poems live or die, will preserve a niche for him in the history of music as a man who loved his art, despised money, attracted everybody worth knowing in the nineteenth century, lived through the worst of it, and got away from it at last with his hands unstained.

THE REDEMPTION AT THE CRYSTAL PALACE
(*The Dramatic Review*, 8 May 1886)

Why should the Handel Festival occur only once in every three years? Would it pay to make it biennial, annual, half-yearly, quarterly, weekly? Cannot something be made out of our gold-laden visitors from the colonies this year by a festival or two? An experiment in the direction of answering these questions was made last Saturday at the Crystal Palace, when M. Gounod's Redemption was performed at the Crystal Palace by the Handel orchestra, with three thousand singers in the choir, and four hundred players in the orchestra. Additional solemnity was given to the occasion by the prohibition of the sale of intoxicating liquor at the refreshment bars during the performance (so I was assured by a neighbor on his return from a short and unsuccessful absence); and nothing was allowed to distract the attention of the audience from the oratorio except a large signboard with the inscription "OYSTERS," which was conspicuous on the left of the orchestra. The audience behaved much like a church congregation, stolid, unintelligent, and silent, except once, when Madame Albani took her place on the orchestra after the first part, and again when one of her highest notes excited the representatives of that large and influential section of the public which regards a vocalist as an interesting variety of locomotive with a powerful whistle.

M. Gounod is almost as hard to dispraise as the President of the Royal Academy. Both produce works so graceful, so harmonious, so smooth, so delicate, so refined, and so handsomely sentimental, that it is difficult to convey, without appearing ungracious or insensible, the exact measure of disparagement needed to prevent the reader from concluding that M. Gounod is another Handel, or Sir Frederick Leighton another Raphael. And indeed M. Gounod does not express his ideas worse than Handel; but then he has fewer ideas to express. No one has ever been bored by an adequate performance of The Messiah. Even a Good Friday tumble through it at the Albert Hall—ordinarily the worst thing of its kind in the whole cosmos—inspires rage and longing for justice to Handel rather than weariness. But the best conceivable performance of the Redemption would not hold an audience to the last note if the half-past five train back to town from Sydenham were at stake, much less make them impatient for a repetition of the oratorio, which is, in truth, an extremely tedious work, not because any particular number is dull or repulsive, but because its beauties are repeated *ad nauseam*. We all remember how, at the awakening of Margaret in the prison scene of Faust, we were delighted by the harmonic transitions from phrase to phrase by minor ninths resolving on stirring inversions of the common chord of a new tonic (technically unskilled readers will kindly excuse this jargon), as her voice rose semitone by semitone to the final cadence. It was a charming device; and M. Gounod used it again and again in his other operas. But when he gives us a long oratorio, consisting for the most part of these phrases on successive degrees of the chromatic scale, not only do we get thoroughly tired of them, but the pious among us may well feel scandalized at hearing the central figure in the tragedy of the atonement delivering himself exactly in the love-sick manner of Romeo, Faust, and Cinq Mars. No one expected M. Gounod to succeed in making the Redeemer differ from Romeo as Sarastro, for example, differs from Don Giovanni; but he might at least have made him as impressive as Friar Lawrence. Instead, he has limited himself to making the Prince of Peace a gentleman; and one cannot help adding that he could have done no less for the Prince of Darkness.

And such a smooth-spoken gentleman! There is a plague of smoothness over the whole work. The fact that M. Gounod has put too much sugar in it for the palate of a British Protestant might be condoned if the music were not so very horizontal. There is nearly always a pedal flowing along, and the other parts are slipping chromatically down to merge in it. Mr Compton Reade used to be fond of calling Handel the great Dagon of music. But when, at the end of the second part of the trilogy, the celestial choir demands Who is the King of Glory? words cannot express the longing that arises to have done with M. Gounod's sweetly grandiose periods, and to hear great Dagon answer concerning The Lord strong and mighty; the Lord mighty in battle. And again, in the chorus of mockers at the crucifixion, *Ah, thou that dost declare*, though the composer's dramatic instinct does make a faint struggle against his love of suave harmony, the lamenting listener's memory reverts enviously to the sinister turbulence of great Dagon's sardonic *He trusted in God that he would deliver him*. If Mr Compton Reade, or anyone else, still doubts that M. Gounod is to Handel as a Parisian duel is to Armageddon, let him seek greater wisdom at the next Crystal Palace performance of the Redemption or Mors et Vita. Depend upon it, he will be forced either to change his opinion, or to accuse Handel of an extraordinary lack of variety in rhythm and harmonic treatment, and an essentially frivolous sentimental piety in dealing with a subject which, to a genuinely religious Christian composer, must be the most tremendous in universal history.

The execution of the work on Saturday last was as fine as one has any right to expect under mundane conditions. No doubt a choir of angels would sing M. Gounod's ethereal strains better than a massive detachment from the ranks of the British *bourgeoisie*; but no reasonable exception can be taken to the steady middle-class manner and solid middle-class tone of the Festival choristers. The basses seemed to me to be weak; but that may have been due to our relative positions. Some of the orchestral effects were enhanced by the vast space. Thus, at the beginning of the second part, the chords of the violins pulsating above the veiled melody of the horns, answered by the clear and brilliant notes of the trumpets in the gallery, transported us all into cloud-land. Later, in an orchestral interlude full of mystery, entitled The Apostles in Prayer, the perpetual tonic pedal ceased to be tiresome, and almost excused M. Gounod for being unable to tear himself away from the few devices which he uses so exquisitely. Of Madame Albani, Miss Marriott, Madame Patey, Mr Lloyd, Mr King, and Mr Santley, nothing need be said, except to congratulate them on the easiest Festival engagement that ever fell to the lot of six such vocalists.

HOW TO BECOME A MUSICAL CRITIC

MEMOIRS OF A FAMOUS FIDDLER

(Unsigned review of Sara C. Bull's *Ole Bull. Pall Mall Gazette*, 5 *July* 1886)

We have at last an English memoir of Ole Bull, not before it was urgently needed. For, it being nearly a quarter of a century since the great Norwegian violinist played publicly in the United Kingdom, it had come about that while young America knew Ole Bull as well as we know Joachim and Sarasate, young England very commonly supposed him to be an octogenarian negro. That we failed to attach him to us as a yearly visitor was rather our misfortune than our fault. It is true that he was intrigued against and cheated here; but there was nothing peculiar to us in that. Bull invariably assumed his fellow men to be honest until he found out the contrary; and it is due to the alert commercial spirit of Europe and America to say that, to his cost, he almost invariably did find out the contrary. In whatever quarter of the globe he sojourned he found the general public ready to heap gold upon him, and the particular man of business equally ready to relieve him of it. In America a hasty speculator, who had just made a large haul in this way, was foolish enough to attempt to take off by poison the goose that laid the golden eggs. On another occasion a ruder pioneer of civilization, coveting a diamond which sparkled in the magic fiddle bow, approached the player, knife in hand, with a view to its extraction. But Ole Bull, like Sinfjotli, instinctively saw death in the cup, and refused to drink, whilst the unfortunate pioneer with the bowie knife took nothing by his enterprise except a rough estimate of how much nerve and muscle go to the making of a Norseman who can play the violin in four-part harmony.

Ole Bull's gain, on the whole, greatly exceeded his loss. Wherever he went he soon found himself the focus of all the hero-worship in the place. He knew everybody worth knowing; he never was sea-sick; and he never grew stout. His strength, courage, and skill did not wane as his popularity grew. Though he ventured to start a colony in America, and was even rash enough to attempt the foundation of a national theatre in his own country, he died a rich man with fair estates. Illnesses, brought on by overwork and misadventures in the course of his traveling, occurred sufficiently often to impress upon him the value of his happier hours. Litigation and the demoralizing worry of being cheated he probably brought upon himself by his unbusinesslike habits; but as these meant nothing more than a natural repugnance to treat men as knaves by tying himself and them down with stamp and signature in the strong bonds of the law (which is the essence of businesslikeness), perhaps he gained as much as he lost even on this point. For, gold magnet as he was, even he found men honest occasionally. On the whole, there is reason to believe that though he suffered, like all great artists, from the hucksterdom of his environment, he yet succeeded in doing it more good than it did him harm. Genius was not in him a disease: he enjoyed robust moral as well as physical health, and, indeed, illustrated in his person the interdependence of the two.

As a violinist, he was of no school, and somewhat of Paganini's sort. His beginnings scandalized the orthodox disciples of Lafont, Rode, and Baillot; and, though he subsequently assimilated the essence of the Italian classical tradition, he became famous, not as an interpreter of the great composers, but as the utterer of a poetic inspiration which he claimed to have had direct from the mountains of Norway. He played his own music; but he had the power of making all genuinely popular music his own. Wherever he went, he found either folk songs, which he immediately regenerated for the people so that they no longer sounded hackneyed; or else, for audiences too highly civilized or sophisticated to be won over in this way, he played his own Norse music, and brought the foreigners under the spell it had laid on himself. His physical aptitude for his instrument enabled him to acquire a prodigious command of it; and in displaying his power in all its phases and in all its exuberance he did not escape the reproach of charlatanism. But he must have been far more than a charlatan to have conquered the world as he did, and to have gained the respect of so many artists who thoroughly knew the value of a player's work. His appreciation of and capacity for music of the highest class is proved by his successful devotion to the music of Mozart, which, whilst it makes extraordinary demands on an artist's sensibility, affords no cover for his shortcomings. Besides his mastery of the manipulative difficulties of violin-playing, Ole Bull knew well the shades of tone and expression of which the alternative resources of the four strings afford such rich variety, and which only a born fiddler can exhaustively learn and use.

Mrs Sara Bull's memoir of her gifted husband is for the most part an itinerary, enlivened with anecdotes and favorable newspaper criticisms. As her personal knowledge of him dates only from the year 1868, its advantages hardly counterbalance the partiality entailed by close and affectionate relationship. In truth, the Ole Bull described in her pages is no real man, but an ideal Norse hero—a Berserk or Viking, with a dash of Orpheus and the Pied Piper—a product, not of nature, but of nineteenth-century imaginative literature. A widow's biography of her husband has necessarily something of the defect and excess of an epitaph: it omits faults, and records common instincts as special virtues. But a widow who regards her husband as the embodiment of a poetic ideal which grew up in the course of her reading and day-dreaming before she knew him must be even less than ordinarily trustworthy as a critical biographer. That Ole Bull was thus idealized by his second wife is much to his credit; but he must surely have had a failing or two. One would like to hear the devil's advocate before pronouncing a verdict.

The anecdotes concerning Ole Bull are very like the anecdotes about Paganini, Liszt, and the rest of the great *virtuosi*. It is inspiriting to learn that he did not need police protection against canine pets, though his kicking the Princess Dameroud's snappish doggie into the chandelier is not so suggestive of tenderness towards animals as the mode of his touching reconciliation with the Danish poet Ohlenschläger, who narrates it as follows:—

When he at one time, on board the steamer, had caused my displeasure by a too severe criticism of the Swedes, and I had taken my seat on a bench, he came leaping towards me on his hands and feet, and barked at me like a dog. This was a no less original than amiable manner of bringing about a reconciliation.

On a Mississippi steamer he astonished a rowdy who was shocked at his unnatural objection to whisky by performing upon him the feat known to British wrestlers as "the flying mare." When the rowdy came to, he offered his bowie knife as a tribute to the strongest fiddler he had ever seen.

Fiddle-fanciers will find much to interest them both in the memoir and appendix. Ole Bull was a fancier as well as a player, and, like Paganini, never used a Stradivarius, preferring the purer, if less even, tone of the masterpieces of Amati and Guarnerius. Eventually he used almost exclusively a violin by Gaspar da Salo, whom he believed to be identical with Gaspar Duiffoprugcar, a lute-maker patronized by Francis I. His instrument must therefore have been the oldest of its kind in use. His bow was a heavy one, exceeding the customary length by two inches.

A BOOK FOR ORATORS AND SINGERS

(Unsigned review of Morell Mackenzie's *Hygiene of the Vocal Organs*. *Pall Mall Gazette*, 26 *July* 1886)

Though there must by this time be in existence almost as many handbooks for singers and speakers as a fast reader could skip through in a lifetime or so, publishers still find them safe investments. Young people who are born into that fringe of the musical and theatrical professions from which we draw our great stock of deadheads are generally much at a loss when the question of earning a living comes home to them. They find, to their surprise, that they can neither read nor write the various languages in which they have so often chattered to the musical foreigner. Their knowledge of the ways of mummers and minstrels will no more pass with managers and *impresarios* as artistic skill and culture than a sexton's opportunities of helping the beneficed clergy into their surplices would recommend him to a bishop as preacher or theologian: yet they do not recognize their unfitness for an engagement, as a sexton, to do him justice, recognizes his unfitness for ordination. Their ineptly stagey manners and appearance, like their morals, are the impress of an environment of bismuth and rouge, overcoats with Astrakhan collars, moustaches, sham concerts for the benefit of sham singers out of engagement, and an atmosphere which creates an unquenchable craving for admission without payment to all sorts of public entertainments, especially to the Opera. An engagement at £200 a night at Covent Garden usually strikes them as a peculiarly eligible means of subsistence; and their parents, eager to have a *prima donna* in the family to exploit all to themselves, encourage the project while there is a spark of life in it. Unsuspicious of their own futility, they have some distorted ideas of practice, but none of study. They are always in search of a method—especially the old Italian one of Porpora; and they will even pay cash for a handbook of singing, a set of unintelligible photographs of the larynx, or an ammoniaphone from which to suck a ready-made compass of three octaves, with the usual fortune attached. They are not damped even by the reflection that if *prima donnas* could be made on these terms the supply among the Western nations would exceed the demand by several millions, and the market value of an Elsa or Valentine sink to eighteen shillings a week exclusive of expenses. Madame Patti can build castles because, besides the wages of a highly skilled workwoman, she enjoys the rent of her monopoly of a highly popular form of ability. If everyone with a musical turn could do as much as she after a course of complimentary tickets and a few whiffs from the ammoniaphone, there would be no more castles for poor Madame Patti: she would at once be reduced to the needy ranks of unskilled labor.

It may seem unjust to Dr Morell Mackenzie to harp in this place on a parasitic class to which his book is not specially addressed. But he has himself created the association by a certain facetiousness and quotativeness that would vanish from his mind in the presence of an audience upon whose scientific and artistic culture he could rely. There is hardly a chapter in which he does not seem to be making allowances, with good-humored contempt, for the untrained reason of vulgar readers in one sentence, and in the next writing down to their level with a sort of jocoseness permissible at a musical at-home, but decidedly not good enough for a carefully weighed treatise. It is ill to be dull even when correct; excellent to be lively, witty, and vernacular as well as correct; but intolerable to be chatty and trivial in manner merely to reconcile slovenly people to the correctness and authority of your matter. Dr Morell Mackenzie's backsliding in this direction would not be worth insisting on but for the importance of his book, which is the most interesting English record of laryngoscopic investigation since Madame Seiler's. He recognizes two vocal registers, which he calls long reed and short reed respectively, asserting that in chest voice "the pitch is raised by means of increasing tension and lengthening of the cords," whilst in head voice the same result is brought about "by gradual shortening of the vibrating reed." He does not regard the closure of the cartilaginous ends of the cords as a change of register, because the reed still lengthens as the pitch rises. It is when "stop closure" of the ligamentous glottis takes place, and the reed begins to shorten with the ascent of the voice, that he admits a change of register. He has discovered eminent singers, tenor and soprano, singing throughout the whole compass in the long reed register, although the quality of tone seemed unmistakeably that proper to the short reed, the laryngoscope thus ruthlessly discrediting judgment by ear. His table of fifty voices examined by him is full of curious points; and his remarks on the difficulty of learning to manipulate the laryngoscope and read the image aright, carrying all the authority of his exceptionally extensive practice with the apparatus, are very suggestive as to the contradictory observations of previous investigators. His general hints to singers and speakers are practicable: he does not irritate the reader by prescribing habits, clothes, diet, and hours that would cut an artist off from human society under existing arrangements. There is the inevitable warning against tight lacing, high heels, open mouths, sudden changes of temperature, and excesses of all kinds, which will probably prove just as effectual as previous admonitions to the same effect. With respect to what is called the "breaking" of the voice in adolescence, he points out that only about seventeen per cent. of boys' voices actually crack; and he declares his ignorance of any reason for disusing the voice during the change that would not justify disuse of the limbs during the growth of the long bones of one's skeleton.

Dr Mackenzie is perhaps the greatest living authority on such matters, and, notwithstanding the defects of style which we have pointed out, this volume deserves to be widely read, as a most authoritative treatise on a subject in which we are all of us interested.

WAGNER ON ORCHESTRAL CONDUCTING

(Unsigned review of Richard Wagner's *On Conducting*, translated by Edward Dannreuther. *Pall Mall Gazette*, 28 May 1887)

When this little work was published at Leipzig in 1869, it was not worth any publisher's while to have it translated into English. To the few who had then heard of him here, Wagner was known as a pretentious and quarrelsome person who persisted, on principle, in writing ugly music in spite of repeated failure, and who had been dropped by the Philharmonic Society (admittedly the greatest authority on music in the world) after a couple of trials as conductor. Times have changed now with a vengeance. No other music than his can be depended on to draw large audiences to orchestral concerts; the intensity of Beethoven's popularity is waning as that of the newer tone poet's waxes; and selections and arrangements from his operas take precedence of symphonies and concertos in programs that are nothing if not classical. And this concise treatise of his on orchestral conducting will be sought for today as a monograph, unique of its kind, by the greatest composer, conductor, and critic of our own time.

It is perhaps as well to explain that Ueber das Dirigiren is not an academic textbook of time-beating. It does not offer diagrams supposed to be traced by a *bâton* indicating four in a bar, six in a bar, &c.; nor advice as to how to manage the three simultaneous dances in Don Giovanni. Nor does it contain the slightest recognition of that adroitness in driving inefficient orchestras through scratch performances which many professional musicians, and even some critics, regard as the first and last qualification of a conductor. "The whole truth of the matter is," says Wagner, "that in a proper performance the conductor's part is to give always the proper *tempo*." His insistence on this may do us some service; for we suffer much from conductors who can do everybody else's business in the orchestra so well—even to counting their rests for them, and shewing them how to finger difficult passages—that no one dares to hint that their own special function of choosing the proper *tempo* is never successfully discharged when really great work is in hand. The illustrations given from the Freischütz overture, the Eroica, C minor, and choral symphonies, and Mozart's symphony in E flat will come home to all loving students of these works. It is as true here as in Germany that, "if music depended on our conductors, it would have perished long ago." How well, too, we have reason to groan with Wagner at the habitual opera mutilation which provoked such a passage as "Cut! Cut!—this is the *ultima ratio* of our conductors: the pleasant and never-failing means of accommodating to their own incompetence the artistic tasks which they find impossible." Again—"They have no notion that, with even the most insignificant opera, a comparatively satisfactory effect on educated minds can be secured by correctness and completeness in performance." Does Mr Carl Rosa agree here; and, if so, would it be too much to ask him to give us Lohengrin, if not complete, at least without such butcherly cuts as that sometimes made in the instrumental prelude to the second act? Much that Wagner has said about famous orchestras trading on the departed excellence they were wrought up to by some deceased or seceded conductor, might have been written of the Covent Garden orchestra when, though some of its nightly performances would have disgraced a circus, it was still generally spoken and even written of as the first orchestra in England, merely because it had been so under the direction of Costa, who had then returned to the rival house, and had of course taken the orchestral supremacy with him. To this day there are people who talk of the Covent Garden orchestra as if there were in the neighboring cabbages a musical magic of which nothing could rob a band in Bow-street.

The disappointing impressions which Wagner complains of having received from public performances of classical music in his earliest youth were common and indeed inevitable experiences in London before he brought Herr Richter to conduct his festivals at the Albert Hall. The new conductor certainly had his work cut out for him. He had to reveal Wagner; to save Beethoven from vulgarization; and to restore Mozart, whose music was almost extinct. For when Herr Richter first conducted the great Symphony in E flat here, concert-goers had fallen into the habit of expecting nothing from Mozart but a certain vapid liveliness—the English phase of that "Mattigkeit der Mozartschen Kantilene" which so astonished Wagner when he, too, began to suffer from incompetent conductors. That such a difference could have been made by merely changing the man who noiselessly waved the stick has puzzled many people, and reduced them either to incredulity or to irrelevant statements—offered with an explanatory air—as to Herr Richter's extraordinary memory and his practical acquaintance with the art of playing the horn. Those who desire some more intelligent account of what constitutes a good conductor will find it in this book, which will, it is to be hoped, be read or re-read by the expert as well as by the general reader and the student. Mr August Manns, for example, might take, as to the slow movement of the Ninth Symphony, a hint from Wagner which would come as an impertinence from any ordinary critic. And Sir Arthur Sullivan might find something to interest him in the trenchant passages in which Wagner points out that the modern Mendelssohnian "culture," with all its refinement, its elegance, its reticence, and its "chastity," is far too negative to equip a conductor for a struggle with Bach or Beethoven.

Mr Edward Dannreuther is not responsible for the wording of all the passages quoted above. His version of them, though adequate when taken with the context, happened to be inconvenient for quotation. The variations are therefore by no means offered as improvements. Mr Dannreuther has done his manuscript very conscientiously, and with an evident sense of its being well worth doing for its own sake. The acknowledgment must, however, be strictly limited to the manuscript. "Procrustus" and "ultimo ratio" are only mild examples of the results of careless proof correction, undiscovered even by the compiler of the list of errata, which is itself an inexcusable adjunct to a book of one hundred and twentytwo pages.

THE DON GIOVANNI CENTENARY

(*Pall Mall Gazette*, 31 October 1887; signed "By our
Special Wagnerite")

When I was requested by the Pall Mall Gazette to attend the
centenary concert recital of Don Giovanni on Saturday last at
the Crystal Palace, I felt strongly disposed to write curtly to the
Editor expressing my unworthiness to do justice to the beauties
of eighteenth-century opera. However, I was by no means sure
that the Editor would have appreciated the sarcasm (editors, as a
class, being shocking examples of neglected musical education);
and, besides, I was somewhat curious to hear the performance.
For though we are all agreed as to the prettiness of Mozart's
melodies, his *naïve* touches of mild fun, and the touch, ingenuity,
and grace with which he rang his few stereotyped changes on the
old-fashioned forms, yet I have observed that some modern
musicians, in the face of a great technical development of harmony and instrumentation, and an enlargement even to world
spaciousness of our views of the mission of art, yet persist in
claiming for Mozart powers simply impossible to a man who had
never read a line of Hegel or a stave of Wagner. I am not now
thinking of the maudlin Mozart idolatry of M. Gounod, whom I
of course do not consider a great musician; but rather of the unaccountable fact that even Richard Wagner seems to have
regarded Mozart as in some respects the greatest of his predecessors. To me it is obvious that Mozart was a mere child
in comparison with Schumann, Liszt, or Johannes Brahms;
and yet I believe that I could not have expressed myself
to that effect in the presence of the great master without
considerable risk of contemptuous abuse, if not of bodily
violence.

So I resolved finally to venture hearing poor old Rossini's pet
dramma giocosa. Before starting, I took a glance at the score, and
found exactly what I expected—commonplace melodies, diatonic harmonies and dominant discords, ridiculous old closes
and half-closes at every eighth bar or so, "florid" accompaniments consisting of tum-tum in the bass and scales like pianoforte

133

finger studies in the treble, and a ludicrously thin instrumentation, without trombones or clarionets except in two or three exceptionally pretentious numbers; the string quartet, with a couple of horns and oboes, seeming quite to satisfy the Mozartian notion of instrumentation. These are facts—facts which can be verified at any time by a reference to the score; and they must weigh more with any advanced musician than the hasty opinions which I formed at the concert when in a sort of delirium, induced, I have no doubt, by the heat of the room.

For I am bound to admit that the heat of the room produced a most extraordinary effect upon me. The commonplace melodies quite confounded me by acquiring subtlety, nobility, and dramatic truth of expression; the hackneyed diatonic harmonies reminded me of nothing I had ever heard before; the dominant discords had a poignant expression which I have failed in my own compositions to attain even by forcibly sounding all the twelve notes of the chromatic scale simultaneously; the ridiculous cadences and half-closes came sometimes like answers to unspoken questions of the heart, sometimes like ghostly echoes from another world; and the feeble instrumentation—but that was what warned me that my senses were astray. Otherwise I must have declared that here was a master compared to whom Berlioz was a musical pastrycook. From Beethoven and Wagner I have learned that the orchestra can paint every aspect of nature, and turn impersonal but specific emotion into exquisite sound. But an orchestra that creates men and women as Shakespear and Molière did—that makes emotion not only specific but personal and characteristic (and this, mind, without clarionets, without trombones, without a second pair of horns): such a thing is madness: I must have been dreaming. When the trombones did come in for a while in a supernatural scene at the end, I felt more in my accustomed element; but presently they took an accent so inexpressibly awful, that I, who have sat and smiled through Liszt's Inferno with the keenest relish, felt forgotten superstitions reviving within me. The roots of my hair stirred; and I recoiled as from the actual presence of Hell. But enough of these delusions, which I have effectually dispelled by a dispassionate private performance at my own pianoforte. Of the concert technically, I can only say that it was practically little more than a rehearsal of the orchestral parts.

BOÏTO'S MEFISTOFELE

(The Star, 18 *July* 1888; unsigned)

Boïto's Mefistofele is chiefly interesting as a proof that a really able literary man can turn out a much better opera than the average musician can, just as he can turn out a much more effective play than the average poet. We have by this time accumulated such a huge stock of orchestral effects, rhythms, and modulations, all of which are quite accessible to any person who starts with sufficient musical gift to pick up He's all right when you know him by ear, that the composition of a passable opera or ballet will be as mechanical an achievement before the end of the century as the writing of a passable novel is now. Meanwhile, let us take Mefistofele as seriously as Die Zauberflöte, and suggest to Mr Harris that the effect of the oncoming of night in the first act with the gradual melting of the town ramparts into the gloom of Faust's study, should not be performed with lights turned up, and stage carpenters bustling through the gauze and cheerfully shouting, "Pull it back, sir? Yessir. Go on, Tom," and so forth. One would also suppose that such inexpensive articles of *diablerie* as will-o'-the-wisps might be supplied more plentifully in the Brocken scene, if only to give some point to the erratic flights of tootling in the orchestra. However, these are but details, only to be noted at Covent Garden, because so much is there sacrificed to spectacularism on the highest scale.

The singing was—as to the chorus—hurried, jaded, flat, and ineffective in the prologue, where it most needs to be majestic and penetrating; as to the principal persons, various. Signor Ravelli, much used up, spurted bravely at times, but hardly did justice to his part. Signor Edouard de Reszke, as the fiend, used his fine voice with great effect in certain passages, but left extensive room, as usual, for intelligence and variety. The honors of the evening were carried off by Miss Macintyre. She played Margaret like a novice, but her novitiate is full of promise and charm. Of Helen let it suffice to say that she received, amid scanty applause, a vast basket of flowers, which was not generally believed to be a spontaneous tribute from the front of the house. The audience seemed well pleased throughout, and Mefistofele will probably be brought forward oftener next year. The last act, one of the best sections of the opera, made a marked impression in spite of the late hour; and it is a pity that it is not likely to be secured an earlier hearing by the omission of the Brocken business, which is musically and scenically childish. So many scenes have already been cut from the original score that the additional injury to the composer's feelings would hardly be felt by him.

SUCH A THUMPING OF PIANOS

(The Star, 10 *October* 1888; unsigned)

The recorded humors of musical enterprise include few more entertaining freaks than that of Mr Alexander Alexandroff at the Albert Hall. It will be especially relished by those who know that London is a city of high schools for girls, and how on prize distribution day, every half-year, the British parent attends school to be entertained by a performance of the overture to Masaniello, or perhaps, in establishments where taste is severe, the overture to Egmont, played on innumerable pianofortes by his daughters, two to each instrument. M. Alexandroff's idea of engaging fifty young ladies and twentyfour pianofortes to go through this characteristically British performance, and offering it to London as Russian national music, has a certain not unattractive *naïveté* about it. It may well be, of course, that they do this sort of thing in Russia, where the education of women greatly flourishes. But let not M. Alexandroff, or any other intelligent foreigner, suppose for a moment that we do not do it in England. It is a product of the ladies' school, and no nation can boast a monopoly of it. The effect it produces at Kensington can easily be imagined. Everybody knows what a Brinsmead pianoforte is like—its bright dry sound at the top, as of a sonorous brick struck with the edge of a trowel, its precise touch, and its clear tone in the middle and bass. Everybody knows also what a dashing young lady pianist is. Imagine a Brinsmead pianoforte standing to others in the relation of the Albert Hall to the Court Theatre, with two proportionately magnified young ladies playing a duet on it, and you have imagined this speciality "as performed at St Petersburg and Moscow." The public are taking to it amazingly, and it is worthy the attention of those students of instrumentation who look forward to the realization of Berlioz's dream of an orchestra of 467 players, thirty of them pianists. And it must be admitted, in favor of Berlioz, that there is more room at present for innovation in orchestras by the addition of instruments of the lyre type than in any other direction.

As to the singers, the natural material is Russian, but the manufacture is French. The men sing with the fervor, the *vibrato*, and the ruthless and continual slurring that MM. Faure, Maurel, Lassalle, and others have tried for years to make us like, and which we are no doubt often ashamed to confess that we do not like. That, however, is not Russia's fault; and Mr Michael Vinogradoff, for instance, deserves to be acknowledged as a very accomplished and effective singer of his school, with a fine voice. But magnanimity has its limits, even towards the French school; and Mlle Veber's *vibrato* oversteps those limits. She is by no means without expression and artistic feeling; but a lady whose notes are a chain of imperfect shakes is out of court in England. Madame Olga Pouskowa's powerful contralto voice makes everyone in the vast auditorium both feel and hear it. She sings a vocal waltz which, for its combination of triviality with Oriental passion, might have been composed in Maida-vale. The tenor, M. Pavel Bogatyrioff, finds the Albert Hall rather large for his voice. Mr Alexander Laroff is another operatic baritone in the French manner. The choir is not bad; and the orchestra is very good, especially in Glinka's Kamarinskaja, which we have all learned by heart at the Richter concerts. The omissions and delays which called forth so many complaints at the first performance were all remedied last night; and Mr Alexandroff may now fairly claim public support for his enterprise, in spite of the somewhat hackneyed character of some of his novelties.

HOW TO BECOME A MUSICAL CRITIC

MUSICAL MEMS: BY THE STAR'S OWN CAPTIOUS CRITIC

(*The Star*, 15 *February* 1889)

The other evening, at the London Symphony Concert, I had an idea—an invaluable idea. The first movement of the Eroica symphony was being played; but, as usual, it was going haphazard. The band had not really studied it with the conductor; and the conductor was taking his chance with the band. This was nobody's fault; it was caused by the customary length of the program, and the cost of rehearsals relatively to the sum of the payments for admission to St James's Hall. To the orchestral player, as to other men, time is money, and money is livelihood. If he is to devote several days to a thorough study with Mr Henschel of the Eroica—not to mention the other half-dozen items in the program—he must be paid for it. But the hall will not hold money enough. So what is to be done pending the erection of a new hall, with a magnificent orchestra endowed by the County Council, from a poll tax on amateur tenors? Evidently, either put up with scratch performances or else shorten the programs. Now, by this time we all know the Eroica symphony as well as we know Hamlet or Macbeth; and I, for one, am tired of scratch performances of it.

The best rehearsed dramatic companies (this is not a digression: the idea is coming) are those itinerant ones which repeat the same performance half-a-dozen times a day before successive audiences. Why should not Mr Henschel take a hint from them? On Tuesday last he might have dropped the latter half of his program, and concentrated his preparation on the Lohengrin prelude, the song, and the symphony, which are quite as much as a large crowd (even with improved ventilation and electric light) can take in at a time. Then, with the prices reduced to three and ninepence, two shillings, one shilling, and sixpence, he should have begun at eight o'clock instead of half-past. At a few minutes past nine the concert would have been over. Then clear the room, and begin again before a fresh audience at a quarter to ten, finishing at eleven. To this plan there are absolutely no drawbacks. It would not involve the hiring of a single additional assistant or artist, and the cost of the room would remain the same. The public would hear a well-rehearsed performance of just the right length, for half what they now pay for a tedious scratch affair. The suburban amateurs would come to the first concert and get away by early trains in excellent time; the late diners and late risers would patronize the second concert. Above all, the sixpenny admission would bring in the enormous class of patient and serious people with a love for art, who cannot afford a shilling for a concert.

Who is this that, after taking it upon himself to tell me how old Mr Lazarus is, adds that wind instruments are injurious to the player's health? I deny that statement flatly. It is so far from being true that the only difficulty is to restrain enthusiasts from prescribing the trombone for all the diseases under the sun. It has been seriously declared that the workmen of the celebrated firm of Courtois of Paris—a name familiar to all *virtuosos* of the cornet—enjoy immunity not only from affections of the lungs, but from cholera and smallpox. They all, it would seem, die of old age, at a hundred and upwards, breathing their last into an ophicleide. I have often wondered myself why the waits do not die of exposure at Christmas. Everybody wishes they would; but they do not seem even to catch cold—at least I never saw a wait with a cold. There must be something in it.

However, there are two sides to this question. The physical effects of artistic activity, especially musical activity, have never been explained. It is quite certain that although the practice of the finest artists is beneficial to them, yet it is possible to sing, act, or play an instrument with demoralizing and even fatal results. Violent and impatient people, who try to overcome difficulties by force, always come to grief. When you begin to sing, or to play a wind instrument, you have to bring into voluntary action muscles of the throat and lips which are weak and involuntary because you have never used them before. However futile and ridiculous your first attempts may be in consequence, you must "suffer it up" in patience and hope. It is from the people who are in too great a hurry that we get the young lady who lost her voice by singing too often (though she never, for the life of her, could venture upon as much vocal exercise in a week as a good artist gets through with pleasure and benefit in a day), as well as the man who lost his teeth and got hæmorrhage of the lungs by playing the French horn. Further, it is to be carefully remembered that Art pursued for the sake of excitement would be as mischievous as drinking or gambling, if there were as few obstacles to immoderate indulgence in it.

I am a member of the Wagner Society, and am therefore ready to roll its log at all times, but I do not think I shall contribute to its journal, the Meister. I can stand a reasonable degree of editing, but not even from the all but omniscient editor of The Star would I bear a series of footnotes contradicting every one of my opinions. If the Meisterful method were introduced at Stonecutter-street, my criticisms would appear in this wise:

On Tuesday last a numerous and crowded audience were attracted to St James's Hall by the announcement that Miss Pauline Cramer would sing Isolde's death song, that most moving piece of music ever written. (Note by ED.—Surely our gifted contributor has forgotten Let Erin remember the days of old, in making this sweeping statement.) It is unquestionably the greatest of Wagner's works, and is far superior to the compositions of his earlier period. (We agree, on the whole; but would point out that both in his Tannhäuser March and in his well-known William Tell overture, Wagner has attained a more engaging rhythmic emphasis, and, at least, equal sweetness of melody.—ED.) Those who heard Miss Cramer's performance must have forgotten for the moment all previous experiences of the kind. (Has our critic ever heard Miss Bellwood's rendering of What cheer, Ria? If so, we can hardly let this statement pass without a protest.—ED.) And so on.

As to the recital of Tristan und Isolde at the Portman Rooms, with pianoforte accompaniment, it was, of course, a terribly shorn and meagre affair in the absence of an orchestra. But such performances are much better than no performances at all. I hear rumors of following up Tristan with the entire Ring. If this comes off, Mr Armbruster must devote all his energy in the first instance to securing the intelligibility of the performance. Unless the audience hear and understand every word, five-sixths of the Ring will be voted a senseless bore. The singers should read their lines together without music, as if they were rehearsing an ordinary drama. If they cannot do this tolerably well, they will never make anything of the music. I do not believe that any person who heard Tristan for the first time at the Portman Rooms without the assistance of a libretto could have passed the most superficial examination as to what the poem was about.

The paragraphs provoked by the revival of L'Etoile du Nord by Mr Carl Rosa in the provinces prove how soon the lapse of years turns a stale opera into a novelty. I have not seen the new performance, but I am certain that it is not a perfect one, for the simple reason that perfect operatic representations are still economically impossible in this country, the result not being worth the trouble. Besides, Meyerbeer's works are so long that they are always mercilessly cut up for performance; and Mr Carl Rosa is one of the old cutting school of managers whom Wagner so righteously denounced. One of the very worst cuts I can remember was the excision from the prelude to the second act of Lohengrin of the burst of music from the palace. This was at a Carl Rosa performance at Drury Lane, conducted by Mr Randegger. If we only had a few thoroughly vindictive critics, who would never let a manager hear the last of an outrage of this sort, we should bring the opera houses to their senses in half a season. The critic is the policeman of the opera. Unfortunately, sheep make bad policemen.

It has been hinted to me that the responsibilities of The Star are already sufficiently heavy without the addition of an anonymous column of criticism which the unique descriptive genius of the sub-editor has led him to label "captious." My colleague Musigena [E. Belfort Bax] also declares that he goes in bodily fear of being mistaken for me. For my own part I am against anonymous criticism, and therefore sign my name and title in full without hesitation. The di Bassettos were known to Mozart, and were of service to him in the production of several of his works. The title was created in 1770. We are a branch of the Reed family, but I have never been in Scotland in my life. All complimentary tickets, invitations, and bribes meant specially for me should be addressed to the care of The Star.

Corno di Bassetto.

THE GRIEG CONCERT

(The Star, 21 *March* 1889; unsigned)

The Grieg concert yesterday afternoon at St James's Hall is an event which the musical world of London may look back upon with considerable pleasure and satisfaction. The Norwegian composer and his wife will also, no doubt, carry back with them the pleasantest recollections of their enthusiastic reception at the hands of a highly appreciative St James's Hall audience. It is, indeed, a rare occurrence to be present at a concert the program of which not only consists wholly of one composer's works, but which is performed by the composer himself and his wife. The concert opened with his Holberg Suite, or "Suite in old style," as it was called on the program. This suite was composed on the occasion of the Holberg Jubilee in 1884, when the Danes and Norwegians celebrated in great style the 200th anniversary of the birth of Ludvig Holberg, the father of the literature of those countries, and who, by the bye, is a townsman of Mr Grieg. The composer has succeeded in reproducing with much fidelity the spirit of those "good old times," and it is almost unnecessary to say that he rendered his own composition in his elegant and attractive manner. The suite has already been performed at one of the Popular Concerts this season, but it was yesterday again received with hearty applause.

Mrs Grieg sang Ragna and Hope, both characteristic of those "melodies of the heart" which have made her husband famous. The more we hear Mrs Grieg the more we are convinced that no one else can sing these songs so feelingly, and do such justice to them, as she. What would not most composers give for such wives, such better halves, to interpret their songs! Mr and Mrs Grieg next played a piano duet, Norwegian Dances (Op. 35). Here again the wife proved herself a valuable partner, and both she and her husband were enthusiastically applauded. In this composition Mr Grieg shews how ingeniously and artistically he contrives to weave the national melodies of his country into his composition.

The event of the day was, however, no doubt, the performance of his Sonata in C minor (Op. 45) for piano and violin. It was an excellent idea to secure the services of the brilliant violinist, Mr Johannes Wolff, for the violin part in this very spirited composition. It is some time since we heard a violinist who displayed so much fire and power of execution. There were moments when we were forcibly reminded of the style of Grieg's great country-man, the late Ole Bull. No virtuoso on the violin can desire a better accompanist than Mr Grieg. Both Mr Grieg and Mr Wolff were rapturously applauded, and had to appear three times in response to the calls of the delighted audience.

Mrs Grieg sang three more songs, With a Water-lily, Margaret's Cradle Song, and The Rosebud. Forced to sing an *encore* she gave Björnson's well-known song *Dagen er oppe* (Day is breaking) in her most spirited and effective style. In conclusion Mr Grieg played three of his piano pieces, Berceuse, a most original and elegant composition, Humoreske, and the well-known Bridal Procession. The last is, undoubtedly, one of Grieg's most characteristic pieces for the piano, but it is necessary to hear the composition played by the composer himself the better to understand its peculiar character.

THE PHILHARMONIC

(The Star, 24 May 1889)

There was a rush at St James's Hall last night to hear the famous Belgian violinist who had made such a sensation at the previous concert. The cheapest seats were crammed long before the concert began, although the heat was so great that violin strings soon began to snap in all directions. In the last movement of the Mendelssohn concerto Ysaye's *chanterelle* went, and he, like Joachim at a previous performance of the same work at the Philharmonic, had to swap fiddles with one of the first violins, whose instrument was certainly not a Stradivarius.

The concert began with Mozart's Figaro overture. If you want to ascertain whether a musician is hopelessly belated, benighted, out of date, and behind his time, ask him how this overture should be played. If he replies, "In three and a half minutes," away with him at once; he is guilty. I am sorry to have to add that Mr Cowen finished inside the three and a half minutes, and, in order to do it, necessarily made all play of artistic feeling impossible. However, the overture, so treated, is undeniably useful to boil eggs by, though I prefer them boiled four minutes myself. After the Figaro came a new symphony by Mr C. Hubert H. Parry. And here I protest against the cruelty of these professional exercises in four mortal movements. I respect Mr Parry; I enjoy his musical essays; I appreciate his liberal views; I know the kindly feelings his pupils at the Royal College have for him. If he would only be content with an overture, I should praise it to the skies sincerely; for I like to hear just one specimen of shipshape professional composition in sonata form occasionally. But I really cannot stand four large doses of it in succession—*Allegro con spirito*, in C; *Andante sostenuto*, in A minor; *Allegro scherzoso* (*scherzoso* indeed!) in F; and *Moderato*, with variations (two repeats in each)—twelve variations, as I am a living man! I hate to be told that "the figure in the first bar should be observed on account of the prominence to which it is destined in the working out." That is exactly why it should *not* be observed by anybody who can get comfortably to sleep like the man who sat next me, or the man who has a Standard to read, like the lady two bars in front of me—I mean two benches. Mr Joseph Bennett, the programist, says of the symphony:—"It has been described by the composer as a 'little' work; *and amateurs may remember that Beethoven used the German equivalent of the same term in connection with his No. 8.*" I leave the world to contemplate those words in silence: no comment of mine shall disturb its inexpressible thoughts.

Ysaÿe disappointed me. His technical skill is prodigious, his tone strong and steady, his effect on the public unquestionable. But he is an unsympathetic player. In the *cadenza* of the concerto he played every phrase so as to make a point; and the audience whispered, "How clever, and how difficult that must be!" But they did not recognize that the phrase was an integral part of the movement—a fragment of the opening theme. Now when Sarasate played the same *cadenza* on Saturday, everybody recognized the reference, and nobody had the feat of execution obtruded on them. It was the same throughout. The spirit of the composition was always missed, and the wonders of the fiddling always insisted on. At last, by dint of having the virtuosity of Ysaÿe thrust down their throats at the point of the bow, the audience burst into exclamations of astonishment at feats for which other violinists neither expect nor receive any special credit. When it came to one of Paganini's studies and Wieniawski's *polonaise*—which were certainly played with consummate dexterity—they were quite enraptured.

For my part I have no hesitation in saying that Ysaÿe's performance was chiefly valuable as a foil to Miss Janotha's playing of Beethoven's G major concerto. Her execution, like his, is exceptionally dexterous; but it is also beautiful, suggestive, poetic. I first heard this young Polish artist at a Philharmonic concert, and she played the G concerto then also. My comment was that here at last was someone who could replace Madame Schumann. The concerto charmed me last night as much as before. Though Miss Janotha occasionally breaks out in waywardnesses and displays of strength, suggestive of possession by a fitful musical demon, yet I know no pianist of her generation whose playing is more sustainedly and nobly beautiful than hers.

Of Herr Carl Meyer I can only say that I should like to hear him sing Tom der Reimer again. Provided you understand German, you will find in his performance the intelligibility and interest of recitation with the charm of song. I noticed that in playing the Jubilee overture the band did not rise when they came to God Save the Queen. They always used to at the Philharmonic. A Home Rule demonstration, I presume.

C. di B.

HOW TO BECOME A MUSICAL CRITIC

BAYREUTH AND BACK

(*The Hawk*, 13 *August* 1889; signed "By Reuter." The editor considered it necessary to explain the pseudonym in a footnote: "The appreciation of this joke lies in the pronunciation of it")

Oh Bayreuth, Bayreuth, valley of humiliation for the smart ones of the world! To think that this Wagner, once the very safest man in Europe to ridicule, should turn out the prime success of the century! To be reduced to a piteous plea that you always admitted that there were some lovely bits in Lohengrin! To know beyond all shifts of self-deception that, when you got your one great chance of discovering the great man of your age, you went the fools among, and made an utter, unmitigated, irretrievable, unspeakable ass of yourself! To humbly and anxiously ask whether there are any tickets left—to pay a pound apiece for them—to crawl, seasick and weary, hundreds of costly miles to that theatre which you so neatly proved to be the crazy whim of a conceited, cacophonous charlatan, there to listen to Tristan and the Meistersinger with the hideous guilt upon you of having once thought Lucia and La Favorita worth a dozen such. This is the sort of thing that takes the starch out of the most bumptious critic.

Yes, the cranks were right after all. And now—now that it is not merely a question of whether he or Offenbach is the more melodious, but of whether he is to be accepted as the Luther of a new Reformation, the Plato of a new philosophy, the Messiah who is really to redeem the fall and lead us back to the garden of Eden, now that the temple is up and the worshipers assembled, now that we are face to face with pretensions for "The Master" in comparison with which the old simple claim to rank as artist and man of genius was a mere joke, dare we pick up our weapons and resume the fight? No, thank you, the fellow is too dangerous. Better call him a man of extraordinary ability as if we had thought so all along, and then lie low and see whether he will really pull off his philosophic and religious venture as he undoubtedly pulled off his musical one, confound him!

You would not catch me talking in this strain if my own withers were wrung. No, I am not confessing my own mistakes; I am only rubbing in the mistakes of others. The first time I ever heard a note of Wagner's music was in my small boy days, when I stumbled upon a military band playing the Tannhäuser march. I will not pretend that I quite rose to the occasion; in fact, I said just what Hector Berlioz said—that it was a plagiarism from the famous theme in Der Freischütz. But a little after this bad beginning I picked up a score of Lohengrin; and before I had taken in ten bars of the prelude I was a confirmed Wagnerite in the sense the term then bore, which committed me to nothing further than greatly relishing Wagner's music. What it commits a man to now, Omniscience only knows. Vegetarianism, the higher Buddhism, Christianity divested of its allegorical trappings (I suspect this is a heterodox variety), belief in a Fall of Man brought about by some cataclysm which starved him into eating flesh, negation of the Will-to-Live and consequent Redemption through compassion excited by suffering (this is the Wagner-Schopenhauer article of faith); all these are but samples of what Wagnerism involves nowadays. The average enthusiast accepts them all unhesitatingly—bar vegetarianism. Buddhism he can stand; he is not particular as to what variety of Christianity he owns to; Schopenhauer is his favorite philosopher; but get through Parsifal without a beefsteak between the second and third acts he will not. Now, as it happens, I am a vegetarian; and I can presume enormously upon that habit of mine, even among the elect. But for an unlucky sense of humor which is continually exposing me to charges of ribaldry, I should have been elected a vice-president of the Wagner Society long ago.

However, these be matters into which this is not the place for a deep dip. The question of the moment is, what is Bayreuth like? Well, it is a genteel little Franconian country town among the hills and fine woods of Bavaria, within two or three hours' rail from Nuremberg. It is not old enough to be venerable, nor new enough to be quite prosaic; and the inhabitants either live in villas on independent incomes or else by taking in oneanother's washing and selling confectionery, scrap books, and photographs. There are plenty of street fountains, a nonsensically old-fashioned monument to a person generally described by vulgar English visitors as "old stick-in-the-mud," a factory chimney, a barrack, a lunatic asylum, a very quaint eighteenth-century opera house, the Wagner Theatre half-way up the hill, and the inevitable *Sieges Turm,* or tower commemorative of 1870-1, quite at the summit, among the pines. Half the main street is the Maximilian-strasse, and the other the Richard Wagnerstrasse. The Master's house is a substantial villa, undistinguishable from other villas except by the famous inscription:—*Hier wo mein Wähnen Frieden fand Wahnfried sei dieses Haus von mir benannt,* and by a *sgraffito* cartoon much in the manner and taste of Mr Armitage, representing Wotan the Wanderer. Behind the Master's house is the Master's grave; for Wagner, as I heard an indignant Englishman exclaim, is "buried in the back garden, sir, like a Newfoundland dog." I shall never be a true Wagnerite after all; for I laughed at this explosion of bourgeois prejudice, whereas any decently susceptible disciple would have recoiled horror-stricken. At certain hours the gate between the Wahnfried do-main and the Hofgarten is left open; and the faithful go in to deposit wreaths on the colossal granite slab which covers the Master's last bed, and to steal ivy leaves as souvenirs. The only other sentimental journey available at Bayreuth is to the cemetery at the country end of the Erlangenstrasse, near the old town, where you see a boulder of unhewn stone on Jean Paul Richter's grave, and an inartistic and useless outhouse which is the mauso-leum of Liszt.

The imagination rather declines to face the notion of life at Bayreuth without Wagner. Walks on the hills through the scented pine woods are always available; but dwellers in the next county to Surrey do not spend twenty pounds to walk in Bavaria when a few shillings would land them at Guildford or Dorking. There are a couple of show places—the Fantaisie to the south-west, and the Eremitage to the east, which give some sort of aim for a couple of excursions, each capable of slaying two or three hours. They are something between a Wicklow glen and an Isle of Wight chine; and the Eremitage has a château with Temple of the Sun, pseudo-Roman bath, dolphins, tritons, and general rococo. On the whole, Bayreuth has to be put up with for Wagner's sake rather than enjoyed for its own. Business begins at the Wagner Theatre at four; but after two the stream of people up the hill is pretty constant, their immediate destination being the restaurant to the right of the theatre, and their immediate object—grub. At a quarter to four a group of men whom you at once recognize as members of the orchestra, as much by a certain air of Brixton or Kentish Town about them as by the trombones and cornets they carry, troop out of the centre door. These, by fearsome blasts, right and left, proclaim that the entertainment is about to begin. In spite of the vile noise they make, they are audible only for a very short distance, partly because they stand under the portico instead of on top of it, partly because brass instruments should be blown quietly and musically if the sound is to travel (always excepting the nothing-if-not-violent bugle). In ten minutes or so it will be time to go into the famous theatre.

You have already bought your playbill in the street for a penny; and you will have to find your own seat among the fifteen hundred in the auditorium. However, this is easy enough, as your ticket directs you to, say, Door No. 2, Left Side. That door delivers you close to the end of the row in which your seat is, and as each corner seat is marked with the highest and lowest number contained in the row, you can, by a little resolute brainwork, find your place for yourself. Once in it, you have a stare round at the theatre. It is republican to begin with; the 1,500 seats are separated by no barrier, no difference in price, no advantages except those of greater or less proximity to the stage. The few state cabins at the back, for kings and millionaires, are the worst places in the house. All this is pleasant; for if you are an aristocrat, you say, "Good! a man can be no more than a gentleman," and if a democrat, you simply snort and say, "Aha!" The wonder is that though this theatre has been known to the public for thirteen years, yet we have during that time run up a little host of playhouses, and never once dreamt of departing from the old cockpit-and-scaffold model. What a capital architectural feature is that series of side wings, each with its pillar and its branch of globes, causing the stage to grow out of the auditorium in the most natural manner! Sh-sh-sh! The lights are lowered. Sit down, everybody. Why do not the ladies take off their hats as requested by placard? Ah, why indeed? Now the lights are almost out; there is a dead silence; and the first strain of the prelude comes mystically from the invisible orchestra. And so on. When the act is over, there is a pause of an hour for late afternoon tea. After the second act comes a similar pause for supper. Thus do these ascetics emulate the Buddha.

It is too late in the day to describe the three lyric plays now being repeated at Bayreuth. Tristan—would you believe it?— is thirty years old. Die Meistersinger will be twentytwo next October. Certainly, Parsifal is quite a novelty—only ten years and a half; but Parsifal is not an affair to be sketched in a few lines. All that I shall say here, then, is that though the accounts of the tremendous effect they produce in the Wagner Theatre are not exaggerated, yet the process of getting tremendously affected is by no means a blissful one. I am a seasoned Wagnerian; and there is no veil of strangeness between me and the ocean of melody, with all its cross-currents of beautiful and expressive themes, in Die Meistersinger. But at Bayreuth, after the third act, I had just energy enough to go home to my bed, instead of lying down on the hillside and having twelve hours' sleep *al fresco* there and then. That third act, though conducted by Hans Richter, who is no sluggard, lasts two hours; and the strain on the attention, concentrated as it is by the peculiarities of the theatre, is enormous. Consider, too, that the singers are not like De Reszke or Lassalle, refreshing to listen to. They are all veterans—hale and respectable veterans, irreproachably competent, with thick voices and intelligent declamation; but they are terribly dry. You are driven for a reviving draught of beauty of sound to the orchestra. Having heard that before, you are thrown back on the inner interest of the poem, and so forced to renew your grip with a closer and closer application on the very thing you sought a moment's relief from. When it is over you are glad you went through with it, and are even willing to face it again; but you recognize that you have achieved edification by a great feat of endurance, and that your holiday, your enjoyment, your relaxation will come when the work of witnessing the performances is finished, and you are returning home down the Rhine.

Parsifal, in spite of its prolonged and solemn ritual, is less fatiguing than the Meistersinger, although to the Philistine it is a greater bore; for the Meistersinger, long as it is, is bustling, whilst the shorter Parsifal is slow and serious. Not that the boredom saves any Philistine from the spell of the work; the merest scoffer is impressed, and would not unsee it, even if he could get his sovereign back at the same time. Tristan neither fatigues nor bores, except for a while at the end of the second act, if King Mark is dull, and during the first half of the third if the tenor is uninteresting. The rest is one transport; deafness and impotence combined could alone resist it; you come away hopelessly spoiled for Roméo et Juliette after it.

As to the peculiar merits of the Bayreuth mode of performance, they are simply the direct results of scrupulous reverence for Wagner, thorough study, and reasonable care. What has been said lately about the inferiority of the staging to that at the Lyceum is quite true. Admirable as the orchestra is, we can beat it in London as certainly as we can build the theatre the moment we are wise enough to see that it is worth our while. And the sooner the better, say I, for the sake of our English millions to whom Bayreuth is as inaccessible as the North Pole.

THE OPERA SEASON

(Scottish Art Review, September 1889)

It is grim work watching an opera season in London. In his stall sits the English gentleman in evening dress, taking on trust his guinea's-worth of guaranteed Mozart or Wagner as ignorantly as a ploughman takes Cibber or Garrick on trust as genuine Shakespear. He is walled in with a hotly oppressive crimson pigeon-house of private boxes, filled with countless women in white, glittering and chattering, shaking diamonds and flapping fans. Over his head is a monstrous chandelier, hanging by a huge chain, which may snap, he thinks, at any moment; and clustered about it, on the roof of the crimson pigeon-house, swelters a crowd representing the general public, at half-a-crown and five shillings a head. On the stage an opera tumbles along with cuts here and cuts there, the detail of the action sometimes slurred, sometimes omitted, never simultaneous with its indication in the orchestra; the singers' opportunities for display are strung together in no relation more organic than that between the feats in a circus; and the prompter is working desperately to make up for insufficient rehearsal and want of forethought. This is the ordinary "subscription night," upon which the subscriber gets for his money the most perfunctory Traviata or Trovatore that the management can venture upon without loss of prestige or flagrant breach of faith. There is little risk at the hands of the critics; for the standard of excellence is very low; and those who are disposed to screw it up, having once exhausted the possible variations on the same complaint, drop the subject lest they should repeat themselves and seem barren. Besides, a musical critic is too busy during the season to pay much attention to ordinary subscription-night performances, even were his editor able to spare space. Moreover, the shortcomings are everybody's fault: that is, nobody's fault. If Mr Augustus Harris were asked why his melodramas at Drury Lane are so much better done than his operas at Covent Garden, he would reply— if his startled *amour-propre* did not hide the right answer from him—that if he had to put on a different melodrama every night, the shortcomings of Covent Garden would immediately appear at Drury Lane.

The truth of this will be disputed by no one who remembers what "stock company" acting was. The operatic artist of today is a "stock company" artist. He calls himself a *primo tenore* or a *basso cantante* instead of a juvenile lead or a first old man; but the difference is only technical. Just as the stock actors could take any part in their line at short notice by learning or recalling the lines, and applying their stage habits to the action; so within one week do the Covent Garden artists contrive to get through Lohengrin, La Traviata, La Sonnambula, Aïda, and Le Nozze di Figaro. And just as the old stock company performances as wholes had absolutely no artistic quality, and never produced even a momentary illusion except on the merest novices; so these operatic representations are ineffective beyond endurance by musicians of independent and original culture. The public, however, is still in its novitiate, and has always resented the protests of such critics as Schumann, Berlioz, and Wagner, much as a schoolboy resents his father's impatience of the farce and reluctance to wait for the harlequinade. Mere protest against inferior work never educates the public. The only way to make them intolerant of bad work is to shew them better. It was the traveling company with its repertory of one thoroughly mastered play that drove the stock companies from our provincial theatres, not because the actors were individually cleverer than the members of the stock companies, but because their collective performance had a completeness and produced an illusion, after one experience of which the scratch performances of the stock companies could no longer be endured. The stock company accordingly vanished before the "tour." The change has been described, by advocates of the old-fashioned training, as a triumph of superior economic over superior artistic organization; but the slightest analysis of the economic position will shew that the case was exactly the reverse, since the stationary companies saved, without set-off, the traveling expenses which were so heavy an item in the cost of production of the tour.

This season a remarkable event sounded an alarm for stock companyism in opera. An Italian company came to London with one opera—Verdi's Otello—and astonished the frequenters of Covent Garden by the force and homogeneity of the impression made by its performance. The grip of the drama on the audience, the identification of the artists with their parts, the precision of execution, the perfect balance of the forces in action, produced an effect which, for the first time, justified the claims of Italian opera to rank as a form of serious drama united to purposeful music. The usual romantic explanations of this success were freely offered—Italian aptitude, great artists, La Scala, Wagnerian methods, and so on; but thorough preparation was the real secret. The belief in Italian aptitude for lyric drama is a superstition from the Puritani period. Ever since opera began to assume a really dramatic character the Italian singer has lost his place on the stage, and has even come to be recognized as the least teachable and intelligent member of his profession. In the particular case in question there were three parts requiring special artistic excellence for their due presentation. One of them was played by M. Maurel, a Frenchman, who has repeatedly appeared at Covent Garden in leading parts without ever producing a tithe of the effect made by his Iago at the Lyceum. Another, that of Desdemona, was taken by an Italian, who was the one failure of the representation: her artificial stage business, false pathos, and wavering voice being tolerated for the sake of the whole of which her performance was the least worthy part. In that of Otello himself, there was an Italian, Tamagno, undoubtedly a quite exceptional artist, whose voice seems to have reached the upper part of the theatre with overwhelming power, though to others some of the current descriptions of its volume seemed hyperbolical. His voice, at any rate, had not the pure noble tone, nor the sweetly sensuous, nor even the ordinary thick manly quality of the robust tenor: it was nasal, shrill, vehement, sometimes fierce, sometimes plaintive, always peculiar and original. Imitation of Tamagno has ruined many a tenor, and will probably ruin many more; but the desire to produce such an effect as he did with *Addio, sante memorie!* is intelligible to anyone who rightly understands the range of an Italian tenor's ambition. Yet it was certainly not to hear *Addio, sante memorie!* that the audiences filled the Lyceum night after night during the dog-days: it was to hear Otello; and there was always a protest against the inevitable *encore* on the ground of interruption to the drama. Faccio, the conductor, understands Verdi's music as Richter understands Wagner's. He accompanies with perfect judgment, as he conducts with perfect authority. Like the Bayreuth conductors, and unlike the Covent Garden ones, he had only one opera to think about; and the result was a mastery of it quite as complete as Hermann Levi's of Parsifal or Felix Mottl's of Tristan und Isolde. In amplitude and richness of sonority, beauty of tone, delicacy of execution, and distinction of style, the Milan orchestra might justly have claimed precedence of Bayreuth if the tasks of the two had been at all fairly comparable in point of difficulty.

The Otello enterprise was an enormously expensive one, yet we are told that no loss was suffered by the managers. There is hope, then, that the blow which its artistic success dealt to the subscription-night opera of fashion may prove speedily mortal. It has already raised the standard of operatic acting. Ordinarily, the opera singer is satisfied if he can catch some notion of the incidents which come into his own stage business, and of the situations in which he himself figures; and he is usually inoculated with some tradition as to certain characters, as, for instance, that Mephistopheles is a sardonic smiler and *poseur*, Don Giovanni a swaggering libertine. When these vague notions modify his conventional attitudinizing to the extent of giving it an air of energy and purpose, and even suggesting that he knows the story which the opera tells, and is taking some steps to make it clear to the audience, he shines out as comparatively an actor, and is gravely commended by the newspapers in terms which dramatic critics reserve for Mr Irving and Mr Jefferson, Salvini and Coquelin. Thus, at Covent Garden this season, a Monsieur F. d'Andrade made an indifferent De Nevers and a bad Don Giovanni, but displayed some smartness and intelligent interest in his business, and played with much natural expression and sincerity as Telramond in Lohengrin. He was at first acclaimed as a new histrionic genius. But after Maurel's Iago, nothing more was said of d'Andrade. Maurel played like a man who had read Shakespear and had conceived an Iago with which he was thoroughly preoccupied. Having repeated the impersonation for a long period without interruption or distraction, he was practiced in identifying himself with it—had got into the skin of it, as the phrase goes. He had, too, emancipated himself from the prompter, and thus left himself nothing to think about but Iago. The result was that he made a considerable reputation as an actor by the ordinary standard, whereas formerly at Covent Garden, where he was expected to play Peter the Great, Valentine, Telramond, Hoel, and Don Juan within a fortnight, he was only an actor by courtesy, and by contrast with colleagues who were still more superficial than he. Now he is an actor on the same plane as Mr Edwin Booth, and may claim to be one of the notable Iagos of his time. It is a strong exaggeration to speak of him as the best Iago on the stage; for he is demonstrative and pretentious to a degree that would hardly pass without a smile at the Lyceum in winter; and the raillery of the critic who described his Iago as "twopence colored" was not without point. But it was none the less a new departure of the most hopeful kind in operatic acting.

At Covent Garden Mr Harris kept up the reputation of his management by the production of some newly-prepared and carefully-rehearsed works. Bizet's Pearl Fishers was not worth the trouble. The scale of the performance was too large; the staging was stupidly unimaginative; and Talazac, the Opéra Comique tenor, whose former appearance in London at the Gaiety Theatre with Miss Van Zandt seemed to be quite forgotten, did not interest the public. He is now a short, stout man, with an odd air of always being in the way on the stage, and nothing attractive in his singing except the power of sustaining for a long time a sweet but rather wheezy *mezza voce*. Gounod's Roméo et Juliette, which followed after the usual padding of ordinary subscription-night performances, was produced on the ground, artistically quite irrelevant, that Madame Patti, having recently appeared as Juliette in Paris, had given the opera a valuable advertisement. As a "grand opera" it has never been satisfactory. Its delicate music requires an exquisite tenderness of handling which would be lost in Covent Garden; and the great length of the work, which, except the fiery third act, is in the same vein throughout, makes it tedious in spite of the beauty of the music. The Shakespearean original itself seldom passes without an occasional yawn; but if four of the acts had been rewritten by Lamartine we should go fast asleep over it, though the result would have been a perfect literary analogue to Gounod's opera, enjoyable only under conditions more favorable to contemplative serenity than a fashionable opera house affords.

A more important event was the production of Die Meistersinger, or as much of it as there was time for between half-past seven and a quarter-past twelve. In neither of these sufficiently arduous achievements was there any drawback that can justly be laid to the charge of the management. The preparation was elaborate and thorough, the mounting costly even to extravagance. Unfortunately the all-important functions of the conductor, with whom it lies to make much or little of the opportunities provided by managerial expenditure, were not quite adequately discharged. Signor Mancinelli's industry was most praiseworthy; he has his work at heart—which is a hundred points in his favor; and he is fairly competent for something more than the ordinary work of a conductor of Italian opera. But in dealing with works in which violent musical crises have to be marshaled with vigor and coolness—Les Huguenots, for instance—he loses control; and he has never succeeded in impressing on his players that distinction of style which a band always receives from a fine conductor. In Die Meistersinger the performance of the overture was the worst on record in London, and in the broader and more complex sections throughout the instrumental effect was noisy and confused. The close comparison with Richter at St James's Hall and Faccio at the Lyceum brought all these shortcomings into mercilessly strong relief. A conductor of Richter's calibre would soon win for Covent Garden the artistic rank which its wealth of artistic material renders possible. A strong chief is wanted there all the more because the string band is largely manned by young and very rough players, to whose artistic conscience Signor Mancinelli has not been able to penetrate.

The main strength of the company has been, as usual, vocal, though there has been no attempt to "star" on important occasions. The cleverness of Madame Melba and Miss Russell, remarkable in degree, is commonplace in quality; and Miss Macintyre, though her position is now an assured one, is still too young and amateurish to make it possible to predict whether she will be developed by her internal artistic instinct, or spoiled by her early prima-donnaship. Madame Albani's "heavy lead" was challenged only by Madame Toni Schläger (from Vienna), who, as Valentine, looked like a magnificent woman in deep distress, and sang like a great singer who had for the moment forgotten how to sing. She certainly made her mark; but it is beyond human wit to say whether she failed or succeeded. Though she is a much more tragic person than Madame Marie Roze, she nevertheless resembles her in a curious combination of unusual ability and endowment with a sort of helpless beauty that disarms criticism of her want of skill. The men, on the whole, distinguished themselves more than the women. M. Jean de Reszke's inbred refinement of bearing, the charm of his voice,

and his occasionally inspired declamation made him an ideal
Romeo. M. Lassalle's Sachs far surpassed all his previous achievements: if Theodor Reichmann could only sing the part with
Lassalle's voice, we should have an ideal Mastersinger. As San
Bris in the unfortunate performance of Les Huguenots which
brought forward Madame Schläger, he made much less effect
than Edouard de Reszke, who played it last year, but relinquished
it this time to take the part of Marcel, which proved too low for
his voice, and considerably overtaxed his histrionic intelligence.
The management was at a loss for a heavy basso more than once,
the Commendatore in Don Giovanni coming heavily to grief in
the hands of Signor di Vaschetti, whose failing is a propensity
to sing startling wrong notes. Montariol was not very interesting
as a first tenor; but he was most serviceable as David and Tybalt,
concerning which some ridicule was tactlessly brought on him
by repeated announcements that in condescending to such parts
he was sacrificing his dignity "to oblige the management." The
performance of Roméo et Juliette in the original French was the
most important step in advance made during the season. It
pleased everybody, whereas the perversion of Die Meistersinger
into Italian pleased nobody, except perhaps the lazier members
of the chorus.

Mr Mapleson's attempt at Her Majesty's to interest the public
with the old Italian repertory for its own sake—he had no artists
of special note—was a decisive failure. The Bayreuth performances pointed the moral of this failure, and drove home the
lesson of the Lyceum.

WAGNER IN BAYREUTH

(*The English Illustrated Magazine, October* 1889. An abridged
    version, under the title "Bayreuth Denying the Master,"
    appeared in *The Transatlantic*, Boston, 1 *November* 1889)

There are many reasons for going to Bayreuth to see the
Wagner Festival plays. Curiosity, for instance, or love of music,
or hero-worship of Wagner, or adept Wagnerism—a much more
complicated business—or a desire to see and be seen in a vortex

of culture. But a few of us go to Bayreuth because it is a capital stick to beat a dog with. He who has once been there can crush all admirers of Die Meistersinger at Covent Garden with—"Ah, you should see it at Bayreuth," or, if the occasion be the Parsifal prelude at a Richter concert, "Have you heard Levi conduct it at Bayreuth?" And when the answer comes sorrowfully in the negative, the delinquent is made to feel that in that case he does not know what Parsifal is, and that the Bayreuth tourist does. These little triumphs are indulged in without the slightest re- morse on the score of Richter's great superiority to Herr Levi as a Wagnerian conductor, and of the fact that a performance of the Parsifal prelude by a London orchestra under his direction is often much better worth a trip from Bayreuth to London than a performance by a German orchestra under Levi is ever worth a trip from London to Bayreuth. It is not in human nature to be honest in these matters—at least not yet.

Those who have never been in Germany, and cannot afford to go thither, will not be sorry when the inevitable revolt of English Wagnerism against Bayreuth breaks out; and the sooner they are gratified, the better. Ever since the death of Beethoven, the champions of Music have been desperately fighting to obtain a full hearing for her in spite of professorship, pedantry, super- stition, literary men's acquiescent reports of concerts, and butcherly stage management—all trading on public ignorance and diffidence. Wagner, the greatest of these champions, did not fight for his own hand alone, but for Mozart, Beethoven, and Weber as well. All authority was opposed to him until he made his own paramount. Mendelssohn was against him at a time when to assert that Mendelssohn's opinion was of less weight than his seemed as monstrous as it would seem today to deny it. People do not discriminate in music as much as they do in other arts. They can see that Lord Tennyson is hardly the man to say the deepest word about Goethe, or Sir Frederick Leighton about Michael Angelo; but Mendelssohn's opinion about Beethoven was accepted as final, since the composer of Elijah must evidently know all about music. In England, since not only Mendelssohn, but Costa, the Philharmonic Society, The Times, and The Athenæum were satisfied when they had dried Mozart into a trivial musical box, when the overture to Le Nozze di Figaro was finished within three and a half minutes, when the beautiful trio of Beethoven's Eighth Symphony was made a mere practical joke on the violoncellists, when the famous theme in the Freischütz was played exactly in the style of the popular second subject in the Masaniello overture, the public could only conclude that these must be the classical ways of conducting, and that dulness was a necessary part of the classicism. Wagner did not succeed in putting dulness out of countenance until he became a classic himself. And now that he is a classic, who is to do for him what he did for his predecessors? For he is not going to escape their fate. The "poor and pretentious pietism" which he complained of as "shutting out every breath of fresh air from the musical atmosphere," is closing round his own music. At Bayreuth, where the Master's widow, it is said, sits in the wing as the jealous guardian of the traditions of his own personal direction, there is already a perceptible numbness—the symptom of paralysis.

The London branch of the Wagner Society, unobservant of this danger signal, seems to have come to the conclusion that the best thing it can do for its cause is to support Bayreuth. It has not yet dawned on it that the traditional way of playing Tristan und Isolde will, in the common course of mortality, inevitably come to what the traditional way of playing Mozart's G minor symphony had come to when Wagner heard Lachner conduct it; or, to take instances which appeal to our own experience, what Don Giovanni came to be under Costa in his later days, or what the C minor symphony is today at a Philharmonic concert. The law of traditional performances is, "Do what was done last time": the law of all living and fruitful performance is, "Obey the innermost impulse which the music gives, and obey it to the most exhaustive satisfaction." And as that impulse is never, in a fertile artistic nature, the impulse to do what was done last time, the two laws are incompatible, being virtually laws respectively of death and life in art. Bayreuth has chosen the law of death. Its boast is that it alone knows what was done last time, and that therefore it alone has the pure and complete tradition—or, as I prefer to put it, that it alone is in a position to strangle Wagner's lyric dramas note by note, bar by bar, *nuance* by *nuance*. It is in vain for Bayreuth to contend that by faithfully doing what was done last time it arrives at an exact phonograph of what was done the first time, when Wagner was alive, present, and approving. The difference consists just in this, that Wagner is now dead, absent, and indifferent. The powerful, magnetic personality, with all the tension it maintained, is gone; and no manipulation of the dead hand on the keys can ever reproduce the living touch. Even if such reproduction were possible, who, outside Bayreuth, would be imposed on by the shallow assumption that the Bayreuth performances fulfilled Wagner's whole desire? We can well believe that in justice to those who so loyally helped him, he professed himself satisfied when the most that could be had been done—nay, that after the desperate makeshifts with which he had had to put up in his long theatrical experience, he was genuinely delighted to find that so much was possible. But the unwieldy toy dragon, emitting its puff of steam when its mouth opened, about as impressively as a mechanical doll says "Mamma": did that realize the poet's vision of Fafner? And the trees which walk off the stage in Parsifal: can the poorest imagination see nothing better by the light of Wagner's stage direction in the score than that? Is the gaudy ballet and unspeakable flower garden in the second act to be the final interpretation of the visionary bowers of Klingsor? The Philistine cockney laughs at these provincial conceits, and recommends Bayreuth to send for Mr Irving, Mr Hare, Mr Wilson Barrett, or Mr Augustus Harris to set the stage to rights. It is extremely likely that when A Midsummer Night's Dream was first produced, Shakespear complimented the stage manager, tipped the carpenters, patted Puck on the head, shook hands with Oberon, and wondered that the make-believe was no worse; but even if this were an established historical fact, no sane manager would therefore attempt to reproduce the Elizabethan *mise en scène* on the ground that it had fulfilled Shakespear's design. Yet if we had had a Shakespear theatre on foot since the seventeenth century, conducted on the Bayreuth plan, that is the very absurdity in which tradition would by this time have landed us.[1]

[1] The *Comédie Française*, in performing the plays of Molière, still keeps as closely as possible to the stage arrangements of the author's own time. Even in this

Tradition in scenery and stage management is, however, plausible in comparison with tradition in acting, singing, and playing. If Wagner had been able to say of any scene, "I am satisfied," meaning, not "I am satisfied that nothing better can be done for me; and I am heartily grateful to you—the painter—for having done more than I had hoped for," but "This is what I saw in my mind's eye when I wrote my poem," then successive scene manufacturers might mechanically copy the painting from cloth to cloth with sufficient accuracy to fix at least a good copy of the original scene for posterity to look at with new eyes and altered minds. At any rate the new cloth would not rebel, since it could be woven and cut at will to the pattern of the old picture. But when it is further sought to reproduce the old figures with new persons, then comes to light the absurdity of playing Procrustes with a dramatic representation. I remember once laughing at a provincial Iago who pointed the words "Trifles light as air," by twitching his handkerchief into space much as street hawkers now twitch the toy parachute made fashionable by Mr Baldwin. An experienced theatrical acquaintance rebuked me, assuring me that the actor was right, because he had been accustomed to rehearse the part for Charles Kean, and therefore had learnt every step, gesture, and inflection of that eminent tragedian's play. Unfortunately, he was not Charles Kean: consequently Charles Kean's play no more fitted him than Charles Kean's clothes. His Iago was a ridiculous misfit, even from his own shallow view of acting as a mere external affectation. In the old provincial stock companies, most of which have by this time died the death they richly deserved, there was often to be found an old lady who played Lady Macbeth when the star Shakespearean actor came his usual round. She played it exactly as Mrs Siddons played it, with the important difference that, as she was not Mrs Siddons, the way which was the right way for Mrs Siddons was the wrong way for her. Thoroughly sophisticated theatre fanciers carried the fool's logic of tradition to the

instance, where the tradition has the excuse of being the most trustworthy record of the manners of the period represented, the effect on the plays themselves is sufficiently depressing; and its reaction on the French stage at large is a main factor of the immense superiority of English acting, undrilled and inartistic as our novices are, to French. [Shaw's note.]

extremity of admiring these performances. But of those with natural appetites, the young laughed and the old yawned. Consideration of these cases suggests the question whether we are to be made [to] laugh and yawn at Bayreuth by a line of mock Maternas and sham Maltens? If not, what can Bayreuth do that cannot be done as well elsewhere—that cannot be done much more conveniently for Englishmen in England? If Bayreuth repudiates tradition, there is no mortal reason why we should go so far to hear Wagner's lyric dramas. If it clings to it, then that is the strongest possible reason for avoiding it. Every fresh representation of Parsifal (for example) should be an original artistic creation, and not an imitation of the last one. The proper document to place in the hands of the artists is the complete work. Let the scene-painter paint the scenes he sees in the poem. Let the conductor express with his orchestra what the score expresses to him. Let the tenor do after the nature of that part of himself which he recognizes in Parsifal; and let the *prima donna* similarly realize herself as Kundry. The true Wagner Theatre is that in which this shall be done, though it stand on Primrose Hill or in California. And wherever the traditional method is substituted, there Wagner is not. The conclusion that the Bayreuth theatre cannot remain the true Wagner Theatre is obvious. The whole place reeks of tradition—boasts of it—bases its claims to fitness upon it. Frau Cosima Wagner, who has no function to perform except the illegitimate one of chief remembrancer, sits on guard there. When the veterans of 1876 retire, Wagner will be in the condition of Titurel in the third act of Parsifal.

It would be too much to declare that the true Wagner Theatre will arise in England; but it is certain that the true English Wagner Theatre will arise there. The sooner we devote our money and energy to making Wagner's music live in England instead of expensively embalming its corpse in Bavaria, the better for English art in all its branches. Bayreuth is supported at present partly because there is about the journey thither a certain romance of pilgrimage which may be summarily dismissed as the effect of the bad middle-class habit of cheap self-culture by novel reading; partly by a conviction that we could never do the lyric dramas at home as well as they are done at Bayreuth. This, if it were well founded, would be a conclusive reason for continuing to support Bayreuth. But Parsifal can be done not merely as well in London as in Bayreuth, but better. A picked London orchestra could, after half-a-dozen rehearsals under a competent conductor, put Herr Levi and the Bayreuth band in the second place. Our superiority in the art of stage presentation is not disputed, even by those who omit Mr Herkomer and the Bushey theatre from the account. There remain the questions of the theatre and the singers.

The difference between the Wagner Theatre at Bayreuth and an ordinary cockpit-and-scaffolding theatre is in the auditorium, and not in the stage, which is what any large stage here would be were space as cheap in London as in the Fichtelgebirge. The top of the partition between the orchestra and the seats curves over hoodwise towards the footlights, hiding the players and conductor from the audience. The instruments are not stretched in a thin horizontal line with the trombones at the extreme right of the conductor, and the drums at his extreme left: they are grouped as at an orchestral concert: first violins to the left; seconds to the right; basses flanking on both sides; wood wind in the middle, opposite the conductor; brass and percussion behind the wood wind and under the stage. From the orchestra the auditorium widens; and the floor ascends from row to row as in a lecture theatre, the rows being curved, but so slightly that the room seems rectilinear. There are no balconies or galleries, the whole audience being seated on the cross benches in numbered stalls, with hinged cane seats of comfortable size, in plain strong wooden frames without any upholstery. The most striking architectural feature is the series of short transverse walls with pillars and lamps, apparently suggested by the old-fashioned stage side wing. Each of these wings extends from the side of the room to the edge of the stalls. Between the wings are the doors; and as each ticket is marked with the number not only of the seat, but of the nearest door to it, the holders find their places for themselves without the intervention of attendants. Playbills are bought for a penny in the town, or in the street on the way to the theatre. The wall at the back contains a row of *loggie* for royal personages and others who wish to sit apart. Above these state cabins there is a crow's nest which is the nearest thing to a gallery in the theatre; but the conditions of admission are not stated. The prevailing color of the house is a light dun, as of cream color a little the worse for smoke. There are no draperies, no cushions, no showy colors, no florid decoration of any kind. During the performance the room is darkened so that it is impossible to read except by the light from the stage.

The artistic success of this innovation in theatre-building is without a single drawback. The singers and the players are easily and perfectly heard, the merest whisper of a drum roll or a *tremolo* traveling clearly all over the house; and the *fortissimo* of the total vocal and instrumental force comes with admirable balance of tone, without rattle, echo, excessive localization of sound, or harsh preponderance of the shriller instruments. The concentration of attention on the stage is so complete that the after-image of the lyric drama witnessed is deeply engraved in the memory, aural and visual. The ventilation is excellent; and the place is free from the peculiar odor inseparable from draped and upholstered theatres. The seats between the last doors and the back do not empty rapidly; but in case of fire the occupants could easily step over into the sections which empty at once, and so get out in time to escape suffocation or burning.

Compare this theatre with our fashionable opera houses. In these there is for persons of average middle-class means a stifling atmosphere, a precarious and remote bird's-eye view of the crowns of the performers' hats, and an appalling risk of suffocation in case of panic. For rich people there is every circumstance that can distract the attention from the opera—blazing chandeliers, diamonds, costumes, private boxes for public chattering, fan waving and posing, fashionably late arrivals and early departures, the conductor gesticulating like an auctioneer in the middle of the footlights, and the band deafening the unfortunate people in the front rows of the stalls. Under such conditions a satisfactory representation even of Il Barbiere is impossible. Thus, though we have orchestras capable, under the right conductor, of playing the prelude to any Wagner lyric drama better than it is played at Bayreuth, yet we can never produce the effect that is produced there until we have a theatre on the Bayreuth model to do it in. Why should we not have such a theatre, accommodating 1,500 people, on equal terms at a uniform charge per head. The dramas performed need not always be lyric; for it must not be overlooked that the actual Wagner Theatre is also the ideal Shakespear Theatre.

In considering whether such an enterprise would pay, the practical man should bear in mind that opera at present does not pay in the commercial sense, except in Bayreuth, where the charge for admittance to each performance—£1—is prohibitive as far as the average amateur is concerned. At Covent Garden, Mr Augustus Harris has his subvention, not from the Government, as in Berlin or Paris, but from a committee of private patrons whose aims are at least as much fashionable as artistic. To carry a season through without losing some thousands of pounds is a considerable feat of management. Consequently no demonstration that the money taken at the doors of a Wagner Theatre here would not cover expenses of performance, plus rent, interest, and the ordinary profits of skilled management, is conclusive as against the practicability of London enjoying the artistic benefit of such an institution. The London Wagner Theatre might be an endowed institution of the type suggested by Mr William Archer; or it might be a municipally subventioned theatre. It might be built as an ordinary commercial venture, and let for short periods to tragedians temporarily in want of a Shakespearean theatre, like Mr Mansfield, or to *impresarios* like Mr Harris, Mr Leslie, Mr Mapleson, or the managers of the Carl Rosa company. Its novelty and the celebrity of its original would launch it: its comfort and its enormous artistic superiority to its rivals would probably keep it afloat until the time when its special function as a theatre for lyric drama would be in constant action throughout the year. In any case we should not waste our Wagner Theatre as the Bayreuth house is wasted, by keeping it closed against all composers save Wagner. Our desire to see a worthy and solemn performance of Parsifal has been gratified; but what of the great prototype of Parsifal, Die Zauberflöte, hitherto known in our opera houses as a vapid, tawdry tomfoolery for shewing off a soprano with a high F and a bass with a low E? Mozart is Wagner's only peer in lyric drama: he also made the orchestra envelop the poem in a magic atmosphere of sound: he also adapted a few favorite rhythms, modulations, and harmonies, to an apparently infinite variety and subtlety of accent and purport. If we are asked whether Die Meistersinger is greater than this or that lyric comedy, we say yes with contemptuous impetuosity until Le Nozze di Figaro is mentioned; and then, brought up standing, we quote Michael Angelo's "different, but not better." There is no parallel between Tristan und Isolde and Don Giovanni except in respect of both being unique. At Bayreuth we have heard Tristan und Isolde from the first note to the last, faithfully done according to the composer's score, under the best theatrical conditions possible. But whither shall we turn to hear Don Giovanni? At the opera houses they occasionally try to lick the sugar off it—to sound that part of its great compass which is within the range of the shallowest voluptuary—that part within which the hero is at the level of his ancestor Punch. If the Wagnerites do not ardently desire to hear a dignified and complete representation of Don Giovanni, with the second *finale* restored, they are no true disciples of "The Master." Then there is Fidelio, always grimly irreconcilable with the glitter of the fashionable opera house, and needing, more than any other lyric drama, that concentration of attention which is the cardinal peculiarity of the Wagner Theatre. Verdi, by dint of his burning earnestness about the dramas he has found music for, and of the relevance of every bar of his mature scores to the dramatic situation, has also placed his best operas beyond the reach of Covent Garden. Many persons were astonished at the power of his Otello as performed this year at the Lyceum by the Milan company; but an equally careful and complete performance of his Ernani would have been quite as unexpected a revelation after the intolerable Traviatas and Trovatores of ordinary "subscription nights." Those victims of Wagneritis (a disease not uncommon among persons who have discovered the merits of Wagner's music by reading about it, and among those disciples who know no other music than his) may feel scandalized by the suggestion of Verdi's operas at a Wagner Theatre; but they must be taught to respect the claims of the no less important people for whom Molière and Mozart are too subtle, Schopenhauer and Wagner too abstract. The simple tragedy of Victor Hugo and Verdi is what these novices have to depend on for the purification of their souls by pity and terror; and they have a right, equally with the deepest of us, to the most careful and earnest representation of any art work which appeals seriously to them. As for the composers who were chiefly musicians, or who were dramatic only by fits and starts, or whose dramatic purpose seldom rose above the production of imposing stage effects—Gounod, Rossini, Meyerbeer, and their imitators—a single Wagner Theatre would always have something better to do than to produce their works, pitiful as it would be to abandon them to the incredible slovenliness and flippancy of the fashionable houses. But perhaps the example of a Wagner Theatre might induce rival *impresarios* to consider the moral of the fact that Wagner himself has recorded the satisfaction he enjoyed from an uncut performance of Il Barbiere in which, for once, Rossini's authority was placed above that of the stage manager. Did he not point, in his practical fashion, to the superior artistic completeness gained in ballets through the necessity of giving the artistic inventor his own way on the stage?

The uses of a London Wagner Theatre would by no means be limited to the presentation of the works of Mozart, Beethoven, Verdi, Wagner, and perhaps Goetz. The spoken drama, in spite of the artistic ambition of our actor-managers, is almost as forlorn in England as the lyric. The people for whose use dramatic literature exists have lost the habit of going to the theatre, because they so seldom find anything there that interests them. Occasionally the more enterprising of them may be seen at some amateurish venture of the Browning or Shelley Society, or at the Lyceum. But there is no theatre in London which is the natural home of the plays they want to see. Shakespear's plays, Schiller's, Goethe's, Ibsen's (Peer Gynt and Brand), Browning's—what chance have we at present of knowing these in the only way in which they can be thoroughly known? for a man who has only read a play no more knows it than a musician knows a symphony when he has turned over the leaves of the score. He knows something about it: that is all. Are we then for ever to offer our children the book of the play to read, instead of bringing them to the theatre? The appetite for serious drama exists: that much has appeared whenever it has been put to the proof by a competent manager with sufficient resources to hold out whilst the lovers of serious drama were overcoming their incredulity as to any theatrical entertainment rising above the level of the commonest variety of novel. This year there was a revival of hope because Mr Pinero, in a play produced at the Garrick Theatre, walked cautiously up to a social problem, touched it, and ran away. Shortly afterwards a much greater sensation was created by a Norwegian play, Ibsen's Doll's House, in which the dramatist handled this same problem, and shewed, not how it ought to be solved, but how it is about to be solved. Then came out the deplorable fact that it is possible for men to attend our ordinary theatres as professional critics constantly for years without finding occasion to employ or understand the simplest terms used in metaphysical and psychological discussions of dramatic art. Somebody, for instance, having used the word "will" in the Schopenhauerian sense which has long been familiar to every smatterer in Wagnerism or the philosophy of art, the expression was frankly denounced by one dramatic critic as "sickening balderdash," whilst another adduced it as evidence that the writer could not possibly understand his own words, since they were not intelligible. The truth appears to be that the theatre of today, with its literature, its criticism, and its audiences, though a self-contained, consistent, and useful institution, ignores and is ignored by the class which is only interested in realities, and which enjoys thinking as others enjoy eating. The most cynical estimate of the numbers of this class in London will leave no doubt of the success of any theatre which can once make itself known as a Wagner Theatre in a larger sense than Bayreuth yet comprehends. This theatre need not oust the theatre of today, which will retain its place as long as it retains its use. The two can exist side by side without more friction than perhaps an occasional betrayal of the conviction of each that the literature and criticism of the other is "sickening balderdash."

The doubt as to the possibility of finding singers for an English Wagner Theatre might be disregarded on the ground that

London is accustomed to pick and choose from the world's stock. But this plan has not hitherto answered well enough to justify us in relying upon it in the future. Fortunately, Bayreuth has shewn us how to do without singers of internationally valuable genius. The singers there have not "created" the lyric drama: it is the lyric drama that has created them. Powerful as they are, they do not sing Wagner because they are robust: they are robust because they sing Wagner. His music is like Handel's in bringing into play the full compass of the singer, and in offering the alternative of either using the voice properly or else speedily losing it. Such proper use of the voice is a magnificent physical exercise. The outcry against Wagner of the singers who were trained to scream and shout within the highest five notes of their compass until nothing else was left of their voices—and not much of that—has died away. Even that arch quack, the old-fashioned Italian singing master, finds some better excuse for his ignorance of Wagner's music and his inability to play its accompaniments, than the bold assurance that German music is bad for the voice. Plenty of English singers would set to work at the Niblung Ring tomorrow if they could see their way to sufficient opportunities of singing it to repay them for the very arduous task of committing one of the parts to memory. Singers of genius, great Tristans and Parsifals, Kundrys and Isoldes, will not be easily obtained here any more than in Germany; and when they are found, all Europe and America will compete for them. But Bayreuth does without singers of genius. Frau Materna and Fräulein Malten, with all their admirable earnestness and enthusiasm, are only great Kundrys according to that easy standard by which the late Madame Tietjens passed as a great Semiramis and a great Lucrezia: that is, they have large voices, and have some skill in stage business and deportment; but they do nothing that any intelligent woman with their physical qualifications cannot be educated to do. Perron's Amfortas is an admirable performance; but our next Santley, falling on more serious artistic times, will equal it. Miss Macintyre will have to be very careful and faithful in her career if she wishes to find herself, at Frau Sucher's age, as fine an Isolde; but who can say how many rivals to Miss Macintyre we may have by that time? Theodor Reichmann must have been an excellent Sachs in his time; and he is still worthy of his place at Bayreuth; but we can produce a Hans Sachs of the same order when we make up our minds that we want him. Friedrichs, a capital comedian, and Van Dyck, who makes his mark as Parsifal by a certain *naïveté* and rosy physical exuberance rather than by any extraordinary endowment as a singer, exhaust the list of artists whose perform-ances at Bayreuth this year were specially memorable. Gudehus as Walther and Vogl as Tristan proved themselves as capable as ever of carrying through two very heavy tenor parts; but though their conscientiousness and intelligence were beyond praise, they are neither young nor youthful (it is possible to be either without being the other), and their voices lack variety and charm.

Can we hope to replace the three great conductors? The chief part of the answer is that there is only one great conductor, and him we have bound to us already. Whoever has heard the Tristan prelude conducted by Richter on one of his fortunate evenings at St James's Hall, or the Parsifal prelude as he conducted it on one memorable occasion at the Albert Hall, knows more than Bayreuth can tell him about these works. Herr Levi shews what invaluable results can be produced by unwearying care and ex-haustive study. Herr Felix Mottl's strictness, refinement, and severe taste make the orchestra go with the precision and elegance of a chronometer. Discipline, rehearsal, scrupulous insistence on every *nuance* in a score which is crammed with minute indications of the gradations of tone to be produced by each player: these, and entire devotion to the composer's cause, could do no more. But they are qualities which exist everywhere, if not in everyone. If Wagner's work can call them into action in Germany it can call them into action here. With Richter the case is different. He, as we know, is a conductor of genius. To make an orchestra play the prelude to Parsifal as Herr Levi makes them play it, is a question of taking as much pains and as much thought as he. To make them play the introduction to the third act of Die Meister-singer as they play it for Richter is a question of the gift of poetic creation in musical execution. The perfection attained by Herr Mottl is the perfection of photography. Richter's triumphs and imperfections are those of the artist's hand.

Before Wagner, the qualities which distinguish the Bayreuth performances were rarer in Germany than they are now in England. His work inspired them there: what is to prevent it doing so here? No more of Bayreuth then: Wagnerism, like charity, begins at home.

FAUST AT THE ALBERT HALL
(*The Star*, 31 *October* 1889)

A stroll round the gallery of the Albert Hall last night during the first part of Berlioz's Faust brought me past so many wage-working men of a type unknown at oratorio performances that I must at once say something which members of the Church Establishment had better skip lest they be shocked beyond recovery. It is nothing short of this—that a large section of the most alert-minded, forward, and culture-capable of the London artisan class are eager to gratify their curiosity about this wonderful art of music, if only they can get it dissociated from the detested names—dont be shocked, reader, it is quite true—of St Paul, Elijah, Saul, and the other terrors of the poor man's Sunday school. It is useless to blink the fact. Just as the workman, long after he wanted to give up bad beer and spirits for coffee and cocoa, yet refused to enter the coffee tavern until he could get what he wanted there without a tract and an inquiry as to whether he was saved, so he will keep out of the concert room until he feels certain that he will not be reminded there of the hated "religious instruction" to the hypocrisy of which his own poverty bears unanswerable testimony. He hates fugues because they remind him of anthems; an oratorio makes him feel as if he were in church, which is the most horrible sensation known to him short of actual bodily pain, because there is no place where he is forced to feel the shabbiness of his clothes and the unsocial contempt in which he is held by church-going respectability, as he is forced to feel it there. Therefore, I plead for more secular music for the workman—for picturesque dramatic music that will hold him as a novel holds him, whilst his ear is automatically acquiring the training that will eventually make him conscious of purely musical beauty. Faust he evidently likes, and he would perhaps relish it even more if Mr Barnby could be persuaded to conduct a trifle less canonically. Berlioz has told us how the audience rose in a wild tumult of patriotic enthusiasm when he first gave them his version of the Rákóczy March. At the Albert Hall last night the audience, with admirable self-control, kept their seats, and did not even encore the march. Mr Barnby is certain to be made a knight some day in the ordinary course; but before it is too late let me suggest that he should be made a bishop instead. At the same time I must again bear testimony to the enormous pains he has taken to drill that huge and stolid choir, and to the success with which he has taught them to produce genuine vocal tone and to do their duty with precision and some delicacy, if not with intelligence. I wonder he was not killed by the struggle with their thousandfold pigheadedness (this is not polite, I know; but, bless you, the Albert Hall choristers never read Radical newspapers). I had to leave at the end of the first part, and so did not hear Margaret. Mr Iver McKay, the Faust of the evening, was not in brilliant voice; he was more often flat than not. Mr Henschel sang the Mephistopheles music, which suits his peculiarities, cleverly—more cleverly, perhaps, than could any of his rivals in the part, except Mr Max Heinrich. Mr Ben Grove was an excellent Brander, again shewing himself to be what I declared him when he sang King Mark's music at Mr Armbruster's recital of Tristan, a capable, trustworthy, self-respecting, and Art-respecting singer.

C. di B.

THE WELL-TEMPERED CRITIC

(The 1890's)

CONCERTS

(The Star, 3 March 1890)

On Friday evening last I went to the Wind Instrument Society's concert at the Royal Academy of Music in Tenterden-street. Having only just heard of the affair from an acquaintance, I had no ticket. The concert, as usual, had been kept dark from me: Bassetto the Incorruptible knows too much to be welcome to any but the greatest artists. I therefore presented myself at the doors for admission on payment as a casual amateur. Apparently the wildest imaginings of the Wind Instrument Society had not reached to such a contingency as a Londoner offering money at the doors to hear classical chamber music played upon bassoons, clarionets, and horns; for I was told that it was impossible to entertain my application, as the building had no license. I suggested sending out for a license; but this, for some technical reason, could not be done. I offered to dispense with the license; but that, they said, would expose them to penal servitude. Perceiving by this that it was a mere question of breaking the law, I insisted on the secretary accompanying me to the residence of a distinguished Q.C. in the neighbourhood, and ascertaining from him how to do it. The Q.C. said that if I handed the secretary five shillings at the door in consideration of being admitted to the concert, that would be illegal. But if I bought a ticket from him in the street, that would be legal. Or if I presented him with five shillings in remembrance of his last birthday, and he gave me a free admission in celebration of my silver wedding, that would be legal. Or if we broke the law without witnesses and were prepared to perjure ourselves if questioned afterwards (which seemed to me the most natural way), then nothing could happen to us.

I cannot without breach of faith explain which course we adopted: suffice it that I was present at the concert. The first item, a septet in E flat, which is, for Beethoven, a tea gardens sort of composition, was not made the best of. Mr Clinton led the first movement, which should be brisk and crisp, slowly and laboriously. The bassoons were rough and ready; the horns rough and not always ready. On the whole, with such artists the performance ought to have been several shades finer. The Spohr septet, a shining river of commonplaces, plagiarisms, and reminiscences, went more smoothly; but then the fiddle, 'cello, and piano had a hand in that. The piano, by the bye, was played by Mr Septimus Webbe, who, though in his earliest manhood, has, if I mistake not, been a notable player for at least fourteen years past. What a fortune he would have made had the Hofmann-Hegner boom happened when he was in his prime at eight! One movement of an octet by the late, highly respectable Franz Lachner was enough for me. I am much afraid that Wagner's pithy description of him in Ueber das Dirigiren will survive all the obituary notices that were so complimentary to him.

Madame Backer-Gröndahl seems to have brought from Norway a witch-like power of letting loose the elements on her audiences. Last year she played Beethoven's E flat concerto amid storm and thunder, the lightning scaring the veterans of the Philharmonic Society into vain remorse for their misspent musical lives. On Saturday she came to the Crystal Palace in clouds of boreal snow. I should not have minded her bringing the snow if she had left Grieg's concerto at home. I hinted last year, and I now explicitly repeat, that Madame Gröndahl's powers of interpretation are wasted upon scrappy work like Grieg's. If it had been Señor Albéniz, or Mr Vladimir de Pachmann, or Miss Essipoff, or the composer himself, I should have been content with Grieg. But when you are longing for Mozart in D minor or Beethoven in G, or the E flat over again, then Grieg is an impertinence. The program, as far as the pianoforte was concerned, would have infuriated a saint. Madame Gröndahl put Grieg where she should have put Beethoven, and Chopin where she should have put Grieg. The audience gave repeated proofs of a quite exceptional imbecility. A splendid performance of Mozart's Idomeneo overture, a noble and seldom heard composition, was hardly noticed; whilst a sentimental show piece for the strings by Dvořák was received with rapture. Sir George Grove's "analysis" of Beethoven's second symphony was such a shameless piece of special pleading that I hasten to remark emphatically that nothing can extenuate the insufferable kitchen clock tum-tum which pervades the first two movements of that overrated work. The *scherzo* and the *finale* are fine if you like; and the band surpassed itself in playing them. The *scherzo* in particular was a triumph of orchestral execution. Mr Braxton Smith's singing pleased the audience, though he does not, as skilful bowlers do, vary his delivery: his organ has but one stop. The two pieces by Saint-Saëns were clever trash.

On our way back to Victoria, a signal stopped our train in the snow, and when it fell the engine gasped and refused to budge. At last another train overtook us, and butted us into Clapham, where, in a paroxysm of ill-temper, I resolved to say nothing more about Madame Gröndahl until after her recital at Steinway Hall on Wednesday afternoon.[1]

C. di B.

MR HENRY SEIFFERT'S CONCERT

(The Star, 7 March 1890)

Yesterday evening Mr Henry Seiffert gave something between a violin recital and a concert at Steinway Hall. Miss Fillunger sang, very sympathetically and earnestly; and Madame de Llana played. Indeed, Madame de Llana had to contribute out of all conscience to the work of the evening; for, besides her solos, she had to follow Mr Seiffert vigilantly through a troublesome transcription of the orchestral score of Wieniawski's second concerto,

[1] See review of 7 March 1890, in *London Music in 1888–89* (1937).

and to play the heavy and difficult pianoforte part in Rubinstein's violin sonata in A minor. Her chief solo, Chopin's Ballade in A flat, got shifted to the end of the concert. The result of this inconsiderate departure from the program was that at one complicated passage her memory and her fingers failed her for a moment; and she had to pause for breath. Unlike M. de Pachmann, who passes off mishaps of this sort so effectively that he has been suspected by evil-minded persons of bringing them about on purpose, Madame de Llana looked very angrý with herself, perhaps because she is too young to know how often the same thing has happened to players of the first rank, from Liszt down to Miss Marie Krebs. In fact it happens to them all at one time or another, genius being but mortal. Mr Seiffert's playing was remarkable, as usual, for breadth of tone, for a strength of style in *cantabile* passages which promises to mature into grandeur and passion, and for extraordinary freedom and intrepidity of execution. He is still apt to slur over the very details which, because they are uninteresting in themselves, depend for their interest on the finesse of the player; in themes like the first subject of the *finale à la zingara* of the Wieniawski concerto one misses in his impetuous attack the smooth, perfectly equal touch and the precision of intonation which Sarasate has associated with passages of that character; and his *pizzicato* is curiously ineffective. But all these imperfections may be expected to disappear long before Mr Seiffert is as old as Sarasate. His talent, striking as it is, is not yet by any means fully developed; and I shall wait for a few years yet before stereotyping my opinion of him.

C. di B.

THORGRIM

I

(The Star, 23 April 1890)

There are two possible reasons for Mr Cowen's consenting to set Mr Joseph Bennett's Thorgrim to music. 1. Because its poesy and dramatic force inspired him. 2. Because he was afraid to offend the critic of The Daily Telegraph by refusing. In order to help the reader to an unprejudiced choice of these alternatives, I give the following samples of the verse:—

> Dear lady, what sorrow
> Thy young heart oppresseth?
> May we not cheer thee
> With music's diversion?

The following rises involuntarily to the lips of the heroine when she beholds the hero. It is in rhyme.

> With noble mien and moving words he pleads,
>   His form is grace, his voice makes music sweet,
> And I would follow wheresoe'er he leads—
>   This must be love, since joy and anguish meet!

The punctuation is copied from the libretto. Another sample, one of the best I can find. It is from the love duet:—

> This moment fades the world away,
>   Far, far from thee and me,
> And lost the thought of yesterday
>   In love's immensity.
> The cruel morrow may us part—
>   To Fate's decree we bow.
> There is no time but Now, dear heart;
>   There is no time but Now.

One more specimen, again a specially favorable one:—

> Thine through all the future years,
> Thine in gladness, thine in tears,
> Thine amid the summer flowers,
> Thine in winter's dreary hours,
> Thine on land and thine on the sea,
> Thine wherever thou shalt be.
> Love till I this life resign,
> Everywhere and always thine.

The story, the drama, the interest, the characterization, the subject even need not detain us. There are none. Mr Cowen conducted the performance himself. I was sorry for him; I would as soon have sat in the pillory, in spite of the applause. I did not wait for the fourth act.

I was agreeably surprised to find that Miss de Lussan, whom I had not heard since her solitary appearance as Carmen at Drury Lane two years ago, has added to the cleverness and self-possession she then exhibited, an artistic feeling and a degree of vocal skill and tact that must make her a valuable acquisition to the Carl Rosa company. Her voice has gathered color and individuality; and she knows how to use it, a refreshing thing in a company where every *prima donna* screams more or less. I look forward with interest to seeing her in some part which has dramatic importance, and which has vitality enough to keep the stage long enough to give her time to mature her conception of it. If Thorgrim is done again, Mr Harris would do well to withdraw the girls who dance with the swords in the first act. They should be replaced by men. If Mr Crotty and Mr McGuckin were engaged at an ordinary theatre to play Charles and Orlando in As You Like It, they would be expected to study their wrestling match as Mr Irving and Mr Bancroft studied the duel in The Dead Heart. Being operatic artists, they gave themselves no such trouble, and simply shoved each other back and forward as drunk and disorderly persons do when they quarrel and do not know how to fight. They evidently have made a shrewd guess at the number of times they are likely to have to play in Mr Cowen's opera.   C. di B.

II

(The Hawk, 6 May 1890; unsigned)

The criticizing of Thorgrim is really not so easy a matter as might be supposed. The librettist is a brother critic; and there is fellow-feeling and *esprit de corps*, not to mention the terror spread by Mr Sala's onslaught on Mr Furniss, all prompting one to do the safe and the genial thing—to swear, in fact, that there never was such a libretto and such a score produced since English opera was born as this joint effort of the most widely circulated of our critics and the most popular of our song purveyors. But then the fact is so very obvious that Thorgrim is not good. It is worse than that: it is bad—desperately bad, confoundedly bad, unbearably bad, infernally bad; and everybody knows it. How is this to be put delicately, printably, unlibelously? It is easy for the irresponsible pittite to lean across to his neighbor and dismiss the work as "tommy rot"; but you cant use such expressions in a public paper: it is bad form—vulgar; English criticism, being untempered by duelling, could not be carried on if the rough edge of the truth were not taken off better than that. Rather let it be led up to gently by a reference to one of the sister arts.

Nobody can complain of an art critic admiring his favorite old or new master. Nobody can complain of his buying a picture by that master. Nobody can take exception to his praising that master more than ever when he has had a piece of his work for a year over the sideboard. Nobody can be injured if the American millionaire, educated by the English critic, and yearning consequently to possess a masterpiece by the favored limner, should make golden offers for the picture over the sideboard—offers which the critic has obviously a perfect right to accept. A set of circumstances involving less blame to everybody concerned could not possibly be imagined. And yet, when that critic next goes enthusing, the thought that he may possibly have another deal in view enters the mind unbidden, and discounts his raptures in spite of the utmost resolution to think no evil. And so people get [to] saying that a critic should never be a dealer, even in an amateur way—as if he had not as good a right to buy in the cheapest market and sell in the dearest as any other Briton.

Mr Joseph Bennett, the author of Thorgrim, is the victim of a somewhat cognate prejudice. He is credited with enormous power as musical critic to The Daily Telegraph and editor of The Musical Times. We are all familiar with his demonstrations of the objectionable character of Wagner's music. He provides "books of words" for oratorios; and these are performed at the great provincial English festivals and published by Messrs Novello. He writes analytic programs for the concerts of the Philharmonic Society. And he composes opera librettos. Now his position as critic gives him such power and independence that it is idle to pretend to believe that the Philharmonic gets off any the more easily in The D.T. because the writer of the notices is in the employment of the Society as a programist. And his connection with the Novello firm as editor of their paper and poet of their oratorios probably only makes him more scrupulous in dealing with their publications and with Festival performances than he would otherwise be. And it would be unreasonable jealously to expect a man so variously gifted to confine himself to a single department of literary activity—and that none too well-paid a one—for the sole purpose of narrowing his own influence. Surely that influence should rather be accepted as the inevitable concomitant—nay, the just reward—of many-sided talent.

But look at it from the point of view of the *impresario* or the composer. When Mr Harris makes up his mind to commission Mr Cowen to compose an opera, the advantages of enlisting Mr Bennett as author of the libretto are, through Mr Bennett's merit and not through his fault, too obvious to be disregarded. The libretto is accordingly ordered, executed, and handed to Mr Cowen. Perhaps Mr Cowen is delighted, inspired, fitted to a hair. If so nothing need follow save general rejoicing. But what if on the other hand he is disappointed, and is fain to protest that there is no plot; that the incidents have no organic *raison d'être*; that the verse is doggerel; that Mr Bennett is Fitzball without even Fitzball's folly. Will not the startled *impresario* reply that it would be madness to make an enemy of The Daily Telegraph; that the book is really a very good one when you get used to it; that The Daily News will declare that "some of Mr Bennett's lines fairly yearn for musical expression"; that the musical papers will vouch for it that he is "a man of undoubted literary ability"; that, in short, to secure his co-operation is to secure such a backing of press bluff and press butter as would push and slide anything into good repute for a season at least. It is easy to imagine Mr Bennett's pain and indignation at the assumption that his impartiality as a critic would be affected by the verdict of the composer on his attempt at poetry; but it is not easy to imagine the composer himself feeling quite so sure of that. The tempted musician would certainly try hard to persuade himself that the libretto might have been worse, before he would face the crushing responsibility of rejecting it, especially if he had contracted beforehand to supply the score without reserving any right to a voice in the matter.

Enough! Let us not blame Mr Bennett for failing to see that he was not born a poet or dramatist; and let us forgive Mr Cowen for not having had the courage to tell him so.

CARL ROSA OPERA COMPANY: LOHENGRIN

(*The Star*, 28 *April* 1890)

Lohengrin is so much the best thing the Carl Rosa company has done this season—unless Romeo and Juliet, which I did not see, was better—that the more they give us of it, and the less of Maritana, Lurline, and so on, the better their position will be at the end of their season in London. The choral parts and the stage business have had something approaching a due proportion of the total available Drury Lane energy put into their preparation; and the result is that all the great situations in the first and second acts produce an immense effect. The work is, of course, mutilated; one particularly exasperating aggravation of the atrocious cut in the prelude to the second act has been perpetrated by cutting out the whole of the dawn music with the exception of two beggarly trumpet calls and their echoes. I hope the next world may see a great gulf fixed between me and the man that made that cut. But what is done is done very well, considering the possibilities of the case—well enough, at any rate, to convey much of the force and feeling of Wagner's conception of his work.

The excellence of Miss Amanda Fabris's Elsa was a surprise to the house. I am not sure that they all quite saw where the unwonted charm of it lay. It was not altogether in her singing, though that was pleasant at its weakest, and intelligent and full of appropriate expression at its best. Nor was it in her acting, in the deeper sense of acting, though in that she was successful, as a matter of course. I say a matter of course because no woman ever fails as Elsa, just as no man ever fails as Hamlet, even when they are unable to play much simpler parts. The novel and characteristic element in her impersonation is her admirable pantomime. If I might hazard a guess, I should say that Miss Fabris was either trained in the first instance as a dancer, or has had the good sense and artistic conscience to voluntarily go through that part of a dancer's education which deals with dramatic pantomime. She filled up all the long intervals of orchestral illustration without turning them into something dangerously like stage waits, as so many Elsas have done through sheer pantomimic incompetence. And she was never for a moment out of her part. Altogether, with her long eyes, her slim figure, Tuscan school profile, and Botticellian grace, she made a very marked impression which the audience gave vehement emphasis to after each descent of the act-drop. The other notable success of the evening was that of Ffrangçon Davies, who sang up to the promise of his stupendous Christian name in a fresh, unspoiled baritone voice which pleased the audience immensely. Mr Barton McGuckin, who is, on the whole, second only to Jean de Reszke (a less indisputably pure tenor) among the singers familiar to Londoners, bore himself with dignity as Lohengrin, and sang well. But cannot Mr McGuckin, who has learnt so much, and who has never fallen into the error, common among tenors, of mistaking the beginning of his reputation for the completion of his education—cannot he get the better of his native tendency to maltreat the first letter of the alphabet? His delivery of Lohengrin's declaration in the last act is not improved by such locutions as "In distant londs . . . a costle stonds . . . Montsolvot," &c.

Miss Tremelli must bear with my old and rooted prejudices against the substitution of attitudinizing for acting, and against a method of singing that involves a gasp for breath between every note almost. I do not like it; and I do not feel called upon to disguise my sentiments on the subject. Mr Max Eugene has done worse things than his Telramond. Mr Goossens conducted, and made an original point or two. The audience waxed impatient at last with the length of the waits, and went so far as to whistle We wont go home till morning, a performance which was interrupted by the now well-known Drury Lane cat, which turned over on its back in the stalls, and rolled about in mockery, amid hearty Wagnerian applause. It was extinguished by the passing skirt of Madame Marie Roze, whom it followed out with some show of indignation. I am not in a position to chronicle its subsequent proceedings. I must add, for Mr Harris's information, that there was a good deal of noise made on the stage during some of the preludes. A hint from him on the subject would probably have some weight with the carpenters.

C. di B.

MODERN MEN: HANS RICHTER

(*The Scots Observer*, 28 *June* 1890; unsigned. Reprinted in *Twenty Modern Men from the National Observer* (2nd series), London, 1891)

Dr Richter came to London in 1877, with Wagner. Well, London had plenty of conductors in 1877. There was Mr Cusins at the Philharmonic; and the Philharmonic was on the verge of extinction. Then there was Costa—Sir Michael Costa—the autocrat of Her Majesty's, whose band—brazen, cold, correct—never presumed to play anything as if it enjoyed it, except perhaps a score of Rossini's. At Covent Garden there was Vianesi; and inasmuch as a Parisian has an exquisitely tasty way of being vulgar and childish—that being, in effect, what he supposes art to mean—while a stolid Brixton band can only respond to the call of the Parisian ideal by bumptiousness and blaring, Vianesi who does well enough for Paris is an artistic failure here. Arditi was an operatic conductor pure and simple: he was content to compose Il Bacio and to pull through scratch performances of the old Italian repertory, leaving Costa to conduct the Handel Festival and compose Eli and other sacred contributions to that school of oratorio in which inspiration is a sin. Arthur Sullivan was very neat, tolerated no want of refinement, and got over the ground as fast as possible lest Beethoven should sound tedious and Mozart vapid, yet never made an orchestra go fast enough for that, though every *allegro* was what Mozart would have called a *prestissimo*. Leaving Mr Barnby, with his hopelessly expressionless horde of middle-class oratorio choristers aside as lost to living music, there remained only two conductors of any pretensions; and they were much the best of the set. One was the enthusiast August Manns, who was absorbed by the Crystal Palace concerts, and the other Mr Weist Hill, who was presently drawn off into the Guildhall School of Music founded by the City of London. And none of these could draw the town to orchestral concerts except Manns and Weist Hill, who would certainly have established the Viard-Louis concerts permanently if capital had been forthcoming to tide over the initial wait for remunerative success.

At that time nobody in London except a few readers of Wagner's hard and clotted, desperately German prose saw any point in the term "Mendelssohnian Conductor." As to its being reproach, that would have seemed a paradox. When Wagner came over here in 1877 to try and retrieve the pecuniary losses of his triumph at Bayreuth in 1876, many admirers, professed disciples of his, were not behindhand in misrepresenting him. They talked and wrote as if it were eminently Wagnerian to decry Mozart and to find deep meanings in Brahms and Schumann. "The Meister" himself, as might have been expected, was bored by Brahms, indifferent to Schumann's "deeper" meanings, fond of Don Giovanni like the rest of us, given to ask pianists to play him the Hebrides overture on the piano, as pleased with Masaniello as the greenest, slow to outgrow the childish delight with which he used to conduct the pleasant operas of Boïeldieu, and with a passion for Beethoven far surpassing that of the late Edmund Gurney: in short, a man of strong commonsense, whose tastes were the most simple and obvious to be found on his plane. As his music made extraordinary and continuous demands on the orchestra for expression and "vocality," he was always at war with incompetent conductors, whom he named without the slightest fear of consequences whenever it was necessary to give a practical illustration of what he complained of; and naturally they urged that, as he had also denounced Mendelssohn and Meyerbeer with the envy of an unsuccessful inferior, his spleen should not be a hurt to them. The unsuccessful inferior theory is perhaps a little *passé*[1]; but Wagner is still unappreciated as a

---

[1] W. E. Henley, editor of *The Scots Observer*, audaciously injected into the article a few anti-Wagnerisms, drawing from Shaw the retort: "I had heard of [your] deplorable darkness as to Wagner, and so had to overcharge my article to

critic; for the musical critics, though they see that Richter produces noble results with poor materials, are able to give no intelligible account of the process, but seem to suppose the man to have some natural magic which eludes analysis. Sometimes they try to explain that the charm consists in his ability to play the horn and trumpet, his remarkable memory, and his address in giving cues to his band, on all which irrelevant points he is equaled not only by several distinguished musicians who are hopelessly weak conductors but by dozens of military bandmasters. Wagner had the advantage of knowing what he was talking about when he said: "The whole business of a conductor is to give the right time to the band."

This seems simple; but as nothing short of a complete and original comprehension of the composer's intention, and above all of the melody with which modern symphonic movements, the fast as well as the slow, are saturated, can guide anyone to the right time, it is evident that a man may know that *adagio* means slow and *allegro* fast, his *coup d'œil* over a score may be swift and unerring as far as the notes and entries are concerned, he may be able to play The Last Rose of Summer with variations on every several instrument in his orchestra; and yet he may conduct Beethoven's Coriolanus overture in such a fashion that every honest novice will vote it as meaningless as Zampa, and not half as pretty. A conductor who takes the time from the metronome and gives it to the music is, for all conducting purposes, a public nuisance: a conductor who takes the time from the music and gives it to the band is, if he take and give it rightly, a good conductor. This is what Richter does and would do if he were as incapable of playing the horn as Beethoven himself. And this enables him also to understand what is wrong with the ordinary pseudo-classical orchestra. The Philharmonic band, with all its "refinement," never produces sustained tone: the players attack a note and then let it go without feeling or gripping it; there is no heart in their *forte*, no sensibility in their *piano*; and their conductors find that the only way to avoid an intolerable

receive your misguided watering down. On the whole you have done your spi—
I mean your watering most artistically, and without lacerating my feelings; for
though your 'perhaps a little *passé*' was maliciously intended, it reads like a keen
Wagnerian sarcasm." (Unpublished letter, 1 July 1890.)

insipidity is to take Mendelssohn's famous advice, and scamper along as fast as possible. This is all very well in a Bach *allegro* with not a sustained note in it, or in a piece of rattling Margate Pier music like Signor Mancinelli's Venetian Suite; but imagine the effect of it in Beethoven, with his pregnant and terrible pauses on held notes and his restless ground-swell of melody! In all Beethoven's symphonies there is one movement, and only one, that the Philharmonic band can play, and that is the *finale* of the Fourth, which consists almost entirely of semiquavers. Yet this vapid and useless orchestra needs but a good conductor —a conductor who at rehearsal would do something more than race it through a symphony with an occasional wry face, and a superior "O, coarse, gentlemen! *so* coarse!" or "Cant you bring that out a little more?" or some other equally futile expression of helpless dissatisfaction—to be the best in the world. But for Richter, it would be as true now as in 1869 that, as Wagner declared, "the real reason of the success of Beethoven's music is that people study it not in concert rooms but at their own pianos; and its irresistible power is thus fully learnt, though in a roundabout way. If our noblest music depended solely on our conductors, it would have perished long ago."

Richter is the man who felt what Wagner wanted, as indeed we all felt it—as even Mr Cowen, Villiers Stanford, Dr Mackenzie, Mr Cusins, and all the other captains of the *bâton* feel it more or less acutely, if they had but the courage, the energy, the belief in themselves, and the power over their orchestras that these carry with them, to insist on bringing their want to its fulfilment. Richter has these qualities; and in addition he has the teaching and the confirmation of Richard Wagner. But that teaching is still open to everyone who is capable of appreciating it. There is no celestial arcanum about the Richter orchestra. The tremendous *fortes* of the Rienzi overture, the delicate *piano* of the Meistersinger prelude (that to the third act), the insistence on the melodic character of the Beethoven *allegro*, the smoothing-out of all the old jerks and jigs and *sforzandos* from the surface of the stream of melody, the substitution of the natural movement of the music for the detestable *presto*—all these reforms are obvious enough now that Richter has carried them through. It is time for younger men to make these qualities a matter of course; but whilst music in London is dominated to the extent it is by musicians to whom music is a mere phase of gentility—or "culture," as they call it—the capital for musical enterprise will not easily find its way into the right hands. Still, the thing will be done. Richter has his post (with its pension) at Vienna to attend to; the Crystal Palace concerts are far off and expensive; the opening for a new man is plain. He may lack Richter's genius; but if he also lack some of his fortyseven years, some of his growing tendency to trust for victory to the excitement of the evening, he may be—(should he prefer his work to society and royal patronage)—at least as great a man as Habeneck, of whom you are told that although he had not a scrap of genius he achieved *the* classic performance of the Ninth Symphony at the Paris Conservatoire.

MODERN MEN: SIR ARTHUR SULLIVAN

(The Scots Observer, 6 September 1890; unsigned)

If a boy wishes to waste his life by taking himself too seriously, he cannot do better than get educated in a cathedral choir with a view to winning the Mendelssohn Scholarship and devoting himself thenceforth to the cultivation of high-class music. Once fortified with a degree of Mus. Bac. and a calm confidence in his power to write a Magnificat in eight real parts, to "analyze" the last movement of the Jupiter Symphony, and to mention at any moment the birthday of Orlandus Lassus, he enters life as a gentleman and a scholar, with a frightful contempt for Offenbach and a deep sense of belonging to the same artistic caste as Handel. Not that he thinks himself as good a man as Handel; but his modesty is of the *anch' io son pittore* kind—for he, too, can write a fugue. Presently he finds that nobody wants fugues—that they are never asked for, nor properly relished when offered gratuitously. Publishers issue them at the composer's expense only: a rule which applies also to Magnificats, Tantum Ergos, and other fearful wild-fowl. He begins to feel the force of that old professorial "wheeze": "Learn to write a fugue; and then dont do it."

Hereupon he asks himself, How is a man to live? Well, there are still young people who have not yet realized the situation; and these want to be taught to write fugues. Accordingly, the Mus. Bac. takes pupils and a church organ, which is a highly serious instrument, lending itself to counterpoint by its construction, and reserved for music of the exclusive kind—Jackson in B flat, Goss in F, Handel's anthems, and the like. Then, there is the prospect of promotion to a church with an important musical service, perhaps to a cathedral. The provincial festivals may commission an oratorio once in twenty years or so; and the Philharmonic might even rise—(such things have been!)—at an overture. An occasional Christmas carol (or even anthem) to keep one's hand in is sure, on attaining a hearing in his own choir, to create that acceptable awe with which an impressionable public regards the man who understands the "theory of music."

This is no bad life for one whose turn for music does not include inventiveness, nor grace of workmanship, nor humor (creative originality is here left out of account, as it must always fight and conquer as best it can). But if he has these three gifts, his proper sphere is the theatre—not the "Royal Italian Opera," but the Savoy, the Prince of Wales, and the Lyric. Now the pedigree of such houses will not bear investigation: in vain do they imply that they are first cousins to the Opéra Comique: their common and all-too immediate ancestor was the Bouffes Parisiennes; and he who composes for them must risk being cut by the decorous and eminently gentlemanly remnant of the Sterndale Bennett set, and must mix with that of the profane and scandalous Offenbach. Anyone who knows the number of foot-pounds of respectability under which an organist lies flattened can imagine the superhuman courage required for such an act of self-declassation. Not even the present writer, though shrouded in anonymity and wholly independent of the organ, dares positively assert that Offenbach was a much greater composer than Sterndale Bennett, although he submits that the fact is obvious. Grove's Dictionary of Music gives nine columns of eulogy, tombstone-like in its fervor and solemnity, to Bennett; whilst Offenbach has one shamefaced column, recalling by its tone an unspeakable passage in Robertson's history of Queen Mary, in which apology is made for the deplorable necessity of mentioning one so far beneath the dignity of history as Rizzio. Grove— the institution, not the individual Sir George—owes it to society not to mention that La Grande Duchesse, as an original and complete work of art, places its composer heavens high above the superfine academician who won rest and self-complacency as a superior person by doing for Mendelssohn what Pasteur has done for the hydrophobia virus, and who by example and precept urged his pupils never to strive after effect. This counsel, worthy of the best form of Mrs General, was not only, as Wagner remarked, "all very well, but rather negative": it was also a rebuke to Offenbach, who was always striving after effect, as every artist who is not ashamed of his calling must unceasingly strive from his cradle to his grave.

The reader is now in a position to understand the tragedy of Sir Arthur Sullivan. He was a Mendelssohn Scholar. He was an organist (St Somebody's, Chester-square). He wrote a symphony. He composed overtures, cantatas, oratorios. His masters were Goss and Sterndale Bennett himself. Of Magnificats he is guiltless; but two Te Deums and about a dozen anthems are among the fruits of his efforts to avoid the achievement of an effect. He has shewn his reverence for the classics in the usual way by writing "additional accompaniments" to Handel's Jephtha; and now he has five columns in Grove and is a knight. What more could a serious musician desire? Alas! the same question might have been put to Tannhäuser at the singing-bee in the Wartburg, before he broke out with his unholy longing for Venus. Offenbach was Sullivan's Venus as Mendelssohn was his St Elizabeth. He furtively set Cox and Box to music in 1869, and then, overcome with remorse, produced Onward, Christian Soldiers and over three dozen hymns besides. As the remorse mellowed, he composed a group of songs—Let Me Dream Again, Thou'rt Passing Hence, Sweethearts, and My Dearest Heart—all of the very best in their *genre*, such as it is. And yet in the very thick of them he perpetrated Trial by Jury, in which he outdid Offenbach in wickedness, and that too without any prompting from the celebrated cynic, Mr W. S. Gilbert. When

HOW TO BECOME A MUSICAL CRITIC

Offenbach wrote Orphée aux Enfers he certainly burlesqued *le classique*; but he spared Gluck: it is no parody of *Che farò* that he introduces in the Olympus scene, but the veritable air itself; and when some goddess—Diana?—says an affectionate word of recognition, one feels that for the moment *opéra bouffe* has softened—has taken off its hat to the saintly days of yore. But Sullivan wantonly burlesqued *D' un pensiero* in the quintet with chorus beginning A nice dilemma. Had it been *Chi mi frena* or *Un di si ben* one might have laughed; but the innocent, tender, touching, beloved-from-of-old *D' un pensiero*! Nobody but an irreclaimable ribald would have selected that for his gibes. Sullivan murdered his better nature with this crime. He rose to eloquence again for a moment in setting certain words—

> I have sought, but I seek it vainly,
> That one lost chord divine.

No wonder. This was in 1877, when he was thirtyfive. But no retreat was possible after A Nice Dilemma: not even a visit from the ghost of Sterndale Bennett could have waved him back from the Venusberg then. The Sorcerer belongs to 1877 as well as The Lost Chord; and everybody knows Pinafore and The Gondoliers and all that between them is; so that now the first of the Mendelssohn Scholars stands convicted of ten godless mockeries of everything sacred to Goss and Bennett. They trained him to make Europe yawn; and he took advantage of their teaching to make London and New York laugh and whistle.

A critic with no sense of decency might say out loud that in following Offenbach Sir Arthur has chosen the better part. The Mendelssohn school—with all its superficiality of conception, its miserable failure to comprehend Beethoven or even Weber, and the gentlemanlike vapidity which it deliberately inculcated as taste, discretion, reticence, chastity, refinement, finish, and what not—did undoubtedly give its capable pupils good mechanical skill. Their workmanship is plausible and elegant—just what it should be in comic opera. And the workmanship of our comic operas is often abominable. The technical work of Planquette, for instance, compared to that of Sullivan and Cellier, is crude, illiterate, hopelessly inept. Auber himself could not have written the concerted music in Patience or Pina-fore without more effort than it is worth. The question remains, would the skill that produced these two works have been more worthily employed upon another oratorio, another cantata? When all our musicians are brought to their last account, will Sullivan dissemble the score of the Pirates with a blush and call on the mountains to cover him, whilst Villiers Stanford and Hubert Parry table The Revenge, Prometheus Unbound, and Judith with pride? With which note of interrogation let us pass.

THE MUSIC SEASON IN LONDON

(Bradford Observer, 30 *November* 1891; unsigned)

The musical season here demands a long-delayed word from me. . . . The operatic experiments have ended rather variously, financial success and artistic excellence having been attained in the inverse ratios. Signor Lago, who closed his doors at the Shaftesbury Theatre the other day, is said to have made some money by the success of Cavalleria Rusticana, a clever and vigorous, straightforward bit of work, which could have been as well done by one of our young lions. Signor Lago has pro-duced a few miserably-mounted fragments of worn-out Italian operas by way of *levers de rideau* for Cavalleria. He has tried to revive his old success with Gluck's Orfeo, without Giulia Ravogli; and he has ventured, with the most desperately inadequate equipment, upon Wagner's Flying Dutchman. But the only possible criticism of these efforts is that he had much better have confined himself to Cavalleria. Sir Augustus Harris, meanwhile, has "exercised his right of legitimate competition" by opening Covent Garden with a capital French company, which, by dint of co-operative artistic spirit rather than individual excellence, has won and deserved golden opinions from all sorts of critics. He has produced Gounod's Philémon et Baucis and Bruneau's setting of a dramatic idyll founded by Gallet on Zola's Le Rêve. This is a charming piece of work, full of delicate and noble themes in what I may call the celestial style of Gounod, and woven together in the fashion of Wagner, as far as such a very

French composer as Bruneau is either capable or desirous of acquiring the unmatched German craftsmanship of the composer of Die Meistersinger. Sir Augustus has certainly triumphed over Lago on the artistic side, but he is said to have lost money on the experiment. Mr D'Oyly Carte, too, has at last given up the struggle to recover his large expenditure on Sir Arthur Sullivan's Ivanhoe, and disbanded his company, except as to those artists who are playing in Messager's La Basoche, which is likely to have a long run. He has also given up his attempt to screw up prices, and has adopted the ordinary scale for first-class theatres, of half-a-guinea for the stalls and half-a-crown for the pit. La Basoche is just the work for the English Opera House, elaborate and polished in style, without being pretentiously and emptily heavy, and amusing without being slangy or vulgar. It is exceptionally independent of any extraordinary powers on the part of the performers and, as great pains have been taken by Mr and Mrs Carte with its preparations, it is uncommonly well done.

London is still as badly off as ever for orchestral concerts; for the Crystal Palace concerts are too far away, and cost too much to count for much with amateurs of modest means. Sir Charles Hallé and Mr Henschel, encouraged by the advertisement they obtained from their ill-success at the beginning of last season, when the whole press overflowed with sympathy, have returned to the charge. Hallé, unfortunately, began with the Eroica symphony, which is quite the worst card in his hand. If he had chosen one of those works of Berlioz of which the Manchester has an unrivaled knowledge, he would have drawn a much larger audience. Henschel, with his London Symphony Concerts, is gaining ground. He still worries the orchestra by too often handling his *bâton* as if he were actually executing the passages with it; but there is a marked improvement in finish of execution at his concerts, and it looks as if the Henschel band were destined to become the classical band of London, as Richter is not adding to his old laurels, and Mr Manns's retirement cannot, in the strength of nature, be very remote now, since, vigorous as he looks, he is nearer seventy than sixty. Ysaÿe, the Belgian violinist, played Mendelssohn's concerto lately for Henschel better than any other living violinist could have played it, as far as London knows. He has been leading the quartet at the Popular Concerts, where Mr Chappell has at last awakened to the fact that his stock players were becoming what vestry politicians call an old gang. Popper, the famous violoncellist, the other evening took the place of the veteran Piatti, as Mr Edward Howell has also done on several occasions; in fact Piatti has not taken his old seat on the platform this season. Popper gave a concert on Wednesday, and played several compositions of his own, all somewhat slight, but elegant and finished, occasionally reminding one of Bizet, though without Bizet's originality. Popper's playing more than justifies his great reputation.

As young Gerardy is playing in London again, the violoncello cannot complain of being neglected at present. Another boy prodigy, Max [Mark] Hambourg, a pianist, gave a recital recently at Steinway Hall, where he again shewed, by his faults and his qualities, that he has real genius as a player and has not merely been coached up for the prodigy market. Paderewski, during his recent visit, played technically better than before, and with, of course, the same largeness of artistic comprehension which is the secret of his success—for his rivals would have no difficulty in doing his fingerwork if only they could do his brainwork. His immense vogue has made matters difficult for all later arrivals. Stavenhagen is making a bold bid for his old place as first favorite among the younger pianists; but since Liszt's death he has been all astray, oscillating between affected little exhibitions of crisp dexterity, for which he uses Beethoven's early concertos as stalking-horses, and wildly violent wrestlings with Chopin polonaises and Lisztian *fantasias*. In both moods he wastes much energy and technical accomplishment, and steadily loses ground, without, however, quite forfeiting the interest which his earlier visits aroused.

THE MOZART CENTENARY

(The Illustrated London News, 12 *December* 1891)

Wolfgang Mozart, the centenary of whose death on December 5, 1791, we are now celebrating, was born on January 27, 1756.

HOW TO BECOME A MUSICAL CRITIC

He was the grandson of an Augsburg bookbinder, and the son of Leopold Mozart, a composer, author, and violinist of good standing in the service of the Archbishop of Salzburg. When he was three years old he shewed such an interest in the music lessons of his sister, four and a half years his senior, that his father allowed him to play at learning music as he might have allowed him to play at horses. But the child was quite in earnest, and was soon composing minuets as eagerly as Mr Ruskin, at the same age, used to compose little poems. Leopold Mozart was a clever man up to a certain point, "self-made," untroubled by diffidence or shyness, conscious of being master of his profession, a practical, pushing man, ready to lay down an ambitious program for his son and bustle him through it. Seeing that Wolfgang had talent enough to qualify him for the highest attainable worldly success as a composer and *virtuoso*, he at once set about founding a European reputation for the future great man by making a grand tour through Vienna, Paris, London, Amsterdam, and many other towns, exhibiting his two children at Court and in public as "prodigies of nature." When the boy made a couple of tours in Italy in 1769–71, he knew everything that the most learned musicians in Europe could teach him; he became an unsurpassed harpsichord and pianoforte player; and as an organist he made old musicians declare that Sebastian Bach had come again. As a violinist he did not succeed in pleasing himself. Leopold insisted that nothing but self-confidence was needed to place him at the head of European violinists; and he may have been right; but Mozart never followed up his successes as a concerto player, and finally only used his skill to play the viola in quartets. On the whole, it must be admitted that the father, though incapable of conceiving the full range of his son's genius, did his utmost, according to his lights, to make the best of him; and although Mozart must, in his latter years, have once or twice speculated as to whether he might not have managed better as an orphan, he never bore any grudge against his father on that account.

Mozart's worldly prosperity ended with his boyhood. From the time when he began the world [*sic*] as a young man of twenty-one by making a trip to Paris with his mother (who died there) to the day of his early death, fourteen years later, he lived the life

of a very great man in a very small world. When he returned to
settle in Vienna and get married there, he burst out crying with
emotion after the ceremony. His wife cried too; and so did all
the spectators. They cried more wisely than they knew, considering what the future of the couple was to be. Mozart had three
means of getting money—teaching, giving concerts, and using
such aristocratic influence as he could enlist to obtain either a
Court appointment or commissions to compose for the church
or the theatre. None of these ways were fruitful for him, though
between them all, and a good deal of borrowing, he just managed
to die leaving his wife in possession of £5, exactly £15 short of
what they owed to the doctor. As a teacher, he got on very well
while he was giving lessons for nothing to people who interested
him: as a fashionable music-master he was comparatively a
failure. The concerts paid a little better: he wrote one pianoforte
concerto after another for them, and always improvised a *fantasia*, and was overwhelmed with applause. But there was then
no great public, as we understand the term, to steadily support
subscription concerts of classical music. His subscribers were
people of fashion, inconstant except in their determination only
to patronize music in "the season." His failure to obtain anything
except a wretched pittance at Court for writing dance music was
due to the extreme dread in which he was held by the cabal of
musicians who had the ear of the Emperor. Salieri frankly said
afterwards, "His death was a good job for us. If he had lived
longer not a soul would have given us a crumb for our compositions." Mozart was badly worn out by hard work and incessant
anxiety when his last fever attacked him. He even believed that
someone had poisoned him. A great deal of false sentiment has
been wasted on the fact that the weather was so bad on the day
of his funeral that none of the friends who attended the funeral
service at St Stephen's Church went with the hearse as far as
the distant graveyard of St Mark's. The driver of the hearse,
the assistant gravedigger, and a woman who was attached to the
place as "authorized beggar," were the only persons who saw the
coffin put on top of two others into a pauper grave of the third
class. Except to shew how poor Mozart was, the incident is of no
importance whatever. Its alleged pathos is really pure snobbery.

Mozart would certainly not have disdained to lie down for his last sleep in the grave of the poor. He would probably have been of the same mind as old Buchanan, who on his deathbed told his servant to give all the money left in the house away in charity instead of spending it on a funeral, adding, in his characteristic way, that the parish would have a pressing reason to bury him if they left him lying there too long.

It must not be supposed, however, that Mozart's life was one of actual want in the ordinary sense. He had immense powers, both of work and enjoyment; joked, laughed, told stories, talked, traveled, played, sang, rhymed, danced, masqueraded, acted, and played billiards well enough to delight in them all; and he had the charm of a child at thirty just as he had had the seriousness of a man at five. One gathers that many of his friends did not relish his superiority much more than Salieri did, and that, in spite of society and domesticity, he, on his highest plane, lived and died lonely and unhelpable. Still, on his more attainable planes, he had many enthusiastic friends and worshipers. What he lacked was opportunity to do the best he felt capable of in his art—a tragic privation.

It is not possible to give here any adequate account of Mozart's claims to greatness as a composer. At present his music is hardly known in England except to those who study it in private. Public performances of it are few and far between, and, until Richter conducted the E flat symphony here, nobody could have gathered from the vapid, hasty, trivial readings which were customary in our concert rooms that Mozart, judged by nineteenth-century standards, had any serious claim to his old-fashioned reputation. One reason among many for this mistake may be given. Leopold Mozart undoubtedly did his son the great harm of imposing his own narrow musical ideal on him, instead of allowing him to find out the full capacities of the art for himself. He taught the boy that when a piece of music sounded beautifully, and was symmetrically, ingeniously, and interestingly worked out in sonata form, nothing more was to be expected or even permitted. Mozart, if left untutored, would probably have arrived at the conclusion that a composition without a poetic or dramatic basis was a mere luxury, and not a serious work of art at all. As it was, he was trained to consider the production of "absolute music" as the normal end of composition, and when his genius drove him to make his instrumental music mean something, he wasted the most extraordinary ingenuity in giving it expression through the forms and without violating the usages of absolute music, bending these forms and usages to his poetic purpose with such success that the same piece of music serves as a pet passage of tone poetry to the amateur who knows nothing of musical formalism, while the pedant who is insensible to poetry or drama holds them up as models of classic composition to his pupils.

This combination of formalism with poetic significance has been much applauded, not only for its ingenuity, as is natural, but as a merit in the music, which is perverse and absurd. Mozart apologizing to his father for some unusual modulation which he could not justify except on poetic grounds cut but a foolish figure. If he had written his G minor quintet, for instance, in the free form contrived by Liszt for his symphonic poems, the death of his father, which immediately followed the composition of that work, would, no doubt, have been attributed to his horror on reading the score; but there is not the slightest ground for pretending, with Wagner's works to instruct us, that the quintet would have been one whit less admirable. Later on, when Mozart had quite freed himself, and come to recognize that the forbidden thing was exactly what he was born to do, he still, from mere habit and mastery, kept to the old forms closely enough to pass with us for a formalist, although he scared his contemporaries into abusing him exactly as Wagner has been abused within our own time. The result is that since Mozart, under his father's influence, produced a vast quantity of instrumental music which is absolute music and nothing else, and since even the great dramatic and poetic works of his later years were cast mainly in the moulds of that music, we have hastily concluded that all his work is of one piece, and that an intelligent dramatic handling of his great symphonies would be an anachronism. In his very operas it is hard, nowadays, to get the most obvious dramatic points in his orchestration attended to, even the churchyard scene in Don Juan being invariably rattled through at Covent Garden as if it were a surprisingly vapid quadrille.

HOW TO BECOME A MUSICAL CRITIC

Fortunately, the persistence with which Wagner fought all his life for a reform of orchestral execution as to Mozart's works, the example set by the conductors inspired by him, and such authoritative utterances as those of Gounod on the subject of Don Giovanni, not to mention social influences which cannot be so simply stated, are at last letting the public into the important secret that the incompetence and superficiality of Mozart's interpreters are the true and only causes of the apparent triviality of his greatest music. Properly executed, Mozart's work never disappointed anybody yet. Its popularity is increasing at present, after a long interval. The appetite for riotous, passionate, wilful, heroic music has been appeased; and we are now beginning to feel that we cannot go on listening to Beethoven's Seventh Symphony and the Tannhäuser overture for ever. When we have quite worn them out, and have become conscious that there are grades of quality in emotion as well as variations of intensity, then we shall be on the way to become true Mozart connoisseurs and to value Wagner's best work apart from its mere novelty. The obstacle to that at present is the dulness of our daily lives, which makes us intemperate in our demands for sensation in art, and the bluntness of mind which prevents us from perceiving or relishing the essentially intellectual quality of the very finest music. Both these disqualifications are the result of deficient culture; and while that lasts Mozart will have to lie on the shelf. But that is so much the worse for the uncultured generation—not for the composer of Don Juan.

BRAHMS, BEETHOVEN, AND THE BARBER OF BAGDAD

(The World, 23 December 1891)

The admirers of Brahms are to be congratulated on the set of vocal quartets which have just been sung at the Popular Concerts for the first time by Mrs Henschel, Miss Fassett, Mr Shakespeare, and Mr Henschel. For once in a way, Johannes has really distinguished himself. In these quartets we have, it goes without saying, the extraordinary facility of harmonic workmanship which Brahms shews in everything he does, from the colossally stupid Requiem, which has made so many of us wish ourselves dead, to those unmitigated minor bores, the Liebeslieder Waltzes. But we have also in them a feeling which is thoroughly roused— a vivacious, positively romantic feeling—graceful, tender, spontaneous—something as different as possible from his usual unaroused state, his heavy, all-pervading unintelligent German sentimentality. Besides, they shew good handicraft in another sense than that of doing easily what other men find very difficult. Brahms has always had the mere brute force of his amazing musical faculty. No one can deny that he all but equals our most famous native orators in respect of having a power of utterance that would place him above the greatest masters if only he had anything particular to say. But this time he has shewn imaginative workmanship, especially in the play of color of the four voices, which are combined and contrasted and crossed and interwoven in a delightful way. Much of the effect was, no doubt, due to the four singers, each of them a soloist of distinguished merit; but that does not account for everything, since quite as much has been done for previous compositions of Brahms without for a moment producing the same charm. He evidently composed the quartets in one of those fortunately-inspired moments to which we owe all that is valuable in his work.

I wish I could go on to say that the instrumental quartet (Beethoven's in E flat, Op. 74) was as well rehearsed as the vocal ones. But had that been so, the first movement would not have been the scramble it was. Madame Neruda's solo was Mozart's Adagio in E, which she played, it seemed to me, as well as she could possibly have played it even in her prime, in justice to which golden period I must not pretend that she can now secure her former rapidity and boldness of execution in quick movements without some sacrifice of the old delicacy of hand and purity of intonation. Miss Adeline de Lara earned the tremendous applause she got for her performance of Schumann's Symphonic Studies by the not too common feat of holding the attention of the audience unwearied from the first bar to the last. Nevertheless, the element of nobility of style, which is essential to a completely adequate interpretation of Schumann's intention in this

composition, was lacking in Miss de Lara's romantic reading of
it. Brahms's Sonata for violoncello and pianoforte, Op. 38, a long
elaboration of nothing whatever, was played by Miss de Lara
and Mr Howell. It may seem an impertinence to tell an artist of
Mr Howell's experience that he is improving; but the change
from the orchestral desks in St James's Hall, at which there is no
chance of asserting one's individuality except when the overture
to William Tell or the accompaniment to *Batti, batti* comes into
the night's work, to the Popular Concerts, where the whole
audience have often to be held by the 'cellist single-handed, is
one to which the most hardened veteran could not conceivably
be insensible. The fact is that the orchestra, though it levels many
players up, levels down others, who retain for a long time their
power of rising to the occasion when the occasion comes. Unfortunately, it too often never comes—at least, not in the focus
of London criticism. Only in the suburbs or the provinces can
our many excellent orchestral players get a taste of the bracing
responsibility of solo-playing.

I paid the Royal College students the very considerable compliment (from a critic) of going a second time to see their performance of The Barber of Bagdad. The improvement from the
elimination of stage fright was enormous; and I am disposed to
retract something of what I said about the absence of evidence
of training in voice-production. Mind, I do not retract it altogether; but I now believe that the tenor's habit of thickening his
tongue at the root until he might almost as well have a potato
there, is one against which his teachers have vainly warned him,
because he fought with it successfully all through his first song.
Not until he rose from his couch and was fairly upon his legs
did it get the better of him. Will he believe me that, if he would
only cultivate his sense of beauty in vocal tone, and then face the
ordeal of listening to himself with manly fortitude, he would
never need any warning beyond that of his own ear? Like all the
rest, he sang much better on the 16th than on the previous occasion. Mr Villiers Stanford also was less anxious, and gave his forces
their head when they were disposed to make the pace lively.
Under these bettered circumstances, The Barber of Bagdad revealed itself as a lighter and more fantastic work than it seemed

before. Several passages, of which the shape and intention were obscured on the first occasion by timidity of execution, came out as burlesques of particular points in the reigning grand operas of thirty years ago, Meyerbeer being the chief victim of these pleasantries. Thus, the Barber's long *cadenza* on the word Morgiana, which sounded at the first performance like a somewhat overdone parody of the operatic *cadenza* in general, became recognizable as a gibe at Peter's elaborate *cadenza* on the name Caterina in the tent scene in L'Etoile du Nord, from the last act of which opera, by the bye, Cornelius borrowed the leading phrase of Noureddin's first song. An odd coincidence of this kind occurs in the first act, after the Barber has driven away the servants, when Noureddin, flattering him, breaks out mellifluously with a stave of In happy moments, day by day, from Maritana. The clever *trio* at the beginning of the second act, He comes! he comes! oh, blessed be the day! is an unconscious echo of Daland's entry in the *trio* at the end of the second act of The Flying Dutchman. Many other points illustrate Cornelius's way of assimilating music in all directions, and adapting it in a thoroughly artistic way to his own purpose. If Mr D'Oyly Carte in course of time amasses a repertory at the Royal English Opera, he might do worse than include The Bagdad Barber in it. I am quite prepared to listen to it a third time: in fact, I am in the stage of going about the house fitfully bawling out scraps of "Sally Maleikum" (or whatever it is), to the astonishment of my people, before whom I seldom unbend in this way.

The students of the Royal Academy of Music gave a concert on Thursday afternoon at St James's Hall. The program was an extremely liberal one, consisting of a composition of symphonic proportions, in four movements, for pianoforte, chorus, and orchestra, by Raff, entitled Die Tageszeiten, with three concertos, a *suite de ballet*, and four airs. I held out until after the second concerto; and everything that I heard was well prepared and creditably executed. The orchestra was more heavily reinforced by first-rate professional players than that of the Royal College— too much so to be taken as a genuine students' orchestra; but the tone from the string band, which was largely manned by the pupils, was excellent. The only performance which rose above student level into the region of beautiful execution and sympathetic interpretation was that of Beethoven's fourth concerto by Miss Ethel Barns, who very far surpassed Stavenhagen's recent performance of the same work at the Crystal Palace. The Rubinstein *cadenzas* were, of course, beyond her physical powers; but she succeeded in suggesting their effect vividly to those who recollect Rubinstein's style. Next in order of interest came Goldmark's violin concerto, one of the many compositions of this kind which are not worth the time and trouble of listening to them. It was played by a young gentleman named Philip Cathie, who has not as yet developed any style, but whose touch and intonation are remarkably good. In fact, his fine quality of tone and natural musical feeling would be a sufficient equipment on the technical side for a violinist of considerable eminence. But such a position is not to be attained by mere fiddling. Every generation produces its infant Raphaels and infant Rosciuses, and *Wunderkinder* who can perform all the childish feats of Mozart. But if they are commonplace in character and general capacity, nothing ever comes of their phenomenal excess of special faculty; unless, indeed, they are pretty *prime donne*, in which case they may make a world-wide reputation with a surprisingly small share of artistic honor and conscience. Mr Philip Cathie must, then, take it to heart that having made a fiddler of himself everything now depends on his success in making a man of himself.

I cannot say that I was favorably impressed with the singing at this concert. I heard three very good voices, a soprano, a contralto, and a *basso cantante*. But they were all trained more or less on the old system of grinding the voice to a fine edge, and controlling it by steady pressure. I am a hopeless infidel with regard to that system. No doubt, gifted dramatic singers have made reputations with it in spite of the disadvantage it put them at. I have even heard a singer or two to whom it seemed natural— who could sing in no other way, and could produce a free, rattling tone with it, and be none the worse. But all the cases I have met with of prematurely worn-out voices, and patients whose doctors have had to forbid them to sing, are due to vocal grinding, which begins so promisingly with a great increase in the "strength" and clearness of the voice. And, on the other hand, I have found that veterans like Sims Reeves, who are proof against everything except old age, avoid it as if it were the plague. Fortunately, it has lost much of its old authority, especially of late years, when the superiority of rival methods has been so repeatedly demonstrated by the success of American singers. The Royal College teaching staff evidently warns its pupils not to depend on the old formula of "tension of cords and force of blast," which is, at least, a valuable negative counsel. But at the Academy the grindstone is not wholly discarded yet. However, my opinion on the subject is only my opinion. The Academy tradition claims descent from the great Garcia, whom I am not in a position to criticize, as he died sixty years ago at the age of fiftyseven. No doubt he was a famous teacher; and his son, our Royal Academy Garcia, born in 1805, was his pupil. But if I find by observation that certain ways of singing produce, with persons of average capacity, premature deterioration and failure, whilst opposite ways give the vocal powers their full natural lease of life, I am forced to draw my conclusions without respect of persons or institutions. Therefore, though I do not question the value of the instruction that is to be obtained on many important points in Tenterden-street, much less pretend that individual professors on the staff do not make highly beneficial departures from the typical Academy teaching, yet, on the whole, I am not in the habit of advising novices to lay the foundations of their vocal methods in the R.A.M. And I cannot say that the concert the other day did much to disarm my prejudices in that respect, although I recognize the natural talent shewed by the three young singers, especially the lady who sang the Inflammatus from Dvořák's Stabat Mater.

THE SUPERIORITY OF MUSICAL TO DRAMATIC CRITICS

(The Players, 6 January 1892)

I suppose no one will deny the right of the fully accomplished musical critic to look down upon the mere dramatic critic as

something between an unskilled laborer and a journeyman. I
have often taken a turn at dramatic work for a night merely to
amuse myself and oblige a friend,[1] whereas if I were to ask a
dramatic critic to take my place, I should be regarded as no less
obviously mad than a surgeon who should ask his stockbroker
to cut off a leg or two for him, so as to leave him free for a trip
up the river. Clearly, I may without arrogance consider my
dramatic colleagues—I call them colleagues more out of politeness than from any genuine sense that they are my equals—as at
best specialists in a sub-department of my art. They are men who
have failed to make themselves musical critics—creatures with
half-developed senses, who will listen to any sort of stage diction
and look at any sort of stage picture without more artistic feeling
than is involved in the daily act of listening to the accent and
scrutinizing the hat of a new acquaintance in order to estimate
his income and social standing. Their common formula for a
notice is as follows. First, they trace the origin of the play to any
previous foreign work which happens to contain similar incidents
—as, for example, the unexpected reappearance of a long-lost
husband just in time to rescue his young and beautiful grass
widow from the toils of a villain, or a complication arising from
one character being mistaken for another extremely like him.
Next, they tell the story of the play, more or less accurately. Then
they offer some remarks, in their best taste, on the moral to be
drawn, and its probable reaction on the domestic purity of the
nation. If the conclusion arrived at in this section is harsh to the
author, they easily avoid all unpleasantness by assuring him privately that they agree with every word he says, but that people
are such fools that it would hardly do to avow as much. Finally,
a run through the names in the playbill enables them to do any
little good turns or pay off any old scores that may be outstanding. This last section is the only one which is common to both the
theatrical notice and that higher art form, the musical criticism.

All this is such child's play that I once formed the design of
becoming a dramatic critic myself, in order to shew how the

[1] Shaw had served on several occasions as substitute dramatic critic for William
Archer on *The Manchester Guardian*, A. B. Walkley on *The Star*, and a journalist
named Law on *The Scottish Leader*. He had also written a few dramatic reviews
for *The Pall Mall Gazette* and *Our Corner*.

thing might be done by a really competent hand; and I actually sacrificed my dignity to the extent of telling the editor of a new journal, who had asked me to contribute, that I should like to become his dramatic critic. He replied that he had had applications for the post from the entire literary profession in London (not a single member of which would have dreamed of presuming to consider himself qualified for the post of musical critic), and that, foreseeing this, he had promised the post beforehand to a veteran journalist whose pre-eminent claims would excite no ill-feeling, since they were founded entirely on prescription. A young man could only have been selected on the ground that he was the best man, an implication that would have cost the editor all his friends at one blow. So the veteran was duly appointed; and when he found, as he soon did, that he had neither time nor inclination to do the work, an able junior unobtrusively slipped into his berth without offense to anyone, the vacancy being forgotten by that time. As for me, I resolved to effect my purpose in another way by some day taking apprentices and teaching them the whole critical business, which comprehends writing, esthetics, and technique of the various arts. This is the more necessary, since even in my own superior branch the dignity of the profession is too often compromised by *littérateurs* who have no ears and musicians who cannot write, both varieties being often so destitute of analytic faculty and training that when, after protracted and desperate writing round and round a performance, they are forced at last to give an account of its quality, they have to fall back on the most helpless generalities of praise or blame, and can no more *describe* an artist than a tailor can dissect his customer. Any of these defects, and *a fortiori* all three of them, will lame a critic to such an extent that unless he is magnificently endowed with the superb quality which we dishonor by the ignoble name of Cheek—a quality which has enabled men from time immemorial to fly without wings, and to live sumptuously without incomes—he becomes diffident and deferential in his style. Now, a critic cannot be anything worse than deferential. To aggravate the mischief, the deference is shewn less to the performers than to the *entrepreneurs* who speculate in their attractions; so that the actor who takes a theatre of his own instantly receives from the press a huge unearned increment of consideration far beyond what is due to the sense of advertisements to come.

In consequence, these men of business are rapidly sinking to the level of the artists they employ; and the *impresario*, manager, or agent of the future, instead of being a reasonable man of the world, with a good knowledge of art from the business point of view, promises to be a vain, petulant creature, regarding the critic as a poor dependant to whom he dispenses a magnificent hospitality, and reading press notices with a morbid susceptibility to their bearing on his own personal vanity. Nothing but a timely revival of uppishness on the part of the critics can check this demoralization of the *entrepreneur*; and how can a man be uppish if he is a mere scribbling play-goer, an amateur who can be replaced at a moment's notice by dozens of incipient barristers or *dilettanti* from the upper division of the Civil Service with a taste for complimentary first night stalls? Dramatic criticism has fallen to the level of an amusement for gentlemen: musical criticism remains the scarce product of highly-skilled labor. Between the Richter and the Crystal Palace concerts, the musical critic has opportunities of hearing at least once a week the masterpieces of musical art executed by highly trained performers; whilst the theatrical critic, from lack of familiarity with the masterpieces of dramatic poetry, becomes at last so illiterate that when he is forced, once in a blue moon, to endure a night of Shakespear (performed mostly by actors who deliver blank verse much as a *ripieno* cornet from a Salvation Army band might play one of Handel's trumpet *obligati*) he cannot conceal his dislike, his weariness, his disparagement, his longing to be back at his usual work of discussing plays that only prove how the old reproach has passed from music to the drama, since it now needs no Beaumarchais to discover that when a piece is too silly to be read one acts it.

It is conceded that a musical critic who was nothing but an opera-goer would be a gross impostor; and yet no man could go to the opera for ten years and be as ignorant of "absolute music" as a dramatic critic may be of absolute literature (if I may so transfer the term) after twenty years of play-going. And accordingly, we find that even the great mistakes of the musical critics are far less discreditable than the great mistakes of the dramatic critics. Take, for example, the apparently cognate cases of the failures to appreciate Wagner and Ibsen. The opposition to Wagner was provoked by the extreme strangeness of the sound of his music to the ears of critics saturated with Handel, Haydn, Mozart, Beethoven, Schubert, and Mendelssohn. Clearly the musical critics were misled by sheer intensity of culture, just as Spohr and Weber were betrayed into attacking Beethoven. But the anti-Ibsenite dramatic critics cannot allege that Ibsen staggered them with unwonted tonic discords and unprepared major ninths—that his words were unknown to dictionary makers and his syntax to grammarians. No critic saturated with Goethe (the dramatic contemporary and peer of Mozart and Beethoven) could possibly have come so desperately to grief over Ibsen as most of our dramatic critics now rue having done. The proof is that the two dramatic critics who most triumphantly escaped the pitfall—and that without at all accepting the Ibsenist philosophy —were not only accomplished literary critics, but one of them had practiced musical criticism as well, and the other was the author of a life of Wagner. They were in no more danger of taking the "suburban egotist" view of Ibsen than I, through my poor opinion of most of Brahms's music, am of mistaking that composer for an organ grinder. Besides, compare the anti-Wagnerite documents with the anti-Ibsenite ones. Read Hanslick, Edmund Gurney, or even the belated Mr Statham on the hopeless subject of the fallacy of Wagner's art theory. Set against their criticisms the best of the current indictments of A Doll's House and Ghosts; and then deny, if you can, that even in making an ass of himself the musical critic towers majestically over the little specialist of the playhouse.

One important point of inferiority which the dramatic critic cannot very well help, considering the limits of his experience, is his gullibility on the subject of "the palmy days" of theatrical art. As it happens, the palmy days are in full swing at the opera still. I know all about them. At Covent Garden the bill changes every night, and always from one heroic work to another: coats and waistcoats are as unfamiliar to me on the stage as they were

to Mrs Siddons. The artists to whom I am accustomed do not
play the same little bit of ephemeral comedy for five hundred
nights at a time, and find their wigs becoming grey before they
have played one classic part. No: they receive that "thorough
all-round training," and acquire that "readiness of resource"
which is only to be gained by playing a fresh leading part in a
great work every night, as actors used to do in such famous old
schools of acting as the provincial stock companies, mostly extinct at present, and deeply regretted by all those who are too
young to know at first hand what they are talking about. And the
strong opinion I have formed from my experience is, that of all
the —— but I find that I have no room left. I am very sorry; but
I am strictly limited in point of space, and really cannot go on
any longer.

THE ROSSINI CENTENARY

(The Illustrated London News, 5 March 1892)

Fifty years ago Rossini would have been described as one of
the greatest of modern composers, the equal, if not the superior,
of Beethoven. At present, such an estimate of him seems as
ridiculous to us all as it seemed then to Berlioz and Wagner; and
the danger now is that all the centenary notices of him which are
not mere compilations from the musical dictionaries will revenge
upon his memory the excesses of the Rossinian age, when even
scholarly musicians regarded him as an Italian Handel. Mendelssohn himself was captivated by his genius, although it is not too
much to say that Rossini never produced a single secular composition of any length without padding or spicing it with some
gross claptrap which Mendelssohn would have hanged himself
rather than put before the public as his own work. Indeed,
Rossini was one of the greatest masters of claptrap that ever
lived. His moral deficiencies as an artist were quite extraordinary.
When he found the natural superiority of his genius in conflict
with the ignorance and frivolity of the public—and the musical
ignorance and frivolity of the Venetians and Neapolitans can
hardly be overstated—he surrendered without a struggle. Although he was so able a man that it was easier and pleasanter to

him to do his work intelligently than to conventionalize it and write down to the popular taste, he never persevered in any innovation that was not well received; and it is hardly possible to doubt that the superiority of William Tell to his other operas is due solely to the fact that it was written for the Grand Opéra in Paris, where the public had been educated by Gluck to expect at least a show of seriousness in an *opera seria*. He rose to the occasion then as a matter of business, just as he would have sunk to it had the commission come from Venice; and it was characteristic of him that he did not rise an inch beyond it: in fact, he adapted all the old claptrap to the new conditions instead of discarding it. This may be seen plainly enough in the overture which every reader of these lines probably knows by heart. Rossini's previous overtures had all been composed according to a formula of his own. First came a majestic and often beautiful exordium, sometimes extending, as in Semiramide, to the dimensions of a slow movement. Then he fell to business with an irresistibly piquant "first subject," usually a *galop* more or less thinly disguised, working up into the conventional *tutti*, with the strings rushing up and down the scales and the brass blaring vigorously. Then a striking half-close, announcing a fresh treat in the shape of a "second subject," not a *galop* this time, but a spirited little march tune, leading to the celebrated Rossini *crescendo*, in which one of the *arabesques* of the march pattern would be repeated and repeated, with the pace of the accompaniment doubling and redoubling, and the orchestration thickening and warming, until finally the big drum and the trombones were in full play, and every true Italian was ready to shout *Viva il gran' maestro!* in wild enthusiasm. And then, since everybody wanted to hear it all again, the whole affair, except, of course, the introduction, was repeated note for note, and finished off with a Pelion of a *coda* piled on the Ossa of the *crescendo*, the last flourish being always a rush up the scale by the fiddles, and a final thump and crash for the whole band. As Rossini's invention never flagged in the matter of *galops* and marches, he was able to turn out overtures of this sort without a second thought. They soon overran Europe; and those to Tancredi, L' Italiana in Algeri, La Gazza Ladra, and especially Semiramide, are still as familiar to military bandsmen as God Save the Queen. When William Tell was ordered, Rossini understood that Paris would expect something more than a mere reshaking of his old box of tricks; but he knew better than to risk his popularity by giving them any really novel or profound work. All he abandoned was the wholesale repetition and the *crescendo*. By way of repudiating all noisy pomp in the exordium, he made it a charming concerted piece for the violoncellos alone. The *galop* and the *tutti* he presented in the most ingenious metamorphosis as the approach and final bursting of a tremendous storm. The second subject was a charming pastorale, with variations on the flute which no school-girl could misunderstand. Suddenly came a trumpet-call, and then such a quickstep as the world had never heard before. Not one of his old *galopades* or *crescendos* could keep pace with it for a moment: it was the very quintessence of all his claptrap. Hackneyed as it has become, it is hard to this day to keep an audience from encoring it when it is well played. The whole opera bears the same relation to his other operas as the overture to his other overtures. It was meant for an audience which included a certain percentage of serious and cultivated musicians. He just surpasses himself far enough to compel the admiration, if not the respect, of these few, without losing his hold of the rest. Had the percentage been higher, he would have taken a little more trouble: if it had been lower, he would have taken less. The success of William Tell, added to the results of a prudent marriage, and the friendship of the Rothschilds, who looked after his savings for him, secured his future pecuniarily. From that time, although he had not turned thirtynine, he wrote no more operas. For the forty years of life which remained to him he could afford to be idle, and he was idle, except that he composed a mass and a Stabat Mater, in which again he rose with consummate ease just to the requirements of his church, still without sacrificing a jot of his popularity. The Stabat, with its *Cujus animam* set to a stirring march tune, its theatrically sublime *Inflammatus*, and the ingenious sham fugue at the end, shews that he was the same man in the church as in the theatre. In so far as he was ever great, he was great in spite of himself. When he was a lad learning counterpoint, his master one day disparaged him as only knowing enough to compose mere operas. He immediately replied that all he wanted was to compose operas, and refused to carry his studies a step further. Among musicians, therefore, his name is famous, but not sacred. He was captivating and exhilarating; he was imposing to the last degree in his splendid moments; he was clever, and full of fun; his practicality was largely due to good sense; he did not settle down to offering the public frivolous work until it had snubbed him for taking himself more seriously; he may be credited with some sincerity in his admissions that he was not a great composer as Mozart was a great composer; and it cannot be denied that he was exceptionally unfortunate in respect of the illiteracy, the Bohemianism, the ignorance, narrowness, and squalor of his environment during childhood. On all these grounds, and some others, there is a case to be made out on Rossini's side which cannot be adequately stated here; but when the utmost has been made of it, it will not entitle him to pre-eminence even among modern Italian composers, whilst as to a place in the hierarchy of the greatest modern masters, from Bach to Wagner, that is quite out of the question.

THE RELIGION OF THE PIANOFORTE

(The Fortnightly Review, February 1894)

The other day somebody went to Rubinstein and said, "Is the pianoforte a musical instrument?" That is just the sort of question people put nowadays. You call on the Prince of Wales to ask, "Is England a republic?" or on the Lord Mayor with, "Is London a city?" or on Madame Calvé to take her opinion, as an expert, on "Is Cavalleria Rusticana an opera?" In treating such questions as open ones you have already achieved a paradox; and even if the Prince of Wales should have the presence of mind to simply say No, and the Lord Mayor and Madame Calvé, Yes, and have you immediately shewn out, still you are in a position to fill the contents bill of one of our weekly scrap papers with, "Is England a republic?—What the Prince of Wales says"; and so sell off an edition to people who cannot bring themselves to think that the plain explanation of the mystery is that you are a foolish person.

Yet it will not do to reply to "Is the pianoforte a musical instrument?" by a simple Yes. That would be an understatement of a quite extraordinary case. The pianoforte is the most important of all musical instruments: its invention was to music what the invention of printing was to poetry. Just consider the analogy for a moment. What is it that keeps Shakespear alive among us? Is it the stage, the great actors, the occasional revivals with new music and scenery, and agreeably mendacious accounts of the proceedings in the newspapers after the first night? Not a bit of it. Those who know their Shakespear at all know him before they are twentyfive: after that there is no time—one has to live instead of to read; and how many Shakespearean revivals, pray, has an Englishman the chance of seeing before he is twentyfive, even if he lives in a city and not in the untheatred country, or in a family which regards the pit of the theatre as the antechamber to that pit which has no bottom? I myself, born of profane stock, and with a quarter-century of play-going, juvenile and manly, behind me, have not seen as many as a full half of Shakespear's plays acted; and if my impressions of his genius were based solely on these representations I should be in darkness indeed. For what is it that I have seen on such occasions? Take the solitary play of Shakespear's which is revived more than twice in a generation! Well, I have seen Mr Barry Sullivan's Hamlet, Mr Daniel Bandmann's Hamlet, Miss Marriott's Hamlet, Mr Irving's Hamlet, Signor Salvini's Hamlet, Mr Wilson Barrett's Hamlet, Mr Benson's Hamlet, Mr Beerbohm Tree's Hamlet, and perhaps others which I forget. But to none of these artists do I owe my acquaintance with Shakespear's play of Hamlet. In proof whereof, let me announce that, for all my Hamlet-going, were I to perish this day, I should go to my account without having seen Fortinbras, save in my mind's eye, or watched the ghostly twilight march (as I conceive it) of those soldiers who went to their graves like beds to dispute with him a territory that was not tomb enough and continent to hide the slain. When first I saw Hamlet I innocently expected Fortinbras to dash in, as in Sir John Gilbert's picture, with shield and helmet, like a medieval Charles XII, and, by right of his sword and his will, take the throne which the fencing foil and the speculative intellect had let slip, thereby pointing the play's most characteristically English moral. But what was my first Hamlet to my first Romeo and Juliet, in which Romeo, instead of dying forthwith when he took the poison, was interrupted by Juliet, who sat up and made him carry her down to the footlights, where she complained of being very cold, and had to be warmed by a love scene, in the middle of which Romeo, who had forgotten all about the poison, was taken ill and died? Or my first Richard III, which turned out to be a wild *potpourri* of all the historical plays, with a studied debasement of all the best word music in the lines, and an original domestic scene in which Richard, after feebly bullying his wife, observed, "If this dont kill her, she's immortal"? Cibber's Richard III was, to my youthful judgment, superior to Shakespear's play on one point only, and that was the omission of the stage direction, "Exeunt fighting," whereby Richmond and the tyrant were enabled to have it out to the bitter end full in my view. Need I add that it was not through this sort of thing, with five out of every six parts pitiably ill acted and ill uttered, that I came to know Shakespear? Later on, when it was no longer Mr Blank's Hamlet and Miss Dash's Juliet that was in question, but "the Lyceum revival," the stage brought me but little nearer to the drama. For the terrible cutting involved by modern hours of performance; the foredoomed futility of the attempt to take a work originally conceived mainly as a long story told on the stage, with plenty of casual adventures and unlimited changes of scene, and to tight-lace it into something like a modern play consisting of a single situation in three acts; and the commercial relations which led the salaried players to make the most abject artistic sacrifices to their professional consciousness that the performance is the actor-manager's "show," and by no means their own or Shakespear's: all these and many other violently anti-artistic conditions of modern theatrical enterprise still stood inexorably between the stage and the real Shakespear.

The case of Shakespear is not, of course, the whole case against the theatre: it is, indeed, the weakest part of it, because the stage certainly does more for Shakespear than for any other dramatic poet. The English drama, from Marlowe to Browning, would practically not exist if it were not printed. To extend the argument to literature in general it is only necessary to imagine the nation depending for its knowledge of poetry and romance on the recitations of elocutionists and the readings with which some of our sects replace the "lessons" of the Church of England. Such a conception dies of its own absurdity. Clearly, the literature which the private student cannot buy or borrow to take home and puzzle out by himself may be regarded as, at best, in a state of suspended animation.

But what has all this to do with the pianoforte? Well, can anything be more obvious? I decline to insult the intelligence of the public by explaining.

Let me, however, do an unsolicited service to thousands of fellow creatures who are huddling round the fire trying to kill time with such sensations as they can extract from novels, not suspecting a far more potent instrument stands dumb by the wall, unthought of save as one of those expensive and useless pieces of show furniture without which no gentleman's drawing room is complete. Take a case by way of illustration. You are a youth, let us suppose, poring over The Three Musketeers, or some romance of Scott's. Now, in the name of all that is real, how much satisfaction do you get out of mere *descriptions* of duels, and escapes, and defiances, and raptures of passion? A good deal, you think (being young); but how if you could find a sort of book that would give you not merely a description of these thrilling sensations, but the sensations themselves—the stirring of the blood, the bristling of the fibres, the transcendent, fearless fury which makes romance so delightful, and realizes that ideal which Mr Gilbert has aptly summed up in the phrase, "heroism without risk"? Such a book is within your reach. Pitch your Three Musketeers into the waste-paper basket, and get a vocal score of Meyerbeer's Huguenots. Then to the piano, and pound away. In the music you will find the body and reality of that feeling which the mere novelist could only describe to you; there will come home to your senses something in which you can actually experience the candor and gallant impulse of the hero, the grace and trouble of the heroine, and the extracted emotional quintessence of their love. As to duels, what wretched printed list of the thrusts in *carte* and *tierce* delivered by D'Artagnan or Bussy d'Amboise can interest the man who knows Don Giovanni's duel in the dark with the Commandant, or Romeo's annihilation of Tybalt (not Shakespear's, but Gounod's Romeo), or Raoul's explosion of courage on the brink of the fight in the *Pré aux Clercs*. And mark, it is only at the piano that that *Pré aux Clercs* fight is really fought out—that Maurevert comes out of the darkness with his assassins to back San Bris, and that Marcel, in extremity, thunders his *Eine feste Burg* at the door of the inn, and brings all the Huguenot soldiers tumbling out to the rescue with their rataplan. Go to the theatre for that scene, and there is no sense in what passes: Maurevert is cut; Marcel is cut; everything that makes the scene grow and live is cut, because the opera is so long that even with the fourth act omitted it is impossible to present it unmutilated without an ungentlemanly curtailment of the waits between the acts. Besides, it is a curious circumstance that operatic stage managers never read operas, perhaps because, since they never conceive cause and effect as operating in the normal way, the composer's instructions would only lead them astray. At all events, we have Meyerbeer at the same disadvantage on the stage as Shakespear.

Here I can conceive our Musketeer-loving youth interrupting me with some impatience to explain that he cannot play the piano. No doubt he cannot: what of that? Berlioz could not play the piano; Wagner could not play the piano; nay, I myself, a musical critic of European reputation, *I* cannot play. But is any man prevented from reading Othello by the fact that he cannot act or recite? You need not be able to play your Huguenots: if you can read the notes and bungle over them, that is sufficient. This only leads our youth to put his difficulty more precisely: he cannot even read the notes. Of course not; but why? Because he has never discovered that they are worth learning. Pianism has been presented to him as a polite accomplishment, the object of which is to give pleasure to others—an object which has not been attained, he has observed, in the case of his sisters. To him, therefore, I seem to propose that he shall, in pure and probably unsuccessful altruism, spend so many hours a day for a year over

Czerny's, Plaidy's, or Cramer's exercises in order that he may be able to play Beethoven's Pathetic Sonata slowly and awkwardly, but note-accurately, to the manifest discomfort and disturbance of all within earshot. Now, he does not care two straws about the Pathetic Sonata, and would not spend twelve hours, much less twelve months, over Czerny to save all Beethoven's works from destruction, much less to oblige me. Therefore, though he will learn to smoke, to skate, to play billiards, to ride, to shoot, to do half-a-dozen things much more difficult than reading music, he will no more learn his notes than a sailor will learn ploughing. Why should he, since no pleasure can come of it for himself? As to giving pleasure to others, even sisterless youths know, first, that there are not ten men in Europe among the most gifted and arduously-trained professionals whose playing gives pleasure to enough people to fill St James's Hall; and second, that the effect of ordinary amateur playing on other people is to drive them almost mad. I learnt my notes at the age of sixteen or thereabouts; and since that time I have inflicted untold suffering on my neighbors without having on a single occasion given the smallest pleasure to any human being except myself. Then, it will be asked, Why did I begin? Well, the motive arose from my previous knowledge of music. I had been accustomed all my life to hear it in sufficing quantities; and the melodies I heard I could at least sing; so that I neither had nor desired any technical knowledge. But it happened one day that my circumstances changed, so that I heard no more music.[1] It was in vain now to sing: my native woodnotes wild—just then breaking frightfully—could not satisfy my intense craving for the harmony which is the emotional substance of music, and for the rhythmic figures of accompaniment which are its action and movement. I had only a single splintering voice; and I wanted an orchestra. This musical starvation it was that drove me to disregard the rights of my fellow lodgers and go to the piano. I learnt the alphabet of musical notation from a primer, and the keyboard from a diagram. Then, without troubling Czerny or Plaidy, I opened

[1] The reference here is to the departure of Shaw's mother and two sisters for London in 1872. For a fuller account of this phase of Shaw's musical education, see his preface to *London Music in 1888–89* (London, 1937).

Don Giovanni and began. It took ten minutes to get my fingers arranged on the chord of D minor with which the overture commences; but when it sounded right at last, it was worth all the trouble it cost. At the end of some months I had acquired a technique of my own, as a sample of which I may offer my fingering of the scale of C major. Instead of shifting my hand by turning the thumb under and fingering $\frac{C\,D\,E\,F\,G\,A\,B\,C}{1\,2\,3\,1\,2\,3\,4\,5}$, I passed my fourth finger over my fifth and played $\frac{C\,D\,E\,F\,G\,A\,B\,C}{1\,2\,3\,4\,5\,4\,5\,4}$. This method had the advantage of being applicable to all scales, diatonic or chromatic; and to this day I often fall back on it. Liszt and Chopin hit on it too; but they never used it to the extent that I did. I soon acquired a terrible power of stumbling through pianoforte arrangements and vocal scores; and my reward was that I gained penetrating experiences of Victor Hugo and Schiller from Donizetti, Verdi, and Beethoven; of the Bible from Handel; of Goethe from Schumann; of Beaumarchais and Molière from Mozart; and of Mérimée from Bizet, besides finding in Berlioz an unconscious interpreter of Edgar Allan Poe. When I was in the schoolboy-adventure vein, I could range from Vincent Wallace to Meyerbeer; and if I felt piously and genteelly sentimental, I, who could not stand the pictures of Ary Scheffer or the genteel suburban sentiment of Tennyson and Longfellow, could become quite maudlin over Mendelssohn and Gounod. And, as I searched all the music I came across for the sake of its poetic or dramatic content, and played the pages in which I found drama or poetry over and over again, whilst I never returned to those in which the music was trying to exist ornamentally for its own sake and had no real content at all, it followed that when I came across the consciously perfect art work in the music dramas of Wagner, I ran no risk of hopelessly misunderstanding it as the academic musicians did. Indeed, I soon found that they equally misunderstood Mozart and Beethoven, though, having come to like their tunes and harmonies, and to understand their mere carpentry, they pointed out what they supposed to be their merits with an erroneousness far more fatal to their unfortunate pupils than the volley of half-bricks with which they greeted Wagner (who, it must be confessed, retaliated with a volley of whole ones fearfully well aimed).

Now, in this fragment of autobiography, what is it that stands as the one indispensable external condition of my musical culture? Obviously, the pianoforte. Without it, no harmony, no interweaving of rhythms and motives, no musical structure, and consequently no opera or music drama. But on the other hand, with it nothing else was needed, except the printed score and a foreknowledge of the power of music to bring romance and poetry to an enchanting intimacy of realization. Let a man once taste of the fruit that brings that knowledge, and no want of technical instruction will prevent him from doing what I did, if only he can get access to a piano and ten shillings' worth of cheap editions of operas and oratorios. I had not the key to the instrument, but I picked the lock by passing my ring finger over my little finger, driven as I was to that burglarious process by my craving for the booty within. It was easier than learning to read French; and how many of us learn to read French merely to satisfy our craving for a less reticent sort of novel than England produces! It is worth anyone's while to do likewise for the sake of Meyerbeer, Gounod, and Verdi alone—nay, for the sake of Offenbach and the Savoy operas. For one must not affright people of moderate capacity by promising them communion with the greatest men, whom they are apt to find dry. On the other hand, let me not lead those older and abler souls to whom the heroics of Verdi, the seraphic philanderings of Gounod, and the pseudo-historical effect-mongering of Meyerbeer are but children's entertainments, to suppose that there is no music at their level. Music is not always serenading Jessica and Lorenzo: it has higher business than that. As one of those swaggering bronzes from the furniture-shops—two cavaliers drawing their swords at one another from opposite ends of the mantelpiece—is to a statue by Praxiteles, so is an opera by Meyerbeer to one by Mozart. However you may despise romantic novels, however loftily you may be absorbed in the future destiny of what is highest in humanity, so that for mere light literature you turn from Dante to Goethe, or from Schopenhauer to Comte, or from Ruskin to Ibsen—still, if you do not know Die Zauberflöte, if you have never soared into the heaven where they sing the choral ending of the Ninth Symphony, if Der Ring des Nibelungen is nothing to you but a newspaper phrase, then you are an ignoramus, however eagerly you may pore in your darkened library over the mere printed labels of those wonders that can only be communicated by the transubstantiation of pure feeling for musical tone. The greatest of the great among poets, from Æschylus to Wagner, have been poet-musicians: how then can any man disdain music or pretend to have completed his culture without it?

Thus to the whole range of imaginative letters, from the Bab Ballads to Prometheus Unbound, you have a parallel range of music from Trial by Jury to Tristan und Isolde, conveying to your very senses what the other could only suggest to your imagination. Only, to travel along this higher range rather than along the lesser one, you must use your piano. This is the mission of the pianoforte, to assert which adequately is such an answer to "Is the pianoforte a musical instrument?" as will send the questioner away an abashed idiot.

Now let us consider the drawbacks to culture by pianoforte as opposed to culture by ordinary reading. To begin with, people do not read aloud; consequently half-a-dozen persons can sit in the same room and enjoy six different books by the light of the same lamp. Imagine these people going to six pianos and simultaneously striking up The Mikado, Dinorah, Faust, Aïda, Fidelio, and Götterdämmerung. Nay, imagine them doing it, not in the same room, but even in the same house, or in the same square, with the windows open in summer! In German towns they have a music curfew, and will not let you play after a stated hour in the evening. When Liszt was teaching at Weimar, playing the pianoforte with the window open was a public misdemeanor punishable by fine. The only wonder is that the piano is permitted at all except in lighthouses and other detached residences. At present unmusical people get used to the noise of a piano just as they get used to the noise of cabs clattering past; but in the end the pianos will make most people musical; and then there will be an end of the present anarchic toleration. For just in proportion as you like bungling on a piano yourself does the bungling of others offend and disturb you. In truth, just as the face a man sees when he looks in the glass is not his face as his neighbor sees it, so the music we hear when we play is not what our neighbors hear. I know no way out of this difficulty just at present. We cannot go back to the clavichord unless we listen to it through a microphone; for though you can play Bach fugues on a clavichord, you cannot play *Suoni la tromba*, or *Di quella pira*, or the Rákóczy March, or the Ride of the Valkyries—at least, not to your heart's content. Even good playing and good pianos are eternally impossible. For the laws of nature forbid good playing with our keyboard, which defies the human hand and only gives us the run of the twelve keys on condition that they are all perceptibly out of tune. And the laws of nature equally seem, so far, to decree that the pianoforte string which gives the most beautiful tone and the pianoforte action which gives the most perfect touch will not last; so that if you get an ideal piano at a cost of some hundreds of pounds, in five years you will want a new one. But you are far more likely, as the income-tax returns prove, to be compelled to put up with a twentyfive pound piano on the three years' system; and though excellent French pianets (considering) are to be had at that price, the ordinary British householder prefers a full-sized walnut piano of the sort that justifies the use of dynamite. Thus we appear to be driven to this lamentable alternative: either to give up the best part of our culture or else make it a curse to the people downstairs or next door. We seem hardly to have the right to hesitate; for now that the moral basis of pianism as a means of giving pleasure to others is exploded, and shewn to correspond to the exact opposite of the facts of the case, it appears to be our plain duty to forbid amateur music altogether, and to insist on romance and poetry being restricted to their silent, incomplete, merely literary expression.

But this, I submit, we dare not do. Without music we shall surely perish of drink, morphia, and all sorts of artificial exaggerations of the cruder delights of the senses. Asceticism will not save us, for the conclusive reason that we are not ascetics. Man, as he develops, seeks constantly a keener pleasure, in the pursuit of which he either destroys himself or develops new faculties of enjoyment. He either strives to intensify the satisfaction of resting, eating, and drinking, the excitement and exercise of hunting, and the ardor of courtship, by "refining" them into idleness, gluttony, dipsomania, hideous cruelty, and ridiculous vice, or else he develops his feeling until it becomes poetic feeling, and sets him thinking with pleasure of nobler things. Observe, if you please, the order of development here: it is all-important, as I shall shew, even at the cost of a digression. It is feeling that sets a man thinking, and not thought that sets him feeling. The secret of the absurd failure of our universities and academic institutions in general to produce any real change in the students who are constantly passing through them is that their method is invariably to attempt to lead their pupils to feeling by way of thought. For example, a musical student is expected to gradually acquire a sense of the poetry of the Ninth Symphony by accumulating information as to the date of Beethoven's birth, the compass of the *contra fagotto*, the number of sharps in the key of D major, and so on, exactly analogous processes being applied in order to produce an appreciation of painting, Greek poetry, or what not. Result: the average sensual boy comes out the average sensual man, with his tastes in no discoverable way different from those of the young gentleman who has preferred an articled clerkship in a solicitor's office to Oxford or Cambridge. All education, as distinct from technical instruction, must be education of the feeling; and such education must consist in the appeal of actual experiences to the senses, without which literary descriptions addressed to the imagination cannot be rightly interpreted. Marriage, for instance, is admittedly an indispensable factor in the education of the complete man or woman. But in educational institutions appeals to the senses can only take the form of performances of works of art; and the bringing of such performances to the highest perfection is the true business of our universities.

This statement will surprise nobody but a university man. Fortunately there is no such thing as an absolutely pure specimen of that order. If it were possible to shut off from a boy all the influence of home, and to confine him absolutely to public-school life and university life, the resultant pure product of what we call "education" would be such a barbarous cub or insufferable prig as we can only conceive by carefully observing the approaches to these types which are occasionally produced at present. But such a complete specialization is not possible. You cannot wholly shut art out now, even with the assistance of modern architects. Though my name is to be found on the books of no Oxford college, I have enjoyed all the real education which the university has to offer by simply walking through the university and looking at its beautiful old quadrangles. I know fairly-educated Oxford men—though, to be sure, they are all truants and smugglers, connoisseurs of the London theatres and galleries, with pictures, pianofortes, and beautiful things of one kind or another in their rooms, and shelves upon shelves of books that are never used as textbooks. I remember conversing once with the late Master of Balliol, an amiable gentleman, stupendously ignorant probably, but with a certain flirtatious, old-maidish frivolity about him that had, and was meant to have, the charm of a condescension from so learned a man. In Oxford he was regarded as a master educator. I would ask what right he had to that distinction in a country where Hallé had made, and was conducting, the Manchester band; where August Manns, with Sir George Grove, had created the Crystal Palace orchestra; and where Richter was teaching us what Wagner taught him? Sir Frederick Burton, as master of the National Gallery, Sir Augustus Harris, as master of the Royal Italian Opera, were and are worth to England, educationally, forty thousand Masters of Balliol. Which is the greater educator, pray—your tutor when he coaches you for the Ireland scholarship or Miss Janet Achurch when she plays Nora for you? You cannot witness A Doll's House without *feeling*, and, as an inevitable consequence, thinking; but it is evident that the Ireland scholarship would break up Oxford unless it could be won without either feeling or thinking. I might give a thousand illustrations, if space permitted, or if criticism of the university system were my main purpose instead of my digression.

Taking it, then, as established that life is a curse to us unless it operates as pleasurable activity, and that as it becomes more intense with the upward evolution of the race it requires a degree of pleasure which cannot be extracted from the alimentary, predatory, and amatory instincts without ruinous perversions of them; seeing, also, that the alternative of "high thinking" is impossible until it is started by "high feeling," to which we can only come through the education of the senses—are we to deliberately reverse our Puritan traditions and aim at becoming a nation of skilled voluptuaries? Certainly. It may require some reflection to see that high feeling brings high thinking; but we already know, without reflection, that high thinking brings what is called plain living. In this century the world has produced two men—Shelley and Wagner—in whom intense poetic feeling was the permanent state of their consciousness, and who were certainly not restrained by any religious, conventional, or prudential considerations from indulging themselves to the utmost of their opportunities. Far from being gluttonous, drunken, cruel, or debauched, they were apostles of vegetarianism and water-drinking; had an utter horror of violence and "sport"; were notable champions of the independence of women; and were, in short, driven into open revolution against the social evils which the average sensual man finds extremely suitable to him. So much is this the case that the practical doctrine of these two arch-voluptuaries always presents itself to ordinary persons as a saint-like asceticism.

If, now, relieved of all apprehensions as to the social safety of allowing the world to make itself happy, we come to consider which of the arts is the most potent to this end, we must concede that eminence to music, because it alone requires for its enjoyment an artistic act on the part of its reader, which act, in its perfection, becomes such an act of re-creation as Wagner found in Liszt's playing of Beethoven's sonatas. There is no need in this account to set up the musician above the painter, the master-builder, or the sculptor. There are points at which all rivalry between the arts vanishes. When you are looking at the Turner water-colors in the National Gallery, the poetic feeling which they so exquisitely and sufficingly express completely delivers you from that plane on which mere hero-worshipers squabble as to whether the painter or the composer of music is the better man. None the less, in the National Gallery the feeling is expressed by the painter and not by you, although your feeling, too, struggles for expression, sometimes almost painfully. You stand dumb, or at best you turn to your neighbor and say, "Pretty, aint it?" of which remark most art criticism is but an elaboration.

Now suppose the feeling were aroused, not by a picture, but by a song! At once your tongue is loosed: you sing the song, and thereby relieve one of your deepest needs—strange as that may sound to people who sing songs solely to gain the applause of others. Further, you gain by practice the power of expressing feeling, and with that power the courage to express it, for want of which power and courage we all go miserably about today, shrinking and pretending, misunderstanding and misunderstood, making remarks on the weather to people whose most nourishing sympathy or most salutary opposition we might enjoy if only we and they could become fully known to each other by a complete self-expression. Music, then, is the most fecund of the arts, propagating itself by its power of forcing those whom it influences to express it and themselves by a method which is the easiest and most universal of all art methods, because it is the art form of that communication by speech which is common to all the race.

This music wisdom has been urged on the world in set terms by Plato, by Goethe, by Schopenhauer, by Wagner, and by myself. As a rule, when, in order to obtain concreteness, I couple my teachings with the name of any individual who enjoys opportunities of carrying out my ideas, he threatens me with legal proceedings, on the ground that I have taken him seriously. And indeed the commonsense of the country under present circumstances feels that to take music as seriously as religion, morals, or politics is clear evidence of malicious insanity, unless the music belongs to an oratorio. The causes of this darkness are economic. What is the matter with us is that the mass of the people cannot afford to go to good concerts or to the opera. Therefore they remain ignorant of the very existence of a dramatic or poetic content in what they call "classical" or "good" music, which they always conceive as a web of learnedly and heavily decorative sound patterns, and never as containing a delicious kernel of feeling, like their favorite Annie Laurie. Consequently they do not crave for pianos; and if they did they could not afford to buy them, and would perforce fall back on the poor man's piano—the German concertina or accordion. At the same time, our most gifted singers, instead of getting ten or fifteen pounds a week and a pension, have to be paid more than Cabinet Ministers, whose work turns them prematurely grey, or officers in the field, or musical critics. All this must be altered before any serious advance in culture can be effected. The necessity for change in the social structure is so pressing that it drives the musician into the political arena in spite of his own nature. You have Wagner going out in '48 with the revolutionists because the State declined to reform the theatre, just as I am compelled, by a similar obtuseness on the part of our own Governments, to join the Fabian Society, and wildly masquerade as a politician so that I may agitate for a better distribution of piano-purchasing power.

If I were now to string all these points in their logical order on the thread of a complete argument, to prove that the future of humanity depends at present on the pianoforte, I should render my case repugnant to the British mind, which sensibly objects to be bothered with logic. But let me, in allowing the British mind to jump at its conclusion, plead for a large construction for the word pianoforte. An organ, an harmonium, a vocalion, an æolion, an orchestrion, or any instrument upon which the full polyphony of an opera or symphony can be given, may obviously replace the pianoforte; and so far as the playing can be done, wholly or partly, by perforated cards, barrels, or other mechanical means of execution, by all means let it be so done. A fingering mechanism so contrived as to be well under the *artistic* control of the operator would be an unspeakable boon. Supply me with such a thing and I will make an end of Paderewski.

Finally, let no one suppose that because private readings and performances are better than nothing, they are therefore an efficient substitute for complete dramatic and orchestral representations. Far from it; they are makeshifts, and very miserable makeshifts too. In Italy, when you go from the picture gallery to the photograph shop, you are revolted by the inadequacy of the "reproductions" which turn Carpaccio's golden glow into sooty grime. At Bayreuth when, on your way back of an evening from the Festival Playhouse, you hear someone strumming a pianoforte arrangement of the overture to Die Meistersinger, you wonder how the wretch can bear to listen to himself. Yet, after a few months in England, when you pull out your photograph, or sit down to the pianoforte score of Die Meistersinger, you are very pleasantly and vividly reminded of Carpaccio or Wagner. Also, however diligently you may read your Shakespear or your Ibsen, you must date your full acquaintance with any work of theirs from the time when you see it fully performed on the stage as they meant you to. The day will come when every citizen will find within his reach and means adequate artistic representations to recreate him whenever he feels disposed for them. Until then the pianoforte will be the savior of society. But when that golden age comes, everybody will see at last what an execrable, jangling, banging, mistuned nuisance our domestic music machine is, and the maddening sound of it will thenceforth be no more heard in our streets.

BEETHOVEN'S EIGHTH SYMPHONY

(Unsigned sub-leader in *The Daily Chronicle*,
6 *November* 1895)

In the last instalment of Mr Ashton Ellis's translation of the prose works of Richard Wagner occurs a well-known story about the third movement of Beethoven's Eighth Symphony. Says Wagner:—

I once was in Mendelssohn's company at a performance of this symphony in Dresden, conducted by the now deceased Kapellmeister Reissiger, and told him how I had—as I believed— arranged for its right performance by Reissiger, since he had promised open-eyed to take the trio of the minuet slower than of wont. Mendelssohn quite agreed with me. We listened. The third movement began, and I was horrified to hear the old familiar Laendler tempo once again. Before I could express my wrath, Mendelssohn was rocking his head in pleased approval, and smiling to me: "Thats capital! Bravo!" So I fell from horror into stupefaction. Mendelssohn's callousness towards this curious artistic *contretemps* inspired me with very natural doubts as to whether the thing presented any difference at all to him. I fancied I was peering into a veritable abyss of superficiality—an utter void.

A quarter of a century ago, when this was written, and for long enough after it, every conductor in England used to murder the Eighth Symphony exactly as Reissiger murdered it; and every violoncellist in the Philharmonic orchestra used to dread the trio of the third movement. It was not likely that we were going to alter our ways at the suggestion of a man blasphemous enough to consider the composer of Elijah superficial, [and] who produced abominably cacophonous music like that of Tannhäuser. For we little thought then that before the century was over the man who thought Mendelssohn superior to Wagner would enjoy about as much authority in musical criticism as a literary critic who should assume that Longfellow was obviously greater than Shakespear, still less that on the wettest day in winter, with the stalls at 15s., St James's Hall could be sold out on the announcement of an orchestral program three-fifths Wagner and the rest Beethoven and Berlioz, without even an allusion to Mendelssohn's Italian Symphony or Spohr's Consecration of Sound, which we used to call The Power of Sound because consecration was too metaphysical to seem good sense to us. That happened last Monday, and was by no means a remarkable or unprecedented event. It is mentioned here solely because the concert began with that very Eighth Symphony whereby the Mendelssohn tale hangs.

Last year, it will be remembered, Siegfried Wagner visited us for the first time, and was handsomely received. But on his second visit he conducted the Eighth Symphony and the overture to Der Freischütz—also much mentioned in the Essay on Conducting quoted above—and conducted them, of course, "à la Wagner" as best he could. Unhappily this time the band was in a bad temper; and the youthful conductor, staggering under the weight of a great name, yet had the hardihood to introduce himself as a composer by a symphonic poem which, though certainly a good deal better than his father used to turn out at his age, might have been replaced with great advantage by the Italian Symphony. The result was that, though Richter sat in the front row and applauded demonstratively, especially after the *allegretto* of the Eighth Symphony, the press turned and rent poor Siegfried; so that for a moment it seemed as though he would share the fate of the son of Mozart, and be crushed by a name to which no mere mortal could live up. The fact is, however, that Siegfried scored many charming points both in the symphony and the overture, and seems to need nothing but the tact and authority which a very young man necessarily lacks to hold his own in London, where, to confess the truth, we have not only put up with, *faute de mieux*, but wantonly glorified and bragged of much worse conductors than the one who stands in Siegfried's shoes.

We are still, with all our crowding to hear Richter and Mottl, a horribly unmusical city. You can tell this by our Gargantuan musical digestion. When a Theatre Royal performs nightly a favorite *comédietta*, a celebrated sensational drama, a Shakespearean tragedy, a grand Christmas pantomime, and a screaming farce to wind up with, you do not conclude that the taste for dramatic literature is in a flourishing condition in that town: quite the contrary. But what then must we say of the program of the last Richter concert? Let us premise that a single Beethoven Symphony is quite as full a meal as any real musician can digest at one sitting. Now for the horrible particulars. The Eighth Symphony, Berlioz's King Lear overture, the Tannhäuser overture with the Venusberg bacchanal, the first act of Die Walküre from the exit of Hunding to the end, and, by way of a liqueur at the end, the Ride of the Valkyries. Will future ages be able to credit such monstrous, undiscriminating gorging and gormandizing? Even the Ninth Symphony is not enough for one concert —an overture and a concerto, or perhaps Schubert's Unfinished Symphony, with Adelaida sandwiched between, must be thrown in to give the audience value for its money. This means, of course, that the British amateur does not follow the development of a symphony at all: he only listens for a pretty bit here and there, like a child picking raisins out of a stodgy cake. How schoolboyish he is can be seen by his love of the Ride of the Valkyries and the Venusberg orgy, which have no business in a concert room at all. Indeed, the popularity of the Seventh Symphony, which Richter repeats *ad nauseam*, is evidently due to the galloping rhythm of the first movement, and the stamping, racing vigor of the last, not to mention the simple hymn-tune form of the pretty *allegretto*. In all subtler respects the Eighth is better, with its immense cheerfulness and exquisite playfulness, its perfect candor and naturalness, its filaments of heavenly melody suddenly streaming up from the mass of sound, and flying away cloudlike, and the cunning harmonic coquetry with which the irresistibly high-spirited themes, after innumerable feints and tantalizing invitations and promises, suddenly come at you round the most unexpected corners, and sweep you away with a delightful burst of joyous energy. The man who, being accessible to all this, asks for more—and such a lot more—or even supposes himself capable of entertaining it, is an inconceivable person.

Richter, by his handling of the Eighth Symphony, again shewed himself a consummate Beethoven conductor. There was no Reissiger-Mendelssohn mistake about the trio, no confusion of the movement "in the time of a minuet" (as danced) with the old brisk Haydn Symphony minuet, which is such a very different thing. It goes without saying that the unforgetable second theme of the last movement—perhaps the most ravishing of those aforesaid filaments of melody—was divine; but what unhappily does not go without saying in this unhappy country was the masterly phrasing of the chain of passages which follows it. It is at such points that the connoisseur in finely intelligent execution recognizes the master. Yet it now turns out, as was perhaps inevitable, that the perfect Beethoven conductor, even when taught by Wagner—though, depend on it, a conductor like Richter is nobody's pupil but his own—cannot also be the perfect Wagner conductor. Anyone who has heard Mottl conduct Wagner has found out that Richter conducts him like a drill-sergeant. The discipline is perfect, and the tone fine in quality and majestic in volume; but listen to the ruthless rigidity of the *tempo* and the stiffening of the melodies! What clarionet player, giving us the song of Venus in the Tannhäuser overture, would care to be pulled up short in his cadence by Richter after being coaxed into caressing the audience with it by Mottl? And in Die Walküre, when the woe-devoted Siegmund sits by the fire crooning dreamily to the warm glow, until, as it dies out, he compares it to the fire without light in his own heart, would Mottl be capable of going straight on from the light to the darkness without the faintest inflection of the *tempo*, even under the influence of the paralyzing Philistinism of Mr Edward Lloyd, who, finding the deep gloom of the low notes to which the words *Tief in des Busens Berge* are set uncomfortably for his voice, cheerfully sings them an octave higher, a proceeding to which the attention of the Recording Angel has probably been very seriously called by Wagner? And yet Mottl can do comparatively nothing with Beethoven: there Richter has his revenge. Levi, who was good at both, has paid for his ambidexterity with his reason, like Faccio. Let us wish him a speedy recovery and a trip to England to confirm it. The only wonder is that our inhumanly long programs have not by this time driven us all mad, as they would if we really knew how to listen to them.

BASSETTO AT BAYREUTH

(*The Star*, 22-25 *July* 1896)

I

19 JULY.—There are moments when Providence takes a joke seriously by way of restraining our sense of humor. We all know (or ought to know) the moment near the close of Das Rheingold, when, the ring being disposed of to the giants, and Freia and her apples of eternal youth restored to the gods, Donner, mounting the rock, calls the clouds to him, and, when their black legions, crowding about him, have hidden him in their mists, swings his hammer, splits them with a thousand blinding ribbons of lightning, and reveals the skiey towers of Valhall, with Froh's rainbow-bridge spanning the valley to the gate of the wonderful castle—the home of the gods. The effect of this on the stage of the Wagner Theatre is magnificent, but the management, not content to wait for this, took advantage of the Bayreuth custom of summoning the audience by sound of trumpet, to blare out Donner's call to the real heavens before the performance began. What was the result? No sooner was the call

sent echoing from hill to hill than the cloudless sky darkened, and the trombones were answered by a distant roll of thunder. I was up in the pine woods at the time, discussing high themes with the brilliant editor of a paper which I will disguise as the D***y Chr*****e. He had persisted in whistling I dreamt that I dwelt in marble halls all the way from Victoria to Nuremberg (the turbulent part of the Channel excepted), and I was trying to get him off that subject when I heard the brazen voices sending forth their

He da! He Da!
Duftig Gedünst
Donner ruft euch zu Heer.

The thunder—the real thunder—answered, and we sprang up from our carpet of scented pine needles and made for the theatre precipitately. Just as we reached it the rain came down in torrents. Consequently the entry of the audience to the first performance, usually a gay, busy, eager, hopeful function, was this time a damp scuttle. Nearly every seat in the house was filled a quarter of an hour before the performance began.

Das Rheingold, being only the prologue to the colossal music-drama of The Niblung's Ring, which takes three nights to perform, is not divided into acts, and therefore compels the audience to sit for about two hours and a half without a rest. I sat it out without turning a hair; and my companion did not whistle a single bar during the hundred and fifty minutes; but some of the audience found their powers of endurance somewhat strained. One lady fainted, and her removal, with the curious flash of bright daylight into the dark theatre and across the lurid picture of Nibelheim as the door was opened to let her out, made an unwelcome disturbance.

The performance was, on the whole, an excellent one. Its weakest point was Perron's Wotan, a futile impersonation. The orchestra, although it was too good, as orchestras go, to be complained of, was very far from being up to the superlative standard of perfect preparedness, smoothness, and accuracy of execution expected at Bayreuth. We in London have taught Richter to depend too much on his reputation, and on his power of pulling a performance through on the inspiration of the moment. The result of our instruction is now apparent. The effect of the Das Rheingold score was not the Bayreuth effect, but the London effect: that is, it sounded like a clever reading of the band parts at sight by very smart players, instead of an utterance by a corps of devotees, saturated with the spirit of the work, and in complete possession of its details. The strings were poor; the effects were not always well calculated—for instance, the theme of the magic helmet was hardly heard at first; and in the prelude, the great booming pedal note—the mighty ground tone of the Rhine—was surreptitiously helped out, certainly with excellent effect, by the organ.

The stage management is—I can no longer conceal it—radically bad at all the points where ordinary amateur intelligence, devotedly exercised, is not sufficient to find out the right way. The plain truth is that Madame Wagner does not know what acting can and cannot do, or how much the imagination of the audience will do when the situation goes beyond the resources of acting. Over and over again, when overwhelming crises of emotion are reached—crises which occur in the minds of the spectators as they follow the drama, and which, though they are supported with the most powerful sympathy by the orchestra, are not provoked by any particular action of the figures on the stage, and are utterly beyond expression by any such means—we find the Bayreuth artists making the most violent demonstrations, striking the most overcharged attitudes, and attempting to look ineffable things at the very moment, in short, when the slightest betrayal of any share on their part in the excitement of the audience must mar the whole effect—the moment, consequently, when a skilled actor allows the play itself, helped by the imagination of the spectators, to do all the work. This is the whole secret of the amateurishness of Bayreuth. Madame Wagner is beyond question a very clever lady, and a most able woman of business; but she knows so little how dramatic effects are produced technically that at the very points where her husband's genius and the emotions to which it appealed are producing their most searching effects she assumes that no effect will be produced at all if the *prima donna* does not exhibit the most demonstrative consciousness of it. I call this amateurish, but from the Bayreuth point of view it is even worse than amateurish: it is heretical, being the most foolish characteristic of Italian operatic acting. I do not say that Wagner himself was free from it. Though his tendency always seemed to me to be to err in the direction of taking too much of the work for the music—that is, for himself—and leaving too little to the actor, who is often instructed to stand motionless for long periods whilst the orchestra conveys, often with the most extraordinary vividness, not only how he feels, but what he is thinking about, yet it may be that the vehemence of Wagner's imagination, and the success with which he had himself enlarged the limits of forcible expression by mechanical means in the orchestra, may have led him occasionally to demand superhuman demonstrations from his actors. But I rather doubt this in view of the care with which his scores, with all their wealth of instrumentation, are contrived so as not to overwhelm the singer. He was perhaps the most practical of all the great composers, and the last man in the world, apparently, to demand impossibilities. At all events, whether the fault lies with the Wagner tradition or Madame Wagner's present supervision, there can be no doubt of the fact that a stage manager who understands acting—if the world can produce so unusual a phenomenon—is badly wanted at Bayreuth.

There is a good deal to be done, too, in the way of getting rid of mere old-fashionedness. Probably it is not possible at present to convince a German *prima donna* that Mrs Leo Hunter was not thoroughly right and ladylike in wearing a modish gown along with her helmet when she impersonated Minerva. I do not for one moment dare to suggest that the Rhine maidens should take a hint from our "living pictures," and dress like Rhine maidens. The world is not decent enough for that yet. But is it necessary for the three ladies to go to the other extreme and swim about in muslin *fichus* and teagowns? They gave me a strong impression that they had forgotten their gloves and hats; and even a parasol to save their complexions when the sunlight came shimmering down through the water on the Rhinegold would hardly have been out of keeping with their costumes. Happily, their movements were fairly mermaidenly. The old fire escape machinery of

1876 has been discarded; and the three are now suspended from above, like Mlle Enea, or Miss Kate Rorke in Mr Buchanan's last play, with plausible and graceful results.

Another antiquated stage trick which Bayreuth clings to is that of attitudinizing on the stage with a corner of your mantle held between your fingers, in the manner of the antique Niobe. But whereas Niobe held up her mantle to screen herself and her children from the arrows of Apollo, the Bayreuth *prima donna* does it solely to display her drapery in the German historico-classical manner, with unspeakably ridiculous and dowdy effect.

One more disparagement. In 1876 the use of jets and clouds of steam for stage effects was a novelty. We all remember how it was transferred from the Bayreuth stage to the Lyceum by Sir Henry Irving in the late W. G. Wills's version of Faust. But it cannot be denied that from the very first it carried with it a prosaic flavor of washing day, totally irreconcilable with the magical strangeness of the wishing cap or *tarnhelm*. It is effective only for one purpose—that of producing an illusion of a cloud of fire when a powerful light is turned upon it; and to that use, I suggest, it cannot be too strictly limited.

For the rest, I have nothing but praise, although there certainly was a Rhine-daughter whose top note was distressingly flat. The singing, on the whole, was much better than I expected it to be. The Germans are evidently becoming conscious that there are in the world De Reszkes and other people who have demonstrated that Wagner's music can be sung beautifully, and that even a basso should not deliver himself as if the Bayreuth audience were a Hyde-park demonstration. I admit, of course, that Friedrichs, as Alberich, occasionally howled and shouted in the old Wagnerian style; but he also sang at times—even at most times—and sang not badly either. The veteran Vogl, who played Loge at Bayreuth twenty years ago, played it again last Sunday with a vocal charm which surpassed the most sanguine expectations. Both he and Friedrichs acted with great spirit and intelligence. Burgstaller, who is to play Siegfried presently, took the small part of Froh, and made his mark in it by a certain radiant sensitiveness and enthusiasm which became him very well. Frau Heink Schumann, who will be remembered in London as the contralto of the Munich company brought over by the late Sir Augustus Harris, was magnificent as Erda. Calvé herself could not have surpassed her in dramatic power and beauty, and her voice was at its best. Marie Brema, the only English member of the cast, was Fricka, never a very popular goddess, her modern name being Mrs Grundy. Miss Brema sang very well and shewed no diminution of her old energy; but she devotedly does (and occasionally overdoes) what she is told to do by Madame Wagner, besides wearing what she is told to wear. No human *prima donna* could make a perfect success under these conditions, and I urge Miss Brema, whose ability is of a very high order, to take her fate into her own hands for the future. Acting is her own business: it is not Madame Wagner's; and the sooner that is realized, the better for Bayreuth. The rest of the cast was adequate—Breuer as Mime perhaps a trifle more than that.

You shall hear further from me presently. My friend the editor has now got I dreamt that I dwelt mixed up with the Rhine-daughters' *trio*. The combination of Balfe and Wagner is novel, and somewhat trying at first, but it grows upon one with use.   C. di B.

P.S.—The first act of Die Walküre has just been rescued from a *succès de sommeil* by the perennial and passionate Sucher, who suddenly broke into one of her triumphs as Sieglinde. Gerhäuser, as Siegmund, made up as a stout middle-aged gentleman in sheepskins and a red beard, has been as null and wooden as anybody could desire. With the assistance of Wachter as Hunding, he all but put us asleep in the first half of the scene. In pulling the sword from the tree he was much less exciting than an English vestryman taking his hat from a peg. But Sucher carried everything before her. She could not transfigure Gerhäuser, but she made us forget him and remember only the Siegmund of Wagner's poem—that poor devil of a hero to whose moment of happiness our hearts all go out. Bravo Rosa!

II

20 JULY.—Die Walküre is endured by the average man because it contains four scenes for which he would sit out a Scotch

sermon, or even a House of Commons debate. These are the love
duet in the first act, Brynhild's announcement to Siegmund of
his approaching death in the second, the ride of the Valkyries
and the fire charm in the third. For them the ordinary play-goer
endures hours of Wotan, with Christopher Sly's prayer in his
heart—"Would twere over!" Now I am one of those elect souls
who are deeply moved by Wotan. I grant you that as a long-
winded, one-eyed gentleman backing a certain champion in a
fight, and letting himself be henpecked out of his fancy because
his wife objects to the moral character of the champion, he is a
dreary person indeed, and most ungodlike. But to those who
have seen on the greater stage of the world how Religion has
fortified itself by an alliance with Law and Order and Morals and
Propriety; how it has gained temporal power at the cost of that
eye which is not the eye to the main chance; how it has become
so entangled in these alliances and bargains that when new and
higher forces are born of its holiest wisdom it is driven first to
use its authority over them to make them war against Truth as
dangerous, and Love as an unnatural vice, and then when they
defy its authority, in spite of that filial love, to silence them in
sleep (since they cannot be killed), and surround their couch
with juggling fires to scare away mankind from waking them—
to those who have seen all that, there is nothing trivial, nothing
tedious in Die Walküre.

Wotan's one eye is not ridiculous; his spear, the symbol of his
temporal power, with the runes and bargains engraved on its
shaft, is no mere stage property; his wife Fricka, shuddering with
horror and wrath at her broken moral laws, and forcing him to
abandon his love-child to the "justice" of her worshiper, is no
mere henpecking Mrs Caudle; and when Brynhild, the child of
his wisdom, rebels against the command which Fricka has forced
from him, and is put to sleep on the mountain peak, surrounded
by the fires of Loge, there is more in it than the somewhat
fifth-of-Novembery pyrotechnics—mostly squibs and steam—
of the Bayreuth stage machinist. You, Mr Star Editor, familiar
as you are with the tragedy of Religion married (for money) to
the State; with a people frightened away from truth and knowledge by a display of brimstone that can scorch no hand that is

fearlessly thrust into it; and with other matters which are no doubt mentioned in your political columns—you would understand Die Walküre well enough. And in a dim way, many of the people who have no general ideas, and who yawn and fidget when Wotan is at the seven hundred and seventyseventh bar of one of his disquisitions, with no sign of any intention of stopping, do perceive that something of public importance is going on and must be put up with. They may not exactly see how or why the god finds that all the power he has built up has only enslaved himself—still less do they understand the apparent contradiction of his secret hope and longing for his own downfall and destruction even whilst he is working with all his might to defend himself and make Valhall impregnable and eternal; but they see his trouble; and, after all, it is trouble that moves us to sympathy, and not the explanation of the trouble.

At the same time let me confess that Die Walküre at full length, beginning at four and ending at half-past nine, and involving three hours and a half of concentrated attention, is hard work for a critic, and a considerable test of the endurance of an amateur, except when the performers are sufficiently gifted to make you forget everything but the drama. The Bayreuth artists cannot all do this; in fact, some of them rather excel in the art of making five minutes seem like twenty. In Die Walküre the all-important performer is Wotan; and, as I hinted in my last communication, Perron is not the ideal Wotan. He is a tall but awkward and straddling person, and is perhaps as clever in private life as many other people who appear stupid on the stage. His acting consists of striking a graceless attitude and holding on to it until the fear of cramp obliges him to let go. Why then, you will ask, was he selected for such a part on such an occasion? Well, simply because he has an excellent voice, of which he takes commendable care. From its low G to its top F it comes without effort, is clear, resonant, powerful without noisiness or roughness, and agreeable in quality. At the end of Die Walküre he shewed no sign of fatigue. And that is why he takes the place which so many keener artists, without this physical endowment of his, must deeply envy him. Gerhäuser's voice has matured since he sang the part of Lohengrin here a couple of years ago; but as

Siegmund the Unlucky he was quite overparted—conscientious, but slow, dull, and resourceless almost beyond bearing. Wagner has provided such formidable lengths of dumb show in this work that, unless an actor is inventive, highly accomplished in pantomime, and able to make himself personally fascinating, he must inevitably be left again and again helplessly staring at the conductor and waiting for his cue. And that is just what Siegmund and Hunding were doing most of the time. Of Sucher's great success as Sieglinde I told you in the hurried postscript which I dispatched after the first act. The second act began with a very fine performance of Fricka's scene by Miss Marie Brema, whose performance entitles us to say in England that we have produced one of the very best living Wagnerian artists. It was a first-rate piece of work, having the vocal qualities that the Germans neglect as well as the dramatic qualities they value, with, to boot, the excellent quality of Miss Brema's own individuality, which happily got completely the better of the Bayreuth tradition this time. Miss Lilli Lehmann, now Frau Lehmann-Kalisch, played her old part of Brynhild; but she was ill, and had to be helped by both prompter and conductor in passages which she has had at her fingers' ends for many years.

Die Walküre has the advantage over Das Rheingold of being much more frequently performed. Probably everybody concerned, from the stage carpenters to the *prima donna*, knew it better. The difference was very noticeable in the orchestra. Richter was in his best form, interpreting the score convincingly, and getting some fine work from the band. In the scene of the apparition of the Valkyrie in the second act, the effect of the wind instruments was quite magically beautiful. The deep impression made, in spite of the fact that none of the men could cope with their parts, and that Brynhild, though capably played, was not altogether suitably impersonated, was due very largely to the force with which Richter, through his handling of the orchestra, imposed Wagner's conception on the audience.

The weather here is excellent; and we all wish that the old plan of giving the audience one day's holiday were in force. Parsifal also is badly missed. But Der Ring is Der Ring, and there is an end. Among the visitors the Germans seem to be in a large majority this year, but no doubt the American and English tourists will turn up and assert themselves later on.

C. di B.

P.S., 6.15 p.m.—The first act of Siegfried has been the worst disappointment so far. Grüning, as Siegfried, is hardly to be described without malice. Imagine an eighteenth-century bank clerk living in a cave, with fashionable sandals and cross garters, an elegant modern classic tunic, a Regent-street bearskin, and a deportment only to be learnt in quadrilles. Or, rather, do not imagine it; but pray that I, who have seen the reality, may not be haunted by it in my dreams. He only needed a tinder-box instead of a furnace, and a patent knife-cleaning machine instead of an anvil, to make him complete. I really cannot conscientiously advise Englishmen to come to Bayreuth until Grüning comes to England. Fortunately there was some relief. Breuer was excellent as Mime; and Perron, in the Wanderer Scene, where voice alone can do almost everything, and the costume makes awkwardness impossible, was at his best. And the orchestra is keeping up to its Walküre standard.

III

22 JULY.—With all possible goodwill towards the Bayreuth management, I cannot bring myself to congratulate it on Siegfried. If the performance had been given at an ordinary German theatre, with ordinary German prices, I should have been delighted with the orchestra and the mounting; but I should have roundly denounced the choice of the principal artist. And since Siegfried is a drama which depends as much on the actor who plays the title-part as Hamlet does, my condemnation of Herr Grüning practically gives away the whole performance. I must add that Madame Wagner—who is understood to be responsible for the casting of Der Ring—is not in this case the victim of an unexpected collapse. Herr Grüning is no novice. I have never yet succeeded in visiting Bayreuth without hearing him sing. He has played Parsifal and Tannhäuser, and Madame Wagner knows to a hair's breadth, as well as I do, what he can do and what he

cannot do. Consequently the people who have made tedious and costly pilgrimages from the ends of the earth to Bayreuth, as the one place in the world where Wagner's music-dramas can be witnessed in their utmost attainable excellence and fidelity of representation, have every right to remonstrate indignantly at being deliberately put off with a third-rate Siegfried. As far as I can judge, there can have been no attempt even to make the best of him by careful rehearsal. We have seen Alvary manage the business of the Wagnerian stage with the precision of a French pantomimist, at a scratch performance in London, with everything behind the scenes at sixes and sevens and only enough interval between the acts to clear away one scene and tumble another on. Why cannot the same result be obtained here, where the intervals are an hour long, and the simple-minded pilgrims are fed all day with stories of the months of rehearsal, the scrupulous observance of the Master's wishes, the inexorable conscientiousness of Madame Wagner? The truth is that all these devout professions are borne out by the carpenters, machinists, and gasmen, and by them alone. The changes of scene, the wonderful atmospheric effects, the jets of steam, and so on are worked with a smoothness and punctuality that are beyond praise. Once only, in the change of scene from the depths of the Rhine to Valhall, did I hear something tumble with a thud behind the gauzes, accompanied by a strenuous whispering of instructions. That was no doubt an accident—a very trifling one to me, who have so often sat in Covent Garden during the change from the second to the third scene of Boïto's Mefistofele, listening to the mysterious strains of the orchestra, whilst dim figures of stage carpenters stumbled and rushed wildly about in the stage twilight, stimulating and exhorting oneanother in language which owed its frantic force to profanity rather than to grammar. At Bayreuth the clouds move, night follows day, and calm follows storm apparently without human agency. But it is one thing to drill a staff of workmen, and quite another to drill a tenor. If any of the men at work in the flies had botched his work last night as Grüning several times botched his, he would be an unemployed man this morning.

Yet, on the whole, the tenor was more conscientious than the *prima donna.* Frau Lilli Lehmann-Kalisch is famous for her Brynhild—famous in America. She has a bright soprano voice, brilliant at the top, but not particularly interesting in the middle —just the wrong sort of voice for Wagner. When dressed as the warmaiden, she is plump, pretty, very feminine, and not at all unlike our clever comedienne, Miss Kate Phillips—therefore just the wrong sort of person for Brynhild. She is clearly conscious that her golden hair is hanging down her back, and since she refuses, as she lies asleep on the mountain top, to allow her face to be covered by the vizor of her helmet, she is, in that attitude, so unmistakeably and indeed aggressively a conventionally pretty woman, emphasizing a well-developed bust with a toy cuirass, that Siegfried's assumption that she is a man, and the emotional shock with which he subsequently discovers that the supposed sleeping warrior is a young woman, are made incredible and ridiculous. And this, if you please, is Bayreuthian fidelity to "The Meister."

However, I quite admit that Frau Lehmann-Kalisch is an artist of considerable qualifications; and I should like to see her as Marguerite in Gounod's Faust. Her singing is open to exception in the matter of phrasing: in fact, she absolutely destroys one of the most characteristic turns in that section of the great duet (excuse the word; but it *is* a duet, and actually has a concerted *cadenza* in it) with which the familiar Siegfried Idyll begins. But her offences in this respect were as nothing beside Grüning's. Even in the sword-forging scene, when he was comparatively cool, the swinging triplets which occur in the bellows music were too much for his powers of execution; and at the end, when he was wrecked with emotion over which he had not an artist's mastery, the manner in which he gasped his way from note to note, producing effects which had exactly the same relation to Wagner's shapely phrases as a heap of broken glass has to a crystal goblet, is not to be described.

In justice to Herr Grüning, let me add that he has some agreeable points. He is handsome and, in a pleasant, robust, very German way, elegant in the manner of the last century. In a periwig, as a sympathetic young man of sensibility, with a not too exacting vocal part, he would pass as a tenor who ought to be doing better things. Apparently he loves Wagner, and is anxious to do him justice; and when he fails, he fails honestly. But I must not insult him by an open attempt to spare his feelings on this occasion; and I have no desire to spare the feelings of the managers. He was overparted in Siegfried; and I repeat that they knew beforehand that it would be so. The guarantee of a first-rate performance—that guarantee which is the basis of the authority and prosperity of the Wagner Theatre—has been broken, and broken deliberately, not for the first time.

Let me now forget Marguerite-Brynhild and her young man, and recall the moments when neither were on the stage. Then, I grant you, the representation was splendid. Perron, with his straddling legs, knock knees, and unhappy expression hidden by the gown, the beard, and the wide hat of the Wanderer, and with his fine voice in full play, did nothing to contradict the majesty of the Wotan music. He missed the humor of the passages with the dwarf and with Siegfried at the foot of the mountain; but that was only a small deduction from the satisfaction of the general effect. Breuer, as Mime, repeated himself a good deal; but his play was so clever that it was worth repeating. Frau Heink Schumann as Erda, and Friedrichs as Alberich, sustained the impression they made in Das Rheingold; and the orchestra was again very fine, especially in Mime's nightmare after Wotan's visit, and in the tragic thunderclouds of music in the first scene of the third act. Die Götterdämmerung tonight will probably redeem all that was lost last night, since it depends so much less on Siegfried. At all events, we are full of hope.

C. di B.

P.S.—There is joy over Die Götterdämmerung: Grüning has vanished, and Burgstaller, the alternative Siegfried, reigns in his stead. So far, the improvement is due more to the faults of Grüning than the qualities of Burgstaller, but he promises well. We are all somewhat exhausted after a first act lasting two hours, yet most of us are ready to go through it again. The scene between Brynhild and Waltraute has affected us beyond all my adjectives: not even Frau Heink Schumann's combination of black-blue Valkyrie armor and shield with a summer gown and fashionable sleeves could spoil its sublimity. I shall start

for London after the performance (unless it kills me). The
interval is too short [to write] more.

IV

23 JULY.—The completion of the first cycle of the Nibelungen
tetralogy at Bayreuth has been celebrated by applause lasting
for seven minutes, the object being to bring Richter and the
principal artists before the curtain. But at Bayreuth nobody takes
a curtain call, except the—well, the dove in Parsifal. Nevertheless the audience hammered and bravoed very lustily, the English
taking an unmistakeable lead in the noisier part of the demonstration, but failing to keep the Germans up to the standard of
perseverance set by the first night of The Rogue's Comedy at
the Garrick, when a vain attempt to call out Mr Henry Arthur
Jones was kept up for twentyfive minutes. The enthusiasm was
certainly justified by the performance. The new Siegfried, Burgstaller, a product of Bayreuth and its Wagner school, won the
audience over completely in the second and third acts. In the
first act he was a little handicapped by a certain novelty (after
the Germanically handsome Grüning) in his aspect, and by a
helmet which had to be rescued from falling off whenever he
ventured on an impulsive advance to Brynhild.

He is a young man, of the build and features which we associate rather with Syria and Maida-vale than with the primeval
Rhineland, and in his make-up he aimed only partly at Siegfried,
and chiefly at—say, Parsifal. But he has none of the pretentious-
ness and lack of simplicity which sometimes distinguish the
clever Oriental from the stupid Saxon. On the contrary, his
chief personal charm lies in a certain combination of courageous
shyness and a touch of the unformedness of youth in his movements, with impulsive enthusiasm and an artistic judgment very
remarkable at his age. In the third act, when he came to tell that
story of the ring and the helmet, the sword and the dragon,
which everybody in the tetralogy tells at full length whenever
the smallest opening for it is perceptible, he quite charmed us
by his bright delivery. In narrating the incident of the woodbird, he was far more interesting than the woodbird itself had

been; and this result was largely due to clever and skilful singing. Not only did he give us some very pretty contrasts of tone, but he made the rhythms dance in a way that was quite delightful after the trudging and trampling of those who had been over the same ground before him. He has, too, qualities of joyousness and humor in his temperament that are invaluable in relieving the heavy earnestness which occasionally oppresses Bayreuth. In the first act he accidentally slipped into his head register on a high note, the effect being by no means unhappy; and immediately the foolish people whose ears are just sharp enough to distinguish the note of a piccolo from that of a trombone began to wonder whether his voice would stand the strain of the performance. They might have spared their anxiety; his voice was never in the slightest danger. His success was complete and legitimate; and I hope that Mr Schulz-Curtius will some day induce him to make a trip to London and tell his Götterdämmerung story for us at a Mottl concert.

Nobody who is acquainted with Der Ring will need to be told by me that The Dusk of the Gods brought the sensation of the tetralogy to a climax. The truth is—I may dare to say so now that I am clear of Bayreuth in full flight for London—Das Rheingold, Die Walküre, and the first two acts of Siegfried are music-drama in the fullest possible integrity of that genre; but Die Götterdämmerung, like the end of Siegfried, is opera. In it we have choruses and finales; we have a great scena for the *prima donna* with the chorus looking on very much as they used to do when Semiramide was singing *Bel raggio*; above all, we have the tenor stabbed to death and then coming to life to sing pretty things about his love before he finally expires, just like Edgardo in Lucia di Lammermoor. The resemblance is not shirked at Bayreuth. When two stalwart members of the chorus picked up the slain Siegfried, and pretended to support him whilst he stood up and had a few more bars about Brynhild, it was impossible not to see that we had come round again to Valentine in Gounod's Faust. It is true that we had come round, like the Hegelian spiral, on a higher plane—a prodigiously higher plane; but the fact remains that Wagner, instead of abandoning opera for ever after Lohengrin, only abandoned it for a time to invent and create the music-drama, since his great world-poem could not find its musical expression otherwise. But the powers which he acquired in creating Das Rheingold, Die Walküre, and most of Siegfried—powers so gigantic in comparison with those which Meyerbeer, Gounod, and others acquired by practice in mere opera-composing on the old scale that it is hardly possible now to conceive Meyerbeer and Wagner as beings of the same order and species—completely changed the situation for him. It gave him a technical command over dramatic music which made him as complete a master of the opera as Beethoven was of the symphony, Bach of the fugue, or Mozart of the decorative forms into which he poured his apparently spontaneous and unconditioned dramatic music. Die Götterdämmerung, Die Meistersinger, and Tristan are just as much operas as anything else: the fact that they are dramatic poems, and that Il Barbiere and Fra Diavolo are not, is no more an objection to the inclusion of the four under the same general heading of opera than the fact that Beethoven's Ninth Symphony is a dramatic poem is an objection to its being called by the same technical name as Haydn's Surprise Symphony. On the other hand, I should hesitate to call Das Rheingold an opera, since it deliberately excludes all operatic features, whereas Die Götterdämmerung excludes nothing, the composer like a true past-master of his art availing himself of all forms and methods with entire freedom, even when they led him, as they sometimes did, to all the outward and visible signs of Italian opera.

No doubt this is the explanation of the popularity of those works of Wagner which followed his relapse, as music-drama doctrinaires should call it, into opera in the last scene of Siegfried. Certainly the effect of Die Götterdämmerung was very rich and splendid on Wednesday. The music is from beginning to end the very luxury of sound woven into a gorgeous tissue by a consummately skilful master. I shall make no attempt to describe it: those who know the music will understand when I say that the conductor and the band understood their work, and that Waltraute's description of Wotan waiting in Valhall for his doom surpassed expectation in its beauty of sound, majesty of movement, and psychological luck in producing the golden moment of the first act. And to those poor barbarians who do not know the work, why should I address myself at all, since they would not understand me?

In point of technical execution, perhaps, the worst feature of the performance was the Hagen of Grengg. His voice, once described to me by Levi as "the best bass voice in Germany," is coarsened and shaken by abuse. He breaks his phrases in the worst pseudo-Wagnerian style, pumping out almost every note with a separate effort, and seldom conveying more than the roughest broken outline of the phrase. His acting is heavy and undistinguished. They are possibly proud of him at Bayreuth; but I am prepared to back Mr Bispham to drain a tankard of laudanum and then play Hagen twice as smartly and ten times more artistically. The English singer, Miss Marie Brema, had been announced as one of the Norns, but she did not appear, to my great disappointment, as her Fricka in Die Walküre proved her to be, by temperament, physical qualifications, voice, and skill, one of the most powerful and accomplished Wagnerian heroines Madame Wagner has yet discovered. Her place was filled by the somewhat provincial expedient of doubling the part of the first Norn with that of Waltraute. Madame Heink Schumann has thus played three parts in the tetralogy, the third being Erda, and in all of them she has made a deep impression by her fine contralto voice and the passion and power of her delivery. The contrast, vocally, was a little hard on the other Norns, one of whom was no less an artist than Sucher. In the river scene, the Rhinemaidens, no longer suspended by ropes, but still clinging to their *fichus*, rose out of the river with their hair elaborately dressed like three wax heads in a Bond-street shop window, and would have been exceedingly ridiculous if the music and the drama and Siegfried had not swept away all such considerations. Frau Lilli Lehmann-Kalisch's high notes, bright and true, and her saturation with the feeling of a part so magnificent that no woman with a heart and brain could possibly play it without rising far out of her ordinary self, achieved a triumph which makes it ungracious to qualify a very warm commendation of her performance. I must not, however, call her a great Brynhild. She acts intelligently, sings effectively and in tune, and is attractive enough, attaining in all these respects a degree of excellence that makes it impossible to call her commonplace; but for all that she is conventional, and takes the fullest advantage of the fact that plenty of ideas suggested by Wagner will attach themselves to her if only she stands her ground impressively. Gunther and Gutrune did their work without distinguishing themselves remarkably one way or the other; and the chorus bellowed with a will, substituting real primeval roughness for an artistic representation of roughness, which is a very different and more difficult thing.

But these criticisms of executive details, though they are important inasmuch as it is only by the most vigilant and unsparing activity in making them that Bayreuth can be kept conscious of the fact that it must conquer fresh prestige from performance to performance, and never for a moment rest on its reputation and the Master's laurels, must yet seem trivial and impertinent to those who can feel nothing but the tremendous impression made on them by a representation, complete in every word, note, and picture, of the mightiest art work our century has produced. I exhort all those who have lazily made up their minds that Bayreuth is too far, or that they cannot spare the money for the trip, to reconsider their decision and insist on the ever-resourceful Mr Schulz-Curtius finding them tickets for one of the remaining cycles. If even I, to whom Bayreuth has no novelty, and who can detect faults at the rate of about three in each bar, can say that I have been more than overpaid for the trouble and expense of my trip, how much more will not a visit be worth to those who can add the enchantments of a fool's paradise to the genuine recreation—I use the word in its highest sense—to be gained from the prodigious sum of really successful artistic effort which each performance represents? Therefore hesitate no longer, but buy your tickets, pack up your traps, and away with you. Only, if you value a cordial welcome, perhaps you had better not mention that you come on my recommendation.

C. di B.

HOW TO BECOME A MUSICAL CRITIC

WHAT IT FEELS LIKE TO BE SUCCESSFUL

(*The Star*, 16 *January* 1897)

Well, how do I know? I am amazed—overwhelmed—at
having such a question put to me, of all living men. Who says
I am successful? Everybody knows I am brilliant, paradoxical,
eccentric, witty, and all the rest of it. But *how* do they know it?
Simply because I have told London so every week at two or
three thousand words' length during the whole of the nine years
of The Star's existence.[1] Englishmen dont find out these things
for themselves: they require to be told what to say and think
about me just as much as about Shakespear.

And, pray, when did I ever say I was successful? Would you
call the Ancient Mariner a successful man merely because people
could not help listening to him, even when they heard the loud
bassoon? Did anybody believe him? Did anybody consider him
an agreeable character? Was he in a position to entertain people
at Metropole banquets like the late Colonel North, or to get
knighted like the late Sir Augustus Harris? No. Very well, then,
am I better off than the Ancient Mariner? Have I any money?
Am I respectably dressed? Do people read me except to laugh
at me and at the victims of what they call my sarcasm? Why, the
first time a journalist saw me draw a cheque, the fact was considered so extraordinary that it was mentioned in half-a-dozen
papers. Success! What use have I for success, what time for it?
Can you eat success without losing your wind, or drink it without hobnailing your liver, or wear it without bagging it at the
knees, or feel it without secretly knowing yourself to be a
humbug?

And will you tell me this? What tribunal now existing has the
right to decide whether I am successful or not? Public opinion,
perhaps! You forget that it is my function, as critic, to judge for
the public, not theirs to judge for themselves. What do they
know about it? Or posterity! If I did not hope that posterity will

---

[1] Shaw does not imply here that he has written weekly feuilletons for *The Star*
for nine years, but merely that he has been so employed throughout this period
by various London journals and newspapers.

soon have grown out of all possibility of ever understanding what any creature of this rascally century could write, should I take the trouble to be a Socialist, do you think? And what a nice successful thing it is to be a Socialist, isnt it?

Besides, Mr Star Editor, have you reflected that success is death? What is the summit? The last step before the descent. I thank my stars that the crags still tower above me. If you think I have yet succeeded, I hope you underrate my destiny.

What made the success of The Star? I reply, emphatically, the articles of Corno di Bassetto. You habitually misprinted him; and you sometimes felt that your good fortune in discovering him was almost more than you could bear. But you *did* discover him; and that was success, beyond a doubt. What does it feel like?

Corno di Bassetto.

OLD THEMES AND NEW MUSIC

(The Twentieth Century)

MUTILATED OPERA

(To *The Times*, London, 31 *May* 1904)

Sir,—I am loth to say a word that could hamper Mr [H. V.] Higgins in his plucky, but hopeless, duel with your critic.[1] When a gentleman explains that in announcing Don Giovanni without cuts he meant Don Giovanni with cuts, he makes his position clear; and there is nothing more to be said except to apologize for having misunderstood him.

But I have a protest to record against the implied doctrine that when a composer or dramatist is driven by circumstances to allow his work to be performed with cuts, or even to make the cuts himself sooner than trust the scissors to somebody else, he thereby publishes the mutilated score or prompt-book as a revised "version" of his work. When the Deutsches Theater of Berlin accepted for production my play entitled Cæsar and Cleopatra, I myself proposed the total omission of the third act in order to bring the performance within the customary limits of time. But I shall be greatly surprised if the Deutsches Theater announces the performance as " without cuts," and unspeakably staggered if Dr Richter describes, or allows it to be said that he describes, the performance without the third act as "the correct version." A cut score or book is not a "version" at all; for instance, there are two versions of Beethoven's Leonore overture, No. 2 and No. 3 (No. 1 is virtually an independent work); but

---

[1] A criticism on 3 May by the musical critic [J. A. Fuller-Maitland] of *The Times*, that the Royal Opera, after announcing uncut productions, had not performed them in their entirety, resulted in extended correspondence between manager H. V. Higgins, the critic, and *Times* readers. Shaw here refers to Higgins's letter of 25 May.

the old mutilation of No. 3, made at a time when it was considered too long for performance, is not a third version.

Take again Meyerbeer's Les Huguenots, always outrageously mutilated, and now performed at Covent Garden without the last act. Meyerbeer was forced to let the earlier mutilations pass because of the Procrustean tyranny of the fashionable dinner-hour. But I venture to say that if he were alive now, and compelled to cut the same number of bars, he would cut the work in a very different way, sacrificing such dragged-in irrelevancies as the chorus of bathers in the third act for the sake of restoring the dramatic coherency of the third. What is performed of any opera at the opera house is only that part of it which survives from the composer's struggle with the public, always ten years behind the composer, and the *impresario*, always twenty years behind the public. To call the result "the correct version" is—well, it is what Mr Higgins accuses Dr Richter of.

No doubt the finale to Don Giovanni is "an anti-climax." To the many people who do not wait even for the statue scene, that is an anti-climax too. And the third part of The Messiah is an anti-climax after the Hallelujah chorus. And Bach's St Matthew Passion should end with the thunder and lightning chorus. For all who sit out the mutilated last scene of Don Giovanni simply because they want to see the ghost, not only should the finale be cut, but the preliminary pages also; in fact, a surprisingly compact selection from the opera would satisfy them better than what they get at present. But for those to whom an *impresario* pretends to appeal when he announces Don Giovanni without cuts, and takes it out of the hands of the third-rate conductors by whom this great work has been outraged and insulted for so many years past at Covent Garden, the finale is not only indispensable to its integrity, but contains, in its last ecstatic *fugato*, one of the most delightful and intensely characteristic of all Mozart's personal outbursts. We never expected its restoration from Mr Higgins; why should we? But we did expect it from Dr Richter; and I hope that, if his authority is again brought into question in this correspondence, it may not be offered at second-hand.

Yours truly,

G. Bernard Shaw.

SUMPTUARY REGULATIONS AT THE OPERA

(To *The Times*, London, 3 *July* 1905)

Sir,—The Opera management at Covent Garden regulates the dress of its male patrons. When is it going to do the same to the women?

On Saturday night I went to the Opera. I wore the costume imposed on me by the regulations of the house. I fully recognize the advantage of those regulations. Evening dress is cheap, simple, durable, prevents rivalry and extravagance on the part of male leaders of fashion, annihilates class distinctions, and gives men who are poor and doubtful of their social position (that is, the great majority of men) a sense of security and satisfaction that no clothes of their own choosing could confer, besides saving a whole sex the trouble of considering what they should wear on state occasions. The objections to it are as dust in the balance in the eyes of the ordinary Briton. These objections are that it is colorless and characterless; that it involves a whitening process which makes the shirt troublesome, slightly uncomfortable, and seriously unclean; that it acts as a passport for undesirable persons; that it fails to guarantee sobriety, cleanliness, and order on the part of the wearer; and that it reduces to a formula a very vital human habit which should be the subject of constant experiment and active private enterprise. All such objections are thoroughly un-English. They appeal only to an eccentric few, and may be left out of account with the fantastic objections of men like Ruskin, Tennyson, Carlyle, and Morris to tall hats.

But I submit that what is sauce for the gander is sauce for the goose. Every argument that applies to the regulation of the man's dress applies equally to the regulation of the woman's. Now let me describe what actually happened to me at the Opera. Not only was I in evening dress by compulsion, but I voluntarily added many graces of conduct as to which the management made no stipulation whatever. I was in my seat in time for the first chord of the overture. I did not chatter during the music nor raise my voice when the Opera was too loud for normal

255

conversation. I did not get up and go out when the statue music began. My language was fairly moderate considering the number and nature of the improvements on Mozart volunteered by Signor Caruso, and the respectful ignorance of the dramatic points of the score exhibited by the conductor and the stage manager—if there is such a functionary at Covent Garden. In short, my behavior was exemplary.

At 9 o'clock (the Opera began at 8) a lady came in and sat down very conspicuously in my line of sight. She remained there until the beginning of the last act. I do not complain of her coming late and going early; on the contrary, I wish she had come later and gone earlier. For this lady, who had very black hair, had stuck over her right ear the pitiable corpse of a large white bird, which looked exactly as if someone had killed it by stamping on its breast, and then nailed it to the lady's temple, which was presumably of sufficient solidity to bear the operation. I am not, I hope, a morbidly squeamish person, but the spectacle sickened me. I presume that if I had presented myself at the doors with a dead snake round my neck, a collection of blackbeetles pinned to my shirtfront, and a grouse in my hair, I should have been refused admission. Why, then, is a woman to be allowed to commit such a public outrage? Had the lady been refused admission, as she should have been, she would have soundly rated the tradesman who imposed the disgusting headdress on her under the false pretense that "the best people" wear such things, and withdrawn her custom from him; and thus the root of the evil would be struck at; for your fashionable woman generally allows herself to be dressed according to the taste of a person whom she would not let sit down in her presence. I once, in Drury Lane Theatre, sat behind a *matinée* hat decorated with the two wings of a seagull, artificially reddened at the joints so as to produce an illusion of being freshly plucked from a live bird. But even that lady stopped short of the whole seagull. Both ladies were evidently regarded by their neighbors as ridiculous and vulgar; but that is hardly enough when the offense is one which produces a sensation of physical sickness in persons of normal humane sensibility.

I suggest to the Covent Garden authorities that, if they feel bound to protect their subscribers against the danger of my shocking them with a blue tie, they are at least equally bound to protect me against the danger of a woman shocking me with a dead bird.

Yours truly,
G. Bernard Shaw.

STRAUSS AND HIS ELEKTRA

(To *The Nation*, London, *March–April* 1910)

[Ernest Newman reviewed a performance of Richard Strauss's *Elektra* in *The Nation* on 26 February 1910. To Bernard Shaw the Newman appraisal was not only harsh, but ill-judged and unreasonable. The following extracts from Newman's review exemplify his critical approach to the work, and clarify Shaw's response: "All but the Strauss fanatics will admit that, though he is undoubtedly the greatest living musician, there is a strong strain of foolishness and ugliness in him, that he is lacking in the sensitive feeling for the balance of a large work that some other great artists have, and that consequently there is not one large work of his, from 'Don Quixote' onward, that is not marred by some folly or some foolery . . . much of the music is as abominably ugly as it is noisy. . . . The real term for [what some call Strauss's complexity] is incoherence, discontinuity of thinking. . . . Strauss in 'Elektra,' indeed, is like a huge volcano spluttering forth a vast amount of dirt and muck, through which every now and then, when the fuming ceases and a breath of clear air blows away the smoke, we see the grand and strong original outlines of the mountain. . . . We may detest the score as a whole for its violence and frequent ugliness, but the fine things in it are of the kind that no other man, past or present, could have written. . . . One still clings to the hope that the future has in store for us a purified Strauss, clothed and in his right mind, who will help us to forget the present Strauss —a saddening mixture of genius, ranter, child, and charlatan." Shaw's letter of protest appeared in *The Nation* on 12 March.]

HOW TO BECOME A MUSICAL CRITIC

Sir,—May I, as an old critic of music, and as a member of the public who has not yet heard Elektra, make an appeal to Mr Ernest Newman to give us something about that work a little less ridiculous and idiotic than his article in your last issue? I am sorry to use [such] disparaging and apparently uncivil epithets as "ridiculous and idiotic"; but what else am I to call an article which informs us, first, that Strauss does not know the difference between music and "abominable ugliness and noise"; and, second, that he is the greatest living musician of the greatest school of music the world has produced? I submit that this is ridiculous, inasmuch as it makes us laugh at Mr Newman, and idiotic because it unhesitatingly places the judgment of the writer above that of one whom he admits to be a greater authority than himself, thus assuming absolute knowledge in the matter. This is precisely what "idiotic" means.

Pray do not let me be misunderstood as objecting to Mr Newman describing how Elektra affected him. He has not, perhaps, as much right to say that it seemed ugly and nonsensical to him (noise, applied to music, can only mean nonsense, because in any other sense all music is noise) as Haydn had to say similar things of Beethoven's music, because Haydn was himself an eminent composer; still, he is perfectly in order in telling us honestly how ill Elektra pleased him, and not pretending he liked it lest his opinion should come to be regarded later on as we now regard his early opinion of Wagner. But he should by this time have been cured by experience and reflection of the trick that makes English criticism so dull and insolent—the trick, namely, of asserting that everything that does not please him is wrong, not only technically but ethically. Mr Newman, confessing that he did not enjoy and could not see the sense of a good deal of Elektra, is a respectable, if pathetic, figure; but Mr Newman treating Strauss as a moral and musical delinquent is—well, will Mr Newman himself supply the missing word, for really I cannot find one that is both adequate and considerate?

When my Candida was performed for the first time in Paris, the late Catulle Mendès was one of its critics. It affected him very much as Elektra affected Mr Newman. But he did not immediately proceed, English fashion, to demonstrate that I am a perverse and probably impotent imbecile (London criticism has not stopped short of this), and to imply that if I had submitted my play to his revision he could have shewn me how to make it perfect. He wrote to this effect: "I have seen this play. I am aware of the author's reputation, and of the fact that reputations are not to be had for nothing. I find that the play has a certain air of being a remarkable work and of having something in it which I cannot precisely seize; but I do not like it, and I cannot pretend that it gave me any sensation except one of being incommoded." Now that is what I call thoughtful and well-bred criticism, in contradistinction to ridiculous and idiotic criticism as practiced in England. Mr Newman has no right to say that Elektra is absolutely and objectionably ugly, because it is not ugly to Strauss and to his admirers. He has no right to say that it is incoherent nonsense, because such a statement implies that Strauss is mad, and that Hofmannstahl and Mr Beecham, with the artists who are executing the music, and the managers who are producing it, are insulting the public by offering them the antics of a lunatic as serious art. He has no right to imply that he knows more about Strauss's business technically than Strauss himself. These restrictions are no hardship to him; for nobody wants him to say any of these things: they are not criticism; they are not good manners nor good sense; and they take up the space that is available in The Nation for criticism proper; and criticism proper can be as severe as the critic likes to make it. There is no reason why Mr Newman should not say with all possible emphasis—if he is unlucky enough to be able to say so truly—that he finds Strauss's music disagreeable and cacophonous; that he is unable to follow its harmonic syntax; that the composer's mannerisms worry him; and that, for his taste, there is too much restless detail, and that the music is over-scored (too many notes, as the Emperor said to Mozart). He may, if he likes, go on to denounce the attractiveness of Strauss's music as a public danger, like the attraction of morphia; and to diagnose the cases of Strauss and Hofmannstahl as psychopathic or neurasthenic, or whatever the appropriate scientific slang may be, and descant generally on the degeneracy of the age in the manner of Dr Nordau. Such diagnoses, when supported by an appeal to the symptoms made with real critical power and ingenuity, might be interesting and worth discussing. But this lazy petulance which has disgraced English journalism in the forms of anti-Wagnerism, anti-Ibsenism, and, long before that, anti-Handelism (now remembered only by Fielding's contemptuous reference to it in Tom Jones); this infatuated attempt of writers of modest local standing to talk *de haut en bas* to men of European reputation, and to dismiss them as intrusive lunatics, is an intolerable thing, an exploded thing, a foolish thing, a parochial boorish thing, a thing that should be dropped by all good critics and discouraged by all good editors as bad form, bad manners, bad sense, bad journalism, bad politics, and bad religion. Though Mr Newman is not the only offender, I purposely select his article as the occasion of a much needed protest, because his writings on music are distinguished enough to make him worth powder and shot. I can stand almost anything from Mr Newman except his posing as Strauss's governess; and I hope he has sufficient sense of humor to see the absurdity of it himself, now that he has provoked a quite friendly colleague to this yell of remonstrance.—Yours, &c.,

G. Bernard Shaw.

[Newman's reply, in the same issue, was a peevish one, beginning with an attack upon Shaw's lack of manners as well as upon his peculiar logic. He scored the dogmatism and offensiveness of a man who had confessed he had not yet heard *Elektra*, and protested that his arguments had been distorted: "To say that a man at times writes ugly music does not imply that at other times he cannot write beautiful music; and to say that Strauss's large and wonderful previous output, plus the wonderful passages of 'Elektra' prove him to be the greatest of living composers . . . is not inconsistent with the opinion that in recent years Strauss has sometimes done vulgar and stupid and ugly things. I hope this is clear, even to Mr. Shaw." His parting shot, after the injection of several gratuitous insults, was that he agreed with Shaw "that his letter—so rich in knowledge, so admirable in reasoning, so perfect in taste, so urbane in style—should teach the music critics something, even if only in the way that the language and the antics of the drunken helots were held to be

useful for teaching the Spartan youths the advantages of sobriety."
Shaw's response to this rebuttal appeared on 19 March.]

Sir,—It is our good fortune to have produced in Professor
Gilbert Murray a writer and scholar able to raise the Electra of
Euripides from the dead and make it a living possession for us.
Thanks to him, we know the poem as if it were an English one.
But nothing Professor Murray can do can ever make us feel
quite as the Electra of Euripides felt about her mother's neglect
to bury her father properly after murdering him. A heroine who
feels that to commit murder, even husband murder, is a thing
that might happen to anybody, but that to deny the victim a
proper funeral is an outrage so unspeakable that it becomes her
plain filial duty to murder her mother in expiation, is outside
that touch of nature that makes all the ages akin: she is really too
early-Victorian. To us she is more unnatural than Clytemnestra
or Ægisthus; and, in the end, we pity them and secretly shrink
from their slayers. What Hofmannstahl and Strauss have done
is to take Clytemnestra and Ægisthus, and by identifying them
with everything that is evil and cruel, with all that needs must
hate the highest when it sees it, with hideous domination and
coercion of the higher by the baser, with the murderous rage in
which the lust for a lifetime of orgiastic pleasure turns on its
slaves in the torture of its disappointment and the sleepless
horror and misery of its neurasthenia, to so rouse in us an overwhelming flood of wrath against it and ruthless resolution to
destroy it, that Electra's vengeance becomes holy to us; and we
come to understand how even the gentlest of us could wield the
axe of Orestes or twist our firm fingers in the black hair of
Clytemnestra to drag back her head and leave her throat open
to the stroke.

That was a task hardly possible to an ancient Greek, and not
easy even to us who are face to face with the America of the
Thaw case, and the European plutocracy of which that case was
only a trifling symptom. And that is the task which Hofmannstahl and Strauss have achieved. Not even in the third scene of
Das Rheingold, or in the Klingsor scenes in Parsifal, is there
such an atmosphere of malignant and cancerous evil as we get
here. And that the power with which it is done is not the power

of the evil itself, but of the passion that detests and must and finally can destroy that evil, is what makes the work great, and makes us rejoice in its horror.

Whoever understands this, however vaguely, will understand Strauss's music, and why on Saturday night the crowded house burst into frenzied shoutings, not merely of applause, but of strenuous assent and affirmation, as the curtain fell. That the power of conceiving it should occur in the same individual as the technical skill and natural faculty needed to achieve its complete and overwhelming expression in music is a stroke of the rarest good fortune that can befall a generation of men. I have often said, when asked to state the case against the fools and money changers who are trying to drive us into a war with Germany, that the case consists of the single word, Beethoven. Today I should say, with equal confidence, Strauss. That we should make war on Strauss and the heroic warfare and aspiration that he represents is treason to humanity. In this music-drama Strauss has done for us just what he has done for his own countrymen: he has said for us, with an utterly satisfying force, what all the noblest powers of life within us are clamoring to have said, in protest against and defiance of the omnipresent villainies of our civilization; and this is the highest achievement of the highest art.

It was interesting to compare our conductor, the gallant Beecham, bringing out the points in Strauss's orchestration, until sometimes the music sounded like a concerto for six drums, with Strauss himself, bringing out the meaning and achieving the purpose of his score so that we forgot that there was an orchestra there at all, and could hear nothing but the conflict and storm of passion. Human emotion is a complex thing: there are moments when our feeling is so deep and our ecstasy so exalted that the primeval monsters from whom we are evolved wake within us and utter the strange tormented cries of their ancient struggles with the Life Force. All this is in Elektra; and under the *bâton* of Strauss the voices of these epochs are kept as distinct in their unity as the parts in a Bach motet. Such colossal counterpoint is a counterpoint of all the ages; not even Beethoven in his last great Mass comprehended so much. The feat is beyond all verbal description: it must be heard and felt; and even then, it seems, you must watch and pray, lest your God should forget you, and leave you to hear only "abominable ugliness and noise," and, on remonstrance, lead you to explain handsomely that Strauss is "vulgar, and stupid, and ugly" only "sometimes," and that this art of his is so "ridiculously easy" that nothing but your own self-respect prevents you from achieving a European reputation by condescending to practice it.

So much has been said of the triumphs of our English singers in Elektra that I owe it to Germany to profess my admiration of the noble beauty and power of Frau Fassbender's Elektra. Even if Strauss's work were the wretched thing poor Mr Newman mistook it for, it would still be worth a visit to Covent Garden to see her wonderful death dance, which was the climax of one of the most perfect examples yet seen in London of how, by beautiful and eloquent gesture, movement, and bearing, a fine artist can make not only her voice, but her body, as much a part of a great music-drama as any instrument in the score. The other German artists, notably Frau Bahr-Mildenburg, shewed great power and accomplishment; but they have received fuller acknowledgment, whereas we should not have gathered from the reports that Frau Fassbender's performance was so extra-ordinary as it actually was. A deaf man could have watched her with as little sense of privation as a blind man could have listened to her. To those of us who are neither deaf nor blind nor anti-Straussian critics (which is the same thing), she was a superb Elektra.

Whatever may be the merits of the article which gave rise to the present correspondence, it is beyond question that it left the readers of The Nation without the smallest hint that the occasion was one of any special importance, or that it was at all worth their while to spend time and money in supporting Mr Beecham's splendid enterprise, and being present on what was, in fact, a historic moment in the history of art in England, such as may not occur again within our lifetime. Many persons may have been, and possibly were, prevented by that article from seizing their opportunity, not because Mr Newman does not happen to like Strauss's music, but because he belittled the situation by so miscalculating its importance that he did not think it worth even the effort of criticizing it, and dismissed it in a notice in which nothing was studied except his deliberate contemptuous insolence to the composer. It would have been an additional insult to Strauss to have waited to hear Elektra before protesting, on the plainest grounds of international courtesy and artistic good faith, against such treatment of the man who shares with Rodin the enthusiastic gratitude and admiration of the European republic, one and indivisible, of those who understand the highest art. But now that I have heard Elektra, I have a new duty to the readers of The Nation, and that is to take upon me the work Mr Newman should have done, and put them in possession of the facts.

And now Ernest, *"Triff noch einmal"*!—Yours, &c.,

G. Bernard Shaw.

[Shaw's second letter goaded Newman into an even more vigorous drubbing of *Elektra* than in his original article. He labeled von Hofmannstahl's drama (on which the opera was based) "a most unpleasant specimen of that crudity and physical violence that a certain school of modern German artists mistake for intellectual and emotional power." In setting this violence to music Strauss had tried "to out-Herod Herod," but failed. "My complaint against 'Elektra' is that he frequently fobs us off with the merest make-believe." Shaw had reported that the capacity audience "burst into frenzied shoutings . . . of strenuous assent and affirmation," but there were two possible explanations for this: "Some people have been swept off their feet by the first excitement of the thing; others have been astonished and delighted to find that, so far from the Strauss idiom being so advanced and recondite as they had been led to believe, many of the tunes . . . are of the most friendly and accommodating commonplace." He scored the banality of the Chrysothemis theme and asked Shaw to examine it as such. Much of *Elektra*, he insisted, "is merely frigid intellectual calculation simulating a white heat of emotion." His final barb was reserved for "this purist [Shaw] who yells so deafeningly for moderation in criticism," but who was himself frequently immoderate in his critical utterances, particularly where Shakespear was concerned.

A review, on 26 March, of *Elektra* as a play, written by H. W. Massingham, editor of *The Nation*, prompted Newman's third letter, especially as Massingham had revealed himself as generally sympathetic to Shaw's view. Surely, insisted Newman on 2 April, "the real question is not 'What kind of a drama has von Hofmannstahl written?' but 'What kind of music has Strauss written?' " Shaw's final reply (to Newman's second letter) also appeared on 2 April.]

Sir,—Just a last word with Mr Newman. I make no apology for bullying him: the result has justified me. I leave it to your readers to say whether I have not wakened him up beneficially, as well as put a very different complexion on the case of Strauss and Elektra. The anti-Strauss campaign was so scandalous that it was clear that somebody had to be bullied; and I picked out Mr Newman because he was much better able to take care of himself than any of the rest. Most of them I could not have attacked at all: as well strike a child or intimidate an idiot.

I will now repeat my amusing performance of knocking Mr Newman down flat with a single touch. He asks me, concerning a certain theme in Elektra, to look at it honestly and tell him whether it is not banality itself. Certainly it is. And now will Mr Newman turn to the hackneyed little "half close" out of which Handel made the Hallelujah chorus, and tell me honestly whether it is not—and was not even in Handel's own time— ten times as banal as the Chrysothemis motif? Strange how these men of genius will pick up a commonplace out of the gutter and take away our breath with it; and how, as they grow older and more masterful, any trumpery diatonic run, or such intervals of the common chord as have served the turn of thousands of post- boys, dead and alive, will serve their turn, too!

Fancy trying that worn-out banality gambit on an old hand like me!

Now for Mr Newman's final plea, with its implicit compliment to myself, which I quite appreciate. That plea is that he did to Strauss only as I did to Shakespear. Proud as I am to be Mr Newman's exemplar, the cases are not alike. If the day should ever dawn in England on a Strauss made into an idol; on an outrageous attribution to him of omniscience and infallibility; on a universal respect for his reputation accompanied by an ignorance of his works so gross that the most grotesque mutilations and travesties of his scores will pass without protest as faithful performances of them; on essays written to shew how Clytemnestra was redeemed by her sweet womanly love for Ægisthus, and Elektra a model of filial piety to all middle-class daughters; on a generation of young musicians taught that they must copy all Strauss's progressions and rhythms and instrumentation and all the rest of it if they wish to do high-class work; in short, on all the follies of Bardolatry transferred to Strauss, then I shall give Mr Newman leave to say his worst of Strauss, were it only for Strauss's own sake. But that day has not yet dawned. The current humbug is all the other way. The geese are in full cackle to prove that Strauss is one of themselves instead of the greatest living composer. I made war on the duffers who idolized Shakespear. Mr Newman took the side of the duffers who are trying to persuade the public that Strauss is an impostor making an offensive noise with an orchestra of marrow-bones and cleavers. It is not enough to say that I scoffed, and that therefore I have no right to complain of other people scoffing. Any fool can scoff. The serious matter is which side you scoff at. Scoffing at pretentious dufferdom is a public duty; scoffing at an advancing torchbearer is a deadly sin. The men who praised Shakespear in my time were mostly the men who would have stoned him had they been his contemporaries. To praise him saved them the trouble of thinking, got them the credit of correct and profound opinions, and enabled them to pass as men of taste when they explained that Ibsen was an obscene dullard. To expose these humbugs and to rescue the real Shakespear from them, it was necessary to shatter their idol. It has taken the iconoclasm of three generations of Bible smashers to restore Hebrew literature to us, after three hundred years of regarding the volume into which it was bound as a fetish and a talisman; and it will take as many generations of Shakespear smashers before we can read the plays of Shakespear with as free minds as we read The Nation.

Besides, what I said about Shakespear, startling as it was to all the ignoramuses, was really the classical criticism of him.

THE REMINISCENCES OF A QUINQUAGENARIAN

That criticism was formulated by Dr Johnson in what is still the greatest essay on Shakespear yet written. I did not read it until long after my campaign against Bardolatry in The Saturday Review; and I was gratified, though not at all surprised, to find how exactly I had restated Johnson's conclusions.—Yours, &c.,

G. Bernard Shaw.

(On the broader issue raised here, is not the trouble precisely this: that Mr Shaw appears to claim for himself the possession of a perfect criterion for distinguishing " duffers " and " torch-bearers" and for naming other persons qualified to perform the same task of discrimination?—ED., Nation.)

[The final letter in the debate was Newman's, on 9 April. It was, at best, a carping letter, attempting to force a few more variations out of already overworked themes, and adding nothing but "the last word" to the controversy. His one effective riposte, however, was the provision of a suggested new telegraphic address for Shaw: " 'Infallibility,' London."]

THE REMINISCENCES OF A QUINQUAGENARIAN

(Shaw's improvised address was delivered before the meeting of the Musical Association on 6 December 1910. As it "unfortunately defied verbatim reporting," Shaw provided the following report for the Proceedings, 37th Session, 1910–11. This was reprinted in The New Music Review, New York, August 1912, but the verbatim report of the ensuing discussion and of Shaw's rebuttal was omitted)

A good deal of what I said need not be reported. It served its purpose of keeping the audience in good humor for the moment; and there is no reason why it should survive.

The important points were these:—

That musical reminiscences are usually valueless except as anecdotage, and even at that are seldom witty unless they are also incredible. They might, however, be made really instructive and supply material for genuinely scientific treatises on art, if musical veterans, instead of mentioning that they once played a pianoforte duet with Chopin, and that the night they first heard

Jenny Lind sing was the wettest they can remember, would try to recall faithfully what things in the music that was new in their time sounded strange to them, or even scandalous and intolerable. It is not easy for a musician today to confess that he once found Wagner's music formless, melodyless, and abominably discordant; but that many musicians now living did so is beyond all question. I myself was deeply interested in Wagner's music, and I supported him enthusiastically to the utmost of my opportunities; but I had to listen to his music and that of his successors for many years before I could say, as I can say now, that the overture to Tannhäuser sounds as hackneyed, as far as its chords and progressions and modulations are concerned, as the overture to William Tell did forty years ago.

The technical history of modern harmony is a history of the growth of toleration by the human ear of chords that at first sounded discordant and senseless to the main body of contemporary professional musicians. By senseless I mean, in the case of a discord, that you cannot foresee its resolution or relate it to a key. Great composers anticipate the rank and file of us in this sort of perception, and consequently in the toleration of combinations which seem unbearable in the absence of any such perception. Musicians had to confine themselves to thirds and fifths until somebody—we used to say it was Monteverdi—ventured to pile a minor third on top of the fifth in a very cautious way, introducing the new note first as a third, fifth, or unison in the previous chord, and letting it sweeten itself into a concord again in the following one: preparation and resolution, as we call it. It took quite a long time before the battle over the toleration of this discord of the seventh was so thoroughly won that it could be exploded without preparation on an audience in any position. I can still remember the time when its last inversion—with the seventh in the bass—sounded strange and dramatically momentous, as in the first *finale* in Don Giovanni, and especially in Beethoven's early Prometheus overture, which opens with an abrupt third inversion of the seventh, *fortissimo*. By that time, however, minor ninths, then called diminished sevenths, were familiar; and Wagner's battle began with unprepared major ninths, which, joyously blared forth in the second act of Tannhäuser, sounded as scandalous as anything in Richard Strauss's Sinfonia Domestica does today. Who cares about an unprepared major ninth now, or an eleventh, or a thirteenth? Yet when you have accustomed people to these, you have conquered the whole diatonic scale, and may sound every note in it simultaneously, leaving nothing for future generations to discover but the art of making chords out of combinations of different keys, an art in which we are already making experiments.

Parallel with this line of advance goes the training of our ears and minds in alertness in passing from key to key: that is, from mood to mood. Formerly we needed to have a change of key broken to us very gently, by modulation, and even then only to a very closely related key: that is, a key consisting as nearly as possible of the same notes. As an example of the violent throwing off of such precautions, let me cite the point in the third act of Lohengrin, where the full close of the Wedding Chorus in B flat is succeeded without a note of warning by a discord belonging to the key of E natural. Nowadays this produces no effect except that of its admirable dramatic propriety. We are accustomed to such changes. We are even beginning to consider effects like the alternations of the common chords of A flat and A natural in The Ring as cheap and pretty. But I assure you that when I first heard Lohengrin I literally did not know where I was when I was flung into that sharp key out of the flat one without modulation. I thought Wagner had invented some novel and extraordinary chord, undreamt of by Mozart or even by Bach, who anticipated everybody and everything in music.

I submit that this sort of reminiscence has some real historical value. If we would all make notes of the progressions that puzzled or surprised, startled or shocked us, when we first heard them, and that we have lived to see added to the commonplaces of the music-hall, we should be providing materials for a really scientific history of music, and, what is more, for a really vital way of teaching students. I do not know how they are taught now; but in my time nobody except Stainer did anything but explain that Wagner's practice was "wrong," and that everything depended on your having correct views as to the true root of the chord of the supertonic, all this nonsense about roots being the result of a wildly absurd attempt to dress up the good old rule-of-thumb thoroughbass with Helmholtz's discovery of overtones, partial tones, combination tones, and the like.

But what is of far greater importance than the theoretical instruction of the musician—for, after all, the follies of the academic treatises did not prevent academy students from writing music if they had it in them—is the question of the practical training of composers. I want to make an earnest protest against the gentleman amateur in music and all other arts. I do not deny that gentlemen amateur artists have done remarkable and even great things since artists unfortunately became gentlemen—more or less—in the seventeenth century. Though Hogarth was the last English painter who could boast of being a skilled tradesman until the Pre-Raphaelite revival began, yet Reynolds was a fine artist and Turner a very great one indeed, even when they daubed and smudged in a way that would have thrown Van Eyck or Memling into ecstasies of derisive laughter. None the less, if a carriage-builder were to daub a brougham or a house-painter a hall-door as crudely as most of our gentleman painters daub their Academy pictures, he would be bankrupt in a fortnight. Have we anything analogous in the musical profession? Certainly we have. As far as I know, there is only one way in which an orchestral composer can become a really skilled tradesman, in the Van Eyck sense of the word, in this country, and that is by working in the theatre. In the theatre, when I want a piece of music for a certain purpose, I can get it. If I want it a certain length, I can get it exactly that length. If in the course of rehearsal I want it altered to suit some change in the stage business of my play, I can get the alteration made. The conductor does not say that his inspiration cannot be controlled in this way, and that he must work his movement out as his genius prompts him and as its academic form demands. He does not tell me that he cannot do what I want without eight horns and four tubas, half-a-dozen drums and a *contra fagotto*. He has to do it with one oboe generally. He is really master of his materials, and can adapt them at a moment's notice to any set of circumstances that is at all practicable. And it is precisely because he can do these small things when other people want them that, if he has talent enough, he can do great things when he himself wants them. This is the way of the true master.

Mozart was able not only to write Don Giovanni to please himself and his friends: he was also able to sit in a tavern garden with Schickaneder and write Die Zauberflöte just as Schickaneder wanted it for the stage, and cut it about without spoiling it when it did not fit. This did not prevent him from telling the king who complained that there were too many notes in his scores that there were just the right number, or from having his own way when he knew it was the right way. My point is that he was master of his trade and of his materials, and could do a thing in a dozen different ways and on a dozen different scales according to circumstances. If you want to know who was the greatest master of the orchestra in London in the days when I was a critic of music, I can tell you at once. It was Mr James Glover, of Drury Lane Theatre. I tried to induce him once to write a treatise on orchestration for the benefit of those who have to arrange full concert scores for small theatre bands, and, above all, to explode the superstitions of the big standard treatises as to the limitations of wind instruments. Yet I doubt whether Mr Glover ever wasted an hour over the pages of Berlioz or Gevaërt. You all know the drum and trumpet parts of Mozart and Beethoven— the quaint writing in dots and dashes forced on those composers by the gaps in the scale on the old horns and trumpets. I have heard these ridiculous dot and dash passages conscientiously imitated by our gentlemen amateur composers and professors when Mr Glover was not only handling his cornets with the freedom of a military bandmaster, but was producing effects of extraordinary brilliancy in the Drury Lane pantomime by filling the stage with a battery of the modern instruments known as Bach trumpets. He had also, in a ballet at the Palace Theatre, written an accompaniment for a scene representing a Channel crossing which for humor and daintiness of handling could not have been surpassed by any English composer. Yet this was all in his night's work. It was never performed as a concert piece. Nobody wrote solemn criticisms of it any more than of the work of the scene-painters, who, by the way, are also masters of their art. We read the story, quoted by Ruskin, of the Pope's messenger who asked Giotto for a sample of his skill, and to whom Giotto replied by lifting his hand and drawing a perfect circle on the wall. Our gentlemen painters are deeply impressed by this anecdote; but I have seen Mr Hemsley, the scene-painter, raise his hand like Giotto and do this very same thing in sketching a plan of a scene for me in his studio. Now I do not know whether Mr Glover will ever want to write a symphony or a mass or an opera, or any of the things that our academic musicians aim at; but of this I am certain, that if he does, he will make his orchestra do what he wants, and not let it make him do what the textbooks say it ought to do. If Sir Charles Stanford and Sir Hubert Parry had graduated by occupying for four or five years the posts held by Mr Glover at Drury Lane and the late Mr Jacobi (an equally skilful if less original bandmaster) at the old Alhambra, I venture to say that they would have expressed themselves not only more copiously but much more fully and freely in their essays in the highest class of composition. I repeat, until a composer has learnt how to turn out music to order for other people and for practical use, he will not be able to turn out work to his own order, no matter how many exercises he may have labored through. And though this generation has many more opportunities of hearing orchestral music, and even of practicing it, than existed thirty years ago, it is still true that the theatre is the only place where a young man who aspires to mastery of the orchestra can make himself what I call a real tradesman.

This is the more important as England is now taking her old place, after an interval of two centuries, as a productive nation musically. Sir Edward Elgar, whose genius, like that of Burne-Jones, achieved a finished technique by study and by making opportunities of practice, produces neither second-hand Handel like Arne, second-hand Mozart like Bishop, [nor] second-hand Mendelssohn like Bennett—to come no nearer our own time—but music which is as characteristically English as a Shropshire country house and stable is characteristically English. I am not here raising the question whether it is good music: that is to say, whether you happen to like it or not (though as a matter of fact I like it myself). My point is that, whether you like it or not, it is the characteristic expression of a certain type of English breeding, and very good breeding at that. Before Elgar came such a thing did not exist on the symphonic plane in England. You had to go back to Purcell for it.

Before concluding, let me say that there is still, as there has always been in England, a huge body of mere brute musical faculty, and a sort of connoisseurship which is exactly like that of the football field and cricket pitch. Our musical festivals are for the most part horribly unmusical. Our notion that you can give majesty to Handel's music by having it roared and growled and wheezed and screamed simultaneously by 4,000 people who do not know how to sing is too silly for human patience. But the people who go to hear this sort of thing are often quite keen critics of certain points of execution. They will listen to a tenor singing Deeper and deeper still to discover whether he can sing the ascending passages without an obvious break and change of register; and if he achieves this feat as successfully as Santley in Honor and Arms they will applaud him, though he will please them all the more if he interpolates a high note at the end that would infuriate any really cultivated musician. But silly as these people are, they are musical, and only need plenty of opportunities of hearing good music, especially real English music like Elgar's (not sham English music produced by simply writing in the old English dance forms), to provide a demand which will give all our young composers as much practice as they want without having to choose between the theatre band or the church organ and no practice at all.

DISCUSSION

THE CHAIRMAN [W. H. CUMMINGS].—On my own behalf, and I am sure I may add on yours also, I tender most sincere thanks to Mr Shaw for the very entertaining and eloquent discourse he has given us. I remember we have had comic histories of England, and I was sometimes reminded of these when Mr Shaw was speaking; but we must remember that a comic presentation of facts may nevertheless enforce great truths, and at the back of Mr Shaw's remarks there are many important lessons to be learned.

HOW TO BECOME A MUSICAL CRITIC

A few years ago I happened to be at a country town, and the Mayor apologized for the feebleness of an "octogeranium." I hope you will make some allowance for me on the same grounds. The last subject discussed was Elgar. He had told an audience that he taught himself to compose by taking a score of Mozart and filling it up with his own parts bar by bar. That shews we must build on the old foundations. Mr Shaw has made an amusing reference to our unfortunate orchestras, but he told us how we afterwards learned to play Wagner. There was a great deal of truth in his remarks. Wagner was at first abhorred; but that is nothing wonderful. If you take up a Greek book—say Homer's Iliad—and do not know the alphabet, could you appreciate it? So you have to learn the language of Wagner, and you may find it good or bad. I do not think Mr Shaw's history of English music is quite correct. There is one man who might have done great things in the direction Mr Shaw has indicated—Sir Henry Bishop. When at Drury Lane he tried to copy Mozart and Beethoven. Mr Shaw's final sentences are the best we can take away with us. We want our own language, our own thoughts, our own expressions, our own brutality if you like; and if he can help us to that I am sure we shall all be delighted.

Mr [JAMES] GLOVER.—As you seem to be amused by the reminiscences of one Irishman, perhaps you will hear a few words from another. I am the Mr Glover to whom reference has been made. Mr Shaw has spoken of the practical side of the more or less trifling or important music for which I have been responsible. With respect to trumpets, I was limited. I found very few trumpet players, and those who had only a few notes invariably played them out of tune. But my manager insisted on engaging twelve trumpets. You know that to have twelve trumpets blowing the same few notes all through the night is too awful. I did have a trumpet with a valve attachment which gave us all those chromatic beauties of which Mr Shaw has spoken. I remember Sir Arthur Sullivan sending round to me between the acts, and asking how I did it. There is one phase of Mr Shaw's remarks that I should like to enlarge on, and that is the apathy of eminent musicians to popular demands during the last twentyfive or thirty years. I formed a musical association, and tried to encourage the better class of musicians—I mean the musicians who compose—to give us something more for a smaller orchestra. Nine-tenths of the populace know Sir Edward Elgar's Pomp and Circumstance. This was published in Germany with a French title. Sir Edward did not write impossible orchestration; it is scored for a small orchestra by Adolph Schmidt, who did the same for Madame Wagner in order to popularize her husband's works. If I ask about the first violin part of a composition, and am told there are eight first violin parts, it is evident I can have no use for it. There are hundreds of things of Sir Charles Stanford's I would gladly introduce into the pantomime, but I cannot because I am barred by the complications of the instruments. Everybody for the last thirty years has been complaining that the better class of music gets no encouragement from the State. But, as I have pointed out where I am allowed to write, an Act of Parliament was passed in 1907 entitling every borough to charge a penny rate for music; and there are not three towns that have taken advantage of it. I do not complain of this; but what I do complain of is that there is not a single person connected with the higher music of London who has called a meeting for promoting the adoption of the Act. A penny rate in the little town of Bexhill, where I go for my week-ends, means £428. If I can get Bexhill to take it up, I will see that the £400 is spent on music. If you add up the rateable value of the entire country there is £500,000 waiting for English music, and there is not a person in London who is prepared to stand up for it. It is waiting for every member who writes works that nobody wants to hear. Many years ago, when I was at Covent Garden, and had the pleasure of first introducing the Valkyrie, a man from over the way said, "This is the place for you"; but I said, "Not for me." But it does seem to me that what we want is the education of the public taste, not in a too academical sense. Those who are at the head of affairs have not the pluck or the commonsense to agitate for it.

Dr [Thomas Lea] Southgate.—I should like to call attention very briefly to an inconsistency on the part of our lecturer. He commenced by deprecating reminiscences, and he has given us reminiscences. He reminded me of an ancient hero who was called in to curse, and remained to bless! His reminiscences practically took the form of one branch of history. History is always entertaining, especially to old members, and the Chairman and I are among the oldest. I remember very well those reminiscences to which our lecturer has referred, and can name the gentleman he has in mind, Mr G. A. Osborne: he has long been dead, so we need not mind mentioning his name. I must say I found his experiences very interesting, because he had had a wide range of knowledge of music and musicians in many parts of the world. I should like to make one protest, and that is against the lecturer's statement that in his early days composers did not write English music. Now when I think of Sir Sterndale Bennett, who has sometimes been ignorantly represented as an imitator of Mendelssohn, but was nothing of the kind; of Macfarren, whose Chevy Chase overture I still remember; of Sullivan, whose music was distinctly English; of Hatton; and of Bishop, to whom our Chairman has referred, I think his stricture that these men did not write English music is not justified. He has forgotten one branch of music of which we are all justly proud— I mean our English church music; surely Sir John Goss wrote noble cathedral music! The moral to be deduced from the lecture we have heard is a very old one: Practice makes perfect. According to the theory laid down, the music heard at the Crystal Palace and elsewhere did not give satisfaction because the players did not master the parts! I was surprised to hear that assertion about Manns's orchestra. We must remember that those Saturday concerts were only the weekly ones. There were also the daily ones, so the orchestra had plenty of opportunities of practicing together. May I set Mr Shaw right on one point? He thought Ouseley and Stainer belonged to different Universities, though I daresay the remarks he made with regard to the views of each on chords and harmony were true. But I rather think he referred to the idea that, when Macfarren was Professor at Cambridge, not many got through on Stainer's book on Harmony. Macfarren, who believed so passionately in Day's theory, was not in sympathy with the theories that obtained at Oxford.

A MEMBER.—Mr Shaw suggests that we are dependent on the machinery we find. Does not the artist often invent his own machinery?

Mr BERNARD SHAW.—It is, of course, true that artists are inventive. I suppose every great artist does add a brick or so to the general structure of art. But even if you take the case of Wagner at Bayreuth, I think you must admit that if there had been no orchestras or theatres in Paris or elsewhere, it would not have been possible for him to construct his theatre. Had he been a Sandwich Islander he could have done nothing. He could not have done the work he did if the way had not been prepared by all the great modern musicians from Bach onward. He simply took the structure that had been raised by other great men and added his own little contribution. You must take up the art at the particular point to which it has been built up.

Why did Dr Southgate get up and give Osborne away? I did not mention his name. I do not know that I particularly disliked his reminiscences, because there was always a sort of dramatic touch about his accounts of Berlioz and Chopin, and those whom he had known. I cannot agree that Sir Sterndale Bennett wrote English music. Of course it is quite possible that his most characteristic work was written before he saw any of Mendelssohn's, but he must have come across a good deal that was inspired by Mendelssohn, such as some of Spohr's works. His music was very charming, and I wonder why one or two of his compositions are not more frequently performed; but they are in no sense English. The May Queen appears to me to express what is not English. There is a certain feeble sentimentality about it; but if you are an Englishman and can get up and say you find everything that is characteristic of your country in the music of Sterndale Bennett, I shall really wonder whether you have any clear idea as to what English music is. I do not say that English characteristics do not occasionally shew themselves in Sterndale Bennett and Macfarren, e.g. in Tis jolly to hunt, or the end of the Chevy Chase overture; but that is not exactly what I am talking about. I was thinking of the soul of England. If you were to present Tis jolly to hunt to a man from Asia, he would fail to recognize the soul of England in it.

I have a certain sympathy for the way in which Dr Southgate contended for Sterndale Bennett and Macfarren; but if one really thinks that is English music, he does not know what English music is. I remember how Goetz sent over to the Philharmonic Society a Spring Overture, and Macfarren had to write an analytical program—a very terrible thing it is when you have to write an analytic program for a Society. Yet here Macfarren said, "This seems to me a collection of consecutive 7ths." What he meant was that Goetz had no right to compose in consecutive 7ths; and I say a man who is in that frame of mind has lost sight of what music really is. One of the secrets of the success of Chevy Chase was that Macfarren in his early youth had learned to play a brass instrument, and consequently for once he got a genuine inspiration. I make Dr Southgate a present of Sullivan, and Hatton, and the rest of them; they wrote very nice things. I need not speak against Goss. But if I want to speak well of English music, I have to go further back. I cannot rise to any enthusiasm about Goss. A real omission I made was in speaking of the theatrical conductors as the only musicians; I should have mentioned another class of practical men—the church organists. I did not mean to speak disrespectfully of the Crystal Palace band, because they were thoroughly practical men; but whenever they essayed pieces that were very seldom played, they could not do them well. A performance under Manns of a Mozart symphony was deplorably like two young ladies at Brixton playing a pianoforte duet. Mozart is the test; he is the master of masters. I am obliged to Dr Southgate for setting me right about the rival examiners.

CAUSERIE ON HANDEL IN ENGLAND

(Shaw's causerie was written to be read to a society of musicians in France, in a translation by Augustin Hamon. It was never published in England, but Shaw sanctioned American publication in *Ainslee's Magazine, May* 1913. An unauthorized reprint, under the title "Bernard Shaw on Handel," appeared in *The Boston Evening Transcript,* 21 *June* 1913)

Handel is not a mere composer in England: he is an institution. What is more, he is a sacred institution. When his Messiah is performed, the audience stands up, as if in church, while the Hallelujah chorus is being sung. It is the nearest sensation to the elevation of the Host known to English Protestants. Every three years there is a Handel Festival, at which his oratorios are performed by four thousand executants, collected from all the choirs in England. The effect is horrible; and everybody declares it sublime. Many of the songs in these oratorios were taken by Handel from his operas and set to pious words: for example, *Rende sereno il ciglio, madre: non piange più* has become Lord, remember David: teach him to know Thy ways. If anyone in England were to take the song from the oratorio and set it back again to secular words, he would probably be prosecuted for blasphemy. Occasionally a writer attempts to spell Handel's name properly as Händel or Haendel. This produces just the same shock as the attempts to spell Jehovah as Jahve. The effect is one of brazen impiety.

I do not know of any parallel case in France. Gluck, almost unknown in England until Giulia Ravogli made a success here some twenty years ago in Orfeo, was, and perhaps still is, an institution in France; but he was an operatic, not a religious, institution. Still, there is some resemblance between the two cases. Gluck and Handel were contemporaries. Both were Germans. Both were very great composers. Both achieved a special vogue in a country not their own, and each of them remained almost unknown in the country which the other had conquered. I can think of no other instance of this.

Handel's music is the least French music in the world, and the most English. If Doctor Johnson had been a composer he would have composed like Handel. So would Cobbett. It was from Handel that I learned that style consists in force of assertion. If you can say a thing with one stroke unanswerably you have style; if not, you are at best a *marchand de plaisir*; a decorative *littérateur*, or a musical confectioner, or a painter of fans with cupids and *cocottes*. Handel has this power. When he sets the words Fixed in His everlasting seat, the atheist is struck dumb: God is there, fixed in his everlasting seat by Handel, even if you live in an Avenue Paul Bert, and despise such superstitions. You may despise what you like; but you cannot contradict Handel. All the sermons of Bossuet could not convince Grimm that God existed. The four bars in which Handel finally affirms "the

Everlasting Father, the Prince of Peace," would have struck
Grimm into the gutter, as by a thunderbolt. When he tells you
that when the Israelites went out of Egypt, "there was not one
feeble person in all their tribes," it is utterly useless for you to
plead that there must have been at least one case of influenza.
Handel will not have it: "There was not one, not one feeble
person in all their tribes," and the orchestra repeats it in curt,
smashing chords that leave you speechless. That is why every
Englishman believes that Handel now occupies an important
position in heaven. If so, *le bon Dieu* must feel toward him very
much as Louis Treize felt toward Richelieu.

Yet in England his music is murdered by the tradition of the
big chorus! People think that four thousand singers must be
four thousand times as impressive as one. This is a mistake: they
are not even louder. You can hear the footsteps of four thousand
people any day in the Rue de Rivoli—I mention it because it is
the only street in Paris known to English tourists—but they are
not so impressive as the march of a single well-trained actor
down the stage of the Théâtre Français. It might as well be said
that four thousand starving men are four thousand times as
hungry as one, or four thousand slim *ingénues* four thousand
times as slim as one. You can get a tremendously powerful *fortissimo* from twenty good singers—I have heard it done by the
Dutch conductor, De Lange—because you can get twenty
people into what is for practical purposes the same spot; but all
the efforts of the conductors to get a *fortissimo* from the four
thousand Handel Festival choristers are in vain: they occupy too
large a space; and even when the conductor succeeds in making
them sing a note simultaneously, no person can hear them simultaneously, because the sound takes an appreciable time to
travel along a battle front four thousand strong; and in rapid
passages the semiquaver of the singer farthest from you does not
reach you until that of the singer nearest you has passed you by.
If I were a member of the House of Commons I would propose
a law making it a capital offence to perform an oratorio by
Handel with more than eighty performers in the chorus and
orchestra, allowing fortyeight singers and thirtytwo instrumentalists. Nothing short of that will revive Handel's music in

A NEGLECTED MORAL

England. It lies dead under the weight of his huge reputation and the silly notion that big music requires big bands and choruses. Little as Handel's music is played in France, the French must be better Handelians than the English—they could not possibly be worse—as they have no festival choirs. Perhaps they even know his operas, in which much of his best music lies buried.

The strangest recent fact in connection with Handel in England is the craze he inspired in Samuel Butler. You do not yet know in France that Samuel Butler was one of the greatest English and, indeed, European writers of the second half of the nineteenth century. You will find out all about him in a couple of hundred years or so. Paris is never in a hurry to discover great men; she is still too much occupied with Victor Hugo and Meyerbeer and Ingres to pay any attention to more recent upstarts. Or stay! I am unjust; there are advanced Parisians who know about Delacroix and the Barbizon school, and even about Wagner; and I once met a Parisian who had heard of Debussy, and even had a theory that he must have been employed in an organ factory, because of his love of the scale of whole tones.

However, I am forgetting Handel and Butler. Butler was so infatuated with Handel that he actually composed two oratorios, Narcissus and Ulysses, in the closest imitation of his style, with *fugato* choruses on the cries of the Bourse, the oddest combination imaginable. Butler's books are full of references to Handel, and quotations from his music. But, as I have said, what do the French care for Butler? Only Henri Bergson can understand the importance of his work. I should explain that Mr Bergson is a French philosopher, well known in England. When he has been as long dead as Descartes or Leibnitz, his reputation will reach Paris. Dear old Paris!

A NEGLECTED MORAL OF THE WAGNER CENTENARY

(*The New Statesman*, 31 *May* 1913; unsigned)

Last week the London press descanted on the fact that Richard Wagner stands with Bach and Beethoven as one of the greatest

281

composers of all time. It also reported a naval court martial at which, among other matters, it transpired that a battleship, in a department needing eighteen men for its full equipment, put to sea with three.

What, it may be asked, is the connection between these two items? The connection is that they were both symptoms of our national weakness for writing and speaking without the smallest reference not only to facts, but to our own previous utterances on the same subjects. How did the London press treat Wagner during his lifetime? As an impostor, a charlatan, a musical ignoramus who, being unable to compose a bar of melody, produced a hideous *charivari* by a monstrous abuse of the orchestra and called it "the music of the future." When for one season, by some strange accident, he became conductor of the Philharmonic Society, he was, in spite of the support of Queen Victoria and her Consort, driven off and replaced by a musician [Hans Richter] whom no one now supposes worthy to black his shoes. Not since Handel had a composer written so healthily for the human voice; yet he was said to smash all the voices, though Verdi and even Gounod, with their trick of writing for the upper fifth of the singer's compass alone (the pretty part), were filling Europe with the wrecks of shattered goat-bleaters whilst the Wagner veterans were roaring cheerfully a quarter of a century after their great-grandchildren had started in life and were presumably imploring them to stop. Mr Ashton Ellis devoted his life to the translation of Wagner's prose works; and it was with the greatest difficulty that, after years of effort, a wretchedly inadequate Civil List pension was procured for him in the face of the sedulously inculcated conviction that Wagner was an abominably bad musician, and that, being only a composer, he could not possibly have written books, or if he did they could not be proper ones. Nearly two generations of Englishmen were deprived of the pleasure and edification of Wagner's music, and filled with a purely mischievous contempt for a very great man for no mortal reason whatever, and with no countervailing benefit to any human being. In round figures, we had to do without Wagner's compositions for thirty years because they were not performed here at all; and we were by that time so prejudiced against them that it was another thirty years before we became really familiar with them.

And now, when the Wagner Centenary comes, all the papers say what a great man he was, without making the smallest reference to the fact that they did all that in them lay to blast his reputation and starve him to death. Some of the very men who have written the Centenary articles thought no stone too jagged and no mud too dirty to throw at him; though their only quarrel with him was that The Niblung's Ring was not written in the style of Mendelssohn's Elijah.

Just about the time when even editors of newspapers, though densely ignorant of music, and divided between their Philistine contempt for it as a subject and their deep awe of their critics' jargon about the chord of the supertonic (which did not then suggest a Nietzschean heresy) and "a smoothly contrasted second subject in the dominant," were at last beginning to wonder, with the Richter concerts at the height of their vogue, with Lohengrin more hackneyed at the opera than Il Trovatore had ever been, with Bayreuth almost as fashionable as Goodwood, with Europe, in short, saturated with an enormous popularity such as no musician before had ever attained or dreamt of, whether it could really be the correct thing to go on explaining that Wagner was an obscure and infamous impostor who could not compose a melody, and whose reputation was a passing craze got up by a few long-haired and unwashed victims of neurasthenia, Ibsen reached us. And then it began all over again. Wagner was hastily snatched from the pillory and perfunctorily shoved among the immortals; and Ibsen was thrust into his vacant place of disgrace. And he was treated worse than Wagner, though that seemed impossible. It was, however, easy. We had at least not accused Wagner of obscenity, nor called for the prosecution of Her Majesty's Theatre as a disorderly house after the first performance of Lohengrin. But we did that to Ibsen. And in due course, when we come to Ibsen's Centenary, we shall calmly treat him as the greatest dramatist since Shakespear, hardly even excepting Goethe, without the smallest reference to the fact that at the moment when he delivered his message to mankind we assured the English nation that he was an illiterate, diseased, half-crazy pornographer, and wanted to prosecute the people who performed his plays in spite of the prohibition of the Censor, who actually declared, at a Parliamentary inquiry, that the plays which were not censored were only passed over in contempt as not mattering.[1] And the French kept us in countenance by the now incredible folly of the rejection of the magnificent monument to Balzac by Rodin, glaringly the mightiest sculptor since Michael Angelo.

The latest victim of this sort of stupidity is Richard Strauss; but Strauss is a man of business, and in his case, as in that of the Post-Impressionists, a much more energetic commercial exploitation than Wagner or Ibsen ever enjoyed has met and stemmed the torrent of abuse. The press, which never felt its master in Wagner or Ibsen, bows at once to a well-advertized commercial vogue; and the fossilized critics have been forced, sulkily enough, to take their heads out of their sacks and the cotton-wool out of their ears, and to recognize high prices if they cannot recognize fine art. But nobody can doubt that if the newest developments were as unfriended in the City as the old ones were, their fate would be no better.

The other side of the banner is the one that Ibsen tried so hard to turn towards us. For we seem compelled by Destiny not only to vilify what is great, but at the same time to idealize and flatter what is rotten. And of that the court martial is a very mild instance. Take for instance our ideal navy. This navy—the navy of our hopes and dreams—though never large enough to secure that command of the sea to which we have as much right as to the command of the moon and stars, is nevertheless, as far as it goes, perfect in equipment and discipline, ready, aye, ready for anything that may confront it. An inquiry brings out the fact that the real navy puts to sea with three men to do the work of eighteen. We hear such stories on holiday airings at Portsmouth, when we meet the inevitable man who points to our floating fortresses and assures us that "her full complement is eight hundred men; and there aint not a man more nor 123 aboard her if the Germans come over." Which of us has ever dreamt of

[1] See *Report from the Joint Select Committee of the House of Lords and the House of Commons on the Stage Plays (Censorship)*. London, 1909.

believing such tales? And yet here is a court martial, solemnest of official inquiries, at which it comes out that six per cent. of the full complement is considered too ordinary a proportion to excite any surprise or comment. We ask ourselves, with misgiving, is Our Navy as imaginary as the Wagner who could not write a melody, or the Rodin whose Balzac was "unfinished," or the Ibsen who deserved to be prosecuted under Lord Campbell's Act? If so, the matter is serious; for it is one thing to imagine you have a duffer and a blackguard and find you have a prophet and a hero, and quite another to imagine you have a strong tower of defence and find you have only a paper boat. And if we are living in a fool's paradise as to these things—these fleets that cover miles of the sea, and these geniuses whose glory blazes throughout Europe—what is likely to be our condition as to the obscurer things, the unromantic dirty commonplace things, the dry details of Minority Reports, which are nevertheless at the root of all our fortunes? What sort of place does the man in the street conceive England to be? And what sort of place *is* England? Can it be possible that the fact that the man in the street is so much less sensible and direct than a dog is due to the fact that the dog does not read newspapers, does not listen to speeches, and does not make them?

If so, this paper will get into trouble presently through its occasional references to the actual facts of our civilization, and its sense of the value of Ibsen's warning against ideals that correspond to nothing on earth, and of Wagner's Wotan's hint to Alberich, the outwitted capitalist, *Alles ist nach seiner Art: an ihr wirst du nichts ändern.*

GLUCK IN GLASTONBURY

(*The Nation*, London, 6 *May* 1916)

Perfection is inextinguishable. If ever a nation tried hard to extinguish Gluck, one of the attainers of perfection, by the simple British method of ignoring him, that nation is ourselves. At long intervals some dramatic singer, Giulia Ravogli or Marie Brema, has revived Orpheus. Nearly forty years ago there was a

Gluck Society conducted by Malcolm Lawson; and I still recollect very distinctly a performance of Alceste at which Theo Marzials was the Hercules, and the call of Charon was played, as it should be, on one of the most unnatural notes of the old horn without valves, with the player's hand stuffed up the bell. But how many of our inhabitants have ever heard Iphigenia in Tauris? Not I, for one, until I stumbled on it at Easter in a village called Street, close to Glastonbury, the last place on earth where I should have expected it.

It was in some vital respects a better performance than ever Sir Thomas Beecham could have afforded in London. I guessed that it had been rehearsed for three months; I found on inquiry that it had been rehearsed for four. In London musical performances consist mostly of people playing and singing music they do not really know, helped out by the occasional *virtuoso* playing or singing one of the three or four *rôles* or pieces he or she knows far too well. It is a hard and joyless way of earning a living; and the way of the critic who makes his by listening to it is much harder. There was nothing of this mixture of the perfunctory and the state [sic] at Street. The Somerset folk know Iphigenia through and through. Nothing could shake them as they delivered the English version of it (such English as is possible in translations which have to fit music made to fit a French text) in their native dialect. They were utterly unlike that ageless, deathless miracle, the metropolitan opera chorus, with its hollow square of motley nondescripts who have made some unholy compact with the devil, by which they are to live for ever without growing older or younger on condition that they sing perpetually in masterpieces of dramatic music without ever becoming musical or dramatic. The Somerset Scythians and Achaians were both musical and dramatic. Like all natural people on the stage, they tried to be as conventional as an Imperial ballet; for to be natural on the stage in the realistic manner is the last accomplishment of artifice, and, to the performer, the most revolting of all outrages on Nature. They waved their arms and moved with convulsive strides; but they were full of illusions about it, and really meant it and felt it. And the Covent Garden chorus could by no means have shouted them down. Their tone was close, unadulterated with bawling and blowing and wheezing; their attack was prompt, confident, and solid; and every bar sounded as if it meant something.

The principals did not disgrace their parts. Iphigenia (Miss Gladys Fisher) sang very agreeably, and with adequate power and presence, without suggesting that her part presented the slightest difficulty. The audience did not know that there were even any high notes in it. When she becomes a thoroughly sophisticated *prima donna*, and learns to shriek every note above the treble staff as if it were her last gasp, the audience will wonder at her prowess; but she will no longer be Iphigenia. Her costume carried village simplicity a little too far. No doubt Diana and her priestesses were so chaste that nothing could do their virtue justice in Somerset but the white muslin of the British village maiden trimmed with silver foil. Nevertheless, I contend that the village maiden always gets married in the end, and looks it, whereas a priestess of Diana should chill the future as icily as the present. Miss Lillah McCarthy in her wonderful costumes looked ten times chaster than the Somerset maidens, who tend to buxomness, in their muslin frocks; and at the fall of the curtain we all felt that Iphigenia's hand and heart were a sure thing for Pylades. If I were Miss Fisher, I should stand out for a less native and more imaginative dress next time.

Pylades (Mr Louis Godfrey), an excellent tenor, hit off the amiability and sincerity of that almost too virtuous friend to a marvel, singing very agreeably indeed; and Thoas (Mr Bernard Lemon), a good rough *basso cantante*, was a very presentable tyrant.

Orestes had been reached at the last moment by the voice of patriotic duty, and had gone to face a sterner music in Flanders or Salonika. The result was that the conductor had to take up the part; and it may be that some of the freshness and excellence of the performance were due to the fact that there was no conductor. At all events, Mr Rutland Boughton, to whom, and to his collaborator, Miss Christina Walshe, in the scene dock and wardrobe, this whole unexpected organization of the latent artistic resources of the countryside is due, had saved the situation by hurling himself suddenly on the stage in the vestments of

Orestes. I do not know what Orestes was like, and so cannot say whether Mr Rutland Boughton resembled him; but he certainly did resemble a well-known portrait of Liszt so strongly that I felt that Pylades should have been made up as Wagner; and yet when I looked at Pylades he reminded me so strongly of Mr Festing Jones that I felt that Orestes should have been made up as Samuel Butler.

Mr Rutland Boughton did astonishingly well under the circumstances. His ability as a composer stood him in good stead; for when his memory gave out, he improvised Gluck recitatives with felicitous ease, though his modern freedom of modulation occasionally landed him in keys from which the orchestra (Mr Clarence Raybould at a grand piano) had to retrieve the others as best it could. I do not know whether Mr Boughton's voice is a tenor or a bass, nor even whether he can be said to have any voice at all for *bel canto* purposes; but it was all the more instructive to hear how he evaded all such questions by attacking the part wholly and simply from the dramatic point of view.

There was fortunately no scenery and no opera house: in short, no nonsense; but there was a shrine of Diana and sufficient decoration by Miss Walshe's screens and curtains to create much more illusion in the big schoolroom than I have ever been able to feel in Covent Garden.

In the evening there was a performance of Mr Boughton's Snow White (mostly dancing), which has been seen in London. Miss Florence Jolley, of the Margaret Morris school, was extremely wicked and extremely seductive, a popular and delightful combination. Miss Morris has really achieved something in the study of what people who cannot dance, as stage dancing is understood by Fokine and Karsavina, can be made to do without a more arduous training than most earnest amateurs are willing to face. The result was a very enjoyable evening.

Altogether, this Easter exploit of the Glastonbury Festival School, as it is called, was very successful and pleasant. Allowances have to be made in judging such performances; and London critics might exaggerate them because, as they are new allowances, they would be much more conscious of them than of the prodigious allowances that have to be made in grand opera houses in great capitals. But the truth is that there was far less to suffer and far less to excuse and allow for at Glastonbury than at the usual professional performances, which, just because rehearsals are so enormously expensive in money, and all operatic stars are wandering stars, are necessarily all scratch performances. And, anyhow, the London critics who have so far been devoted enough to go to Glastonbury, have tended towards idyllic infatuation rather than to hypercriticism.

If the opera is repeated, may I suggest to the writer of the synopsis of Iphigenia in the program that the total omission of any mention of the pursuit of Orestes by the Furies must, to the Somerset folk who were not familiar with classic tradition, have reduced the Eumenidean scenes to mere madness? Alas! I stand out for snakes in the hair of the Furies. The Glastonbury Furies looked like Macbeth's witches, strayed into the classic drama by mistake. They made great play with skinny fingers; but there was not half a snake among the lot of them.

MOZART WITH MOZART LEFT OUT

(*The Nation*, London, 28 *July* 1917)

Everyone who has seen the new production of Figaro's Wedding at Drury Lane will agree that it is quite the most delightful entertainment in London. It may without exaggeration be described as ravishing. To all Londoners who are at their last shilling and are perplexed as to how to spend it most economically I say unhesitatingly, Spend it at the Drury Lane pay-box when next Figaro is in the bill. Can a critic say more? Can a gentleman say less?

And yet see what has just occurred. An able musical critic, well known to the readers of these columns, and with every reason to make the utter best of Sir Thomas Beecham's enterprise (as indeed what lover of music has not?), volunteers the curious suggestion that Sir Thomas should revive the operas of Paisiello and Cimarosa, in order to teach the public that what they are admiring and enjoying in the Drury Lane performance is a sweetness and a neatness, a featness and discreetness (pardon the

vile jingle) that belongs to all the best eighteenth-century composers no less than to Mozart. This is a shot that hits Sir Thomas
between wind and water. It means that he has given us the charm
of the eighteenth century, but not that strange spell by virtue
of which Mozart, being dead, yet liveth, whilst Paisiello and
Cimarosa are in comparison as dead as mutton. It means that
the same success might have been achieved by a revival of
Paisiello.

The wily critic aforesaid has no difficulty in illustrating his
suggestion by citing several numbers in Mozart's opera which
might have been written by any of his popular contemporaries
without adding a leaf to their now withered laurels. If you doubt
it, turn to Don Giovanni, and pretend, if you can, that the contemporary specimens preserved in the supper scene by the Don's
restaurant band are any worse than, or even distinguishable in
style from *Ricevete O padroncina* or any of the numbers mentioned in Mr Newman's article. The truth is that the eighteenth
century produced a good deal of the loveliest art known to us;
and any of its masterpieces adequately presented to us now
could not fail to make us ashamed of our own violent and vulgar
attempts to entertain ourselves. When you are enchanted at
Drury Lane, you must not say "What a wonderful man Mozart
was!" but "What a wonderful century Mozart lived in!"; and so
it was, for persons of quality, comfortably mounted on the backs
of the poor.

Turn now to the eighteenth-century opinion of Mozart. Far
from finding his contemporaries listening with half-closed eyes
to his delicious strains of melody, and to the melting supertonic
cadence that Wagner made fun of in Die Meistersinger, you are
stunned and amazed by complaints of the horrible noisiness of
his instrumentation, of having to climb an arid mountain of discord to pluck a single flower of melody, of "the statue in the
orchestra and the pedestal on the stage," of "too many notes," of
assaults on the human ear and [on] the human tendency to slumber
in the stalls after dinner. They suggest the Tannhäuser fiasco in
Paris in 1860 or the reception of Ibsen's Ghosts in London in
1890 rather than *Voi che sapete* and *Deh vieni a la finestra*. What
has become of all this disturbing power? In the case of Tann-

häuser we can explain it by the fact that we have only lately become quite accustomed to the unprepared major ninths which made the joyous music of Elizabeth sound so horrible to our grandfathers' ears. But the harmonies which disgruntled Mozart's contemporaries were not new. Mozart could take the common chord and make you jump by just doubling the third in the base; or he could put the hackneyed discord of the dominant seventh in a form so cunningly distributed and instrumented that it would sound as if it came straight from hell or from the Elysian fields across the Ionian Sea, according to his purpose. It is hardly an exaggeration to say that as far as mere grammar and vocabulary go, there is nothing more in the statue scene from Don Juan, which threw open the whole magic realm of modern orchestration first explored by Mozart's forerunner Gluck, than in the exquisite little song of Cherubino, *Non so più*. All the effects are still there, as fresh, and, on occasion, as terrible as the day they were composed: handle them properly, and Lohengrin and Tristan will taste like soothing syrup after them. Unfortunately, nobody seems able to handle them properly. After a long experience of many conductors and many composers, I have come to the conclusion that Mozart and Berlioz are, among the moderns, by far the most elusive and difficult in performance.

As I am only half a critic now, I act up to that character by going to only half an opera at a time. As in the case of Il Trovatore, I did not see the first two acts of Figaro's Wedding. When I entered, Sir Thomas Beecham struck up, by way of instrumental prelude to the third act, the *fandango* (at least Mozart, who had never been in Spain and can certainly never have heard a note of Spanish music, called it a *fandango*) from the wedding scene. What Mozart would have said if he had heard himself thus held up as a miserable nineteenth-century composer, so barren of invention as to have to fall back on tunes out of his opera for preludes, I will not try to imagine, though I hope he would simply have expressed a mild wish that people would not do silly things. However, I was not sorry to hear the *fandango* twice; and I suppose nobody else was, in spite of the bad form involved. Only I began instantly to suspect that Sir Thomas is very fond of eighteenth-century music and does not care twopence about the specific Mozart. When the great duet came presently, he treated the few eloquent notes of exordium as if they were merely pianist's chords to fix the key; and of the wonderful opening-out of feeling which comes with the first words of Susanna I could not detect a trace. The first section was just dapper and nothing else: not until the concerted part came did the conductor warm to it. But the conclusive test was the sestet following Figaro's discovery of his parentage. How fine a piece of music that is, and how much it makes of a rather trivial though affectionate situation Sir Thomas will never know until he has fulfilled his destiny by conducting some of Mozart's greatest church music: say the grand Mass in C which lay so long undiscovered. Nothing came of the sestet, absolutely nothing at all: it might just as well have been omitted, as it was by the Carl Rosa company. But when it came to *Dove sono*, the conductor was really great: he squeezed every drop of nectar it contains out for us to the very last drop, and never relaxed his care, not even for the tiniest fraction of a bar. I will not blame the singer for putting in a little *liaison* of her own at the reprise, though I hope she will creep up to it diatonically instead of chromatically in future; for the chromatic progression is a mannerism of Meyerbeer's, and a patch of Meyerbeer on Mozart does not match nicely. All the rest was like that. The sentimental parts were nursed with the tenderest care; but the dramatic and rhetorical parts were treated as so much purely decorative music, kept going very tightly and strictly and rapidly, and played with perfect precision and prettiness: that is to say, for Mozart's purpose, not played at all. The singers, in these rhetorical and dramatic passages, could do nothing but hold on hard lest they should find themselves in the last bar but one. Mr Newman's complaint that he could find none of the bitterness Beaumarchais gave to Figaro in the air *Aprite un po' gli occhi* was therefore not Mozart's fault. It is true that Mozart made no attempt to write political music in the sense of expressing not only wounded human feeling but the specific rancor of the class-conscious proletarian; but the wounded feeling is provided for very plentifully if only the conductor will allow the singer to put it in instead of treating him as if he were one of the second violins. That unlucky power of juggling with music which enabled Mozart to force dramatic expression upon purely decorative musical forms makes it possible for a conductor to treat any of his numbers as merely a sonata or *rondo* or what not; and this is very much what Sir Thomas Beecham does except when he comes to the beauty bits which appeal to him by their feminine sweetness. In conducting Wagner or Strauss he could not do so, because if he ignored the dramatic element there would be nothing left but senseless-sounding brass and tinkling cymbals. In Mozart's case what is left is a very elegant and pretty sonata movement; and with this Sir Thomas is quite satisfied. But even whilst securing a spirited and polished execution of the music on this plane, he shews a curious want of appreciation of Mozart's personal quality, especially his severe taste. After strangling his singers dramatically, he allows them to debase the music by substituting for what Mozart wrote what he no doubt might have written if he had been, not a great composer, but a conceited singer. Sir Thomas thinks that his singers are better composers than Mozart; he allows Susanna not only to transpose passages an octave up, as if he could not stand her quite adequate low notes, but to alter wantonly the end of *Deh vieni non tardar*, a miracle of perfect simplicity [and] beauty, into what seems by contrast a miracle of artificial commonplace, not to say vulgarity. After conducting Basilio's *aria*—that quaint pæan of meanness which only a great actor could make intelligible—so completely in the spirit of abstract music that not even the roar of the tempest or the growl of the lion is suggested by the orchestra, he allows him to perpetrate the most third-class of all operatic tricks, the bawling of the last note an octave up in order to beg a foolish *encore* by a high B flat. As this is not weakness on Sir Thomas Beecham's part, for he is strict to tyranny in getting what his artistic conscience demands, he must really consider that his singers are improving Mozart. He actually lays himself open to the suspicion of having suggested the improvements. In that case there is nothing more to be said. What is clear so far is that he likes eighteenth-century music in its eighteenth-century form; and that this taste of his, highly creditable so far as it goes, has brought him accidentally into contact with Mozart; but of and for the specific Mozart who was not for the eighteenth century but for all time he knows and cares nothing.

Now this opinion of mine is only an opinion unless it can be brought to the test of experiment. Who am I that I should criticize a conductor of Sir Thomas Beecham's experience, and an artistic director of his proved enterprise and popularity? Simply nobody but a man of letters of no musical authority at all. Well, I propose an experiment, and a very interesting one. Let Sir Thomas Beecham induce Sir Edward Elgar to take over Figaro for just one night. Elgar has not only the technical tradition (which is being so rapidly lost that I wish the Government would at once commission him to edit all Mozart's operas for State publication) but he understands the heroic side of Mozart, which includes the dramatic side. It is sometimes rather a rough side; but Elgar would not be afraid of that. If Sir Thomas does not, after one hearing, blush to the roots of his hair and exclaim "Great Heavens! And I took this great composer for a mere confectioner!" I will pay a penny to any war charity he likes to name.

Mozart's opera scoring does in truth need some editing; for our conductors are spoiled by the copious and minute instructions which have been provided for them ever since they ceased to be a socially humble, professional caste fortified with an elaborate technical tradition instead of coming in from the general body of cultivated gentleman amateurs. Mozart jotted down f or sf in his score where Meyerbeer would have written *con esplosione*. He wrote p where Verdi would have written $ppppp$! He did not resort to abbreviations to anything like the extent that the seventeenth-century and earlier composers did; but compared to nineteenth-century composers, who wrote down every note they meant to be sung, he used conventional musical shorthand to a considerable extent; and we want someone to fill in his scores as Arnold Dolmetsch has filled in the scores of Mozart's predecessors. Sir Thomas Beecham, relying on the existing scores, seems to have no conception of the dynamic range of Mozart's effects, of the fierceness of his *fortepianos*, the *élan* of his whipping-up triplets, the volume of his *fortes*. Even when Mozart writes pp, by which he means silence made barely audible (as in the first section of the Wedding March, for instance), we get at Drury Lane the same *mezzo forte* that prevails, except at a few blessed moments, during the whole performance. When the audience should be holding its breath to listen, or reeling from the thunder of the whole band and all the singers at their amplest, it still gets the same monotonous pretty fiddling that is neither high nor low, loud nor soft.

Yet on Thursday night, when I returned to hear the first two acts, I was carried away by the superb virtuosity of the orchestral execution, and the irresistible vigor and brilliancy of the great *finale* to the first act. Everything except this *finale* was far too fast even for all the instrumental effects, not to mention the dramatic ones; but I could not grudge the conductor his musical triumph; and I was positively grateful to him for audaciously forcing on us between the acts a slow movement for strings that had nothing to do with the opera, so finely was it played. It was pathetic and delightful to see the extraordinary pleasure of the audience, many of whom seemed to be discovering Mozart and going almost silly with the enchantment of it.

I repeat, the Drury Lane performance is charming; and very little additional care and understanding would make it great. It is, by the way, partly a performance of Beaumarchais' Mariage de Figaro; and I think it probable that if Mozart could be consulted as to the propriety of this attempt to make the best of both theatrical worlds, he would say that what he had taken from Beaumarchais he had taken and ennobled, and what he had left he had left for good reasons. To drag the Countess of *Porgi amor* and *Dove sono*, and the Cherubino of *Non so più* and *Voi che sapete* back into an atmosphere of scandalous intrigue was dangerous, but it is not unsuccessful: Mozart carries everything before him. The scenery and costumes are rich and amusing. The idea seems to have been to do something in the style of Mr Charles Ricketts; and the rose-pink crinoline petticoats are certainly as much in the style of Mr Ricketts as the sestet was in the style of Mozart: that is, Ricketts with Ricketts left out. Mr Nigel Playfair did what a man could in looking after Beaumarchais; but it was Mozart that needed looking after, and Mr Playfair could not supersede the conductor. However, I cannot bear to grumble;

only I wish a little more thought had been added to all the money and time and trouble lavished. That last scene, for instance, which should be so cunningly fitted to the music, and is not fitted to anything at all but a vague idea that it would make a pretty picture cover for a summer number of something. When I think of—but there! I think too much to be a reasonable critic.

SCRATCH OPERA

(*The Nation*, London, 22 *June* 1918)

Last week my old professional habit of opera-going reasserted itself for a moment. I heard the last two acts of Don Giovanni at the Shaftesbury Theatre by the Carl Rosa company, and The Valkyrie (Hunnishly known as Die Walküre) at Drury Lane. There was an immense difference between the two performances. One of them might have been an attempt on the part of an opera company, a conductor, and a number of bandsmen, all perfect strangers to oneanother and accidentally marooned in the Shaftesbury Theatre, to wile away the time by reading at sight a bundle of band parts and vocal scores of a rather difficult opera which they had never heard before by a young and very puzzling composer. The other had been rehearsed to the point of achieving, at its best moments, a superb fulfilment of the composer's intention; and the repeated storms of applause which broke out, until the conductor was forced to make several reluctant appearances before the curtain, were not, and could not have been, more generous than he deserved.

And yet they were both scratch performances.

When I was a child I heard certain operas rehearsed by a company of amateurs who, having everything to learn, could not have achieved a performance at all if they had not been coached and trained and rehearsed with a thoroughness impossible in professional music. It would cost too much. These amateurs rehearsed an opera for six months. There were all sorts of weaknesses about their performances; and yet I have never since, even in the course of several years' experience as a professional critic in London, with occasional excursions to Paris, Italy, and the

German capitals, heard any performances as perfect, except some of the most thoroughly prepared productions at Bayreuth and Munich. I may be asked whether the brothers De Reszke, playing Gounod's Faust for the fifty millionth time at Covent Garden, did not display a tolerable familiarity with that work; and, of course, I cannot deny that they did; but the Valentines and Marguerites and Siebels came and went; and there was always the scratch habit which is so hard to throw off. In the ordinary theatre, where thorough rehearsal is the rule, and the conductor (called the producer) and the company have nothing else to do for six weeks or more than to work at the play, I have sometimes had to deal with an actor whose lot has been cast in theatres where a new play had to be presented every week or even every night. In such actors the scratch habit is an incurable disease. At the first rehearsal they astonish everyone, just as London orchestras always astonish foreign conductors and composers, by being almost letter-perfect, and giving such a capable and promising reading of their parts that one feels that after a fortnight's work they will be magnificent, and leave all the others nowhere. And they never get a step further. The fortnight's work is to them useless, unnecessary, and irritating. Even the letter-perfection vanishes: it deteriorates into appeals to the prompter or appalling improvisations. The same thing occurs with opera singers. You hear a performance of some hackneyed opera by singers who have sung in it hundreds of times. It is never accurate. The individual singers are not so accurate, or even nearly so accurate, as when they performed the part nervously and anxiously for the first time, and were much too young to have found out how little accuracy they could make shift with. They could no more give such a performance as Mr Du Maurier's company at Wyndham's Theatre gives of Dear Brutus than a hotel waiter can behave like an old family servant. All experienced travelers have noticed that, however generously they may tip, hotel servants get tired of them if they attempt to reside in the hotel instead of passing on like all the others. There is a hotel psychology, a stock company psychology, and an opera psychology; and all three are modes of the scratch psychology, which is incompatible with thorough excellence.

HOW TO BECOME A MUSICAL CRITIC

I sometimes ask myself whether a thorough representation of an opera is worth while. I do not mean commercially: commercially it is impossible under existing conditions. But suppose money were no object, would the final degrees of perfection be worth the trouble they would cost? I go further than merely saying baldly that I think they would. I am strongly of opinion that nothing but superlative excellence in art can excuse a man or woman for being an artist at all. It is not a light thing in a world of drudgery for any citizen to say, "I am not going to do what you others must: I am going to do what I like." I think we are entitled to reply, "Then we shall expect you to do it devilish well, my friend, if we are not to treat you as a rogue and a vagabond." I have a large charity for loose morals: they are often more virtuous than straitlaced ones. But for loose art I have no charity at all. When I hear a fiddler playing *mezzo forte* when his part is marked *pianissimo* or *fortissimo* (as the English orchestral fiddler is apt to do if he can trifle with the conductor), or a trombone player shirking the trouble of phrasing intelligently, I hate him. Yet I could forgive him quite easily for being a bigamist.

The difference between the Don Giovanni and the Valkyrie performances was that the Carl Rosa company had better not have played Don Giovanni at all than played it as they did, whereas it would have been a positive national loss to us if we had not had the Beecham performance. I grant that there are extenuating circumstances. Mozart's music is enormously more difficult than Wagner's; and his tragi-comedy is even more so. With Mozart you either hit the bull's-eye or miss; and a miss is as bad as a mile. With Wagner the target is so large and the charge so heavy that if you get the notes out anyhow, you are bound to do some execution. It takes a Coquelin, combined with a first-rate *basso cantante*, to play Leporello; but any heavyweight bass, with the voice of a wolf, and very little more power of vocal execution, can put up a quite impressive Hunding. Roll Forbes-Robertson and Vladimir Rosing into one, and you will have an adequate Don Juan; but which of all the famous Wotans could have touched Don Juan with the tips of his fingers? It is the same with the conducting: what conductor of any talent, with the tradition of Wagner and Richter to prompt him, could fail with the scene between Siegmund and Brynhild in the second act of Die Walküre, or with the fire music at the close? Try him with the two symphonic scenes in which Don Juan invites the statue to supper, and in which the statue avails himself of the invitation, and he is as likely as not to be hopelessly beaten. Felix Mottl was one of the very best Wagner conductors produced by Bayreuth. I have heard him conduct Mozart's Nozze di Figaro, Così fan Tutte, and Clemenza di Tito to perfection in Munich. But he was utterly beaten by Don Giovanni. Senor de la Fuente, the Carl Rosa conductor, when he conducted Le Nozze di Figaro last year, handled it brilliantly. It is an easily learnt work: the execution may require exquisite delicacy and immaculate taste; but there is no touch of tragedy in it, nor any touch of passion of the tragic quality. Now, Don Juan is a tragic hero or nothing: his destiny is announced by Mozart from the very first chord of the overture. That the opera is called a *dramma giocosa*, and that there was an early Don Juan who was only a squalid drunkard and libertine, does not weigh against the evidence of the score. Before Shakespear touched Hamlet there was a zany Hamlet who mopped and mowed, and nailed down the courtiers under the arras and set them on fire, going through all the pitiable antics with which the village idiot amused heartless visitors when he was one of the sights of the village instead of an inmate of the county asylum. Well, Mozart abolished the drunken Don Juan as completely and finally as Shakespear abolished the zany Hamlet. Unfortunately, the operatic conductors and stars do not seem to have found this out. When the singer who impersonates Don Juan happens to be a gentleman, he takes the greatest pains to make himself a cad for the occasion. Leporello's agonies of terror are replaced by silly and ineptly executed buffooneries which the Brothers Griffith could do, in their proper place, artistically and funnily. Everyone, the conductor included, is nosing through the score for the vulgar fun which is not there, and overlooking the tragic and supernatural atmosphere which is there. And the result is that they all feel that the thing is not going, that they are missing instead of hitting. They do not know what is the matter, and yet know that something is the matter. They find the music frightfully difficult; cling with their eyes to the conductor; become rattled and flurried and panic-stricken; until at last their passages sound like nothing at all. The conductor has to keep up an air of assurance, but is secretly almost equally puzzled: you know it by the infirmity of the rhythm. Even the ruthless march of the statue music, a rhythm which no conductor ever misses in the music of Wotan or of Rossini's Moses, dwindles into an irresolute buzzing. For example, the terrible address of the statue, which begins *Tu m'invitasti a cena*, is preceded by two ominous bars in which this rhythm is thundered through dead vocal silence as emphatically as the opening of Beethoven's symphony in C minor. The conductor must mark this with Handelian conviction and power; for it is quite as necessary to the effect as the more sensational orchestration of the hellish blasts which follow it, and which only a deaf conductor could underrate. But Senor de la Fuente noticed nothing in it but commonplace rum-tum, which he was too worried to attend to. That is only one instance of the sort of thing that went on all through the symphonic numbers, and that always will go on until some conductor will take the work in tragic seriousness, search the score for what Mozart put into it and not for what he made his reputation by leaving out of it, and finally rehearse it hard for a year or so before letting the public in.

He will find other things besides the tragic intensity of the overture and the statue music. He will find that the window *trio*, *Ah, taci, ingiusto core*, is not a comic accompaniment to the unauthorized tomfoolery of Don Juan making a marionet of Leporello, but perhaps the most lovely nocturne in the whole range of musical literature. And he may also be led to the discovery, greatly needed by all English conductors, and apparently by one Spanish one, that six-eight time does not always mean that the piece is a country dance. In German music it often means an *andantino* of intense and noble sentiment.

I must in fairness make it clear that the shortcomings in the Carl Rosa performance were not the fault of the singers. They were asked to perform under scratch conditions a work which has never yet been satisfactorily or even decently performed under such conditions, and never will. At Covent Garden the directors used to throw it over to some *ripieno* conductor to run through once a season as an easy routine job, and were perfectly successful in making it appear worthy of the ignorant contempt with which they were treating it. The Carl Rosa company at least know it to be an important work; but as they know little else about it except the mere notes, and some of its silliest would-be comic traditions, the result is no better. Why not leave Don Giovanni in peace on the shelf? It is so easy not to perform it.

By the way, there was one original point made. Mr James Pursail is the first Don, as far as I know, to notice that, as Don Juan was not a professional singer, however masterfully he may sing all the dramatic music, he should sing the serenade like an amateur. And this was just what Mr Pursail did. I do not mean that he sang it badly: on the contrary, he sang it very nicely; and I do not quarrel with his unauthorized F sharp at the end, because, for a high baritone with an F sharp which is better than his low D, it is a pardonable flourish, and is not in any case a vulgarity like shouting the last note an octave up, with which Mr Edward Davies discredited an otherwise excellent performance of *Il mio tesoro*. I mean that Mr Pursail sang it, not in the traditionally ardent and accomplished manner, but in the manner of a modest amateur. This is a real new reading which deserves to be noted.

Die Walküre was a very different affair. The singers and the conductor knew much more about the work, and the execution was remarkably accurate. And yet the scratch quality came out sometimes just where the accuracy was closest and the skill most perfect. Take, for example, the sword theme. The seven notes of which it consists are all over Die Walküre. They present no difficulty to such wind players as Sir Thomas Beecham commands; and they are scored so as to give them the prominence of a constellation in the orchestral heaven. Well, a lady who is not unfamiliar with the music made the astounding remark to me that she had detected the sword theme *once*. Before Sir Thomas dismisses that lady as a deaf imbecile, I advise him to engage a mathematician to calculate how many different phrasings can be put upon a seven-note theme. Then let him call a wind rehearsal, and try all the different phrasings. He will be interested to find that whenever the third note is included in a slur, the theme will become unrecognizable as Wagner's sword theme. A single *portamento* in the wrong place will put off any listener who does not know the score. It will veil the star which gives the constellation its characteristic form, and turn it into a mere strip of the milky way. Clearly, in a performance prepared up to the best Bayreuth point, an understanding would be established with all the wind players as to the exact phrasing of this and every other theme. On Saturday night hardly any two wind players gave the same version of it; and the result was that it lost its identity. That is why I reluctantly put this very splendid and valuable revival under the heading of Scratch Opera.

Sir Thomas Beecham was the star of the evening, but the singers ran him close. Miss Agnes Nicholls sang the music of Brynhild beautifully; but I ask how any woman can be expected to look like a valkyrie, or feel like one, or move like one, in the skirt of an ultra-womanly woman of the period when a female who climbed to the top of an omnibus would have been handed [over] to the police as a disgrace to her sex. If Sir Thomas or anyone else imagines that the situation is saved by adding to the womanly skirt a breastplate and a barmaid's wig of that same period, he errs. In 1876, when this ridiculous dress was "made in Germany," it could at least be said that when Brynhild left the theatre in her private character, she wore a long skirt. But before Miss Agnes Nicholls leaves her dressing room for the street she has to put on a short skirt, and to find even that conspicuous for its length in the crowd of knickered *chauffeuses* and booted and breeched female war workers of all sorts. Why on earth does not Sir Thomas throw all this ragbag rubbish of fifty years ago into the dustbin, and make his valkyries look like valkyries and not like Mrs Leo Hunter? This thing is beyond patience; I pass on.

Fricka I did not hear, because I dined, Bayreuth fashion, between the first and second acts. Miss Miriam Licette did as much with Sieglinde as a soprano with a mezzo-soprano part could do against the competition (where there should have been contrast) of Brynhild. Mr Robert Parker was in a similar difficulty: his bright hard voice is not of the right color for Wotan, "the melancholy Dane" of the modern stage. And he really should not dance at Brynhild as if he were going to kick her unless he seriously reads the part that way. He was more Herod than Wotan; but his articulation was the best in the company, and he put in some fine singing. It would be unreasonable to ask for a richer Siegmund than Mr Walter Hyde, who was deservedly very popular. The English version, as far as it got across the footlights, was very helpful to the English audience; but why are the German epithets retained in such passages as *Friedmund darf ich nicht heissen; Frohwalt möcht ich wohl sein: doch Wehwalt muss ich mich nennen?* Polyglot nonsense, I call it. The performance was described in the program as having been "produced." I saw no evidence of the process. The old routine was carried out in all its sacred staleness. The scenery made Old Drury feel young again. Wings, sky-borders, set pieces: nothing was missing. Granville-Barker must have chuckled.

The house was crammed from floor to ceiling, and the applause prodigious. This, for a work of which the hero and heroine are within the tables of consanguinity, written and composed by one classed by our patriotic papers as a congenital scoundrel with a specific lust for the blood of women and children, would probably be accounted for by the patriots on the ground that Old Drury, huge as it is, does not hold 47,000,000 people. I will therefore conclude by mentioning that I never saw a more normal and native British musical audience in my life, or a more enthusiastic one. And now bring along your Dora and hale me to the Tower.

THE FUTURE OF BRITISH MUSIC

(Text of Shaw's address to the British Music Society, "Starved Arts Mean Low Pleasures," revised by Shaw for publication in *The Outlook,* 19 and 26 *July* 1919)

It has never been possible for modern British composers to live by the practice of the higher forms of their art in their own country; but until 1914 Germany provided a market which enabled them to produce a symphony with at least some hope of having it performed and even published. That is now at an end. Performances of British music in Germany have ceased; and remittances are cut off. Thus British composers who have obtained a hearing in that country are suffering seriously from a closing of the most important source of their incomes from classic work; and the economic inducement to our younger composers to keep British music in the front rank of culture no longer exists.

This situation is not creditable to us as a nation. And it has arisen at a moment when the introduction of compulsory military service and the waging of a long war has dealt a heavy blow to the fine arts. To realize the weight of that blow it is necessary to consider what the state of music would have been if Sebastian Bach had been engaged in the Thirty Years War, and Mozart, Beethoven, and Wagner sent to the trenches for the few years (no longer than the duration of the present war) during which they produced, respectively, Don Giovanni, Figaro, the Jupiter Symphony and its successors in G minor and E flat, the Eroica Symphony and the Emperor Concerto, and the Ring Poem and the scores of Das Rheingold and Die Walküre. Such a sacrifice to militarism would have left the world three centuries behindhand in musical development. Yet an instalment of that sacrifice befell British music during the war. We were so little conscious of it that attempts to persuade tribunals that the composition of serious music is work of national importance were received with derision. Almost in the same week we saw one energetic young composer and organizer of musical festivals sneered at and sent into the army by the tribunal in a leading English city, and another exempted elsewhere with something like awe because he had once composed a popular waltz.

Such a state of public opinion is inexcusable in a civilized country once famous throughout Europe for the quality of its music. Yet it has lasted for two centuries, which may be reckoned as the dark ages of British music. During that time musicians have supported themselves by giving piano lessons to young ladies without serious musical intentions, or by composing drawing-room ballads, or as church organists by accompanying hymns and "sacred music" which seldom rose above the level of Jackson's Te Deum. Sterndale Bennett, for example, with a promise as bright and a character as high as Mendelssohn's, was sterilized by a lifetime of drudgery as a piano teacher.

The notion that musical genius is independent of the substantial encouragements which attract men towards other careers is strikingly contradicted by the history of music in England. It is true that British composers of a sort survived when the overwhelming pecuniary temptations of the industrial revolution turned the genius of England to commerce in the eighteenth century; but the outstanding fact about them is that they wrote no British music except trivial drawing-room music or vulgar dance music with less national character than their knives and forks. In the higher departments they produced shoddy Handel, a little Mozart and water, and, finally, a great deal of secondhand Mendelssohn and Spohr. They expressed nothing of the British character or the British imagination: all that their scores convey to us is their love of foreign music and their vain ambition to become great composers by imitating it. With the exception of a few sturdily unfashionable Britons like Pearsall, who kept up the old tradition in his motets and madrigals, our composers posed as Germans as ridiculously as our singers posed as Italians. And the main reason clearly was that it is not in the British character, if indeed it be in any sound character, to accept success in art at the cost of poverty and contempt in the common life of the nation. Under such circumstances art will be practiced only by those who are infatuated with their love of music (the character of the amateur), or who are good for nothing else—and it is a disastrous mistake to suppose that the great artists are good for nothing else. Yet it is a very common mistake: it is even considered a mark of soulful enlightenment in artistic matters to believe that if Phidias had been born an Andaman Islander and Beethoven a Patagonian, they would have produced the Parthenon and the Ninth Symphony by inspiration. Genius, it is supposed, will bridge all chasms and vanquish all difficulties, the inevitable result being that England tends towards the condition of Patagonia or the Andaman Islands as far as the higher forms of music are concerned. Under this false, mean, lazy, and stupid assumption that it is sordid and Philistine to regard music as a product of national respect for it, and national practical encouragement of and inducement to it, classical music is left to "irresistible vocation," and perishes accordingly. Even the really irresistible vocations, such as Mozart's or Elgar's, are dependent on the quite easily resistible ones. Mozart could not have occurred except in a Europe in which there had been many generations of thousands of commonplace musicians whose vocation was by no means irresistible, and many of whom had been driven to the first study of their art by blows. Michael Angelo could not have occurred in the England of his day, and did not. He was the product of a great craft of masonry, and of a magnificent patronage of its artistic application. There is not a single case in the whole history of art in which artists have produced the greatest work of which art is capable except as a final step in an elaborate civilization built up and maintained by a multitude of citizens, mostly amateurs employing professional artists of whom not one-tenth [of one] per cent. were original geniuses, but all accepting fine art as an indispensable element in the greatness of States and the glory of God.

Public opinion must be roused to the need for providing in England the conditions in which it will be possible for Englishmen, after a lapse of two centuries, once more to express themselves in genuinely British music with a weight and depth possible only in the higher forms of music. Here there is no question of the sort of "national music" that is produced by forcing music into local dance forms, or into the pseudo-modes which can be imitated by omitting those intervals of our scale which could not be played on primitive forms of the bag-pipe or the harp. All such *bric-à-brac* already receives more than enough encouragement. The language and instrumentation of music are now international; and what is meant by British music is music in which British musicians express their British character in that international language. When Elgar startled us by suddenly reasserting the British character in music he did it in an idiom which was no more distinctively English than the idiom of Schumann; but Schumann could not, or rather would not, have written ten bars of an Elgar symphony.

THE FUTURE OF BRITISH MUSIC

The needs of the situation may be roughly summed up as more performances, more publication, and more advertisement. Taking the [last] first, how many people are aware of the fact that the British Isles can put into the field about forty living composers of serious music without counting those nineteenth-century composers whose names are well known to the public, such as Elgar, Stanford, Parry, Cowen, Bantock, Delius, and others? It is not only possible to find enthusiastic musical amateurs who do not know this, but positively difficult to find any who do know it. Our resources must be advertized.

The most effective advertisements of the fine arts are the performances and exhibitions attended by the critics who deal with them in the press. Mere commerce is never up to date in this matter. The pioneering must be done by societies of enthusiasts. If our critics of the drama know something more of modern dramatic literature than can be picked up by attending commercial performances, they owe their knowledge to the efforts of private societies such as the Stage Society and the Pioneer Players. If there were no other picture exhibitions than those of the Royal Academy, the modern developments of painting would not exist either for the critics or for the public. If the commercial concert-givers are ever to insist on their conductors undertaking the labor of studying new works by troublesome young men, they must be sharply criticized for their neglect, and made to feel that programs without a single novelty, whether British or foreign, are ridiculous. Before the critics can be expected to do that, societies like the British Music Society must bring the new work to their knowledge.

And the performances cannot be followed up unless the music is published at reasonable prices in vocal score or in transcription for the piano in two-handed and four-handed arrangements or in pianola rolls; for it remains as true now as when Wagner said it that music is kept alive on the cottage pianos of the amateurs, and not by commercial performances.

What the British Music Society may be able to do in these directions will depend on the support it receives. It is impossible to feel very sanguine in the face of such facts as the influentially launched Shakespear Memorial National Theatre scheme with, as a result of years of expensive agitation, a single subscription of £70,000 from a German gentleman, or the ruthless seizure during the war of the public picture galleries throughout the country for the commonest office purposes, culminating in a shameless attempt, which fortunately collapsed through some accident at the last moment, to crown the sacrifice by the seizure of the British Museum. These things, be it noted, happened at a moment when we were claiming to be the champions of European civilization against Hunnish barbarism. When at last the Armistice came, what was it that sprang to the front to demand restoration and reconstruction as the first relief and recreation brought by our victory? Racing, hunting, football, cricket. Not a word about music, though perhaps the most ridiculous incident that relieved the tragedy of the war had been the demand for the instant exclusion of German music from the programs of the Promenade Concerts, which, being at once effected amid patriotic cheers, resulted in empty concert rooms for a week, at the end of which an unparalleled outburst of Beethoven and Wagner crowded them again. It need not be said harshly and uppishly that all this is disgraceful to us. But it will be said, and indeed must be said, that it makes our pretensions to be a cultured nation (not, to be quite just, that we often make such pretensions, or seem to be the least bit ashamed of ourselves) so absurd that we ourselves have to laugh heartily at them like the cheerful savages we are on that plane.

During the war we borrowed our music not only from Germany but from Russia. This is a sort of borrowing for which an honest nation should pay in kind. If we have to borrow tea from China and pay for it in hardware, we can at least plead that our soil will not produce tea. Now music it *can* produce. It has done it before and can do it again. The stuff is there waiting for a market to make it worth mining. It is kept waiting because we are a people of low pleasures. And we are a people of low pleasures because we are brought up to them: the British workman finds the public-house and the football field offering themselves to him insistently at every turn; and the British gentleman is actually forced to spend his boyish leisure at cricket and football before he enters an adult society in which he cannot escape hunting, shooting, bridge, and billiards, though he can go through life as a complete gentleman without hearing a Beethoven sonata in any other form than that of a disagreeable noise which he forbids his daughters to make in the schoolroom except during the hours when he is usually out of doors. If you eliminate smoking and the element of gambling, you will be amazed to find that almost all an Englishman's pleasures can be, and mostly are, shared by his dog.

Why is this state of things described always as "healthy"? Simply because there are worse pleasures in ambush for human leisure in our civilization. Compulsory perpetual athletics at school are to send the boy to bed too tired for mischief. The meet in the hunting field is better than the meet in Piccadilly Circus. But what is the worth of a society which has to resort to such barbarous shifts? Are not the Muses always there to give our leisure the most delightful entertainment, and to refine our tastes and strengthen our intellects at the same time? We banish them, and then find that we must resort to the occupations of greyhounds and ferrets, and the migrations of birds, to rescue us from the snares of the pestilential rivals of the Muses.

It is a pitiful state of things; and I, for one, wish the British Music Society luck in its resolve to educate, agitate, and organize against it in the sacred names of Euterpe and Polyhymnia, Thalia and Terpsichore. I am tired of being suspected of being no gentleman because I am more interested in these goddesses than in the mares in the stables of those of my friends who represent the culture of the Empire.

SIR EDWARD ELGAR

I

(Music and Letters, January 1920; *Harper's Baʒar, April* 1920)

Edward Elgar, the figurehead of music in England, is a composer whose rank it is neither prudent nor indeed possible to determine. Either it is one so high that only time and posterity can confer it, or else he is one of the Seven Humbugs of Christendom. Contemporary judgments are sound enough on Second

Bests; but when it comes to Bests they acclaim ephemerals as immortals, and simultaneously denounce immortals as pestilent charlatans.

Elgar has not left us any room to hedge. From the beginning, quite naturally and as a matter of course, he has played the great game and professed the Best. He has taken up the work of a great man so spontaneously that it is impossible to believe that he ever gave any consideration to the enormity of the assumption, or was even conscious of it. But there it is, unmistakeable. To the north countryman who, on hearing of Wordsworth's death, said, "I suppose his son will carry on the business," it would be plain today that Elgar is carrying on Beethoven's business. The names are up on the shop front for everyone to read. ELGAR, late BEETHOVEN & CO., Classics and Italian & German Warehousemen. Symphonies, Overtures, Chamber Music, Oratorios, Bagatelles.

This, it will be seen, is a very different challenge from that of, say, Debussy and Stravinsky. You can rave about Stravinsky without the slightest risk of being classed as a lunatic by the next generation. You can declare the Après-midi d'un Faune the most delightful and enchanting orchestral piece ever written without really compromising yourself. But, if you say that Elgar's Cockaigne overture combines every classic quality of a concert overture with every lyric and dramatic quality of the overture to Die Meistersinger, you are either uttering a platitude as safe as a compliment to Handel on the majesty of the Hallelujah chorus, or else damning yourself to all critical posterity by a *gaffe* that will make your grandson blush for you.

Personally, I am prepared to take the risk. What do I care about my grandson? Give me Cockaigne. But my recklessness cannot settle the question. It would be so much easier if Cockaigne were *genre* music, with the Westminster chimes, snatches of Yip-i-addy, and a march of the costermongers to Covent Garden. Then we should know where we are: the case would be as simple as Gilbert and Sullivan.

But there is nothing of the kind: the material of the Cockaigne overture is purely classical. You may hear all sorts of footsteps in it, and it may tell you all sorts of stories; but it is classical

SIR EDWARD ELGAR

music as Beethoven's Les Adieux sonata is classical music: it tells you no story external to itself and yourself. Therefore, who knows whether it appeals to the temporal or the eternal in us; in other words, whether it will be alive or dead in the twentyfirst century?

Certain things one can say without hesitation. For example, that Elgar could turn out Debussy and Stravinsky music by the thousand bars for fun in his spare time. That to him such standbys as the whole-tone-scale of Debussy, the Helmholtzian chords of Scriabin, the exciting modulations of the operatic school, the zylophone and celesta orchestration by which country dances steal into classical concerts, are what farthings are to a millionaire. That his range is so Handelian that he can give the people a universal melody or march with as sure a hand as he can give the Philharmonic Society a symphonic adagio, such as has not been given since Beethoven died. That, to come down to technical things, his knowledge of the orchestra is almost uncanny.

When Gerontius made Elgar widely known, there was a good deal of fine writing about it; but what every genuine connoisseur in orchestration must have said at the first hearing (among other things) was, "What a devil of a *fortissimo*!" Here was no literary paper instrumentation, no muddle and noise, but an absolutely new energy given to the band by a consummate knowledge of exactly what it could do and how it could do it.

We were fed up to the throats at that time with mere piquancies of orchestration: every scorer of ballets could scatter pearls from the *pavillon chinois* (alias Jingling Johnny) over the plush and cotton velvet of his harmonies; but Elgar is no mere effect monger: he takes the whole orchestra in his hand and raises every separate instrument in it to its highest efficiency until its strength is as the strength of ten. One was not surprised to learn that he could play them all, and was actually something of a *virtuoso* on instruments as different as the violin and trombone.

The enormous command of existing resources, which this orchestral skill of his exemplifies, extends over the whole musical field, and explains the fact that, though he has a most active and curious mind, he does not appear in music as an experimenter and explorer, like Scriabin and Schönberg. He took music where Beethoven left it, and where Schumann and Brahms found it.

311

Naturally he did not pick up and put on the shackles that Wagner had knocked off, any more than he wore his trumpet parts in tonic and dominant *clichés* in the eighteenth-century manner, as some of his contemporaries made a point of honor of doing, for the sake of being in the classical fashion. But his musical mind was formed before Wagner reached him; and his natural power over the material then available was so great that he was never driven outside it by lack of means for expressing himself.

He was no keyboard composer: music wrote itself on the skies for him, and wrote itself in the language perfected by Beethoven and his great predecessors. With the same inheritance, Schumann, who had less faculty and less knowledge, devotedly tried to be another Beethoven, and failed. Brahms, with a facility as convenient as Elgar's, was a musical sensualist with intellectual affectations, and succeeded only as an incoherent voluptuary, too fundamentally addleheaded to make anything great out of the delicious musical luxuries he wallowed in. Mendelssohn was never really in the running: he was, in his own light, impetuous, and often lovely style, *sui generis*, superficial if you like, but always his own unique self, composing in an idiom invented by himself, not following a school and not founding one.

Elgar, neither an imitator nor a voluptuary, went his own way without bothering to invent a new language, and by sheer personal originality produced symphonies that are really symphonies in the Beethovenian sense, a feat in which neither Schumann, Mendelssohn, nor Brahms, often as they tried, ever succeeded convincingly. If I were king, or Minister of Fine Arts, I would give Elgar an annuity of five thousand dollars a year on condition that he produce a symphony every eighteen months.

It will be noted, I hope, that this way of Elgar's, of accepting the language and forms of his art in his time as quite sufficient for anyone with plenty of courage and a masterly natural command of them, is the way of Shakespear, of Bach, of all the greatest artists. The notion that Wagner was a great technical innovator is now seen to be a delusion that had already done duty for Mozart and Handel: it meant nothing more than that the born-great composer always has the courage and common sense not to be a pedant.

Elgar has certainly never let any pedantry stand in his way. He has indeed not been aware of its academic stumbling blocks; for, like Bach, he has never been taught harmony and counterpoint. A person who had been corrupted by Day's treatise on harmony once tried to describe a phrase of Wagner's to him by a reference to the chord of the supertonic. Elgar opened his eyes wide, and, with an awe which was at least very well acted, asked, "What on earth is the chord of the supertonic?" And then, after a pause, "What *is* the supertonic? I never heard of it."

This little incident may help to explain the effect produced at first by Elgar on the little clique of devoted musicians who, with the late Hubert Parry as its centre, stood for British music thirty-five years ago. This clique was the London section of the Clara Schumann-Joachim-Brahms clique in Germany, and the relations between the two were almost sacred. Of that international clique the present generation knows nothing, I am afraid, except that when Madame Schumann found that Wagner's Walküre fire music was to be played at a concert for which she was engaged, she declined to appear in such disgraceful company, and only with great difficulty was induced, after anxious consultation with the clique, to make a supreme effort of condescension and compromise herself rather than disappoint the people who had bought tickets to hear her.

This is too good a joke against the clique to be forgotten; and the result is that poor Clara and Joachim and company are now regarded as a ridiculous little mutual-admiration gang of snobs. I entreat our snorting young lions to reconsider that harsh judgment. If they had heard Clara Schumann at her best, they could not think of her in that way. She and her clique were snobs, no doubt; but so are we all, more or less. There are many virtues mixed up with snobbery; and the clique was entirely sincere in its snobbery, and thought it was holding up a noble ideal on the art it loved. Wagner was about as eligible for it as a 450 h.p. aeroplane engine for a perambulator.

It was much the same at first with Elgar and the London branch of the clique. A young man from the west country without a musical degree, proceeding calmly and sweetly on the unconscious assumption that he was by nature and destiny one of the great composers, when, as a matter of fact, he had never heard of the supertonic, shocked and irritated the clique very painfully. It was not, of course, Elgar's fault. He pitied them, and was quite willing to shew them how a really handy man (they were the unhandiest of mortals) should write for the trombones, tune the organ, flyfish, or groom and harness and drive a horse. He could talk about every unmusical subject on earth, from pigs to Elizabethan literature.

A certain unmistakeably royal pride and temper was get-atable on occasion; but normally a less pretentious person than Elgar could not be found. To this day you may meet him and talk to him for a week without suspecting that he is anything more than a very typical English country gentleman who does not know a fugue from a *fandango*. The landlady in Pickwick whose complaint of her husband was that "Raddle aint like a man" would have said, if destiny had led her to the altar with the composer of the great symphony in A flat, "Elgar aint like a musician." The clique took Mrs Raddle's view. And certainly Elgar's music acted very differently from theirs. His Enigma Variations took away your breath. The respiration induced by their compositions was perfectly regular, and occasionally perfectly audible.

That attitude towards him was speedily reduced to absurdity by the mere sound of his music. But some initial incredulity as to his genius may be excused when we recollect that England had waited two hundred years for a great English composer, and waited in vain. The phenomenon of greatness in music had vanished from England with Purcell. Musical facility had survived abundantly. England had maintained a fair supply of amazingly dexterous and resourceful orchestral players, brass-bandsmen, organists, glee singers, and the like. But they lacked culture, and could not produce a really musical atmosphere for the local conductors who tried to organize them. And the only alternatives were the university musicians who made up the metropolitan cliques, gentlemen amateurs to a man, infatuated with classical music, and earnestly striving to compose it exactly as the great composers did. And that, of course, was no use at all. Elgar had all the dexterities of the bandsmen; sucked libraries dry as a child sucks its mother's breasts; and gathered inspiration from the skies. Is it any wonder that we were skeptical of such a miracle? For my part, I expected nothing from any English composer; and when the excitement about Gerontius began, I said wearily, "Another Wardour-street festival oratorio!" But when I heard the Variations (which had not attracted me to the concert) I sat up and said, "Whew!" I knew we had got it at last.

Since then English and American composers have sprung up like mushrooms: that is, not very plentifully, but conspicuously. The clique is, if not dead, toothless; and our Cyril Scotts and Percy Graingers, our Rutland Boughtons and Granville Bantocks and the rest pay not the smallest attention to its standard. The British Musical Society offers to name forty British composers of merit without falling back on Elgar or any member of his generation. But, so far, Elgar alone is for Westminster Abbey.

As I said to begin with, neither I nor any living man can say with certainty whether these odds and ends which I have been able to relate about Elgar are the stigmata of what we call immortality. But they look to me very like it; and I give them accordingly for what they may prove to be worth.

II

(To *The Daily News*, London, 9 *June* 1922)

The Leeds Choral Union gave a superb performance of Sir Edward Elgar's fine work, The Apostles, yesterday at Queen's Hall in aid of the Westminster Abbey Restoration Fund.

So scanty was the audience that the neglect of such a British masterpiece was a matter of general comment, and Mr Bernard Shaw expresses his feelings in characteristic terms in the letter below. [Editor, DAILY NEWS.]

Sir,—I have just heard at Queen's Hall the finest performance of Sir Edward Elgar's masterpiece, The Apostles, that our present executive resources at their choral best in the North, and their solo and orchestral best in London, can achieve.

It is only at very long and uncertain intervals that such a performance is possible.

HOW TO BECOME A MUSICAL CRITIC

The Apostles is one of the glories of British music: indeed it is unique as a British work. Its quality is such that German music at its highest in this form can put nothing beside it except the St Matthew Passion of Bach, a few samples from The Messiah of what Handel could have done with the same theme, and Beethoven's great Mass in D.

It places British music once more definitely in the first European rank, after two centuries of leather and prunella.

It would be an exaggeration to say that I was the only person present, like Ludwig of Bavaria, at Wagner's *premières*. My wife was there. Other couples were visible at intervals. One of the couples consisted of the Princess Mary and Viscount Lascelles, who just saved the situation as far as the credit of the Crown is concerned, as it very deeply is.

I distinctly saw six people in the stalls, probably with complimentary tickets.

In the cheaper seats a faithful band stood for England's culture.

It was not, as days go this month, an oppressively hot day. The season was at its height.

The occasion was infinitely more important than the Derby, than Goodwood, than the Cup Finals, than the Carpentier fights, than any of the occasions on which the official leaders of society are photographed and cinematographed laboriously shaking hands with persons on whom Molière's patron, Louis XIV, and Bach's patron, Frederick the Great, would not have condescended to wipe their boots.

The performance was none the less impressive, nor the music the less wonderful.

My object in writing this letter is simply to gratify an uncontrollable impulse to let Sir Edward Elgar and the Leeds Choral Union know that I am unspeakably ashamed of their treatment.

I apologize to them for London society, and for all the other recreants to England's culture, who will, I fear, not have the grace to apologize for themselves.

I think the enormous expenses of the performance should be repaid to the public-spirited Yorkshireman on whom, I understand, they will fall.

HANDEL'S MESSIAH

And, finally, I apologize to posterity for living in a country where the capacity and tastes of schoolboys and sporting coster-mongers are the measure of metropolitan culture.

Disgustedly yours,

G. Bernard Shaw.

III

(To *The Times*, London, 20 *December* 1932)

Sir,—I have occasionally remarked that the only entirely creditable incident in English history is the sending of £100 to Beethoven on his deathbed by the London Philharmonic Society; and it is the only one that historians never mention.

Thanks to Sir John Reith it is no longer unique. His action in commissioning a new symphony from Sir Edward Elgar, the first English composer to produce symphonies ranking with those of Beethoven, is a triumph for the B.B.C.

But is it not a pity that Sir Edward has had to wait so long for the advent of a public administrator capable of rising to the situation? The forthcoming symphony will be his third: it should be his ninth. It is true that we have loaded him with honors. I use the word loaded advisedly, as the honors have the effect of enabling us to exact much gratuitous work from him. He has given us a Land of Hope and Glory; and we have handed him back the glory and kept all the hope for ourselves.

I suggest that we make a note not to wait until our next great composer is seventy before guaranteeing his bread and butter while he is scoring his Eroica.

Yours truly,

G. Bernard Shaw.

HANDEL'S MESSIAH

(To *The Times*, London, 14 *October* 1941)

Sir,—Mr Hubert Langley's letter in your issue of September 24 was a very welcome distraction of our attention from the war and the personality of Mr Hitler to the infinitely more important though less pressing subject and greater personality of Messiah and its composer.

But his demand for a performance "as Handel wrote it" is not so simple a matter as he assumes. A composer in writing a score is limited by the economic conditions and artistic and technical resources at his disposal. He must take what he can get and make the best of it. Had the Albert Hall, the B.B.C. orchestra, and the Salvation Army's International Staff band been within Handel's reach the score of Messiah would have been a very different specification. The music would not and could not have been better, but the instrumentation would have been very much richer and more effective. The money taken at the doors would have far exceeded the utmost that the room in Fishamble-street, Dublin, where the first performance took place, could hold at the prices charged for admission in those days. Suppose Handel had all this money to play with. Suppose his trumpets and horns could play chromatic scales instead of the few scattered notes of a posthorn. Suppose he had clarionets as well as oboes (haut-boys), and tubas as well as trombones. Suppose he had an equally tempered modern cinema organ to which all keys are alike, instead of a comparatively simple organ in mean tone temperament in which only a few of the twelve major and minor keys were available. Suppose he could count on sixty strings instead of twenty, on four horns, or eight, instead of two, on wood wind in Wagnerian groups of three instead of two, on the chords from kettledrums used by Berlioz in his Fantastic Symphony. Would his score have been anything like as poor as it stands in his manuscript? Is there no excuse for the conductors and composers who have ventured to guess how Handel would have enriched it under such conditions?

Mr Langley may say that Mozart went beyond this. He certainly did. Take for example the bass air The people that walked in darkness. It is not too much of an exaggeration to say that Handel did not harmonize it at all: he scored it in hollow unisons, perhaps with some intention of conveying an impression of darkness and void. Mozart filled up these hollows with harmonies so enchanting that every musician longs to hear them again and again. I believe Handel would have been delighted with them.

And is it certain that he did not anticipate them? Elgar, who adored them, pooh-poohed the purists by reminding them that Handel was at the organ, and must have put in all sorts of harmonic variations, being a great improviser. Handel's variations are lost; but are we to throw Mozart's after them?

Handel and his contemporaries wrote trumpet parts that became impossible when the pitch rose as it did until they became unplayable. The trumpets had to be replaced by clarionets until at the first performances of our Bach Society Kosleck arrived with a new two-valved Bach trumpet on which all the impossible passages are now brilliantly played. That was a glorious restoration; but its success does not justify a deliberate reduction of our Messiah performances within seventeenth-century limits.

Only, the changes must be made by a master hand. Wagner provided Gluck's Iphigenia overture with a very beautiful ending to replace the conventional rum-tum coda which was considered *de rigueur*, and which still spoils Mozart's Don Giovanni overture at concert performances. Who wants to have the rum-tum back again? When Wagner wrote trombone parts for a chorus in one of Spontini's operas, the composer, instead of being outraged, sent for the parts when he was producing the opera in Berlin, and was kind enough to say it was a great pity Wagner could never become a great composer, as he (Spontini) had exhausted the possibilities of music. Wagner, when he conducted Beethoven's Ninth Symphony, a sacred masterpiece if there ever was one, found that certain themes which were evidently meant to be heard as principal melodies were smothered by their accompaniments. He rescored the passages to correct this. Gounod accused him of sacrilege; but Wagner's version is now played instead of that left by the deaf Beethoven. Passages in which the brass was left idle because it could not play the chromatic intervals have been reinforced by it without anyone protesting.

I could multiply instances; but enough is enough. Besides, I must confine my assent to changes made by master hands like those of Mozart, Wagner, and Elgar. Genius alone has the right to tamper with genius.

I am myself a composer: that is, a planner of performances,

in the special capacity of a playwright. When I began, I had to keep production expenses within the limits of, say, £2,000 at a London West-end manager's bank, and £20 in the provinces. The invention of the cinema has placed capitals running to a quarter of a million at my disposal for modern revivals of my old cheap plays. This enormous economic change enables me to do things I should never have dreamt of in the nineteenth century. A cinema production which confined itself to the old version would be an imbecility. But I do not allow the additions to be made in Hollywood by the nearest Californian barman.

Finally, take the case of Shakespear. He did not write original plays: he wrote "additional accompaniments" to old ones. Has anyone on earth except Tolstoy, who had no ear for English word music, ever suggested that we should go back to the original Lear? Could Mr Langley endure a performance of the old Hamlet after tasting Shakespear's version?

Fifty years ago The Times, greatly daring, ventured to hint, through its music representative the late J. A. Fuller-Maitland, that the Handel Festivals at the Crystal Palace, where 4,000 performers created an uproar which would have infuriated the irascible composer, were barbarous orgies which had no more to do with Handel's intentions than the Cup Ties. Naturally Costa, the once famous but now forgotten conductor, piled up all the brass and blare and percussion he could muster for these occasions. I agree warmly with Mr Langley that these additions should be ruthlessly scrapped. At the same period Shakespear himself was known to play-goers only by horribly mutilated "acting versions" which made Mr Granville-Barker's uncompromising restorations of the real Shakespear seem surprising novelties even to the professional critics. I agreed with Mr Granville-Barker as heartily as I do with Mr Langley; but that did not prevent my reconditioning the last act of Cymbeline to an extent that would have surprised Shakespear. Some changes are inevitable: I can even imagine Mr Augustus John touching up a Goya. It all depends on how it is done.

Yours truly,

G. Bernard Shaw.

RADIO MUSIC

(*The Musical Times, January* 1947)

Radio music has changed the world in England. When I made my living as a critic of concerts and of opera in London fifty years ago I heard a Beethoven symphony once in a blue moon in the old St James's Hall or the Crystal Palace as part of a musical set of perhaps a thousand people who could afford to pay and were quite accidentally musical in their tastes. My own familiarity with the orchestral classics was gained by playing arrangements of them as piano duets with my sister. As to the Ninth Symphony, performances of it were extraordinary events separated by years.

Today, with radio sets as common as kitchen clocks, the Eroica, the Seventh, the Ninth, are as familiar to Tom, Dick, and Harriet as Nancy Lee used to be when it was played incessantly on every street piano. So also are Mozart's three greatest symphonies. Haydn, no longer forgotten, is alive again. Highbrow music is everywhere, as audible in the slums as in the squares. And it is all due to radio.

I affirm this because I am going to criticize the B.B.C., and must not be set down as a Philistine unconscious of the revolution it has made. Only those who, like myself, are old enough to remember the pre-radio London can have any conception of what we owe to it.

But this does not mean that radio music is less in need of the severest criticism than nineteenth-century performances. On the contrary, such criticism has become a matter of national importance. That is why I am induced to return for a moment to my old *métier* and note a few points on which the B.B.C. goes wrong occasionally.

Its 'worst concessions to popular bad taste, real or imaginary, are very horrible. I switch them off so promptly that I am hardly qualified to condemn them. But I protest against the notion that because there are vulgar people with such low tastes that all orchestral wind instruments have to be degraded by mutes to please them, radio music should condescend to a propaganda of musical obscenity instead of musical beauty. I can trace this evil to its source, because when I was an *ex-officio* member of the B.B.C. Council, in virtue of my chairmanship of its Spoken English Committee, I urged that the most critical care should be taken of what were called the music-hall programs. The Council was horrified. I was actually proposing that its members should be on speaking terms with the low class of persons from which our red-nosed comedians and players of freak instruments were mostly drawn. Against this snobbery I could do nothing. Within its limits the Council was an excellent one; but they were ladies and gentlemen first and last, and would not mix with char-ladies' and costermongers' entertainers on any terms.

But later on they did meddle. The elderly members who had fallen to the charm of music-hall singers, like Marie Lloyd, Bessie Bellwood, and Vesta Tilley, tried to revive them by broadcasting their songs. Now these songs, with their interpolated patter, were not only vulgar but so silly as to be hardly intelligible. And the B.B.C. made the outrageous mistake of thinking that the secret of their popularity lay in their vulgarity, though a moment's consideration should have convinced them that vulgar and silly girls could be picked up in any poor street for a few shillings a week. The real secret was that their intonation and rhythm were so perfect as to be irresistible. When Marie Lloyd sang Oh Mister Porter, what shall I do? I want to go to Birmingham and theyre taking me on to Crewe, nobody cared twopence about Birmingham or Crewe; but everybody wanted to dance to Marie's exquisite rhythm, and found the sensation delightful. Bessie Bellwood's patter, assuring us that she was not going to gow on the stije and kiss her ijent, did not draw sixpence into the pay-boxes; but she, too, could sing in perfect tune and measure. Chirgwin earned his salary, not for his make-up as the White-Eyed Kaffir or his substitution of a kerosene tin with one string for a Stradivarius, but for his infallible musical ear, which kept him always exactly in tune. Sir Harry Lauder, still with us, triumphed, not because of his Scotch accent, but because he has a very fine voice and never sings a false note nor misses a beat. The sham Maries and Bessies strove their hardest, not too successfully, to be vulgar in the cockney manner, and took their passable intonation for granted. The revival was a disgraceful failure.

Let us shift to the classics, where this elementary blundering was also apparent. What does singing or playing in tune mean? Most people who sing or play can do so passably in tune with a piano or orchestra to keep them to the pitch. But between that and being really in the very middle of the note there is a world of difference. Experiments by physicists have shewn that if two instruments are tuned to the same pitch and one of them gradually sharpened or flattened, listeners do not at first detect the variation, and they differ in the degree of it they can observe. The effect of these differences is that when a choir of people who can sing only passably in tune are not kept to the pitch by an organ or band and are set to sing motets, madrigals, and glees, they make a most disagreeable noise, because they are all singing in different keys. The fact that the differences are much less than a semitone makes the discord worse. Yet, tested individually, they can all sing passably in tune and are selected, even at an advanced age and with poor voices, because they are good readers and good starters. And however unmusical their performances may be, they are endured, because it is supposed that the music, being old, must be quaint.

Besides, they do not all sing the same scale. Joachim and Sarasate, the greatest fiddlers of their time, had respectively a German scale and a Latin scale. Had they ever attempted to play in unison they would have accused oneanother of being out of tune.

Of all this the B.B.C. seems to know nothing. Because its choir can sing hymns and anthems acceptably to an organ accompaniment, it thinks that it must be equally available for motets by Byrd or Orlandus Lassus. It takes years of practice to train a group of good readers to sing in tune not only passably but exactly, and in the same scale. Not since we were visited half a century ago by De Lange's wonderful Dutch choir have I heard the treasures of fifteenth-century music pleasurably performed. Vaughan Williams's orchestral handlings of Byrd and Tallis are delightfully harmonious. Who can say as much for the B.B.C. choir cavorting desperately through a struggle to "read" the original work of these composers?

Singing in tune is not the only consideration in broadcasting. The microphone gives away all singers' and speakers' secrets: the gutter from which they may have sprung, the cocktails and too recent meals they may have swallowed, their ages and what not. In casting plays to be performed by invisible actors the contrasts of soprano, alto, tenor, and bass are indispensable to an intelligible and agreeable performance. A cast in which all the voices have the same pitch and pace is as disastrous as it would be in an opera.

On broadcast opera generally may I note that one act at a time, thoroughly done without cuts, would often be better entertainment than scrambling through scraps of the whole work. For example, take the operas of Meyerbeer, treated by the B.B.C. as extinct. The Huguenots, a really great opera of its class, raved about by Goethe, Balzac, and even Wagner in his youth, is so long that after its first performance in Paris it was cut to ribbons and has never since been heard in its entirety. Every act is a complete piece by itself, full of numbers that need the intimacy and finish of the radio and are not on the scale of the Paris Grand Opera into which all operas were then forced. It should be given one act at a time, carefully studied and uncut.

And why are such masterpieces as Goetz's Taming of the Shrew, Mozartian in its melody, and Peter Cornelius's Barber of Bagdad, with its delightful *Salaam a leikum* at the end and a great *basso profundo rôle*, shelved for operas by Rossini which our vocalists cannot sing?

I could put other questions; but enough is enough for once. With daily concerts, an orchestra to which the scores of Wagner and Berlioz are child's play, a bevy of first-rate native conductors and two-thirds of a penny for listening in comfort at home: is there any limit to these possibilities?

They stagger my old-fashioned imagination.

BASSO CONTINUO

(To *The Times*, London, 25 *October* 1948; reprinted under the title "G.B.S. and Orchestral Basses" in *Musical America*, *February* 1949)

Sir,—It would be a pity to let this correspondence[1] drop without emphasizing the ever-pressing need for remedying the weakness of the orchestral bass. I do not greatly care whether *recitativo secco* is accompanied by scrapes of the 'cello or by piano or harpsichord. I should rather like to hear the *tromba marina*; but I shall lose no sleep if I do not. Seventy years ago I filled up the figured basses in Stainer's textbook of harmony quite correctly. Any fool could, even were he deafer than Beethoven.

What has worried me through all these years is that I could never hear Beethoven's No. 3 Leonora Overture as he meant me to hear it; and I never shall until his florid basses can hold their own against the thunder of the full orchestra *fortissimo*. When his impetuous figuration rushes down from top to bottom of the orchestra, the first half of it rings out brilliantly and the rest is a senseless blare. When the bass should tremble and rattle, nothing is heard but a noisy growl and a thump.

I have inquired again and again how the bass could be made audible. Elgar thought it could be done by a group of Belgian trombones with five valves which enabled them to play the most florid passages *prestissimo*. But the ophicleide, a giant-keyed bugle with a peculiar tone which moved Berlioz to denounce it as a chromatic bullock, is as agile as five valves can make (and spoil) the trombone. My uncle played it, so I know.

The expense of extra players daunts many conductors: I know one who, when he pleaded to the municipality for third and fourth horns, was told to make the first and second play twice as loud. But nowadays, when Wagner in The Dusk of the Gods and Strauss in Hero Life require eight horns, and bass clarionets, English horns, hexelphones, and other luxuries undreamt of by

---

[1] "Basso Continuo," an article by the musical critic of *The Times* on 17 September, concerning the baffling problem of Bach's accompaniments, was a subject of discussion in the correspondence columns during most of September and October.

Beethoven have to be available for every callow composer, the B.B.C. can afford to damn the expense.

The purists who want the original score and nothing but the score, not even the music, have no case. Elgar defended Mozart's rescoring of The Messiah on the ground that Handel at the organ could improvise equivalent descants and harmonies (and who can believe that in The people that walked in darkness he played only the written unisons and hollow octaves in the score?); but I am all for the replacement of Mozart's clarionet parts by the new Bach trumpet on which they are no longer unplayable. Trumpeters in Mozart's time were a bumptious lot; he hated them and loved the clarionet. Wagner had to rescore passages in the Ninth Symphony to bring out the parts that Beethoven evidently meant to be prominent, but which, great master of the orchestra as he was, he was too deaf to balance for himself. Schumann was no such master; nobody has yet complained of Mahler's rescoring of his symphonies. But it is the Beethoven basses above all that I want to hear; and we have not heard them yet.

Yours faithfully,
G. Bernard Shaw.

MUSIC TODAY

(A Questionnaire in *The Stage*, 20 *April* 1950)

Do you think there has been any appreciable development in musical interest and understanding in this country since the days when you were a musical critic?

Yes, of course. Enormously. The radio has made Beethoven's Ninth Symphony familiar to millions of people who did not know that such a thing as a symphony existed.

Has the radio had an important influence, one way or the other, on musical appreciation?

It has worked both ways. It has corrupted musical taste and degraded musical instruments by the most obscene sort of jazz as well as reviving Haydn's vogue and making Bach a popular composer.

MUSIC TODAY

Now that the day of the patron is over, in what way could, or should, the Government assist musicians, orchestras, &c.?

The Government supports the British Museum, the National Gallery, and the cathedrals. What is to prevent it supporting municipal orchestras and festivals?

Do you think that the Arts Council, for example, is doing the right sort of work to foster musical taste and to cultivate talent?

It is doing what it can within the limits of its tastes and resources. Its existence is an advance towards a Ministry of Fine Arts.

Do you think there has been any notable change in the quality of instrumental playing during the last, say, forty or fifty years?

Yes, a prodigious change for the better. Not only do *virtuosi* such as Heifetz and Menuhin and Kentner surpass Joachim, Sarasate, and Rubinstein technically and have much wider repertories, but the average orchestral player is superior as an artist— I had almost written more of a cultured gentleman (or lady)— than in my time.

Do you agree that musical criticism today is not of a high enough standard?

No. Musical criticism can never be high enough, but the proportion of musically unqualified reporters praising every performance and enjoying unlimited free tickets is much smaller, if not practically extinct.

What significance, if any, do you think may be attached to the war-time enthusiasm for music, when concerts and recitals were more patronized than for many years?

Most concerts used to be advertisements paid for by the artists and attended by their deadhead friends. As I have not been in practice as a critic for fifty years I cannot say how far this still goes on. My impression is that the war-time enthusiasm was for dancing, and was so crazy as to be pathological.

Would you favor any sort of Government aid for individual composers or instrumentalists who require help if they are to develop without wearing themselves out first or being forced to write music for films, &c.?

It depends on the cases helped. Film music has the highest possibilities, and at its worst is better than academic cantatas and sham oratorios manufactured for prestige at the Three Choirs Festival.

Can you account for the rarity of really front-rank British conductors?

What do you call rarity? In my time we had Stanford, Barnby, Mackenzie, and Cusins, none of whom could conduct. Now, without stopping to think, I can reel you off Adrian Boult, Malcolm Sargent, Basil Cameron, Clarence Raybould, Stanford Robinson, Charles Groves, Ian Whyte, &c. &c. &c., all of them as competent as Furtwängler. If they had foreign names nobody in England would question their eminence.

CODA

WE SING BETTER THAN OUR GRANDPARENTS!
(Everybody's Magazine, 11 November 1950)

The notion that singing has deteriorated in the present century is only a phase of the Good Old Times delusion. It has, in fact, enormously improved.

Fifty years ago the singers whose voices lasted because they knew how to produce them were the De Reszke brothers, taught by their mother, Santley, an ex-choir boy from Liverpool, Adelina Patti, and Edward Lloyd.

Every musical period suffers from the delusion that it has lost the art of singing, and looks back to an imaginary golden age in which all singers had the secret of the *bel canto* taught by Italian magicians and practiced *in excelsis* at the great Opera Houses of Europe by sopranos with high C's and even higher F's, tenors with C sharps, baritones with G sharps, and *bassi profundi* with low E flats. Their like, we think, we shall never hear in our degenerate days.

We are now idolizing the singers of sixty years ago in this fashion. This does not impose on me: I have heard them. The extraordinary singers were no better than ours; the average singers were much worse. At the predominant Royal Italian Opera, Mr Heddle Nash would have been impossible so-called; but Signor Edele Nascio would have been as much in order and at home with Signor Foli and Signor Campobello as with Mr Santley, Mr Sims Reeves, Mr Lyall, Miss Catherine Hayes, and the other indispensables who refused to have their names and nationalities disguised. Edward Lloyd alone was excluded because he would not sing in any language but his own.

As to the robust tenors who came between Mario and Jean de Reszke, the educated and carefully-taught ones sang so

329

horribly that they were classed as "Goatbleaters": Heddle Nash is an Orpheus compared to the once famous Gayarré. The rest were proletarians who had developed stentorian voices as newsboys, muffinmen, infantry sergeants, and humble, vociferous cheapjack auctioneers, who mostly shouted their voices away and are forgotten. De Reszke seemed a prince in comparison.

When I was first taken to the opera in my boyhood and heard Il Trovatore, I was surprised to hear in the second scene a voice from behind the scenes: Manrico singing the serenade. I asked the adult who had brought me (a teacher of singing) "What is that?" He replied, "A pig under a gate." I forbear to rescue that tenor's name from oblivion.

Voice production in general is now immeasurably better than it was fifty years ago.

Voices so strained by singing continually in the top fifth of their range that they could not sustain a note without a *tremolo*, nor keep to the pitch, like those of Faure and Maurel; sopranos Garcia-trained to sing nothing but high C's on the vowel Ah, and [who] soon had to have their C's transposed to B flats, were rife in those days; now they are extinct. Genuine Italian singers and conductors to whom Wagner was not music at all (bar perhaps Lohengrin) are dead; and Toscanini is better at German music than at Rossini.

The notion that Wagner's music broke voices, and that opera singers should sing only that of Rossini, Donizetti, Bellini, and Meyerbeer, has been replaced by the truth that Wagner, Mozart, and Handel, who wrote for the middle of the voice with very occasional high notes for exceptional singers, never broke a properly produced voice.

In Don Giovanni, the greatest opera in the world, there are two baritones and two basses, not one of them having a note to sing that is not easily within the compass of Tom, Dick, and Harry.

Where we fall short is in *roulades*, shakes, and *gruppettos*, which many of our singers simply cannot sing at all, though the B.B.C. puts them up to sing Rossini, making them ridiculous when they could be better employed on such neglected masterpieces as Goetz's Shrew and Cornelius's Barber. As to Meyerbeer, whose Huguenots should be broadcast seriously without cuts one act at a time, the B.B.C. has apparently never heard of him.

Let us hear no more of a golden age of *bel canto*. We sing much better than our grandfathers. I have heard all the greatest tenors (except Giuglini) from Mario to Heddle Nash, and I know what I am writing about; for, like De Reszke, I was taught to sing by my mother, not by Garcia.

BIOGRAPHICAL INDEX

This index of musical personages is not intended to be comprehensive, but to provide data (when available) on persons figuring importantly in Shaw's criticism who may not be familiar to the reader.

ALBANI, EMMA (1852–1930), Canadian-born soprano, made her debut as Amina in *La Sonnambula* at Messina, later appeared in same role in London, 1871. Sang all the great soprano roles of Italian opera, but was especially noted for her Elsa in *Lohengrin*, Elizabeth in *Tannhäuser*, Senta in *Der Fliegende Hollander.*

BACKER-GRÖNDAHL, AGATHE (1847–1907), Norwegian pianist whose repertoire consisted primarily of works of masters of the Romantic school.

BARNBY, SIR JOSEPH (1838–96), English organist, conductor, composer, founder of a choral society which he named after himself. Succeeded Gounod as conductor of Royal Albert Hall Choral Society.

BENNETT, JOSEPH (1831–1911), English musical critic (*Daily Telegraph, Pall Mall Gazette*, etc.), writer, librettist. Annotated Philharmonic Society and Popular Concerts programmes. Furnished librettos to A. C. Mackenzie (*Dream of Jubal*), Arthur Sullivan (*Golden Legend*), Frederic Cowen (*Thorgrim*).

BENNETT, SIR WILLIAM STERNDALE (1816–75), considered by many of his contemporaries one of England's greatest composers. Founded Bach Society in 1849, conducted London Philharmonic and Leeds Musical Festival. Composed symphony, four piano concertos, an oratorio (*Woman of Samaria*).

BREMA, MARIE (1856–1925), first English operatic singer to perform at Bayreuth. Sang Gluck's *Orfeo* and Brünnhilde in London, the *Ring* and *Tristan* at the Metropolitan under Mottl and Seidl.

BURNS, GEORGINA, one of Carl Rosa's most popular singers. Appeared as the Messenger of Peace in Wagner's *Rienzi*, Catherine in Meyerbeer's *L'Etoile du Nord*, and in title role in Wallace's *Lurline*. Later toured provinces with husband Leslie Crotty and a company of their own.

CALVÉ, EMMA (1858–1942), French-born soprano, noted for her dramatic ability, excelled in *Carmen* and *Sapho* and as Santuzza in

Cavalleria Rusticana. Endeavoured to interpret her roles with the greatest realism.

CAPOUL, JOSEPH (1839–1924), French tenor, member of Opéra Comique company, 1861–89. Toured America with Christine Nilsson. First appeared in England, 1871, as Faust at the Italian Opera, sang at Covent Garden, 1875–9.

COSTA, SIR MICHAEL (1808–84), Italian composer and conductor, of Spanish parentage. Wrote several successful operas (including *Don Carlos*), oratorio (*Eli*). Directed Handel Festival, 1857–80; from 1871 was "director of the music, composer and conductor" at Her Majesty's. One of the finest conductors of nineteenth century.

COWEN, SIR FREDERIC (1852–1935), English composer of operas (*Pauline, Thorgrim*), oratorio (*Ruth*), cantatas (*Corsair, St Ursula*). Conducted Promenade Concerts at Covent Garden (1880, 1893), Royal Philharmonic (1888–92, 1900–07), Hallé Concerts (1896–9).

FANCELLI, GIUSEPPE (1835–88), Italian tenor, for many years member of Mapleson's company at Drury Lane. Sang Rhadames at La Scala in first Italian performance of *Aïda*. Lacked personality and was a poor actor, but the quality of his voice was superb and his intonation unfailing.

FAURE, JEAN-BAPTISTE (1830-1914), French baritone, was principal baritone at Paris Opéra for seventeen years. In London sang Mephistopheles in *Faust* (1863–6), Iago in Rossini's *Otello* (1870), Lotario in Thomas's *Mignon*. A frequent performer in London in the 1870's.

FOLI, SIGNOR [ALLAN JAMES FOLEY] (1835–99), outstanding Irish basso profundo, began career as a youth singing in church choirs in the United States, later studied in Naples. Made operatic debut in 1862 in Rossini's *Otello*, had a repertoire of more than sixty operatic roles, but in later years sang principally in oratorio and concert.

GARCIA, MANUEL (1805–1906), Spanish voice teacher, trained Jenny Lind, invented laryngoscope to inspect vocal chords while they were in use.

GAYARRÉ, JULIAN (1844–90), Spanish tenor, formerly a blacksmith, the Caruso of his day, sang in every great opera house of Europe. His *Trovatore* and *Favorita* were considered achievements without equal in the art of singing.

GERSTER, ETELKA (1857–1920), Hungarian-born coloratura soprano, one of the most remarkable of her time. Scored instant success in London debut at Her Majesty's, 1877, as Amina in *La Sonnambula*, remained with company for four seasons.

GOLDSCHMIDT, OTTO (1829–1907), pianist, pupil of Mendelssohn and Chopin, accompanist and conductor in America for Jenny Lind, whom he married in Boston in 1852. Founded Bach Choir and was its conductor, 1875–85.

GROVE, SIR GEORGE (1820–1900), distinguished English critic and editor, prepared analytical programmes for Crystal Palace concerts for more than forty years. Most significant work was four-volume *Dictionary of Music and Musicians* (1879–89).

HALLÉ, SIR CHARLES (1819–95), founded Hallé Orchestra in Manchester, 1857, conducted its concerts until his death. Married the popular violinist, Wilma Norman Neruda.

HARRIS, SIR AUGUSTUS (1851–96), English theatre manager and impresario, produced spectacular melodrama and elaborate pantomime at Drury Lane, later produced opera at Her Majesty's and Covent Garden. Did much for the cause of Wagner's music in London.

HENSCHEL, SIR GEORGE (1850–1934), concert baritone and composer, born at Breslau. Conducted symphonic concerts in Boston, 1881–1884, later directed London Symphony and was first conductor of Scottish Orchestra. Composed a *Stabat Mater* (1894) and operas *A Sea Change* (1884) and *Frederick the Great* (1899).

JOACHIM, JOSEPH (1831–1907), Hungarian violinist, first appeared in London (on recommendation of Mendelssohn) in 1844. Was principal attraction for many years with Crystal Palace concerts and Popular Concerts. Organised a celebrated quartet which bore his name.

KREBS, MARIE (1851–1900), brilliant German pianist, performed publicly from age of eleven. Retired on her marriage in 1885 after many years of popularity in England.

LASSALLE, JEAN LOUIS (1847–1909), great French baritone, made his debut at Paris Opéra at nineteen. Sang leading roles in *Hamlet*, *Huguenots*, *Aïda*, *L'Africaine*, *Ascanio*, *William Tell*.

LAWSON, MALCOLM (1849–?), English organist and composer, works include an opera, several symphonies, and much sacred music.

LEHMANN - KALISCH, LILLI (1842-1929), German prima donna, daughter of famous dramatic singer Maria Loewe-Lehmann, from whom she received earliest instruction. Especially popular at Bayreuth and in United States, her phenomenal range and fine acting showed to especial advantage in such roles as Brünnhilde, Fidelio, Carmen, Norma, Isolde.

LEMMENS-SHERRINGTON, HELEN (1834–1906), English singer, made first appearance in London in 1856, soon became leading English soprano both in sacred and secular music. Appeared in opera from 1860, singing in *Norma, Giovanni, Martha, Huguenots*.

LLOYD, EDWARD (1845–1927), English tenor, trained in Westminster Abbey choir, gained international reputation as singer in concert and oratorio. Created tenor roles in oratorios by Gounod, Sullivan, Elgar, but also sang popular songs. Star tenor piece in concert was "The Holy City."

LUDWIG [LEDWIDGE], WILLIAM (1847–1923), Irish baritone, sang for several years in chorus at Old Gaiety Theatre, London. Gained prominence through performance in *Der Fliegende Holländer* when, in 1877, he succeeded Santley as principal baritone in Carl Rosa company. Noted for Wagnerian roles, in which, says Grove, "the sombre tone of his voice was exactly suited to the music."

MAAS, JOSEPH (1847–86), English tenor, was principal tenor for Carl Rosa company, 1878–80, singing Raoul in *Huguenots*, Faust, Radames, Rienzi. Sang Lohengrin at Covent Garden (1883), was the Chevalier des Grieux in first London production of Massenet's *Manon* (1885).

McGUCKIN, BARTON (1852–1913), Irish tenor, first appeared at Crystal Palace concert in 1875. Made opera debut under Carl Rosa in 1880, soon became popular fixture of the troupe, principal roles including Lohengrin, Faust, Des Grieux, Don José. Also well known in oratorio.

MACINTYRE, MARGARET (*c*.1865–1943), Scottish soprano, scored instant success in debut at Covent Garden in 1888, playing Micaela to Nordica's Carmen. Also scored as Margaret in Boïto's *Mefistofele*, Inez in *L'Africaine*, Marguerite in *Faust*, but career as a leading singer was rather brief.

MANNS, SIR AUGUST (1825–1907), German bandmaster and conductor, engaged in 1855 as conductor at Crystal Palace, where he led Saturday Concerts until 1901. Succeeded Costa as conductor of Handel Festival. Fostered work of German composers, notably Schumann.

BIOGRAPHICAL INDEX

MARIO [GIOVANNI MATTEO] (1810–83), Italian tenor, descended from nobility. First appeared in London in 1839 in Donizetti's *Lucrezia Borgia*, was considered most perfect stage-lover ever seen. The beauty of his voice has become legendary. Retired in 1867.

MATERNA, AMALIE (1845–1918), great prima donna of German opera, gained worldwide reputation at Bayreuth in 1876 when she created role of Brünnhilde. Was first Kundry at Bayreuth, 1882.

MAUREL, VICTOR (1848–1923), French baritone, student of Faure. Made his début at Paris Opéra in *Huguenots*, 1868. First appeared at Covent Garden as Renato in *Ballo in Maschera*, 1873. Greatest roles were Iago and Falstaff; sang first Telramund (*Lohengrin*) and Wolfram (*Tannhäuser*) in England.

MOTTL, FELIX (1856–1911), Austrian conductor and composer, took part in first Bayreuth performances of the *Ring*, 1876. Conducted *Tristan* at Bayreuth in 1886, *Ring* cycle at Covent Garden in 1898, *Parsifal* at the Metropolitan in 1903–4. Composed three operas.

NASH, HEDDLE (b. 1896), Milan-trained English tenor, scored immediate success at Old Vic in 1925 as the Duke in *Rigoletto*. Acclaimed at Covent Garden in 1929 for his Ottavio in *Giovanni*. Grove calls his David in *Meistersinger* "incomparable."

NEWMAN, ERNEST (1868–1959), English musical critic (*Manchester Guardian, Birmingham Post, Observer, Sunday Times* 1920–59), wrote brilliant study of Hugo Wolf, "definitive" biography of Wagner, books on Richard Strauss, Elgar, Gluck.

NILSSON, CHRISTINE (1843–1921), Swedish soprano, first appeared in London as Violetta in *Traviata*. Outstanding roles included Martha, Queen of the Night in *Zauberflöte*, Ophelia in Thomas's *Hamlet* (which she created), Donna Elvira in *Giovanni*, Cherubino in *Nozze di Figaro*.

NORMAN NERUDA, WILMA [LADY HALLÉ] (1839–1911), Moravian-born violinist. One of London's most popular soloists, performed every season from 1869 to 1898 at Philharmonic, Crystal Palace, Popular Concerts.

PARRY, SIR CHARLES HUBERT H. (1848–1918), English composer, author, teacher. Bach Choir's performance of his chorale *Blest Pair of Sirens* established him as master of choral writing. Wrote five symphonies, unproduced opera *Guinevere*, four oratorios, several treatises on music.

PATEY, JANET (1842–94), outstanding Scottish contralto, member of

Henry Leslie's choir, later became leading contralto concert singer. Most noted operatic role was Blanche of Devan in Macfarren's *Lady of the Lake*. Has been compared favourably as a singer with Alboni.

PATTI, ADELINA (1843–1919), Spanish-born daughter of Italian parents, one of greatest of all coloraturas. Debut in New York as Lucia in 1859, in England as Amina in *La Sonnambula* in 1861. Repertoire included Lucia, Violetta, Zerlina, Martha. Sang annually, 1861–84, at Covent Garden in repertory of about thirty operas. Career lasted 56 years.

PORPORA, NICOLA A. (1686–1766), Italian composer of some fifty operas. Was Handel's principal rival in London, 1733–6. Also noted as teacher of singing, unrivalled in his day.

RAVOGLI, GIULIA, Italian-born prima donna, whose sister Sofia was also a well-known singer. Repertoire included *Orfeo*, *Lohengrin*, *Aïda*, *Gioconda*, *Carmen*. Very popular with American audiences, in Europe was hailed as one of the greatest dramatic sopranos.

REEVES, [JOHN] SIMS (1818–1900), revered English tenor, started career as second tenor in Macready's company at Drury Lane, later sang Edgardo in *Lucia* at La Scala with marked success. Same role at Drury Lane in 1847 earned him position of actor and singer of first rank. Greatest reputation, however, came from oratorio, particularly performances in Handelian repertory and in Bach's *St Matthew Passion*.

RESZKE, EDOUARD DE (1855–1917), Polish basso, brother of Jean de Reszke, who taught him singing. A favourite at Covent Garden for two decades, noted particularly for Wagnerian roles, considered outstanding singer and actor of lyric stage.

RESZKE, JEAN DE (1850–1925), Polish baritone who developed into a tenor, generally regarded as best tenor since Mario. Principal roles included Faust, Romeo, Radames, Tristan, Tannhäuser, Lohengrin, Siegfried, Samson. Founded operatic singing-school in Paris in 1905 and became celebrated teacher.

RICHTER, HANS (1843–1916), Hungarian-born conductor, friend of Wagner, conducted first performance of *Ring* cycle at Bayreuth in 1876. Frequently conducted concert and operatic performances in England, particularly Hallé concerts in Manchester, 1900–10.

RIGBY, GEORGE VERNON (1840–?), English tenor, first appeared as concert singer. After study in Milan and Berlin, sang Handel's *Samson* at Gloucester Festival, replacing Sims Reeves. Appeared frequently in opera and concert, but never developed into a first-rate performer.

ROSA, CARL (1842–89), German violinist, came to London in 1866, later (1875) organised now famous English opera company, with Rose Hersee and Charles Santley as principal artists, which met with instant success. Introduced Wagner's *Rienzi*, Cowen's *Pauline*, Goetz's *Taming of the Shrew*.

ROZE, MARIE (1846–1926), French soprano, began career at Opéra Comique, 1865–8, was great favourite at Drury Lane and Her Majesty's, 1872–81. Joined Carl Rosa company in 1883.

SANTLEY, SIR CHARLES (1834–1922), sometimes called king of English baritones, performed title role in Mendelssohn's *Elijah* for half a century. Introduced *Der Fliegende Hollander* to London in 1870, but retired from opera in 1877, appearing thereafter only in concerts and oratorio. At 81 he sang with perfect intonation and much of the quality he had revealed fifty years earlier.

SARASATE, PABLO DE (1844–1908), Spanish violinist, performed on two stradivari. First appeared in London at Crystal Palace in 1861. Grove says he had "purity of style, charm, brightness of tone, flexibility, and extraordinary facility." Favoured works of Saint-Saëns and Lalo, frequently performed exquisitely-played solos of his own composition.

SCHUMANN HEINK, ERNESTINE (1861–1936), operatic contralto, born near Prague. English debut as Erda at Covent Garden, 1892. Sang at Bayreuth, 1896, and for several seasons (from 1898) at the Metropolitan. Created role of Klytemnestra in Strauss's *Elektra*, 1909. Noted also for lieder singing.

STANFORD, SIR CHARLES VILLIERS (1852–1924), Irish composer, conductor, teacher, best known for Irish Rhapsodies and "Irish" Symphony. Conducted Bach Choir, 1885–1902, Leeds Triennial Festival, 1901–10. Composed nearly a dozen operas, including *Savonarola* and *Much Ado about Nothing*.

STERLING, ANTOINETTE (1850–1904), American contralto, possessed a voice of extraordinary range. Although she sang classical music (Mendelssohn, Schumann, Bach), was best known as ballad singer of such works as "Three Ra'ens" and "Sands of Dee."

SVENDSEN, OLUF (1832–88), Norwegian flautist, joined Crystal Palace orchestra in 1856. Later performed with Philharmonic Orchestra and, for ten years, in orchestra at Her Majesty's.

TAMBERLIK, ENRICO (1820–89), Italian tenor, first appeared in England in 1850 as Masaniello in Auber's *Muette de Portici*. Remained with Royal Italian Opera until 1864, later sang at Covent Garden and Her Majesty's. Most important roles were Florestan in *Fidelio*, Don Ottavio in *Rigoletto*, title role in Rossini's *Otello*, Manrico in *Trovatore*.

TREBELLI-BETTINI, ZELIA (1838–92), Paris-born mezzo-soprano, made her debut at Madrid, singing Rosina to Mario's Almavįva in *Il Barbiere*. One of her greatest roles was Orsini in *Lucreẓia*, which she sang to thunderous ovation in London debut, 1862. One of London's best-loved singers until retirement in 1889.

WEIST HILL, THOMAS H. (1823–91), English violinist, conductor, teacher, became member of Costa's orchestra at Royal Italian Opera in 1849. Was conductor at Alexandra Palace, 1874–6, later conducted Mme Viard-Louis's orchestral concerts, 1878–9.

YSAŸE, EUGENE (1858–1931), Belgian violinist and conductor, studied under Wieniawski and Vieuxtemps, first appeared in London at Philharmonic concert, 1889. Composed "Variations on a Theme of Paganini" and six violin concertos, popularised Franck's violin sonata, which was dedicated to him.

GENERAL INDEX

Musical personages whose names are preceded by
an asterisk are included in the Biographical Index

Achurch, Janet (1864–1916), 224
ADELAIDA, 230
Aeschylus, 221
Agnesi, Luigi (1833–75), 40
Agoult, Marie, Comtesse d'
["Daniel Stern"] (1805–76), 119
AÏDA, 152, 221
*Albani, Emma (1852–1930), 26-
27, 30-2, 33, 84, 92, 121, 123,
157
Albéniz, Isaac (1860–1909), 176
Albert, Eugen d' (1864–1932), 82
Albert, Prince [England] (1819–
1861), 15, 282
ALCESTE, 286
Alexandroff, Alexander, 136
Alfieri, Vittorio (1749–1803), 14
Alvary [Achenbach], Max
(c.1858–98), 242
Amati, Nicola (1596–1684), 93,
94, 127
Amicis, Anna Lucia de (1740–
1816), 97
Andrade, Francesco d' (1859–
1921), 155
APOSTLES, THE, 315–16
Archer, William (1856–1924),
166, 206n.
Arditi, Luigi (1822–1903), 38; Il
Bacio, 185
ARIADNE AUF NAXOS, xxii
Armbruster, Karl (1846–1917),
141, 173
Armitage, Edward (1817–96), 148
Arne, Thomas A. (1710–78), 272

Auber, Daniel François (1782–
1871), 192-3; Fra Diavolo, 247;
Masaniello overture, 78, 160,
186

Bach, Johann Sebastian (1685–
1750), xix, 48, 51, 60, 61-5, 90,
93, 95-6, 105, 107, 116, 118,
132, 188, 196, 213, 222, 247,
262, 269, 271, 281, 304, 312,
313, 319, 325n., 326; Mass in B
minor, 21-2, 61-4, 96; St
Matthew Passion, 17-18, 254,
316
Bach Choir, 21-2, 61-5
Bache, Walter (1842–88), 56, 58-
61, 118, 120
*Backer-Grøndahl, Agathe
(1847–1907), 176, 177
Bagagiolo, Signor, 27
Bahr-Mildenburg, Anna (1872–
1947), 263
Baillot, Pierre (1771–1842), 125
Baldwin, Thomas S., 162
Balfe, Michael William (1808–
1870), 9, 66, 237
Balliol, Master of, see Jowett
Balzac, Honoré de (1799–1850),
117, 284, 285, 324
Bancroft, Sir Squire (1841–1926),
180
Bandmann, Daniel (1840–1905),
214
Bantock, Granville (1868–1946),
307, 315

341

GENERAL INDEX

*Nash, Heddle (b.1896), 329, 330, 331

Neruda, *see* Norman Neruda

*Newman, Ernest (1868–1959), xx, xxi, 257-67, 289-90, 292

Nicholls, Agnes [Lady Harty] (b.1877), 302

Nietzsche, Friedrich Wilhelm (1844–1900), 283

*Nilsson, Christine (1843–1921), 25, 88

Nordau, Max (1849–1923), 259

*Norman Neruda, Wilma [Lady Hallé] (1839–1911), 9, 201

North, Col. Charles Napier (1817–69), 250

Novello (Vincent) & Co., 181-2

NOZZE DI FIGARO, 72-7, 105, 152, 160, 167, 289-96, 299, 304

O'Connor, T. P. (1848–1929), xvii-xix

Offenbach, Jacques (1819–80), 105, 146, 189, 190-1, 192, 220; La Grande Duchesse, 191; Orphée aux Enfers, 192

Ohlenschläger, Adam Gottlob (1779–1850), 126

ORFEO ED EURIDICE, 192, 279, 285

ORPHÉE AUX ENFERS, 192

Osborne, George A. (1806–93), 276, 277

Osgood, Emma Aline (1849–1911), 20

OTELLO (Rossini), xvii, 25, 30

OTELLO (Verdi), 153-5, 167

Ouseley, Sir Frederick (1825–1889), 276

Pachmann, Vladimir de (1848–1933), 176, 178

Paderewski, Ignace Jan (1860–1941), 4, 195, 227

Paganini, Nicolo (1782–1840), 125, 126, 127, 145

Paisiello, Giovanni (1740–1816), 34, 289, 290

Palestrina, Giovanni da (c.1525–1594), Missa brevis, 80

Palmer, Edward Paget, 65

Parke, Ernest (1860–1944), xvii

Parker, Robert, 302

*Parry, Sir Charles Hubert H. (1848–1918), xx, 144, 272, 307, 313; Judith, 193; Prometheus Unbound, 64, 193; Symphony No. 3 in C, 144

PARSIFAL, 150, 151, 154, 159, 161, 163, 164, 166, 170, 171, 240, 241, 245, 261

Pasta, Giuditta (1798–1865), 4

Pasteur, Louis (1822–95), 191

*Patey, Janet Monach (1842–94), 21, 33, 64, 88, 123

PATIENCE, 193

*Patti, Adelina (1843–1919), 33, 88, 128, 156, 329

PAULINE, xv, 8

PEARL FISHERS, 156

Pearsall, Robert Lucas (1795–1856), 305

Pergolesi, Giovanni (1710–36), xiv

Perron, Karl (1858–1928), 170, 233, 239, 241, 244

Pezze, Alessandro (1835–1914), 11

Phidias, 73, 305

PHILÉMON ET BAUCIS, 193

Phillips, Kate (1849–1931), 243

Phillips, Watts (1825–74), The Dead Heart, 180

353

GENERAL INDEX